Advertising

Related titles in the series

Accounting
Advertising
Auditing
Book-keeping
Business and Commercial Law
Business and Enterprise Studies
Business French
Business German
Business Italian
Commerce
Cost and Management Accounting
Economics
Elements of Banking

Financial Management
Information Technology
Law
Management Theory and
  Practice
Marketing
Office Practice
Personnel Management
Psychiatry
Social Services
Statistics for Business
Teeline Shorthand
Typing

Advertising

Fifth edition

Frank Jefkins, BSc (Econ), BA(Hons), MCAM, ABC, FIPR,
FLCC, FAIE, FInstSMM, MCIM

MADE SIMPLE
B O O K S

Made Simple
An imprint of Butterworth-Heinemann Ltd
Linacre House, Jordan Hill, Oxford OX2 8DP

℞ A member of the Reed Elsevier group

OXFORD   LONDON   BOSTON
MUNICH   NEW DELHI   SINGAPORE   SYDNEY
TOKYO   TORONTO   WELLINGTON

First published 1973
Second edition 1977
Reprinted 1980
Third edition 1982
Fourth edition 1985
Reprinted 1986, 1989, 1990
Fifth edition 1992
Reprinted 1993

British Library Cataloguing in Publication Data
Jefkins, Frank
  Advertising. – New ed.
  (Made Simple Books)
  I. Title II. Series
  659.1
ISBN 0 7506 0325 9

Typeset by Keygraphics, Aldermaston, Berkshire
Printed and bound in Great Britain by Clays, St Ives plc

Contents

Preface to the fifth edition

This book has been a best-seller since it was first published in 1973 with subsequent reprints and up-dated new editions. Now it has been completely rewritten.

It has been rewritten for three reasons. First, the advertising scene has changed enormously in recent years. Second, the London Chamber of Commerce and Industry examinations have become extremely popular worldwide, and thousands of students in the UK and overseas need an up-to-date textbook based on the LCCI syllabus and containing a past exam paper. Third, the CAM syllabuses have been revised, and the CAM examinations in the UK have become an essential part of the training for both advertising and PR personnel. Therefore this edition has been written to meet the requirements of the CAM syllabus, and a past exam paper is also included.

The LCCI and CAM examinations are complementary in that a LCCI Group Diploma in Advertising, Marketing and Public Relations is accepted as an entry requirement for the CAM Certificate. Moreover, distinctions gained in these three LCCI subjects earn exemption from the same subjects in the CAM Certificate.

Part One
The Advertising Scene

1
What is advertising?

1.1 The basic role of advertising and some views on the subject

In an industrialized society almost everyone is touched by advertising. They are surrounded by advertising, indoors and out-of-doors. They respond to it, perhaps depend on it, and they may themselves be advertisers. It is a part of buying and selling, and a vital part of an affluent society, even if there are sceptics who pretend not to be influenced by advertising. In developing countries, where the cash economy is smaller, advertising may be confined mainly to the urbanized, educated and wealthier communities. Consequently, advertising tends to reflect the standard of living and the prosperity of the country.

Moreover, in developing countries advertising is often less sophisticated, sometimes quite crude and exaggerated, and regarded by the public with suspicion. Because it was believed that it unduly aroused the expectations of poor people, the Indonesian government banned television advertising.

Advertising is sometimes condemned for its materialism and for its encouragement to people to buy things needlessly – that it is a parasitical manipulator of minds. This is unfair for it provides choice and, but for advertising, we would be unaware of many of the products and services which we buy and enjoy. It is but a tool of the exchange process, but it can be abused by unscrupulous advertisers. A hammer is a useful tool provided it is not used as a murder weapon. So with advertising.

One of the causes of criticism is that there seems to be such a lot of advertising, and this appears to be extravagant and wasteful. The secret of advertising is *repetition*, and often its task is to ensure that there is a continuous demand to take up factory output or stocks in the shops. People forget very quickly, and those firms which have stopped advertising have simply gone out of business. Some of our most famous advertisers, such as Cadbury, Coca-Cola and Colman have advertised since they first began business, maybe a century or more ago.

Objections to advertising have increased in recent years. The reader of a newspaper or a magazine can be a selective reader of advertisements, and a publication would be formidably dull if it had no advertisers. In contrast, television advertising enters the home and is intrusive and hard to ignore, whereas years ago posters were happily dubbed 'the poor man's art gallery'. The proliferation of direct mail (although less in the UK than on the continent) has earned the ugly nickname of junk mail. Advertising is under fire, and yet it works. Advertisers do not waste their money. Some people would be horrified if they knew that most of the big campaigns cost five to ten million pounds! But Tesco, Sainsburys, Asda and other supermarket chains thrive on it, and build bigger and better superstores to sell more and more advertised goods. In 1990 Sainsburys built 35 new stores.

Something of this was brought out in a MORI survey commissioned by *Campaign* and published in that magazine on September 15, 1989. To summarize very briefly, the survey showed that, by seven to one, respondents said they would be more likely to buy a widely advertised product than one not advertised at all. (Many supermarkets sell unadvertised own label brands.) Nearly three-quarters of those interviewed found television commercials more entertaining than the programmes, which speaks highly of the creative skill of television advertising. But just as many people said they were likely to respond to press advertising as television commercials. The old sceptism remained about advertising expenditure, respondents believing the money would be better spent on improving products. They did not appreciate the necessity for advertising. The poll was remarkable in showing that both men and women respond to advertising, while the survey showed that a higher proportion of young people buy advertised products than older consumers. One shock result was that while bank advertising is mostly directed at young people, one in four young people said they disliked bank advertising. There was contempt for those advertisers who tried to exploit the 'green' bandwagon.

MORI interviewed a quota sample of 2,047 respondents aged 15 plus in 147 constituency sampling points throughout the UK. Interviews were conducted face-to-face in-home between August 17 and 21, 1989.

This book has begun in this fashion because it is important that the reader should understand the climate in which advertising is conducted. Most advertising in the UK is reputable, and it is controlled by the self-regulatory British Code of Advertising Practice, administered by the Advertising Standards Authority, and by more than one hundred statute laws of which the *Consumer Protection Act 1987* is a fairly recent example.

In short, *advertising is the means by which we make known what we have to sell or what we want to buy.*

1.2 Definitions

The above is a simple definition which brings out the point that advertising is not merely a means of making known, like the name of a street or a house. It has to do something such as sell a product or buy labour. Other definitions are more explicit, as with the following from the Institute of Practitioners in Advertising, the trade association of British advertising agencies: *advertising presents the most persuasive possible selling message to the right prospects for the product or service at the lowest possible cost.*

This is a professional definition. It emphasizes that advertising should be planned and created to achieve the most results for the least cost. The 'persuasive... selling message' consists of the copy or wording and the pictorial, layout and typographical presentation of the copy. The right prospects are defined by means of marketing research so that the message can be targeted properly. The lowest possible cost will depend on media planning and media buying skills. All this will be explained more fully in Chapter 5.

Our subject is full of jargon, as seen in the above paragraph, which means that precise meanings are given to words which have more generalized lay meanings. Advertising is itself such a word. People outside the advertising business use the word advertising as a simile for various forms of communication such as publicity, sales promotion, propaganda and public relations, none of which is a form of advertising.

Another definition offered by David Bernstein in his book *Creative Advertising* is: 'advertising is the origination and/or communication of ideas about products in order to motivate consumers towards purchase'.

This certainly brings out the main purpose of advertising which is to sell.

But what about that near relation, *publicity*? We have advertising managers called publicity managers and advertising departments called publicity departments, and a public relations consultancy called Publicity Plus. All very confusing! Sometimes this is a term used because it sounds superior to advertising, or because there is a combination of advertising and public relations. But strictly speaking, *publicity is the result of making known*. In that case there is no control over it and it can be good or bad publicity, and there can be some truth in the saying 'no publicity is bad publicity'. It is sometimes better for a book, a play or a film to be panned rather than ignored. Publicity can therefore be a fickle thing.

Sales promotion is a term which has different meanings in the UK and the USA, and the overseas student taking British examinations should be aware of these different interpretations. In the UK, sales promotion is regarded as a marketing operation to do with special short-term promotional exercises such as free gifts, premium offers, mail-ins and competitions. In the USA, it covers below-the-line advertising such as direct mail, exhibitions, sales literature and point-of-sale displays. (Above-the-line refers to the traditional commission paying media of press, radio, television, outdoor/transportation and cinema). Sales promotion, which used to be called merchandising, may be defined thus: *sales promotion is the function of marketing which seeks to achieve given objectives by the adding of extrinsic, tangible value to a product or service.*

The extrinsic, tangible value is the gift, prize or special offer. The British Code of Sales Promotion Practice refers to sales promotion as *those marketing techniques which are used, usually on a temporary basis, to make goods or services more attractive to the consumer by providing some additional benefit whether in cash or kind. (The benefit may not be enjoyed by the consumer directly but by some good cause which the consumer supports.)* The reference in parentheses concerns charity-linked promotions.

It is important to understand the special nature of sales promotion as this term is often loosely and obviously wrongly applied to advertising. Often, sales promotion is used as an alternative to media advertising.

Propaganda is another term with a multitude of applications, e.g. trade advertising while journalists confuse propaganda with public relations. Its origin probably is a Catholic one when, centuries ago, priests went forth into the world to propagate the gospels. Modern usage is mainly to do with promoting a cause, which may be a good or a bad one. A simple definition is: *propaganda is the means of gaining support for an opinion, creed or belief.*

Unlike advertising, there is no exchange situation beyond the satisfaction which a donor or supporter may feel. It can range from political or religious propaganda to that for a charity or voluntary body. It may use advertising or public relations for this purpose, but it is not a simile for either. This will be referred to again when public relations is defined.

Marketing differs from ordinary selling in the sense that it seeks to sell what the market is willing to buy at a profit to the seller. Ordinary selling is to do with selling what the producer or retailer has to sell without first finding out what the market wants. The Chartered Institute of Marketing defines marketing thus: *marketing is the management process responsible for identifying, anticipating and satisfying customer requirements profitably.*

Or, as the late David Malbert, former City Editor of the London *Evening Standard* put it: *marketing is producing and selling at a profit goods that satisfy customers.*

Both definitions imply the use of marketing research to find out what people will buy, and the responsibility to give satisfaction. The marketing mix is described below as the process of doing this.

Marketing communications is a comparatively new expression about which some confusion exists regarding its scope and limitations. On the one hand these are the limitations of the Chartered Institute of Marketing examination syllabus to the broad use of the term in business names such as 'Marketing Communication' for a public relations consultancy. The limited view is an academic one based on the out-dated Four Ps concept of which promotion is the fourth P, embracing advertising, sales promotion and 'publicity' meaning (presumably!) public relations. But as the definition given below implies, marketing communications takes in most of the marketing mix.

The *marketing mix* spans the whole range of marketing activities from the originating of a product or service to services conducted after the sale – from research and development to the after market. The marketing function is constantly having to communicate with those engaged in selling and distribution and with consumers/users. A salesman's business card is an elementary item of communication. Quite apart from promotional activities, public relations and marketing research, marketing communications inevitably includes branding, labelling, packaging, instructions, sales force communications, dealer relations, market education, and such after-market activities as servicing, spares, guarantees and so on. A comprehensive definition is: *marketing communications consists of every kind of communication relevant to marketing.*

Finally, we come to *public relations*, perhaps the most misunderstood term of all. It is not a form of advertising, not even 'free advertising'. Its purpose is to create understanding and reputation through knowledge. That calls for facts, not fancies. Voice projection and make-up make the stage performer seem natural, and in rather the same way – but without falsity or exaggeration – advertising has to be larger than life to be even noticed. But to be credible, public relations must deal with plain facts. It should provide factual information without embellishment or comment. Thus, the writing of press material is utterly different from copywriting.

Both advertising and propaganda have to be biased in favour of their subject if they are to work, but if it is to be effective – that is, believed – public relations should be unbiased and impartial. That is not easy if one is enthusiastic about one's subject, but the moment a pubic relations message descends into puffery it is doomed. Neither the media nor the audience will accept it, and they will say 'it is only advertising'. They expect advertising to put the best face on things, but once public relations does so all credibility is lost.

Nevertheless, there is a close and important link between public relations and advertising. It is much easier and less costly to advertise a product or service when its supplier has a good reputation, and when the product or service is well understood. That is where public relations can make a valuable contribution to successful advertising. It is far more difficult to advertise something which is handicapped by mistrust or misunderstanding. The definitition by the Institute of Public

Relations reads: *public relations practice is the planned and sustained effort to establish and maintain goodwill and mutual understanding between an organization and its publics.*

This official definition stresses that public relations needs to be planned, and that it is concerned with *mutual* understanding, that is understanding both by and of publics. It also refers to publics which can be more numerous and diversified than the strict target audiences or market segments communicated with by advertising and marketing. Publics can also be internal as well as external, and public relations deals with the private and public sectors, and is not limited to marketing activities. Another, and more specific definition, is the Mexican Statement which resulted from an international public relations conference held in Mexico City in August 1978. This reads: *public relations practice is the art and social science of analysing trends, predicting their consequences, counselling organization leaders, and implementing planned programmes of action which will serve both the organization's and the public interest.*

This splendid definition gives a fuller picture of public relations, indicating the use of research before giving advice to management, and emphasizing the social responsibility of public relations. This brings out the advisory nature of public relations, and challenges those who regard public relations as being unprofessional. For instance, journalists have a bad habit of deriding a political initiative which they dislike as being merely 'a PR exercise', when it has nothing to do with public relations.

The above definitions have been given and discussed to establish the communications environment in which advertising plays its part.

2
Origin and development of advertising

2.1 History of advertising: early days

Where did it all begin? Advertising has been called the second oldest profession, and there are references to it in biblical, Babylonian, Greek and Roman history. One of the earliest recorded advertisements was the offer of a reward for the recapture of an Egyptian slave, while gladiatorial contests were advertised on the walls of Rome.

Most of the world has had its town criers, bringing both news and advertising messages. One of the oldest is said to be the town crier in Athens in ancient times who declared:

> For eyes that are smiling, for cheeks like the dawn,
> For beauty that lasts after girlhood has gone,
> For prices in reason the woman who knows,
> Will buy her cosmetics from Aeselyptoe.

The original Avon lady!

Down through the ages the most simple and effective form of advertising has been the sign, and it still is. The sign can be understood by people of any language, and whether or not people can read. Trades have had their own individual signs such as the red and white barber's pole, the apothecary's peculiarly shaped bottles filled with coloured water, the wheelwright's wheel, the chimney sweep's brush, the horse's head outside a French butcher, or the inn sign. The history of England is told in inn signs. For instance, there are still those which identified the resting places for the drivers of trains of packhorses who, in the Middle Ages carried wool or woollen cloth to London where the merchants shipped 'the golden fleece' to the marts of Antwerp and other cities of the Low Countries. Later came the stage-coaches and the coaching inns where horses were changed, hence inn signs such as The Coach and Horses. Significantly, when bus or tram conductors used to punch bus tickets the fare stages were nearly always the names of public houses along the route and their names were printed on the tickets, e.g. The Greyhound, Swan and Sugar Loaf, Red Deer and Royal Oak.

'Modern' advertising has evolved thanks to the introduction of printing machines, and the first print advertisement in Britain is said to be one produced by William Caxton in 1477 to sell his publication. *The Pyes of Salisbury*.

2.2   Seventeenth century

In Elizabethan times, extraordinary claims about deformed people were made in handbills given away on occasions such as Bartholomew's Fair. The old news-books of those days were gradually replaced by small but regular newspapers such as the *Weekly Newes* of 1622 and the *Newes from Most Parts of Christendom*. Most were short-lived and often they were political sheets. Later came the *Mercurius Britannica* which, on February 1, 1625, contained probably the first advertisement concerning a discourse on a royal match, and a bronze picture of the pair, Charles, Prince of Wales and Lady Henrietta Maria of France.

Newspapers at that time were of course small with local circulations. The following from *Mercurius Politicus* of September 30, 1658 is quoted from E. S. Turner's entertaining book, *The Shocking History of Advertising*:

> THAT Excellent, and by all Physicians, approved China drink, called by Cheans *Tcha*, by other nations *Tay* alias *Tee*, is sold at the Sultaness Head Cophee-House, in Sweeting's Rents, by the *Royal Exchange*, London.

The *London Gazette*, in 1666, was carrying advertisements for coffee, chocolate, tea, and other delights in flamboyant terms, set as classifieds mostly in the same uniform 7 point type, descending for some inches down the column.

Another form of advertising in Stuart times were the wooden signs reaching from one building to another across the narrow street, and these contributed readily to the spread of the fire of London.

2.3   Eighteenth century

The 18th century saw quite rapid development, and in the USA the first American newspaper to carry advertisements was the *Boston News Letter* of 1704. In Britain there were famous journalists such as Steele, Addison and Defoe, and the magazines *Tatler* (1709) and *Spectator* (1711) appeared, containing advertisements. Before long Dr Johnson was commenting on advertising, saying 'The soul of an advertisement is promise, large promise'. But he was ahead of his time when he said, 'the trade of advertising is now so near to perfection that it is not easy to propose any improvement'. He had not reckoned with illustrations.

2.4 Nineteenth century

The 19th century saw some very ingenious advertising as communications improved and urban centres grew so that goods could be sold nationally by firms like Cadbury, Lever Brothers and Lipton. Famous paintings were often used in press ads and on posters, an example being the use of the *Bubbles* painting by Millais for Pears soap. If one looks at old photographs of street scenes one will see many advertisers of today using the sides of horse-drawn buses, trams and vans.

Improvement in press advertising came with the invention of metal plates to reproduce pictures, and of printing type in different sizes and different designs or faces. This revolutionized not only the appearance of press advertisements, but made it possible for space brokers to offer creative services and turn themselves into advertising agents for clients rather than commission salesmen for publishers.

Even so, local town newspapers were still printing the purely typographical advertisement in one size of type, as with this example from the *Croydon Advertiser* of April 6, 1872:

CHEAP BLANKETS
CHEAP BLANKETS
CHEAP BLANKETS
EBBUTT,
94,
NORTH
END
CROYDON
BLANKETS
BLANKETS
BLANKETS

There was a good deal of 'fly posting', that is the pasting up of posters on the walls of buildings. This was often done at night, with rival bill stickers covering up the previous posters. Property owners painted signs, 'Bill stickers will be prosecuted', leading to the joke, 'Who is Bill Stickers?'

The first British advertising agencies were one-man space-broking businesses, the agent – strictly speaking the agent of the media – being paid a commission on the advertising space he was able to sell for a newspaper or magazine. The space broker or space farmer was not unlike an insurance agent, except that he had no specialist knowledge. He merely hawked vacant space to those he could induce to buy it. Circulation figures were anybody's guess, or invention!

Advertising agents in the more modern sense came about with the growth of Government advertising during the Napoleonic wars when money was raised, partly by lotteries. Next, creative agencies emerged when space-selling became more competitive and services like writing slogans, copy and providing layouts had to be provided (out of the commission) to get the business. All this coincided with the growth of mass production and the new mass consumer market, greatly aided by the migration of people from the countryside to the towns and the increase in retail outlets. Railways contributed to this.

The first advertising agents really began to appear at the beginning of the 19th century. Writers and poets such as Charles Lamb were the first copywriters, engaged to 'puff' up products. James White, with the aid of his school friend Charles Lamb, set up the first London agency in 1800. He combined his job of clerk in the treasurer's office at his old school of Christ's Hospital with that of agent for provincial newspapers at 22 Warwick Square 'in the shadow of St Paul's Cathedral'. White's was a comparatively creative agency since Lamb was employed as a freelance copywriter on Government lottery advertisements.

In those days provincial newspapers were like country bankers – there were no national newspapers or national bankers. World and national events were reported in local papers. You would read about, say, an earthquake in Peru in the *Croydon Advertiser*. Although the *Times* made journalistic history by reporting the Battle of Waterloo (about a week after the event) with probably the world's first war correspondent. It was the London and not the national *Times*. Popular national newspapers like the *Daily Telegraph* and Northcliffe's ha'penny *Daily Mail* did not appear until 1855 and 1896 respectively.

Another of the earliest advertising agencies was Reynell and Son of London, established in 1812. The abolition of the advertisement tax in 1853, and the removal of stamp duty from newspapers in 1861, gave fresh incentive to both the sale of space and the use of advertising.

There were, of course, magazines which took advertising, and it will be remembered that originally the long novels of authors such as Charles Dickens and Anthony Trollope first appeared as serials, the author writing each instalment week by week. Trollope was particularly adept at working to measure with a strict word count to fit the journal. Nineteenth century reading was therefore contributing to the growth of media, and the 1870 Education Act began to increase literacy throughout the population.

Some advertisers were extremely competitive, ingenious and even outrageous. Queen Victoria was not amused when Mr Lipton sent her a sample cheese. But perhaps Joseph Beecham was the cheekiest. The son of a shepherd, and the father of the famous orchestral conductor, Joseph concocted a pill made of aloes and ginger packed in hard soap and invented the slogan *Worth A Guinea A Box*. He had boats with sails billowing out the name Beecham, and rows of seaside bathing machines emblazoned with his message. Children learned about his pills through puzzle books, textbooks and story books.

But the best Beecham story is no doubt his sponsorship of hymn books for a church in the slums of Tyneside. Beecham agreed, provided he could insert a small advertisement in the hymn books. When they arrived the South Shields vicar was surprised to find that they were free of any advertising for pills. But on Christmas morning the congregation found itself singing:

Hark, the herald angels sing
Beecham's Pills are just the thing
For easing pain and mothers mild
Two for adults, one for child.

Beecham's pills are still on sale!

2.5 Twentieth century: the inter-war years

A triumph for the advertising world occurred when the Audit Bureau of Circulations (ABC), promoted by the Incorporated Society of British Advertisers (ISBA), was founded in 1931. ISBA also conducted the first newspaper readership survey in 1936. But the story behind the ABC is worth recording. Originally, ISBA was called the Advertisers' Protection Society (APS), and was set up to protect advertisers from being cheated by media owners who often exaggerated their circulation figures by stating print orders rather than the number of copies actually sold. The APS claimed that the circulation of *The Observer* was lower than stated. *The Observer* sued the Society for libel and lost!

Between the two world wars there were a few large advertising agencies and advertising flourished with gift coupon cigarettes, the first popular motor-cars such as the Austin 7, Ford 8 and the Morris Minor, the growth of radio sets and accessories such as batteries, and popular foods and drinks such as breakfast cereals, soft drinks and beers. Famous products were launched of which Ovaltine, Horlicks and Stork margarine remain today.

So much money was invested in promoting Stork margarine that it was advertised throughout the war years, although it was unobtainable, only 'standard' margarine being available on food rationing coupons. When rationing ended, and brands were back, Stork had an advertisement showing a picture of a stork in broad arrow prisoners' clothes being released from prison. No risk was taken of people forgetting this product, as did happen with many others which disappeared during the war years. It is not easy to resuscitate a product after six years' absence.

Humour was often a feature of inter-war advertising, perhaps because these were bleak years following the First World War with much poverty and unemployment. Few people today realize that the Save the Children Fund was launched on behalf of British starving children. Posters were often funny like the Bovril one of a man in his pyjamas astride a large jar of Bovril which was floating on the sea, the slogan being 'Bovril Prevents That Sinking Feeling'. There was the Andrews liver salts ad with a man hunting for the tin, which was stuck in his hip pocket. Pears had a poster for their soap with a picture of a filthy tramp writing a letter which said 'since using your soap I have used no other'. Shell had a two-headed road mender with the slogan 'That's Shell – that was'. Johnnie Walker whisky had a humorous trade character with the slogan 'Johnnie Walker Keeps On Walking'. Greys cigarettes used a series of Langdon cartoons, and presented them in booklet form, and Colman's mustard ran The Mustard Club. The Bisto Kids were true of the times, and may seem incongruous in modern advertising, although the 'Ah, Bisto' slogan is still used. Advertising in the 1930s was very happy, and – amazing to modern readers, no doubt – a lot of the advertising announced price cuts! The power of advertising was often demonstrated by the fact that it created demand which justified economies of scale. The price of Lyons swiss rolls, for instance, enjoyed price reductions as the advertising on the front page of the London *Evening News* boosted sales.

The advent of radio in the 1920s produced commercial radio in many parts of the world, but not in the UK where the BBC was set up as a non-commercial public service broadcaster. Roy Thomson, who came to Britain at the age of 70 to buy *The Scotsman* and set up Scottish Television as 'a licence to print money', had been a commercial radio man in Canada. The BBC programmes were fairly staid, enlivened by only one or two comedy and variety programmes such as Arthur Askey's *Bandwagon*, and a Saturday night variety show. There was a demand for more popular programmes, especially on a Sunday. The European stations Hilversum, Radio Paris, Radio Normandy, Radio Toulouse and Radio Luxembourg began beaming programmes on Britain, supported by British advertisers. Christopher Stone, editor of *The Gramophone*, broadcast a record programme from Radio Paris, identifying the numbers and makers of the records. Commercials for Radio Luxembourg were made in the old swimming bath in the basement of Bush House in London, and the recording flown over to the transmitter. A famous one was the Sunday teatime children's programme, the Ovaltinies, 'We are the Ovaltinies, Happy Boys and Girls,' to promote Ovaltine. This was revived a few years ago as a TV commercial. John Slater, later to star in the television series Z cars, was one of the performers in the Bush House studios of the 1930s. Famous singers like Bing Crosby and Gracie Fields were the stars of some of these continental radio shows, and there were short situation comedies resembling the original American radio soap operas. This term originated from American radio shows sponsored by soap advertisers. When the Second World War came the BBC relented in favour of popular programmes to entertain the Forces, and these were also listened to by audiences at home. The BBC continued to rely on licence fees for its income, and commercial radio – ILR – was not to come until 1973.

The huge Odeon, Gaumont and other cinemas seated 2000–3000 people, and they queued up for hours outside to see films like *Hell's Angels*. The cinema screen was a popular advertising medium and remained so until audiences were stolen by television whose popularity in the UK was sparked off by the Coronation in 1953, after which screen advertising declined, although there has been some recovery recently.

During the twenty years between the two world wars – 1919–1939 – there were more national dailies and Sunday papers, and many more evening papers in London and throughout the UK, than there are today. Among them was the Liberal *News Chronicle*, and the Labour *Daily Herald*, both of which survived until a few years after the Second World War. The *Daily Express* with Beaverbrook's pro-Empire and anti-Co-op bias, was the biggest seller.

It was a time to attract advertising revenue from the big cigarette, food, confectionery, drinks, patent medicine, motor-car, bicycle and radio set advertisers. The *Daily Mirror* was, in the 1920s, a small circulation home interest daily with its Gugnuncs (Pip, Squeak and Wilfred) children's club and was often a second newspaper read by mothers. Increased circulation and a slice of the new advertising revenue called for an utterly different readership profile, especially young male readers. Everard nudes and the Jane cartoon appeared twenty years ahead of *The Sun's* page three girls, and during the Second World War the *Daily Mirror* was the Forces newspaper and is reckoned to have won the post-war General Election for Labour. The *Daily Herald*, backed by the TUC, was the official Labour paper but it could never get above a million circulation if that, and it was never financially viable. It was surrendered by the TUC and Odhams tried to give it a new life as the *Sun*, failed and sold it to the Australian Rupert Murdoch.

During the inter-war period big circulation women's magazines were appearing thanks to the colour printing facilities at Watford. In the mid-30s *Woman* appeared and became the leader. These magazines enjoyed the mass production printing facilities of rotary photogravure, an economical process for large scale colour printing, and printing was on comparatively cheap super-calendered paper. The period also saw the birth of *Picture Post*, a magazine of superb topical picture journalism which was finally destroyed by the instant news of television, and the delightfully satirical pocket magazine *Lilliput* with its juxtaposition photographs (e.g. the hook-nosed Lady Oxford and a chicken).

Advertisers had the benefit of a rich variety of media, but some of them were unscrupulous and unethical. The advertising business set out to defend its good name, beginning with the National Vigilance Committee in 1926, followed by the setting up of the Advertising Association. Its pioneering first general secretary, Russell Chapman, campaigned against misleading advertising throughout the 1930s, and an Advertisement Investigation Department Committee was chaired by Frank Bishop. (After the war Sir Frank Bishop wrote his famous book *The Ethics of Advertising*, and contributed greatly to the British Code of Standards in Relation to the Advertising of Medicines and Treatments of 1948.) The AID and this Code were the forerunners of the independent Advertising Standards Authority and the British Code of Advertising Practice which were set up in 1962. The architects of self-regulatory advertising controls were Russell Chapman, Sir Frank Bishop, and Leslie (Bill) Needham, (advertisement director of the *Daily Express* and chairman of the AID Committee in the 1950s).

Russell Chapman's campaigns were bold and ahead of their time. There were numerous proprietary medicines (often called 'patent medicines') which were of dubious merit but, to the delight of newspaper advertisement managers (who earned fortunes in commission), purchased whole pages to make the most bizarre claims. These far out-reached the flamboyant claims of the Victorian Beecham, and were often downright lies. Today, some of these products are still advertised, but with very meek offers to alleviate ailments, such has been the power of voluntary controls now supported by the media in their own interests.

Advertising in the 1930s flourished with a surfeit of press media, and there was no other really mass media to compete with it. Television did not exist, radio was negligible and foreign-based, direct mail hardly existed, and the main rivals were outdoor and cinema.

Sales promotion had always existed alongside national brands. Samples and free gifts were common. Very popular were gift coupons such as those given with Bournville cocoa, and especially with cigarettes such as Ardath, BDV and Black Cat, while the sets of 50 cigarette cards given for years with Wills' Gold Flake and Players' Navy Cut made them brand leaders. There was a cigarette coupon war leading to their mutual abolition, although the idea has returned in post-war years.

The modern service agency really developed with the arrival of marketing research in the late 1930s and too late to be thoroughly adopted until the removal of wartime controls in the 1950s. Then, with the end of newsprint rationing, the adoption of marketing and marketing research techniques, and finally the arrival of commercial television, the big agencies emerged. Because of the war, the UK was six years behind the Americans where these new developments were well in place after the Depression of the 1920s.

2.6 Post 1945 and conclusion

A feature of the post-1945 advertising world was the measurement of readership and audiences. It was all very well knowing the audited net sale of a journal rather than how many copies were printed, most journals were prepared to submit their figures to the ABC, although the *Daily Telegraph* resisted for many years, but what about *secondary readership?* How many people, and what kind of people, actually read it? It was no use taking the average size of a family and multiplying the circulation figure by that to arrive at a readership figure. This might be correct for one newspaper but not for another, and what about pass-on or waiting room readership? Some newspapers like the *Financial Times* have small circulations but large readerships, whereas the *Reader's Digest* has both. The answer lay in marketing research, and a large national sample of readers had to be questioned.

The magazine publisher, Sir Edward Hulton, set up the Hulton Readership Survey. Not confined to Sir Edward's own magazines, this was a costly, philanthropic, pioneer effort, but research techniques were not perfect, and rival publishers sometimes disputed the Hulton figures. So, in 1954, the IPA (representing agencies) with the support of the publishing bodies, created an independent National Readership Survey, and Hulton ceased his survey in 1956. When ISBA (representing the advertisers) brought in its sponsorship the independence was completed and the tripartite Joint Industry Committee for National Readership Surveys (JICNARS) took over.

Television audience research followed in a similar way with JICTAR in 1967 but, after years of squabbling over JICTAR and BBC audience figures (which were obtained by different research methods – set meters versus street interviews), the Broadcasters' Audience Research Board (BARB) was set up in 1981, combining all television audience research. This followed the advice in the Annan Committee report of 1977 that there should be a joint system of audience research.

A third 'JIC' is JICPAS which handles poster advertising surveys, but these tend to be occasional, while JICRAR measures radio audiences, mainly by means of annual reports based on listeners' diaries.

The history of advertising is a fascinating one, often being a reflection of the society at the time. This is very true in developing countries where advertising may be less in evidence than in industrialized countries simply because there are fewer goods to sell, less money with which to buy them, illiteracy and multi-ethnic populations, and a scarcity of media in which to advertise. But as a society prospers so advertising increases.

In the industrialized world, advertising has followed the growth of urban populations, shopping facilities, transport, education and media, and has become the essential means by which a large producer or seller can reach a large local, national and or even international market. This has been extended by modern forms of communication such as postal services, the telephone, computers, television and satellites. We have come a long way since the coffee house scandal sheets of the 17th century, although maybe scandal sheets still provide the most potent advertising media.

Since this book is likely to be read by CAM students, the evolution of education in advertising is relevant to this chapter, and is part of the history of advertising. The Advertising Association held its first Diploma exams in 1931 and, during the war years, there were British prisoners of war who sat the exams under the auspices of the Red Cross. In the 1940s a joint intermediate exam was held by the AA and the then IIPA, each holding its own finals. The AA qualification was the DAA (Diploma of the Advertising Association) and the IIPA had their MIPA which directors needed for their agencies to be members of the Institute. Later, the DAA became the MAA, giving holders individual membership of the Advertising Association.

In 1970, it was decided to set up a joint examining body for advertising, marketing and public relations. The Institute of Marketing, being a very large and profitable examining body with thousands of students in the UK and overseas, opted out, but the AA, IPA and IPR combined their examinations. At the time, the Institute of Public Relations was on the point of launching its own Diploma, but surrendered this in favour of the CAM Diploma. Advertising was the financially larger business with more employees than public relations, and was able to find some sixteen other sponsoring bodies, and with two public relations papers eventually deleted, the Certificates became advertising dominated.

However, under the new secretariat, and new syllabuses in 1988, greater input by the IPR, requirement of the CAM Diloma for IPR membership in 1992, plus some considerable association of public relations with marketing communications, the Certificate stage has been accepted as providing a basis of broad knowledge for either option of an advertising or public relations diploma.

One curious difference remains between the pre-CAM qualification and the present one. Under the old system sixteen subjects were taken over four years, now only nine subjects can be taken in 18 months. To some extent this streamlining is mitigated by higher entry requirements for CAM, but vital subjects such as commercial art, reproduction and printing have been eliminated, and law and psychology play minor roles. A knowledge of printing would be valuable to both advertising and public relations students, and might be more appropriate than the new Direct Marketing/Sales Promotion paper which could be absorbed under Advertising and Marketing.

A development of recent years has been the intelligent, the caring or the socially responsible buyer. This new consumer is concerned about his or her health, or the health of the environment. Higher prices will be paid willingly for products which have safe or more nutritious ingredients, or organic foods which have been produced humanely or without use of chemicals and fertilizers. Clothing made from animal furs is rejected, while goods made from recycled waste are favoured. Environmentally-friendly products are sought, whether they be aerosols without CFC gases or unleaded petrol. The green consumer market has become a major selling situation for both manufacturers and retailers.

It makes a good closing point for this chapter on the development of advertising, but it also represents a new minefield for self-regulatory controls and possibly legislation. The green bandwagon can be one to be exploited by the hypocritical, and well-meaning people can be misled into buying supposedly 'environmentally-friendly' products. *Caveat emptor* – buyer beware – exists as never before.

3
Kinds of advertising and their purpose

3.1 Why advertise?

We shall now look at some of the reasons why anyone spends money on advertising. What do they expect for their money? That is a very interesting question and not nearly as simple as it looks. It is not just a matter of making known in order to sell. We may have something we want to sell, or someone may have something we want to buy. Alternatively, we may want to give something away, effect an exchange, invite donors or gifts, or even change people's opinions. Generally, however, we want to bring together people who would not otherwise know of the existence of those able to supply and those with a demand, very often complete strangers. This is very different from the face-to-face situation in selling.

Most people use advertising at some time, either privately or in business. And most people respond to advertisements and so enjoy the choices available to them in every sphere of life.

This elementary answer applies whether we want to sell a private house, dispose of kittens, raise funds for a charity, sell the production of a million pound business, buy a second-hand disc player, attract shoppers to our store, launch a new product, engage staff, privatize a state enterprise or simply find a pen friend. The technique is the same: there is merely a difference of magnitude and sophistication between an inexpensive classified advertisement to sell one budgerigar and a national campaign on television to sell bird seed to hundreds of thousands of budgerigar owners.

Consequently, anyone running a business who needs to tell customers what he has to sell has to resort to advertising, otherwise he will simply sit in his office contemplating what he has not sold.

3.2 Specific reasons for advertising

There are many special and specific *reasons* why advertising may be used, in one of its many forms, as the tool for the job and the following 24 examples offer a broader picture of the versatility and value of advertising.

1 To announce a new product or service

Here, prospective customers are presented with details of a new product, and this usually means a costly and dramatic launch. The advertiser literally has to buy his way into the market, perhaps capture a share of an existing market in which others have been established for a long time. Announcements for new chocolate bars, involving television, press and probably poster advertising, are typical examples. So, too, are the much more comprehensive announcements for new investment, savings or insurance schemes. The 'weight' of repetitive advertising makes the campaign hard to miss or overlook, and it will seek out its relevant section of the market.

Is it necessary to spend so lavishly on the launch of a new product? To break into the market with a new product is not easy: the world simply does not beat its way to the better mouse-trap. Novelty is not enough. The buying public is conservative, apathetic and often ignorant. It is apt to be sceptical, hard to shift from established habits, finding it easier to say 'no' than 'yes'.

For decades people thought all doors should be painted brown because they were made of wood, that ice cream was to be eaten only in the summer, and that buses must have conductors. To promote something new the advertising has to be bold, dramatic, persuasive and convincing, whether it be for a complete innovation such as a convenience food or an entirely new kind of motor-car. A solitary big splash will not work: a sustained campaign is necessary. If a fire engine sounds its siren only on leaving the station this warning will not clear the road all the way to the fire. The siren has to be sounded persistently and insistently all the way, and so with advertising.

2 To expand the market to new customers

Good examples of this are when a paint or a fertilizer has been used successfully for industrial or commercial purposes, and is then packaged in smaller sizes, distributed through retailers, and promoted to the consumer market. The do-it-yourself and weekend gardener markets are full of such products, put there by advertising. Alternatively, a retail product may be directed at an extra market, as when sewing machines are sold to girls' schools, motor-cars to fleet owners and domestic equipment to hotels. The advertising in such cases is likely to be more credible and convincing because of proven use in industrial, commercial or professional markets.

In recent years we have seen market expansion among financial services as a result of the deregulation of the Stock Exchange and the Building Societies Act. Banks, building societies, insurance companies, investment brokers and others have extended both their services and their markets, and they have contributed greatly to the rapid development of direct response marketing, whether through direct mail or 'off-the-page' press advertisements.

3   To announce a modification

An existing product may be given a 'face lift' with an additive (as with petrols, toothpastes and household cleaners), a new finish or casing, or perhaps even a new pack or container such as a circular instead of a square tea-bag or a child-proof jar for medicinal tablets. The attempt may be made to revive the sale of a product when the life-cycle is waning too quickly or because of competition (Figure 3.1).

Sales promotion schemes may be used to recover sales.

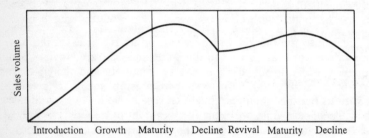

Figure 3.1   Recycled product life cycle showing introduction of modified product to reverse declining sales

4   To announce a price change

Prices can go up or down, as can rates of interest offered by building societies, banks and other finance houses. Such changes may need to be announced quickly, and advertising is a means of making announcements quickly, whether through the media or at the point-of-sale. Press ads for supermarket chains make great play with price cuts.

This has been a costly exercise for banks and building societies as interest rates have risen and fallen, and one way or the other the changes offer opportunities to win more investors.

5   To announce a new pack

This has been touched on above, but it is worth closer examination on its own because a new pack can have many implications. Pack identification at the point-of-sale is always important, especially in self-service stores, and is a reason why packages are illustrated in advertisements. Colour advertisements do this job admirably. This becomes even more important if there is a change of pack as has happened with British confectionery sold on the continent which has required a change of brand names. New sales may be attracted by the opportunity to awaken new product interest. The package may be lighter in weight and unbreakable – plastic instead of glass bottles – capable of preserving the product longer, or be in keeping with modern trends such as a measured sachet instead of a tin from which the product had to be measured. Perhaps a very old-fashioned but old-established container or label has been updated and it is necessary to familiarize customers with the new look while assuring them that the product itself is unaltered or may even be improved. Consumers are apt to suspect that a new pack means a different or inferior product, and the advertising, and the public relations, has to dispel such dangerous misgivings which could easily inhibit sales.

For this reason, unless there is a deliberately dramatic face-lift, packaging changes occur so gradually as to be unnoticed but accepted. This has happened with Guinness labels, Swan Vestas match boxes, Kodak film cartons, Nestlé's chocolate wrappers and McDougall's flour bags.

6 To make a special offer

For various reasons – competition, slack season, policy to expand sales or because of cash flow problems (very evident in the UK in 1989–92 as a result of high interest rates and a stagnant house market) – advertising may be used to make a special offer and boost sales. It could be a banded pack (two bars of chocolate with a price cut), a limited time price reduction, a free gift (such as petrol or insurance with a new motor-car) or special credit terms. New products may be launched with 'introductory' special offers, a ploy often used when launching new magazines. Hotels may offer special packages during their low season. Special introductory offers are virtually a form of sampling.

7 To invite enquiries

Businessmen as diverse as hoteliers, direct response marketers, seedsmen, business-to-business traders and travel agents rely on a flow of enquiries for their services and products. In response to these enquiries they despatch tariffs, catalogues, price lists and sales literature. Enquiries may also provide sales contacts for salespeople. An initial enquiry may lead to a customer who can then become a regular one for years. Firms which sell by mail build up mailing lists in this way, for there is no better prospect now or in the future than someone who has taken the trouble to make an enquiry. This is the basis of much database marketing.

8   To sell direct

Department stores, book and music clubs, and firms specializing in direct response marketing, sell direct to customers. Shopping without shops has become big business, and the largest of these marketers are now the financial houses rather than the club catalogue operators. Customers may buy 'off-the-page' from press advertisements which illustrate or describe the goods and contain an order coupon, or from catalogues and direct mail shots or from TV commercials. Orders may be posted or telephoned. Payment may be by cheque, postal order or credit/charge card and the latter are often illustrated on the order form.

9   To test a medium

Some large advertisers prefer to test a new or untried publication rather than accept or reject the claims made by the publishers. Testing is usually achieved by advertising a free gift – a food manufacturer may offer a recipe leaflet or a sample – and counting the requests received. This response is then related to the cost of the space to arrive at a cost-per-reply figure (which may be compared with that of publications already used) which will indicate the pulling power and economy of the publication.

10   To announce the location of stockists

To support retailers, to encourage the 'selling out' of stocks which the company sales representative (or wholesaler) has 'sold in' and to urge action on the part of readers, space may be taken to list the names and addresses of stockists. With small unit mass market goods (fmcgs) such as foodstuffs, toiletries and proprietary medicines it will be sufficient to say 'at all good grocers' or 'at Boots and other chemists', but with goods sold by appointed dealers – motor-cars, sewing machines, furniture – it is necessary to list the dealers by county and town. There may be only one dealer in a large town, but sales can be lost if prospective customers are not guided to these showrooms or stores. It is not good enough to depend on prospective customers hunting for stockists.

11   To obtain stockists

This is a subtle use of advertising whereby consumers are entreated to ask retailers for the product by name. Their demands encourage retailers to place orders with wholesalers or the advertiser's sales representative. When a manufacturer is trying to get distribution for a new product this is a useful method, but there is the risk that the consumer will accept a substitute and not persist in the search for the advertised product. Obviously, the method is most likely to be successful when the product is novel or the first of its kind.

It is unwise to expect such advertising to act as a substitute for an inadequate sales force, and it can be fatal to advertise something for which adequate distribution has not been set up in advance. Unavailability can only provoke frustration and ill-will. That is wasteful advertising, and bad public relations. Nor can reliance be placed on this method when retail take-up depends on central buyers as with supermarket chains. Astute buying will be guided by trade terms and allocation of shelf space (which may be restricted to so many good selling brands), and the requests of customers at local store level are hardly likely to reach a central buyer for perhaps several hundred stores.

12 To educate customers

Rather unfairly it is sometimes said by critics of advertising that there are two kinds, *informative* and *persuasive*, and that the former is more socially acceptable or ethical than the latter. In fact, organized advertising in the UK has had to fight off EC proposals that advertising should be confined to the informative kind. This would nullify the whole purpose of advertising which is to persuade people to buy what is advertised, not merely tell them what may be bought.

Nevertheless, the educational advertisement is necessary when a commodity, service or an offer needs careful explanation. This technique can also be used to show new uses for a well-established product. The market can often be extended if extra uses can be suggested. Public transport is promoted by suggesting places to visit, while insurance societies and banks will seek to educate people about their financial or family responsibilities and the virtues of thrift. Or it may be that prejudice and ignorance are inhibiting sales of a product whose performance is doubted. Packaged holidays abroad took many years to popularize, and it has taken fish and chips and bingo to overcome fears about funny foreign food and other doubtful pleasures. It is still necessary to educate some people about the merits of air travel, and there were those, long before it was completed, who said they would never travel through the Channel Tunnel. They said that in the 1930s about flying across the Atlantic, and twenty five years before that about flying across the English Channel!

Educational advertisements can also be ingenious or entertaining as with the strip cartoons which have been used to demonstrate how to treat a lawn, protect plants from insects, carry out do-it-yourself jobs such as decorating, or (with maps) how to reach retail premises, exhibitions and sports venues.

13 To maintain sales

Oh, yes! People often think the purpose of advertising is to increase sales, and while that may be welcome, a major objective can be to keep sales as good as they are, or at optimum level (e.g. there is a break-even point with most things such as how many seats have to be filled on an airliner before a profit is made), or to sell the output of a factory.

One of the secrets of successful advertising is its continuity, in one form or another, however seasonal the main emphasis may be. To prove the point one has only to look at one of those old pictures of horse buses jammed together in a crowded London street and to read the names of the advertisers whose placards were fixed to every available space on the vehicles. Many of them will be familiar as the biggest names in trade today. Their advertising has been continuous.

Not all advertising is aimed at promoting new and exciting products. There are everyday products such as beer, mustard, pickles, salt, matches, toothpaste, aspirins, toilet rolls and soap which have been on the market for generations. Guinness, Cadburys, Aspro, HP Sauce, Shell and Kelloggs are good examples of products whose sales have to be maintained, although increased sales are not to be sniffed at. Just how original one can be in advertising an identical product year in and year out can be seen by studying the advertising of those six products over the years.

14   To challenge competition

This motive will be apparent in most of the other sections, and naturally no advertisement is necessarily confined to only one of the possible uses listed here. But the specific purpose of a particular campaign may be to take up the challenge, as when a new substitute material comes on the market, to mention only man-made fibres to which wool has had to give battle through the International Wool Secretariat, while there was the Brick is Beautiful campaign, and the Channel ferry companies have to contend with Eurotunnel. Challenges are frequently seen at the point-of-sale where money-off offers, premium offers, free gifts and other devices are used to capture or re-capture predominant market shares. Some products, like gas and electricity, are engaged in continuously challenging advertising – the heat of the moment versus cookability. The banks and building societies find themselves with such frenetic challenges that it was possible for Abbey National to become a public limited company and virtually a massive bank, while the big five banks have lost business and had to reduce staff. European motor-car manufacturers are having to fight off the challenge of Nissan, Toyota and Honda cars built in the UK and exported to Europe, and at the Paris Motor Show on October 2 1990 Jacques Calvert, chairman of Peugeot, described the UK as 'Japan's fifth major island'.

15   To remind

As Dr Johnson said, 'People more often need to be reminded than to be informed'.

Perhaps this is similar to 'maintaining sales', but not quite. There are products which are bought repeatedly – usually small-unit items like razor blades, tea, margarine, milk, jam, matches and so on – and reminder advertising aims to get people to ask for the same brand and not break their buying habit. Thus, while very similar products, and ones less frequently bought, need advertising to maintain continuity of sales, it is also necessary with repeat purchase goods to encourage re-purchase of that brand. Reminder advertising sustains brand loyalty. Reiteration of brand names by means of signs and posters, or certain positions in publications (like the 'ear' spaces next to the title on some newspapers), and catchy slogans and jingles are used. Some slogans are deliberately perpetuated as a form of reminder advertising to mention only *The Ultimate Driving Machine*, although most of them include the name of the product like *Ah, Bisto*!

Another form of reminder advertising keeps the product or service in mind against some future need. When we go to buy a lawnmower, or a typewriter, a tea-set or a pair of shoes, we are familiar with the makes and often already pre-sold. For months we have said to ourselves 'Next time I buy a so-and-so I'll buy a such-and-such'. Reminder advertising encourages us to stick to that decision, always provided we are satisfied with the earlier purchase.

Much of this kind of advertising concerns *brand names* and it is worth noting that a *brand* is a valuable property which has to be constantly publicized. Moreover, reputation is staked on a brand, and goodwill is involved. Money is invested in promoting brands, and quite rightly they can be balance sheet assets. Companies are bought in order to acquire their brands. There would have been no controversy over the take-over of Distillers by Guinness if Distillers had not possessed such famous brands, and the acquisition was sought at any price.

There is a lot to be said for *paying for the name* because this is a guarantee of satisfaction, and reminder advertising is part of the process of ensuring satisfaction whether it be of a low-price bargain or of an expensive luxury.

Reminder advertising also helps to consolidate an advertising campaign. The brand is advertised in the press or on TV, there may be a time-gap before we visit a stockist, but there is the form of point-of-sale display which is a reminder advertisement.

16   To retrieve lost sales

Again, this is not unlike one or two previously discussed purposes, except that here there is a much more urgent need to use advertising. It has to reverse a negative sales trend, and not just compete. It is an uphill task. Sales may have been lost by default – maybe a foolish cut-back in advertising expenditure or because the product has suffered from a fashion craze or has been temporarily unobtainable due to a strike or restricted imports. Maybe the advertiser is at the mercy of a government that has adopted a policy of high interest rates to the detriment of the economy, and is suffering a cash flow problem which threatens bankruptcy, a situation which provoked recession in the early 1990s. In such circumstances, estate agents, furnishers, do-it-yourself stores and others to do with the domestic home industry found themselves in peril. Some survived by using advertising to retrieve sales, having cut prices, staff, premises and inventories and thereby stimulating cash flow. Trying to retrieve lost sales can be an act of desperation, but there are occasions when a bad situation has been reversed and the advertising has exploited good news, just as Van Den Berghs did when they were able to bring back Stork margarine after the Second World War.

17   To support stockists

Advertising addressed to distributors, such as in the trade press, by direct mail and through exhibitions, aims to *sell in* to the trade, and consumer advertising and sales promotion aims to *sell out* (not in the sense of a shop being 'sold out' but in helping to stimulate turnover). Nowadays, with so many national brands, and 'own labels' of most supermarket chains, distributors cannot afford to tie up money in goods which sit on the shelves or in the showroom. It is a vital question of cash flow. The mark-up or profit margin of most small unit mass market goods (fmcgs) is so small that profitability depends on volume sales. Equally, on more expensive goods which do enjoy a large mark-up, the greater the turnover the greater the profitability and this can apply to items such as domestic appliances (white goods), jewellery and motor-cars. Thus, to be successful any trader has to use and re-use his funds as often as possible.

Nevertheless, whether one is selling cornflakes or lawnmowers, the original manufacturer or supplier can maintain the optimum and profitable turnover of production or imports and not have a stagnant warehouse only by helping to promote sales at the retail end. This may be done by running prize contests, making money-off offers, or giving away plastic toys in packs or, in the case of a motor-car manufacturer, by entering car rallies or participating in the motor show. Allied to this will be public relations activities from press relations to sponsorships.

Dealer support is critical with supermarkets and chain stores which have evolved techniques which permit only a certain area of shelf space to a limited number of accepted brands. Similarly, showrooms have space for only a certain number of models. Some large stores go so far as to test sales of a new product in a single branch where sales are observed, before ordering stock for their chain. Imagine how important this is to a manufacturer whose success lies in selling to say Sainsbury, Tesco, Boots or Woolworth, or to gas and electricity showrooms. It is therefore extremely difficult to break into a market which already carries many competitive brands. Consequently, it takes more than the efforts of a persuasive salesperson to sell goods 'in', and much of the representative's success will depend on adequate advertising success to sell the goods 'out'. The modern retailer, before agreeing to order stocks, is liable to ask: 'Will there be TV advertising?', and the salesperson needs to be armed with proof of advertising support.

This does not mean that advertising appears on TV solely to please retailers, but it is the one medium seen by both consumers and retailers as members of the viewing public, and they may be more impressed by this support (which they can see with their very own eyes) than by advertisements in women's magazines which they may not see. Therefore, it may pay to invite retailers to see TV commercials at their regional independent television station; to send them mailing shots telling them when commercials will be screened; or to make video-cassette presentations of commercials to buyers at their premises. On one occasion Heinz showed a whole series of TV commercials on a Sunday evening so that retailers could see what would be appearing during the weeks ahead.

Broadsheets may be mailed which also refer to other advertising aids to mention only display material, free artwork for cooperative advertising schemes, and offers to meet part of the cost of the retailer's local advertising.

Mention was made above of including stockists' addresses in advertisements and this is, of course, an excellent way of supporting the trade.

18 To please the sales force

Some companies with large field sales forces believe that a bold advertisement in a national publication seen by their sales staff will act as a morale booster. Sales people will tend to boast about their company's whole page advertisement in an appropriate journal. If these advertisements are also independent of the main advertising campaign so much the better.

Sometimes, it is difficult to reconcile sales staff when they see local manufacturers advertising in their sales territories, and they need to be reminded that the company's national advertising is more powerful and is beyond the reach of the local manufacturer.

19 To recruit staff

Recruitment advertising has skills of its own as will be seen from the displayed situations vacant advertising in the press, while Ford, for instance have used television advertising for recruitment purposes. Large employers are conscious of the public relations effort of their 'job ads', and make use of logos and other forms of corporate identity to enhance their efforts to attract employees. These press advertisements are usually described as *displayed classifieds*, and space is booked through the publisher's classified advertisement department.

Among the recruitment advertisements, such as those which appear in the Sunday business newspapers and the trade press, will also be found those inserted by 'head hunting' consultancies and employment agencies.

20 To attract investors

Financial advertising is discussed later under 'classes' of advertising, and the need to raise funds – whether by a building society, an investment broker, a unit trust, a public company or local authority – calls for detailed publicized information about the nature of the investment and its likely return (within legal limits regarding financial forecasts). Interest rates and security, ease of withdrawal of savings, the chance to spread a modest investment over a portfolio of major shares as with unit trusts, life insurance, bank deposit accounts and, in recent years, the opportunity to buy shares in privatized national enterprises (e.g. gas, telephones, steel, water and electricity) are all forms of financial advertising. They are of ever-growing variety and complexity. How else would you tap the market of unknown prospective investors and give the offer the substance which will create confidence? Press, television and direct mail are the chief media used for the purpose, and today the financial houses are great users of database direct response marketing. To this may be added the public relations support of city editors and the business pages of most newspapers, even *The Sun*.

21 To attract donors

Charities rely heavily on advertising, mostly either press or direct mail, to attract funds for their work, and this also extends to the use of direct response marketing to sell goods and seasonal items such as Christmas cards by means of illustrated catalogues. Some brilliantly creative campaigns have been run by some of these charities, often with poignant headlines such as *Save The Children. Now*!

22 To declare ecological responsibility

Many 'green' issues are involved here, such as the use of CFC gases in aerosols, unleaded petrol, catalytic exhausts on motor-cars, indestructible plastic containers, acid rain, radioactive contamination, river and sea pollution, noise abatement, experiments on animals, fur clothing and the protection of wild life. It spreads beyond preservation of the planet to the quality of human life and the social responsibilities of industry. These problems and their costs and solutions differ between companies and their products.

The efforts which have been made to modify (or create) products which are 'ozone friendly', or do not contribute to pollution (and this can include the packaging as well as what it contains), is worth promoting as a well deserved selling plus. However, it can be hypocritical to exploit the issue without justification, and some very dubious claims have been made. The Advertising Standards Authority has issued warnings about this in its monthly ASA Report.

23 To export

Here we touch on a very specialized topic where expert advice can be obtained from advertising agencies with overseas departments, branches or associates. Media outside the UK are usually different. A national press like the UK press is rare, mostly it is regional or local, while commercial radio is generally long established, there may be fewer hours of commercial television, and there may be different kinds of outdoor advertising. Direct mail is more dominant in some countries than in the UK (in spite of the Data Protection Registrar receiving about 1250 complaints a year!) with Swiss adults receiving 90 mailshots a year compared to 30 for UK adults.

Export advertising also requires knowledge of national idiom, traditions, life styles, religions and politics. Translations are best made by a national living in his or her own country who is familiar with the subject. In some cases, brands, like Coca-Cola and Kodak, can be universal, but in other cases the brand name may have to be changed to suit the local market. The Single European Market has produced Eurobrands which are acceptable in every country of the community and can be promoted by cross-frontier or transnational advertising such as on satellite television. There are some extraordinary continental European brand names which would not be acceptable in the UK.

British companies receive excellent assistance from the Central Office of Information and the British Overseas Trade Board which is part of the Department of Trade and Industry. The COI is particularly helpful in securing publicity in foreign media about UK exports, and the BOTB organizes overseas trade fairs, shopping weeks and store promotions, and outward or inward trade missions.

A UK manufacturer wishing to promote export business can make good use of advertising provided the markets are studied carefully, but each market is different. Very few products are capable of being marketed globally, exceptions being Coca-Cola and Kodak as already mentioned above: more often each region of the world and perhaps each country has to be developed individually.

An advertising appeal might be accepted in one country, but not in another. It is easy to offend Islamic attitudes regarding, say, ladies' dresses, or Chinese regarding colours which have special meanings, or innocent-seeming Western words could be phonetically offensive. A black cat may be lucky in the UK, but unlucky in West Africa.

Ethnic groups are scattered throughout the world and people of Indian or Chinese origin or ancestry can be found in almost any country, especially those which were developed by colonialists using indented labour. Such people have to be respected by the exporter, and this may be necessary in the advertising, the packaging or the branding.

Advertisers have been foolish enough to insert press advertisements, or show cinema or TV commercials, which were simply exported as used in the UK. They were not only irrelevant but offensive. This is export advertising on the cheap, and it creates great ill-will towards the exporter. If models or actors are used in such advertisements, they should be nationals dressed in appropriate clothes.

Moreover, export advertising without adequate marketing and media research can be a costly failure. A great mistake is for a company, famous in its own country, to imagine that it is equally well-known in other countries. Before 1969 when the first Datsun cars appeared in the UK, few UK motorists were aware of Japanese motor-cars. Reverse this mental process and it will be realized that when a UK exporter enters a foreign market for the first time a formidable hurdle of ignorance has to be overcome. In fact, in some Middle East markets all products assume the name of the first brand to be sold there so that all trucks are called 'Mercedes', and all sewing machines are known as 'Singers', rather in the fashion of carpet cleaners acquiring the generic name of 'Hoover'.

24 To announce trading results

This is another form of financial advertising and whether a full chairman's annual report is published or there is a digest of essentials for the lay reader's benefit, it is a necessary procedure to announce trading results of a public company. In a good year, it is an opportunity to boast, and there are often original efforts to interest the lay reader by presenting an edited version of the chairman's report, illustrated with charts, sketches or photographs. A copy of the full report is usually offered.

3.3 Jargon

In setting out these 24 reasons for advertising it has also been possible to give an introductory glimpse of the complex but fascinating world of advertising, and its valuable application to many facets of marketing communications for various undertakings. Inevitably, it has been necessary to use the jargon or the special language of the advertising business – and there is plenty of it! – but as the reader proceeds through this book these terms will become easier to understand as they take their natural place in the vocabulary of the topics to which they refer. These terms are indexed at the back of the book, and if the reader is uncertain of the meaning of a term it can usually be cross-referenced by means of the index.

For example, *medium* (singular) and *media* (plural) have been mentioned. The press, radio and television are collectively media and individually each is a medium. *Above-the-line* media are the traditional commission-paying ones of press, radio, cinema, television and outdoor, while *below-the-line* media consist of everything else such as direct mail, exhibitions, sales literature, point-of-sale display material, body media and give-aways. *Displayed* and *classified* advertisements have been mentioned, the first being the creative advertisements with their clever designs and the second being the 'smalls' in which the wording or *copy* is run on line after line. *Displayed classifieds*, such as the designed recruitment advertisements, appear in the classified sections of publications, meaning classified by subject such as situations vacant, houses or motor-cars for sale.

3.4 The eleven classes of advertising

To continue this initial analysis of advertising, eleven distinct and particular classes of advertising will be considered. Each one calls for its own treatment and usually particular media. The great array of advertising media in industrialized countries makes this analysis possible, and it will be seen that because there are hundreds of publications, many television and radio stations, hundreds of outdoor sites of different kinds, and extensive postal services it is possible to address all kinds of advertising to all sorts of people. Such advantages exist on a much smaller scale in developing countries. From the following analysis the diversity of advertising can be appreciated more clearly. The eleven classes of advertising are:

1	Persuasive	7	Cooperative
2	Informative	8	Industrial and business-to-business
3	Institutional		
4	Financial	9	Government
5	Classified	10	Trade
6	Retail	11	Direct response

These 11 classes do not include what is sometimes incorrectly called 'mail order' advertising for two reasons. Strictly speaking, mail order is a form of *distribution* which uses advertising media such as direct mail and the press, catalogues and sometimes television. The expression mail order has been replaced by *direct response*, so direct response advertising has been added as an eleventh class. This compromise enables the inclusion of a fast-growing area of advertising.

1 Persuasive

Also known as 'hard sell' advertising (in contrast to 'soft sell' which presents advertising messages in a more restrained and subtle fashion), this is the most obvious kind which surrounds us in our daily lives, urging us to buy all manner of consumer products and services. Without such sales generating advertising it is hard to imagine how modern society, with its mass production and mass consumption, could survive. It is the lifeblood of free enterprise.

Scathing comments are made about the 'admass', but its critics happen to enjoy the plentiful supply of goods which satisfy their economic needs of food, clothes and shelter. Countless pleasures and former luxuries are also enjoyed simply because economies of scale can be exploited, thanks to advertising and other aids to distribution to local, national and international markets. The argument for advertising is similar to that for the Single European Market.

The alternative to advertising is to revert to the medieval style of life with self-sufficient production and modestly adequate incomes for most craftsmen, little commercial intercourse between towns, exports of certain primary commodities (of which wool predominated in Britain), no banking, no credit and religious antipathy towards money-lending and profits. It is interesting that economic historians have noted the link between capitalism and protestantism with the leap into capitalism in Tudor times and into banking in Stuart times, while much of the industrial revolution concerns non-conformist entrepreneurs. Or the comparison may be made with the primitive conditions, low standard of living and unsophistication of an undeveloped country where there is little or no use for advertising. In developing countries, and especially in the newly industrialized Asiatic countries (NICS), advertising is taking its place alongside industrialization and urbanization. For example, both advertising and public relations play a large part in national family planning, anti-smoking and AIDs campaigns, as well as in the promotion of consumer products and services.

Persuasive advertising is the inevitable companion of industrialization. There is no point in having machines, including the modern use of robotics, if markets cannot be found for their output: *persuasive* advertising probes the markets and keeps the wheels of industry turning by creating and maintaining *demand*. Not only factories rely on advertising: a holiday resort cannot fill its hotel bedrooms, nor can a theatre attract an audience, nor an insurance company attract policy holders, without advertising. Moreover, this kind of advertising persuades people to recognize and consider the huge variety of choices available to them, which is rather different from the criticism that advertising persuades people to buy things they do not want.

The persuasive, hard-selling advertisement must perform five functions if it is to succeed, these being to:

i   attract attention
ii   command interest
iii create desire
iv   inspire conviction
v   provoke action.

When one considers the static nature of a press advertisement, great imagination has to be employed to make those five functions work.

This process means that *attention* has to be attracted from elsewhere, and *interest* held by the message which makes the reader (or viewer or listener) *desire* to own and enjoy the product or service. The message must *convince* the customer of performance or value for money, and some form of inducement, maybe a coupon or special offer, must *provoke* action. All this will require an elaborately planned, created, presented and well-placed advertisement.

Here, then, is the powerful sales-generating advertisement which employs all the imaginative techniques of copywriting, design and media planning to achieve its objectives. And in this we begin to see why advertising calls for such a medley of skills, and why the advertising agency has become the means of providing the advertiser with the brains, talents and experience necessary to plan, create and execute campaigns that succeed in selling their clients' products or services.

2 Informative

Not everything is bought right away. It may have to be thought about very carefully, and there may be quite a bit of window-shopping and budgeting before the final purchase is made. Or it may be one of those once in a lifetime buys, or a present for some lucky person some day in the future. More leisurely and often more expensive purchases can result from a careful study of helpful and explanatory advertisements over a period of time. Central heating, double glazing, motor-cars, designed kitchens, and many technical goods are typical products of this kind which call for very informative copy and pictures. Mostly, they are ones we call *consumer durables*, things that endure and are bought infrequently.

So here we have a very different kind of advertising, less dramatic and compelling perhaps, but nonetheless attractive, interesting and convincing. The pace of the appeal is less strident, there is much more detailed copy to read, perhaps more pictures to look at. The object of the advertisement may be to invite the reader to obtain fuller information by applying for a brochure or arranging for a demonstration.

Of course, a lot of advertisements fall mid-way between the persuasive and the informative. There are exceptions such as proprietary medicines and treatment advertisements which sell by means of facts, evidence, testimonials and other lengthy copy, but generally speaking, persuasive advertisements tend to appear on TV and in the popular press while information advertisements are more likely to appear in magazines or weekend newspapers and their colour supplements which are read more thoroughly or in less hurried circumstances.

There is also the informative advertisement which hardly seems to sell at all, telling us interesting things that are somewhat removed from the product itself, or creating a mood which makes us feel favourably disposed towards the company, product or service. Here we have the 'soft sell' as opposed to the 'hard sell' appeal. A striking example was a whole page advertisement for the Epson printer, headed *A Potted History of Printing From the First Letter to the Last Word*. This intriguing advertisement told of the evolution of writing and typesetting with illustrations of characters. The copy had paragraphs such as:

> Peruvian Quipus – knotted cards of different colours – were used by Inca Civil Servants as a sort of filing system for public records.
>
> They are still used in Lambeth today.
>
> The Quipa may have been alright for beating llamas,
> but as a way of communicating, it couldn't beat writing: 'the greatest invention of man' according to Abraham Lincoln'.

(Pity the poor copywriter could not spell all right!)

Yet another version is the reader or editorial style advertisement which simulates an editorial feature and is very informative. Because reader ads are easily mistaken for genuine editorial, and, after all, that was presumably the original intention, editors object to them and they are usually distinguished by words such as 'Advertiser's Announcement' which virtually nullifies the illusion.

3 Institutional

Also known as *prestige, corporate, image building* or *advocacy* advertising, this is really a kind of advertising used for public relations purposes. It aims to tell the story of an organization, gain credit for its achievements, establish a correct image of its nature and purpose, position it in the market, or, in the case of advocacy advertisements, declare its position in relation to government policy on issues of the day such as pollution and environmental care. For instance, an oil or pharmaceutical company may describe its research skills, or its contribution to society. Such advertisements frequently appear in magazines such as *The Economist* and *Fortune*, and in business newspapers.

They are also used by Gulf banks to position themselves in world markets, and by Asiatic manufacturers who wish to establish themselves overseas. Banks undertake a lot of institutional advertising. Of a more propaganda nature have been advertisements aimed at defending business interests against government intervention, as happened a few years ago with the brewers. It is believed that the brewers (who are among the top donors to Conservative Party funds!) spent £5m on their campaign to stop the proposals of Lord Young and the Monopolies and Mergers Commission to cut the brewers' monopoly of pub ownership.

Corporate advertisements also appear on television and we have seen them for the gas, electricity and water industries, sometimes as a preliminary campaign prior to privatization of state enterprises. The latter has provoked controversy because there did not seem to be a clear distinction between establishing a corporate image and selling shares!

An example of an institutional advertisement was that for the international insurance company Allianz. This was a double-page full-colour spread in *The Economist* with a picture of a North Sea oil rig in stormy seas. The copy was commendably compact:

Talking about the weather.

Some projects face a weather risk.
That's why Allianz experts take
account of regional weather conditions
when drawing up a specialist
insurance cover.
   For 100 years comprehensive
technical and financial resources
have made Allianz a proven partner
for business.
   Chance has played no role in
making us the leader in the demanding
European market. Nowadays,
Allianz insures major industrial and
technical projects all over the world.

Allianz

EUROPE'S LEADING INSURANCE COMPANY

4 Financial

Financial advertising does not have to be sober. Some banks have used humorous TV commercials like the Midland's 'Listening bank' series, and building societies have followed suit with slogans such as 'I am with the Woolwich', while American Express have made a catchword of 'That'll do nicely'.

This can become a very big part of the advertising scene with banks, insurance companies, loan houses, unit trusts, personal equity plans (PEPS), investment brokers, pension funds and others participating, while there are the very detailed and often two page prospectuses for new share issues, and the announcements of interim and annual trading results. Financial advertisements appear not only in the *Financial Times* and business newspapers, but also in the popular press and on television. Today, either as a result of privatization share offers or unit trusts, millions of people own shares, while many more have bank or building society accounts. Financial houses are among the greatest users of database direct response marketing.

Perhaps the chief characteristic of much financial advertising is its detail. Readers usually want and are entitled to know a lot about the offer being made. What are the risks, the safeguards, and the likely rewards – whether it be an advertisement for National Savings or motor insurance? This is also very often highly competitive persuasive advertising, with closing dates for offers or bonuses for quick response. Sales promotion gimmicks have been introduced, such as free gifts by famous insurance companies, which would have been unconventional at one time. Selling financial services has become very marketing oriented and aggressive, especially in its use of direct mail appeals as operated by Norwich Union and Sun Alliance. Organizations such as the Automobile Association adopt persuasive tactics to sell insurance services, while there is tremendous competition to sell a variety of similar services, the building societies becoming virtually banks. Much of this has resulted from legislation which has freed many financial institutions from earlier limitations, but not without consumer protection rules.

5   Classifieds

While a great many classified advertisements ('smalls') are inserted by individuals, others are placed by commercial firms as will be seen, for instance, in the situations vacant columns of both newspapers and magazines. The Personal Column in newspapers is often used by both national and other newspapers for both private and commercial advertisements, although they may be clearly separated. Some newspapers such as *The Times* and *Daily Telegraph* are well-known for personal notices of births, marriages and deaths.

There is a special art in writing a telegrammatic advertisement in a few lines, using a catchy opening to attract attention, squeezing as much abbreviated but intelligible copy into as few lines as possible. The impact of a classified can be lost if the copy is too long because it begins to look like a grey mass. Classified advertisements are charged by the line or word, not by the column depth, and this encourages the advertiser to use short or shortened words and to eliminate prepositions and conjunctions, arriving at something like this:

> First fl.brm to let.Elec.fire.
> Quiet nbhd,nr stn.Call evngs.
> 081 111 0101

Small advertisements are big business by telephone, and for many publishers this is a busy tele-marketing operation, either outwards by telephone sales staff, or inwards by members of the public ringing in their advertisements.

6 Retail

With the exception of production retailers – bakers, florists, hairdressers – most retailers are selling other people's goods, even when they are own label or house brands. Another exception is the shop which sells the manufacturer's own products, such as Boots. But mostly they are selling goods which have been bought via wholesalers or direct from manufacturers for re-sale. Even bakers buy in wrapped bread from plant bakers, florists seldom grow their own flowers, and hairdressers sell products as well as their services. Retail advertising is therefore largely to do with creating turnover, and goods must not be left merely to decorate the shop. It is not enough to expect people to visit the shop of their own volition, although ninety years ago Gordon Selfridge did open his Oxford Street store with the invitation to people to enjoy a day out, visiting his store, and he endeavoured to turn shopping into a pleasure. Generally, retail advertising has four objectives:

i   to sell the *stocks*.
ii   to establish the *identity* or character of the store – a kind of 'image' advertising – and it is interesting to note how different shops selling similar merchandise also have distinct characters.
iii to identify the *location*.
iv   to attract personal, telephone or direct response *shoppers*.

Modern shopping may have special attractions such as one-stop shopping, encouraged by the popularity of the motor-car and provision of parking facilities so that a whole week's shopping, or more with the ownership of domestic refrigerators and freezers, can replace daily shopping.

Obviously, retail advertising has to work very hard, even harder than a persuasive advertisement for a manufacturer. The rewards, or lack of them, will be equally obvious. Such advertising is crucial to the success and survival of a shopkeeper. Not only does the retailer have to buy skilfully, and provide good service for customers, but it is necessary to understand how advertising can achieve the four objectives set out above. This task becomes all the more demanding when one considers what little understanding the smaller trader is likely to have of advertising techniques and that the budget probably does not justify the use of agency services, although local newspapers may be able to offer the creative assistance of their service departments. Some suppliers may offer retailers cooperative advertising schemes.

In announcing stock an economic division may have to be made between types of products, or between departments of a big store. Conversely, the policy may be to offer a bargain, or a 'loss leader' (a sprat to catch a mackerel in the form of a price cut on one item). This will attract what is called *store traffic*, the buyer of the special offer being expected to buy other goods at regular prices.

But the second objective, establishing character, demonstrates the use of and value of advertising in this field. Whether the advertisements are splashed with this week's bargain offers of a supermarket or superstore, or whether they are set out in the sophisticated style of the great department stores, the character emerges to the extent that Tesco and Sainsbury or Harrods and Heals are each clearly differentiated in their own particular way. As a result, customers prefer certain shops as they prefer certain brands. This can be something which also applies to class interests, and stores will adopt certain mark-ups on the same goods to appeal to different classes of people. There are people, for instance, who will deliberately re-use a Harrods' plastic bag and shun a Marks and Spencer one, even though the re-use is to carry, say, potatoes. As an example of this, there was a time in Croydon when four stores, Grants, Allders, Kennards and the Co-op represented four distinct classes of shopper. Today, Grants and the Co-op have gone. Allders is a huge universal department store, and Debenhams has replaced Kennards with a new store with a glass lift and fountains. Shopping today has become less class conscious and stores are more sophisticated with an incredible range of merchandise.

From the above remarks it will be seen that retail advertising is more complicated than advertising by the manufacturers, and reflects great social changes. Many of the chains are selling the store as much as the merchandise to the extent that they carry many own label products, and national brands can be in danger of being de-listed by store buyers. Some manufacturers of national brands, such as Nestlé, make a point – out of self defence – that they do not pack own label products for supermarkets. Meanwhile, the advent of the Single European Market, means that national brands will have to fight hard to keep their brands in the supermarkets, which have the opportunity to offer their customers a huge range of continental brands and so widen customer choice.

Tesco have made great play of this in television commercials, all part of their strenuous campaign to build a quality image.

Location is also important, especially when it offers special advantages such as a traffic-free shopping precinct or an out-of-town site with parking, banking, nursery, hairdressing, dry-cleaning and other facilities. Advertisements may contain maps to direct customers to the location.

Another type of retailer who depends on advertising is the symbol group shop, which may be a small local grocery, which is able to buy comparatively small stocks from one wholesaler, e.g. Spar. The shop is decorated as a Spar shop, carries Spar lines, and benefits from Spar advertising. In some continental countries almost every village or town has its Spar supermarket. Symbol groups should not be confused with stores like Debenhams, Woolworths and Marks and Spencer which have their own branded goods, e.g. St Michael.

Finally, especially since delivery services are not always provided nowadays – another big change in retailing – and because of the competition from direct response marketing companies (shopping without shops), fashion and other stores have adopted direct response themselves, using off-the-page press advertisements or mailing catalogues to potential customers.

7 Co-operative (four kinds)

The four types of co-operative advertising are:

i   *Cooperative society* (Co-op) and agricultural and similar cooperative trading organizations. This is really only a form of retail advertising, and is introduced here merely for the sake of clarifying the succeeding kinds. However, it is worth mentioning as a sign of the times and demise of the once great Co-operative Movement with scores of town or regional societies which had chains of shops and millions of members. They operated on the Rochdale principle of the customer being a shareholder who received a dividend on purchases. Today, the Co-ops are few in number and are either supermarkets or stores which remain open for long hours resembling the 7-Eleven stores.

ii *Joint advertising* placed by a trade association, a national export organization, or a publicity committee set up on behalf of an industry. Members contribute to a pool for joint advertising purposes. Examples of these three versions are the advertisements for the Brick Development Association, the Joint Venture overseas trade fair facilities of the Department of Trade and Industry, and those of the National Milk Council which among other things sponsored the Milk Cycling Race.

iii *Mutual advertising schemes* where two or more firms combine their advertising, as in the case of fashion houses and department stores, bread and butter, packaged holidays and swimsuits. There are also joint sales promotion schemes, e.g. Kelloggs All Bran and a Crown Paint offer and cross-couponing offers when a cash token from one product may be exchanged towards the price of another manufacturer's product.

iv *Dealer support schemes* which are also known as cooperative schemes, the most common use of the term cooperative advertising. The manufacturer may either subsidize the cost of the stockist's local advertising, usually on a 50–50 basis, or supply free advertising material such as camera-ready artwork and copy with space for the stockist's name and address to be inserted, or artwork of products for use in more general advertisements. This will be seen in many advertisements for motor-car dealers which carry pictures of the vehicles and logos of their makers. Such material is also supplied for use in catalogues, direct mail shots and on letter-headings.

8   Industrial and business-to-business

Most industrial advertising offers raw materials, components, capital goods such as machinery, and services to other manufacturers who convert, or use these products, in order to produce finished goods for the consumer market. A house or a motor-car, a television set or a central heating system is an assembly of items made by others. Industrial advertising aims to sell, say, plastic rainwater pipes, pretreated timber, infill panels, wood-block flooring, wall tiles, bathroom equipment, doors, windows, bricks, breeze blocks, cement, roofing tiles, insulation material and so on to housebuilders, probably as specified by an architect. The media in this case of the building industry may consist of the trade press, trade exhibitions, direct mail and displays or demonstrations in building centres. The eventual buyer of a house may have little opportunity of specifying such materials, or even knowing their source. Likewise, with a motor-car it is very difficult to demand certain brands of components such as sparking plugs, battery, wheels or tyres.

Industrial advertisers are sometimes referred to as *secondary suppliers*. Their promotional activities – often making good use of public relations techniques such as press relations, videos and technical seminars – are called *back selling*. The advertiser has the problem that, as mentioned above, his product may seldom or never be known to the final customer, and so sales can rarely be achieved by appealing to the final customer for support. For example, a manufacturer may decide to reduce costs by eliminating a feature of a product, and the supplier of that feature is at the mercy of the assembler.

The sugar industry has suffered from the replacement of sugar by artificial sweeteners in drinks and confectionery. A manufacturer of timers had to fight very hard not to have timers deleted from cookers. We have seen glass containers replaced by plastic ones. Industrial advertisers are constantly having to maintain sales or find new markets.

A principal medium for industrial advertising is the trade and technical press (which also sponsors many of the trade exhibitions or does so in conjunction with trade associations), and the UK is favoured with one of the world's most extensive ranges of specialized journals. They bring industrial advertisers and their markets close together. In this we see just how valuable is the advertising side of the trade and technical press, especially since advertising budgets for industrial advertising are usually modest. Some of these journals also have international circulations, which is useful for companies which export.

The controlled circulation (cc) journal enables advertisers to gain great penetration of the market since a free list is inevitably larger than that of subscribers to a journal with a cover price, that is a retail price. However, controlled circulation journals are not distributed indiscriminately and in order to attain an Audit Bureau of Circulations figure equivalent to a net figure, the mailing list has to be substantially based on requests from readers. For some years controlled circulation journals were able to charge higher rates than bought journals because of their greater penetration of markets. However, the economics of publishing have changed. Printing, paper and postage costs have risen. The sale of space has become more competitive. Trade and technical journals, like newspapers and consumer magazines, have to rely increasingly on cover prices to provide profitable revenue. Consequently, a number of controlled circulation journals now seek to enrol subscribers, retaining a minimal number of free copies. We have seen this with *Direct Response Marketing, Marketing Week* and *PR Week* in our own field. New trade and technical journals are often launched on a controlled circulation basis, but after perhaps a year when the regular readership has been established recipients are asked to pay for future copies.

House journals and membership journals should not be confused with controlled circulation journals.

Business-to-business advertising also consists of selling business goods and services to business. These are not raw materials or heavy machinery, but the means of running a business such as computers, office machines, office furniture and other business equipment. A number of advertising agencies have been set up which specialize in this sphere.

However, industrial and business-to-business advertising has in recent years adopted the overall title of business-to-business advertising in the sense that it comprises all non-consumer advertising. This is in line with the optional CAM Diploma subject, Business-to-Business Advertising, and Martyn Davis' book *Business To Business Promotion and Marketing*.

Advertising media will consist of appropriate trade journals and business newspapers, specialist trade exhibitions, direct mail and catalogues.

With the arrival of so many sophisticated office machines such as personal computers, word processors, copiers and fax machines this has become a growth area in advertising. There has been a corresponding growth in the media servicing the business-to-business industry. This has been a field in which the Japanese have predominated with firms like Brother, Canon, Minolta and Toshiba. They have revolutionized a market which hitherto had been dominated by the older typewriter companies.

9   Government

Some of the earliest press advertising, as described in Chapter 2, was placed by governments. Under this heading is included advertising by central and local government and also by those state-owned enterprises which still exist in spite of privatization. The Government is the biggest advertiser in the UK, and Thatcher Governments (especially with all the multi-million pound privatization flotations) spent more on advertising than any previous government. The electricity privatization campaign in 1990 cost the Government £20m, the Frankenstein character 'Frank' producing even more registrations for information than the 'Sid' campaign for gas shares. Government advertising should not be confused with party political propaganda campaigns, although in the case of the Thatcher Government the difference was sometimes blurred.

Government department or ministry advertising to announce social benefits, run AIDs or road safety campaigns, or recruit nurses or policemen are organized by the Central Office of Information which appoints agencies for the purpose. The role of the British Overseas Trade Board was described under Export in the earlier part of this chapter, and this involves another form of government advertising. The state enterprises and public authorities conduct their own advertising campaigns, appointing their own agents. Local authorities advertise their facilities and amenities such as airports, theatres, sports arenas, industrial estates and so on. They will also use advertising (like central government departments) to recruit staff, and local authorities will also invite investments in short-term fixed interest bonds in order to raise money for projects.

However, most central and local government advertising will be for the purpose of announcing benefits or measures in the public interest.

10   Trade

Sometimes rather misleadingly termed 'trade propaganda' (see definition of propaganda in Chapter 2) trade advertising is addressed to distributors who may consist of agents, wholesalers, brokers, factors, retailers, direct response marketers, importers and exporters, by the manufacturer, producer or supplier.

The media of trade press, direct mail and trade exhibitions are the most commonly used, but TV is used occasionally and TV contractors offer special merchandising schemes by which retailers are told of forthcoming TV campaigns.

The purpose of trade advertising is to secure distribution, that is to 'sell in' to the trade and to gain repeat orders. Its appeal is to the distributors' desire to sell more and make more profit. This appeal has a totally different objective to that of consumer advertising. It promotes not the benefits of the product but the benefits of selling the product. It takes place (or should take place!) prior to consumer advertising because it is folly to advertise something which is unobtainable. Nevertheless, an objective can be to *increase* distribution by finding new outlets.

Trade advertising will urge the distributor to buy stock, either direct or when a representative calls, offering introductory discounts, special trade terms, display material, cooperative advertising schemes, and announcing consumer advertising support. This in turn will be backed up by editorial write ups in the press. With established products, reminder advertising will also occur or be supplied to decorate the premises, particularly outside, like the flags, facia boards, metal signs, and pavement displays that remind passers-by that the shop stocks certain brands. For some lines there will be seasonal campaigns to stimulate demand.

An excellent form of trade advertising is the big broadsheet which reproduces full-size specimens of forthcoming press advertisements and stills from TV commercials, and also illustrates the available point-of-sale display material plus artwork available for local press advertising. This broadsheet will carry an order form so that the retailer can request the supporting material that can be used. This is more economical than dumping display material on a retailer who may discard it. Broadsheets are direct mailed some weeks before the launch or the special promotion, and is one of the ways of establishing direct contact when the product is distributed through wholesalers and there is no direct representation. Otherwise, trade advertising helps to create good relations between the sales force and buyers, helping to narrow the gap in the salesperson's four-or-six weekly journey cycle.

The trade exhibition, usually limited to bona fide trade visitors, tickets being issued in trade journals, or by exhibitors to their customers, or by presentation of a business card at the turnstile, is a means of demonstrating products, especially new ones and prototypes, and of meeting distributors. Some exhibitors regard trade exhibitions as goodwill missions, a blend of trade advertising and dealer relations, aimed at cementing good relations, Many retailers have no personal link with a company beyond the representative who calls, but at exhibitions retailers can meet people from head office. Very often the stand will include a private lounge and bar where distributors are welcomed and entertained.

Trade relations also include education and training, the sales assistants being taught the uses and applications of a product, and also being trained in selling and servicing the product. Evidence of this often appears in shops and showrooms where framed certificates of proficiency are displayed on the wall. We are now impinging on public relations again, and a very effective form of public relations is the *external house journal* specially edited for distributors. The objective is to inform, educate and help the trade to sell the product, and this may be done by suggesting promotional ideas such as window and store displays and by reporting methods adopted by enterprising stockists. Petrol companies publish magazines for the benefit of forecourt attendants and photographic companies issue magazines which explain the technicalities of cameras, films and materials. Window display and other contests can be run through dealer magazines.

11 Direct response

Direct response marketing (or direct marketing as it is sometimes called) has replaced mail-order, and has become a major development in marketing. There is nothing new about selling without shops and the idea was introduced more than a century ago by people such as Montgomery Ward in the USA and Fattorini in the UK.

However, it has taken off in the UK in recent years thanks to the availability of database mailing lists, list brokers, and special Post Office services. Targeting recipients has been made possible by combinations of census figures and post codes with systems of geographic demographic selection such as ACORN, Mosaic and Super Profiles. This has made it possible to use direct mail very effectively. In turn, this has led to a whole industry of designing mailing materials such as special envelopes and inserts.

We have moved a long way from the Littlewoods Mail Order club type of direct response. Today, the biggest users are financial houses and department stores. The latter have resorted to direct response to meet the competition from direct marketers. Selfridge, for instance, send out their fashion and gifts for Christmas catalogues to a selected mailing list.

Direct response is not limited to direct mail with its special envelopes, sales letters, order forms and gimmicks. The catalogue is an important medium which may be mailed, supplied on request, tipped into magazines, or delivered door-to-door. Leaflets are frequently inserted loose in publications, A great deal of direct response advertising is conducted by 'off-the-page' press advertisements which invite orders by post or telephone, and credit card payments are usually accepted. Television commercials are also used to sell goods direct. Piggy-backing is a common technique whereby small catalogues are inserted with other people's mailings such as credit card accounts.

This analysis of eleven different classes of advertising provides an introduction to the widespread nature of advertising and the contribution it makes to the success of the economy. Far from being parasitical it will be seen to be an essential factor of industrial, commercial, business and public life.

4
The advertiser, advertising manager and advertising department

4.1 The tripartite nature of advertising

The three sides of advertising are the *advertisers, advertising agencies* and *media owners*. They are represented in the same order by the Incorporated Society of British Advertisers (ISBA), the Institute of Practitioners in Advertising (IPA) and numerous media organizations such as the Newspaper Publishers' Association (NPA). The three sides are represented on joint bodies such as the Joint Industry Committee for National Readership Surveys (JICNARS).

4.2 The advertiser

Without the advertiser there would be no advertising trinity. The advertiser is the tail that wags the dog. If there are no buyers of print, artwork, agency services, advertisement space, air time or outdoor sites and exhibition space, the entire advertising industry is depressed. This runs right through the economy and is a barometer of the nation's stability and prosperity. It contributes to employment and to living standards. Some advertisers, like Cadbury and Heinz, go on for ever, but many others fail and disappear.

This book discusses advertising at all levels of society, and before proceeding to discuss the advertising manager and the advertising department, let us first consider that the buyer of advertising, in all its many forms, may be a sole trader, a business proprietor or executive, a branch manager or works manager, or a sales manager. In other words, he or she may well be an individual without an advertising department and specialized staff. This individual may be an occasional advertiser as when staff are being recruited, or a regular advertiser like a shopkeeper who takes a regular weekly space in the local press, displays posters on local buses, or buys time on local radio. He or she may be capable of producing advertisements, or may use a freelance copywriter and designer, or take advantage of the service departments of the media. One way or another this advertiser buys and creates advertising.

Alternatively, if the volume of advertising expenditure warrants, a local or national agency will be appointed, and there may still be no advertising department. The job of working with the agency, and of buying various ancillary services such as print, photography, exhibition stands or direct mail mailing lists, may be that of the proprietor, a director responsible for marketing, or of an executive who incorporates advertising in his many tasks, e.g. a marketing services manager. Many industrial companies, producing only a small amount of advertising, work in one of the ways so far described. In organizations where the external communications effort is principally public relations, as happens in many technical and industrial companies and also in local government, the public relations manager may also be responsible for advertising. Generally, consumer product companies depend more on advertising than on public relations, but the reverse is true of technical companies. Rentokil is a good example of a company which spends remarkably little on advertising, has relied for more than 30 years on every kind of public relations technique, and is one of the UK's most successful businesses.

However, when advertising is a major part of the distributive function, the company will have at least an advertising manager, although he may be called a product or brand manager who will handle the total promotion for a product group (e.g. foods, drinks, toiletries) or for a particular brand.

In some companies the advertising manager will have a substantial department, and work will be divided between the agency and the department. A few very large in-house departments are similar to advertising agencies and handle the entire promotional task, even to the extent of claiming commission on media purchases. It is therefore impossible to be absolutely precise about the way companies do or should conduct advertising: each company evolves the kinds of service best suited to its special needs. For instance, some companies in recent years have developed database or direct response marketing, selling by means of off-the-page press advertisements or direct mail. They may do this themselves or be assisted by agencies which specialize in this work.

4.3   The advertising manager

There are two managerial titles which are often confused, advertising manager and advertisement manager. The former works for the advertiser and therefore *buys* advertising services, while the latter works for the *media* and is a sales manager who sells advertisement space, sites or air-time to advertisers. Much of the skill of the advertising manager thus lies in buying ability and this calls for considerable technical knowledge of what is being purchased.

Main types of advertising manager

In spite of the proliferation of titles and 'hats', there are three distinct classifications:

(i)   The advertising manager who is chiefly an administrator and who acts in liaison with advertising agencies and other outside services such as printers.
(ii) The advertising manager who heads a creative department which may use an agency to place advertisements, or may do so direct.
(iii) The brand or product manager who is responsible for product groups or particular brands.

Eight basic responsibilities of the advertising manager

1   To work closely with those responsible for shaping future policy whether it concerns new or modified products, rationalization (reducing the product mix) or diversification (making totally different products, changes in distribution methods, or entry into new markets, market segments or exports). In other words, it is unlikely that a company will go on making and marketing exactly the same product, or only the one product, and the advertising manager – because of the need to plan six months or a year ahead – must have the confidence of those in the boardroom, drawing office, laboratory, production department and, of course, marketing department. He or she should, therefore, sit in on all decision-making committees which will have a bearing on the eventual advertising.

   The advertising manager may become involved in setting up product pre-tests and test marketing exercises to decide whether the product, the marketing strategy or the advertising media and creative techniques are likely to be successful or are capable of refinement. This involvement in initial research may result in the abandonment of the proposed new product, which happened, for instance, with a stout which was intended to rival Guinness. Usually, 50 per cent of procedures test-marketed to see whether a desired percentage of the market can be gained never reach the national market. In a large company the advertising manager will be responsible for initiating research himself. This is another specialist field in which knowledge and experience is required.

2   To interpret the company policy to the advertising agency and other outside services so that their work is produced in accordance with this policy. This is a delicate operation, a matter of clear communi-

cation to others who, inevitably, do not have the benefit of the advertising manager's intimate inside knowledge gleaned over a period of time. Unless the company's requirements are conveyed in easily understandable terms, time, money and patience can be wasted on producing unacceptable campaign proposals, copy, layouts, photographs, artwork, films, videos, exhibition stands and so on.

For example, the company may have developed a *corporate identity*, that is a visual character, which is represented by a standard colour scheme, typography and use of a logo, and everything produced must follow this individual style. A particularly good example of this is an airline which is distinguished from all other airlines by its special corporate identity.

There can also be the *corporate image* – how the company is perceived by others – and it will be necessary that this image is maintained throughout the advertising. This is bound up with the company's reputation, and it would be fatal to this image if, for instance, the company's advertising provoked complaints from the public to the Advertising Standards Authority.

Policy concerns many things. Nescafé do not wish to be thought to provide own label coffees to supermarkets. Audi and BMW believe it would lower the quality image of their cars if they offered sales promotion gimmicks. Guinness have always maintained that the quality of their advertising should reflect the quality of their beer. Curry's challenge customers to find better prices elsewhere. These policies can direct the themes of advertising campaigns.

3   To determine the appropriation, or advertising budget, and to make allocations for different media and purposes. How this may be done is described in a later chapter which examines ways of arriving at the sum to be spent on advertising. The appropriation may be produced in conjunction with the advertising agency, as when advice is sought on what it will cost to reach, say, a certain proportion of the market. One way or another, it will be part of the total marketing budget. It is therefore crucial that proposed expenditure be estimated as accurately as possible, but, of course, success depends very much on how wisely the money is spent.

The product or brand manager may have to present a case for a share of the appropriation in order to promote those products or brands that are this executive's responsibility.

4   Budgeting leads naturally to control of expenditure. With monies dispersed over a diversity of campaigns, media and techniques, the advertising manager has to be a master of budgetary control. This is not easy, and it becomes a primary responsibility. Corrections to advertisements and print have to be avoided because they can be costly. There should be final approval of copy when it is written, not after it has been set. Production costs can escalate if there are

too many changes, such as inserting local addresses in advertisements in regional editions of magazines. The budget may be agreed six months before a campaign is launched, and be operative for the next twelve months during which time costs such as media rates, may increase. A change in postage rates could upset plans for a direct mail campaign. Allocations are usually fixed, and when an advertisement manager of a publication presents a new proposition it may be impossible to accommodate it because funds have been allocated already.

The control of expenditure is also complicated in another way. An advertising agency may cost up a campaign, and this total figure may be approved. But there is no total bill at the end of the campaign. The advertising agency has to meet its on-going costs as they occur, for instance, for artwork or photography, and it will submit separate bills accordingly. The advertising manager has to supervise this expenditure and endeavour to check that all the individual bills rendered over many months will in fact finally agree with the total budget. Failure to do this could lead to financial disaster for the company and the sacking of both the advertising manager and the advertising agency.

5   To co-operate with the advertising agency. Not only is it necessary for the advertising manager to interpret policy to the advertising agency, and to control expenditure, but it is absolutely essential that there is proper day-to-day liaison with the agency. There is a very good saying that an agency is only as good as the client allows it to be. Agencies are not miracle workers, clever though they may be. While their ingenuity must be encouraged they cannot work in a vacuum, and the advertising manager must be responsive in feeding the agency with all the facts, samples, prices and other background information on which the agency work. Good agency-client relations are a two-way exercise.

The advertising manager also has to remember that agency personnel such as visualizers, copywriters and media planners or buyers are not always in direct contact with the client, but have to work through intermediaries such as department heads and, of course, the account executive who liaises with the client. In the agency, especially in a large one, there are a lot of people 'down the line' who are working on a variety of accounts who need to be helped to understand each account properly and the product or service with which they are dealing. One morning they may be working on an insurance account, in the afternoon on a baby food account and next day on one for ladies underwear.

The wise advertising manager can do much to develop a sound relationship. This can be done by means of works visits, invitations to sales conferences and social functions, supply of samples, and regular supply of the company house journal. The advertising manager should endeavour to visit the agency and get to know the people working on his account. It is not just a go-between job between the account executive and the advertising manager. The agency should be seen to be augmenting the advertising department, not an isolated outside service which can be blamed and criticized when mistakes occur.

6   To control the production of all other advertising material not handled by the agency. Some agencies will be asked to carry out everything required by the client. These are what are termed 'through the line' agencies, but agencies tend to handle above-the-line or media advertising which pays commission, e.g. press, radio, television, cinema and outdoor, although at the other extreme some agencies will handle only the booking of space, time or sites. There are media independents who concentrate on the planning and buying of media, and there are *à la carte* agencies which do only creative work. Full service agencies plan campaigns, do the creative work, buy media and produce and deliver finished advertisements or commercials.

Below-the-line items such as exhibitions, videos, direct mail, point-of-sale display material, sales promotion schemes, sales literature, and sponsorships may be handled in-house or through specialist agencies, and the advertising manager will be responsible for all this too. Once again we see the jack-of-all-trades nature of the advertising manager's job.

7   To control or undertake 'product publicity', that is press relations for the product or service. It depends on the structure of the organization, and if the company has a separate public relations department or employs a public relations consultancy, and it will be necessary to liaise accordingly. But he must be careful not to fall into the trap of regarding public relations as free advertising, and think a press release should read like an advertisement. Editors will regard that as 'puffery' and the releases will be binned, not published.

8   To assess the result of advertising, using various forms of research. If advertisements produce direct response this can be measured by means of keys placed in coupons or addresses so that replies can be sorted according to the keys, and the pulling power or cost-per-reply can be assessed simply by dividing the cost of the insertion by the number of replies. A key could be printed in the corner of the coupon, e.g. DE1 for the first insertion in the *Daily Express*. Alternatively, keys can be introduced into addresses, e.g. Room 1 and Room 2, or A. Brown and B. Brown with as many variations as different media used. A further study can be made of the conversion of enquiries to sales and their value.

Other research can include: (i) dealer or shop audit results showing shares of the market held in relation to advertising expenditure and the effectiveness of current advertising and sales promotion campaigns; (ii) recall research to determine how well members of the public read (or saw) advertisements; (iii) impact research to test what people remember of the numerous elements of an advertisement (reading and noting tests); and (iv) tracking studies to measure the long-term effect of advertising and its eventual decay.

These eight basic responsibilities indicate something of the breadth of an advertising manager's job. It calls for a liberal education and sound training in advertising. The CAM Certificate and Diploma exams are particularly relevant to the advertising manager. Cost effectiveness is demanded nowadays, and this requires expert technical knowledge, buying skills and the ability to make constructive criticisms of work produced by outside suppliers.

4.4   The advertising department

After having set out the general responsibilities of the advertising manager we will now take a more detailed look at the specific operations which fall under his direct control, according to the kind of business, and so gain a valuable insight into the working of the advertising department. (Note that a variety of names may be given to the advertising department such as publicity, sales promotion, communications or marketing services department, but we will stick to the simple title which is most appropriate).

Whether the advertising manager uses an advertising agency, buys from a variety of specialist suppliers and freelance workers, or carries out on-the-spot operations in his own self-sufficient in-house department, the following are likely to fall within his control.

Press advertising

In recent years there has been a press media revolution with the demise of Fleet Street, new printing technologies, and new national newspapers, women's, special interest and consumer magazines. Press advertising may be divided into three kinds: (i) consumer or user, to promote sales; (ii) recruitment, to fill jobs; and (iii) trade, to sell to distributors; technical to sell to manufacturers, and professional to sell to professionals.

The advertising manager will be concerned with the right choice of media, based on past results; circulation and readership data; the size, frequency and timing of insertions; copy and layout content; production costs and quality of reproduction. (The last point could range from faithful colour reproduction to show-through of advertising on the reverse side of a newspaper page.)

The *media schedule* produced by the agency will be scrutinized, and it will be necessary to weigh up the merits of the recommended media and the sizes, positions and dates. The agency will doubtless justify the media schedule on the basis of its calculations regarding cost-per-thousand circulation or readership, or bargains negotiated, or the weight of coverage believed necessary. But the advertising manager may have other considerations. Will, for instance, the advertising allow sufficient lead-time for the product to be sold into the shops and delivered so that there is adequate distribution to coincide with the advertising? The advertising manager will either accept or amend the total media allocation so that it fits in with the overall appropriation.

As the insertions appear, the advertising manager must be vigilant to see that good or correct positions are occupied. This is not the fault of the agency but it has happened that an advertisement with a coupon is backed by a similar advertisement with a coupon in the same position so that each nullifies the other. This will be due to the carelessness of the publisher who did not notice the juxtaposition when preparing the paste-up dummy. Another juxtaposition could occur when two advertisements, printed side by side, create an unfortunate effect, such as when the left-hand advertisement says 'Come to Sunny Sicily' and its partner says 'But it's Better at Bali'. These things happen, and the advertising manager will need to complain to the agency, which will complain to the publisher who may offer a free space to keep the peace.

Outdoor advertising

Similarly, the advertising manager will work either with the agency or with the bill posting contractors to secure the most suitable sites, and bookings, designs and printing will have to be approved. It may be that posters can be observed, and if they are seen to be damaged by the weather or by vandals the site can be re-pasted. Some advertisers are anxious to obtain particular sites when they become available, and the advertising manager will request their acquisition.

Television advertising

Here, the advertising manager will be interested in six aspects of the medium:

1 The selection of TV regions or kind of station – ITV Channel 3, Channel 4 – or satellite. The marketing strategy may be to sell the product on a zonal basis and then build up to the national network, or it may be required to give special support to certain weak-selling regions.
2 Approval of the storyboard and script before shooting commences.
3 The air-time schedule. Is it aimed at reaching a given proportion of the market? Are sufficient TVRs calculated to achieve this so that the commercial can be taken off or rested? Do the spots coincide with appropriate programmes? It is easy to accept a bargain 'package' which contains wasteful showings.

4   Approving the casting of performers and presenters, and also jingles or background music.
5   Viewing rushes and the finished film or videotape.
6   Checking the effects of the commercial on sales as revealed by continuous research such as consumer panels, shop audits and tracking studies. Next-day recall tests may also be conducted.

In addition, the advertising manager can view the commercials critically at home, which can be very different from viewing them in the isolation of a studio or on a VCR. Comparison can then be made with other commercials, perhaps rival ones, which are also being aired. Moreover, since this is a family medium he will be made very conscious of what others close to him think of this advertising. Members of the field sales force may also report the reactions of their trade customers.

Radio advertising

Apart from the lack of vision, a major difference between radio and television advertising is that of cost, both production and of air-time. In Britain, under the new Radio Authority, this medium has great potential for advertisers. New developments have already included sponsoring of programmes and split transmissions whereby one station will broadcast to two different audiences on different frequencies. Outside Britain, radio is often a long-established medium with no non-advertising stations like the BBC. Entire sponsored shows are common. If, in countries with a high ratio of illiteracy, radio is used it must be remembered that in a vocal society speech must be apt and to the point, the stations may broadcast in several languages as in Kenya, Nigeria and Zambia. In the UK, national commercial radio has arrived.
An advantage which the advertising manager can exploit is that British radio is often listened to by different people at different times of the day, e.g. commuter motorists in the morning and early evening.

Cinema advertising

This is a medium which lost out to television and became predominantly one for young audiences, but thanks to new types of cinemas (e.g multiplex), audiences have been growing again. The advertising manager of a suitable product may find it useful to produce a cinema version of a TV commercial, so minimizing production costs. In developing countries the mobile cinema can be an important medium, carrying the advertising message from village to village.

Direct mail

The advertising manager may use the services of a direct mail house, or be organized to create, print and dispatch mailings, using a database of addresses or hiring them from a list broker. This will depend on the frequency or size of mailings and the economics involved. A direct response marketer will need instant control of such promotion. The distinction needs to be made here between direct mail and mail order (which is now generally called direct response marketing). The first is an advertising medium while the second is a form of trading or distribution.

Since direct mail is the UK's third largest advertising medium, it is likely to be used by most advertising managers, and as a below-the-line medium it will be an in-house responsibility. Even if consumers are not direct mailed it may be that distributors are.

Exhibitions

Again very much an in-house responsibility, the advertising manager will be responsible for knowing what exhibitions will be held at home and abroad, and for selecting those in which the company should participate. Space in popular shows is booked from year to year, certainly many months in advance, so it is necessary to plan well in advance to secure the most desirable sites. From then on follows responsibility for design and construction of stands, choice of exhibits, staffing and arranging print, samples and liaison with the exhibition press office.

Exhibitions are not limited to public and trade shows, and there can be the company's own private exhibitions which may be toured by road, rail, sea or air. The company may own special exhibition vehicles which it takes to public places or public events, or small portable exhibitions which it sets up in halls and hotels They may be augmented by video shows and talks. The advertising manager will have to organize such exhibits and their tour programmes, perhaps in collaboration with the sales department. Other small exhibits may be displayed in shop premises or supplied as windows displays. A few organizations have permanent exhibitions at their own premises, e.g. Cadbury's World in Birmingham.

Print

While advertising agencies are equipped to design and buy print, this is often another major in-house task of the advertising manager. There may be an in-plant print shop, or outside printers will be engaged for different classes of work. This can involve the advertising manager in many skills such as copywriting, photography, artwork, design and print buying, once again demonstrating his versatility.

Catalogues, data sheets, price lists, instruction manuals, stuffers (leaflets that go in packages), sales leaflets, packaging, showcards, window bills, order forms, stationery and many other items such as print for sales promotion schemes may have to be supplied. All these items have to be stocked, updated and be available as required. Requests may have to be handled, or supplies despatched to retailers. Some companies even sell posters as souvenirs, or supply them (like travel posters) for decorative purposes in various premises. When a prospective customer visits a gas or electricity showroom he or she will expect to be given leaflets describing appliances; motorists expect brochures from motor-car showrooms; exhibition stands need supplies of sales litera- ture, and so print becomes an integral part of the advertising function. It can be a very expensive item which must be estimated for in the annual appropriation. Control of print is therefore a serious matter. There was the case of an offer in an advertisement of a home decorating booklet. The demand was so great that the booklet had to be re-printed, and the advertising manager was fired for exceeding the budget.

Point-of-sale material

This is another area where both adequate supply and avoidance of wastage call for strict control. Not all of this will be print since it can include working models, wire stands, display cases, dumper bins, dummy packs, trade figures, balloons or canvas banners and flags. Knowledge about suppliers, alternative ideas and costs together with buying skill are required here.

Point-of-sale material is costly and must not be damaged in transit, nor frittered away because dealers are inundated with more material than they have space for display. Some seasonal displays can have a very short life, and are then discarded. Yet products need to be displayed, permanently if possible! They must help the retailer to sell. In-store demonstrations need background materials. Advertising campaigns need on-the-spot support. The needs vary from product to product, retail outlet to retail outlet. A dispenser box may be necessary for a credit card company, a display outer for soups, or model aircraft for an airline. If the reader notes the display material in different classes of shop it will be seen how the styles of this material differ and match the particular needs of each trade.

Sales promotion

For some companies, sales promotion has become an alternative to media advertising, and the subject is discussed further in Chapter 18. It has become such big business that there are specialist agencies and its own trade press. Here we go a stage beyond point-of-sale material, and consider special short-term aids to promoting sales, aimed at launching a product, stimulating sales when the life cycle is sagging, or simply to fight competition and maintain sales.

It involves in-store promotions and sampling demonstrations, prize competitions or free draws, money-off offers with flash packs, premium offers, free gifts, cross-couponing offers, High Street redemption and charity schemes which help the retailer to sell out and restock, thus maintaining production flow and sales volume. It will be the advertising manager's job (although in big firms it may be a specialist executive who handles the work) to find new ideas, seek quotations for supplies, organize and supervise with the cooperation of the field sales force, whether the company runs occasional schemes, or a regular series of promotions. Sometimes a promotion will be directed through a particular supermarket chain, as happens with coffee promotions, or there may be a cooperative scheme with another manufacturer, so that two products are promoted simultaneously.

Video-tapes

The advertising manager may be responsible for the production and distribution of two kinds of video-tape, advertising and documentary, although the latter will be the responsibility of the public relations manager if there is one. Some may be used in public cinemas as second features, or on exhibition stands, or in sales showrooms (e.g. ones demonstrating a motor-car), or lent to customers (e.g. travel videos), or shown to private audiences. An advantage of video over film is that it is easier to produce and edit, is less cumbersome than reels of film in cans, and old-fashioned projectors are unnecessary. TV monitors or large screens can be used.

Similarly musicassette tape audio cassettes can be offered in press advertisements and this device has been used by Linguaphone to sell language courses, to sell unit trusts and for recruitment purposes.

The advertising manager will need to understand the use of videos and tapes, the audience for whom they are intended, be able to buy the services of production companies and appreciate treatments, scripts and rushes when asked to approve them. Some large companies may, of course, have their own video studios.

Trade advertising

Keeping wholesalers, brokers, agents and retailers informed about new products, trade terms, price and packaging charges, advertising campaigns and promotional material calls for the use of direct mail, trade press advertising, trade exhibitions and trade public relations efforts. Dealer conferences, work visits and previews of television commercials at regional TV stations may have to be organized.

Dealer cooperative schemes

The supply of free artwork, or part payment of local advertising costs, are ways of encouraging retailers to identify themselves as stockists. These schemes will usually be offered by direct mail, but may also be introduced by visiting sales representatives.

Showrooms and display centres

Some companies maintain public showrooms in city centres, e.g. furniture makers, and it will be the advertising manager's job to supervise their proper use, supplying display materials, and perhaps organizing events and special attractions. Customers may be invited to receptions, demonstrations and audio-visual shows.

Window-dressing services

A number of tobacco, confectionery and toiletry firms maintain a permanent window display service, shops being visited and windows set out at regular intervals. Dummy packs, showcards and perhaps paper sculpture will be used. The advertising manager will have to maintain vehicles, staff and display materials for this purpose.

Organizing sales conferences

The advertising manager's organizing ability and experience with audio-visuals may result in calls for assistance when sales and marketing executives are planning various internal assemblies such as annual sales conferences. The advertising manager may serve as one of the organizing team.

Export advertising

Either through the home advertising agency, or through agencies in overseas sales territories, and in conjunction with the export sales manager, the advertising manager will be responsible for a completely separate and different range of trade and consumer/user advertising services. Much will depend on whether the company exports through foreign agents, has franchise or licensing arrangements with indigenous firms, or has its own overseas plants. One firm may export its products, but another may be multinational or transnational with production plants set up world-wide and sales structures straddling continents. Few products are truly 'global', that is the same product selling anywhere like Coca-Cola. More often they have to be specially designed, modified, packaged and even re-named for particular markets. Some products cannot be sold in, say, Hindu, Muslim or Chinese markets which exist in many parts of the world.

This is therefore a very demanding aspect of an advertising manager's job, and serious blunders have occurred by trying to foist European or American advertising on inappropriate audiences. The advertising manager will need to understand the cultures and customs – say, regarding dress when having overseas advertisements designed – and deal with translators, perhaps knowing one or two suitable languages. This will entail working with printers who are specialists in foreign language typesetting.

Sponsorships

This is a big subject which will be dealt with in a separate chapter (Chapter 19), and sponsorship of sport, the arts, education, expeditions and other worthy causes may be an important part of the overall strategy. Sponsorship can be used to position a product with a particular market segment, e.g. Coca Cola's sponsorship of young people's sports. It can be used to familiarize the market with a name, as achieved by many Japanese companies. There are many advertising, marketing and public relations uses of sponsorship. It is another subject which the advertising manager must understand, and it will be another facet of the appropriation requiring careful budgetary control.

Press relations

This is more properly the preserve of a fully integrated public relations department, or of an outside public relations consultancy, but not every company has either in-house or external public relations services. Consequently, some advertising managers with scant understanding of the difference between advertising and journalism, may have to attempt the public relations role as well. This is seldom successful because public relations is not a form of advertising. From ignorance, the advertising manager is liable to write news releases which resemble advertisements rather than news reports.

House journals

Both internal and external house journals – private magazines not published commercially – are rightly the responsibility of the public relations department and require editing by British Association of Industrial Editors (BAIE) standards. Nevertheless, in smaller firms this task may well fall to the advertising manager, or the house journal editor may be a member of the advertising department staff. Some of these journals are today produced by desktop publishing methods, using a computer to set and design pages, with on-line linkage with the printer's typesetter.

External house journals, addressed to stockists, users, customers and other outside readers, have become an important medium and one which may well come within the advertising department. But the mistake must not be made of producing such a journal which resembles sales literature. To be credible, it should resemble a commercial journal which the reader would normally buy. Something printed like a tabloid newspaper is likely to be more credible – and therefore read – than a lavish full-colour publication printed on heavy paper. That will look like a sales brochure, and will be regarded with the contempt it deserves if it is dressed up with a title and pretends to be a magazine.

4.5   How are advertising managers appointed?

There are probably four main reasons for the choice of an advertising manager:

i   Knowledge of advertising will be essential, and this can come about in three ways. First, the candidate should be well-trained and qualified, holding the CAM Diploma in Advertising, or at least the LCCI Diploma in Advertising, or their equivalent. Second, experience may have been gained in another company. Third, experience may have been gained as an account executive in an advertising agency, servicing the same or a similar account. The latter is a common route, an account executive servicing a client for a number of years and then being invited to join the company.

ii   Knowledge of the industry may be an asset. This may be somewhat related to advertising, e.g. technical authorship, but it could be that a person originally trained in the industry may desire to transfer to advertising.

iii Knowledge of management procedures, including accounts, could also be an asset since the advertising manager will be responsible for departmental management, budgeting, budgetary control and policy interpretation.

iv   Knowledge of marketing, especially if the broad duties of a brand or product manager are to be undertaken. Perhaps he holds the CIM Diploma qualification.

Ideally, a large advertiser will require a mature person who will combine all these qualities. But he will also require younger, able assistants who can learn how to aspire to eventual promotion, or appointment elsewhere, as advertising managers. These assistants are likely to have business studies backgrounds, and should be encouraged to seek the CAM Diploma qualification.

5
The advertising agency

5.1 What is an advertising agency?

The advertising agency has evolved over the last 200 years from a mere
space-broker serving publishers to a sophisticated service for advertisers, but still strictly speaking the agency of the media even though
clients hire and fire agencies and talk about 'their' agencies.

An advertising agency is a team of skilled specialists, appointed by
clients (known as 'accounts') to plan, produce and place advertising
campaigns, but literally acting as the agents of the media which pay
commission on media purchases to those agencies which are 'recognized' for their credit worthiness (ability to pay their bills), and legally
acting as principal (i.e. responsible for payments whether or not they
get paid by their clients).

The agency clearly occupies an anomalous position. Although the
advertiser appoints the agency to do its work, and seeks its loyalty and
confidentiality as if dealing with a normal professional adviser, the
agency is in effect a 'ten per center' and the bulk of its income is derived
from the media owners. Even so, in its curious way the agency acts as
a middle-man between the media and the advertisers, the media literally
subsidizing the advertisers who enjoy many services free of charge out
of the commission. Compare this situation with that applying to a
public relations consultancy. The client enjoys the advertising executive's time free of charge, but (since no commission income is forthcoming) the time of the account executive working for a public relations
consultancy has to be charged as part of the fee. The client has to pay
to talk to a public relations consultancy but not to an advertising agent
who is remunerated by commission.

So, ludicrous though the agency commission system may sound, it
works very well because all three sides of advertising benefit from it.
The media get paid promptly, the agency has a ready income, and the
advertiser gets numerous services for nothing. Of course, the media
would not sell space, and the agency would not prosper, if there were

no clients. We have seen a number of famous agencies crash because their clients went bankrupt, or the agency got into debt through unwise acquisitions of other agencies, or because it simply lost a major client. For all the multi-million pound billings the agency business remains a precarious one.

Perhaps the agency commission system should be scrapped? No one seems very willing to dispense with it, although some agencies do organize their sources of income in different ways. For instance, there is the more professional method of rebating the commission and charging their clients the net price of media purchases, and then charging an hourly or daily fee based on the volume of work done and the value of their expertise. This does enable the agency to get paid for the value of its work, which is more realistic. Another method which has been tried out but is not very popular, is payment by results. This may please the advertiser, but is not fair on the agency which is put in the unprofessional position of, say, a doctor who is paid only if there is a cure, or of a lawyer only if the case succeeds in court. These matters will be discussed more fully later in the chapter.

The foregoing should be sufficient reason for criticizing the mis-use of the expression 'public relations agency' for public relations consultancy, since it is no one's agency and cannot possibly be paid commission by the media. It is therefore physically, financially and legally impossible for a public relations consultancy to be an agency.

5.2   Changes in the 1980s

A number of changes have occurred in the UK agency world, accelerated or provoked by the Office of Fair Trading interpretation of the *Restrictive Trade Practices Act 1976* when it was extended to cover services. Previously, agency recognition enabled agencies to receive standard rates of commission from members of the recognizing bodies such as the NPA, NS or PPA. This standard rate was usually 15 per cent from nationals and ITV, and 10 per cent from regionals and the trade press. Agencies often augmented this by collecting a further 2.5 per cent from their clients because they found the standard commission inadequate.

But in 1979 the OFT ruled that it was a restrictive, monopolistic and therefore illegal practice to guarantee commission rates. The dilemma was resolved by the organizations representing the various media owners recognizing agencies for their credit worthiness and adherence to the British Code of Advertising Practice. From then on, commission rates became negotiable. The conditions for granting recognition are explained in Appendix 7 on media owners.

The essential factor of recognition remained. It endowed no professional status, but simply ensured that agencies had the ability to pay their debts promptly, always bearing in mind that 'the agency acts as principal' and is responsible for debts incurred on behalf of its clients.

In 1990 a new tug-of-war situation arose. The OFT regarded the credit-worthiness requirement as being restrictive, especially when one agency lost its recognition because of non-payment of media bills, and consequently went out of business. In contrast, the media owners decided to tighten up the credit-worthiness requirement because media had lost money through the bankruptcies of agencies. These are new dilemmas facing advertising agencies.

These situations arose because of the bankruptcies of certain agencies that had been caught up in recession and cash flow difficulties which were confronting many businesses in 1990, and the merger of Sky and BSB Television was symptomatic of the period.

5.3 Variations on the commission system

The following are the variations on the straight commission system, and they may depend on the size of the agency or the kind of account. Clearly, a small technical account will produce little commission but incur considerable artwork costs. Agencies may have different ways of charging, in advance or in arrears, and this may depend on the size of the account, the proportion of commission income, and the reputation and financial status of the client.

i   Traditional media commission only, plus charges for work and materials such as artwork, TV commercials, print, etc. Typical of large consumer accounts.

ii Fee plus commission, a basic service fee being paid by the client and the agency taking commission from the media. Typical of medium-sized consumer durable and industrial accounts.

iii Flat fee only. This method applies particularly to technical accounts where commissions are negligible (because of low rates in technical journals and minimum rates of commission), or where there is virtually no above-the-line advertising. The work may consist of sales literature, catalogues, packaging design, exhibitions and displays.

iv Cost plus fee. Here the client pays for the cost of work done together with a fee for agency facilities, overheads and profits. The work is charged 'at cost'.

v   Cost plus. Somewhat similar to the fourth method above, a percentage being added to the cost of work done, this percentage covering overheads and profit. The work is charged 'at cost'.

vi Commission credited. An increasingly popular method, and really the grand compromise with the commission system, this method consists of a fee from the client from which is deducted commission received from the media. Thus the client pays a fee over and above the gross media rates, and the agency loses nothing by rebating part of the commission. This retains the media commission system without the advertiser getting everything for nothing, while the agency enjoys a more professional and less of a 'ten percenter' role.

In other parts of the world there are *accreditation* systems with grades of recognition according to the value of billings.

5.4   Agencies and the Single European Market

The Single European Market provides a great opportunity for British advertising agencies which are respected for their superior creativity, especially in television advertising. Much of that produced on the continent is crude compared with the British, where there is nothing to compare with, say, the Nescafé Gold, Bisto or British Telecom sagas. Nevertheless, the Campaign Report of September 14 1990 on the top 300 European agencies (Table 5.1) revealed some sobering information: the biggest agency in Europe was the French Publicis Conseil, and six of the top ten agencies are French, and one of London's leading agencies WCRS was acquired by the French group Eurocam. However, the number of British entries in *Campaign's* league table exceeded all others, and the forecast for the 1990s is that because of superior talent and expertise London, as a pan-European centre, will emulate the City as a financial centre.

Table 5.1   *Top ten European agencies 1989*

1	Public Conseil	France
2	RSCG	France
3	HDM	France
4	Saatchi and Saatchi	Great Britain
5	BDDP	France
6	J. Walter Thompson	Great Britain
7	Belier WCRS	France
8	Young and Rubicam	France
9	BSB Dorland	Great Britain
10	Young and Rubicam	Great Britain

Source: The Campaign Report 14 September 1990

The future of British adland depends, to a large extent, on how effectively British manufacturers exploit the opportunities not only of the Channel Tunnel but of the rail links which continental Europeans (being wiser than the British) have built towards the tunnel. European manufacturers will be able to pour their goods into Britain and use the international distribution centre at Ashford in Kent, only a few miles from the tunnel.

5.5 Should clients change agencies?

There is clearly merit in an agency–client partnership which becomes richer over the years by its mutual sharing of confidences and knowledge. It can take three years for an agency to reach a proper level of efficiency in dealing with a client's advertising, yet this is the very point when some firms decide they must find a new agency. The following are some of the reasons why clients do seek such a change:

1 Client–agency management got on well before the appointment was made, but liaison is then handed over to an account executive previously unknown to the client. The client feels fobbed off with a substitute as if the agency regards the account as a minor one, which perhaps it is! Nevertheless, the resentment rankles and persists until sooner or later an excuse is made for ending the contract.
2 There is a change of client personnel and with it a 'new broom' attitude which is fatal to the existing agency. Perhaps the new marketing director or advertising manager already knows or has worked for an agency.
3 The agency does not understand the account, and mistakes occur because policy decisions are not interpreted to agency personnel. A fault here may be that agency personnel never have a chance of meeting the client and discovering the policy at first hand.
4 The agency may have got into a rut, and being devoid of new ideas deserves to lose an account which it may have been taking for granted.
5 There may be disagreements over charges and account rendering. This may result from the agency farming out work, imposing an on-cost, and expecting the client to pay two outside profits. The client says if the agency cannot do the work inside with its own staff the client may as well buy direct or use a more comprehensive agency with cheaper services.
6 Agency staff tend to change fairly rapidly. It is a young person's business, and experience can be gained only be moving around. In industry, people are more apt to devote a lifetime, or at least a long time, to employment with one firm. The client may become disheartened by agency staff changes and seek another agency without understanding that agency staff changes are inevitable .
7 There are disappointing results because the client insisted on telling the agency what to do instead of taking the agency's advice.
8 The company's trading figures are poor, and management is looking for a scapegoat.
9 It may be decided to dispense with a full service agency and use the more personal services of *à la carte* agencies and media independents.

These are but a few of the reasons why accounts change hands. Human rather than business reasons predominate, and often the reasons seem unfair and irrational. But they are not unlike the reasons why we stop buying petrol at a certain garage, change our hairdresser or swear we will never eat in that restaurant again. Very largely, it is a matter of human relations and that often means a lack of clear and regular communication. Disenchantment is not always necessary.

5.6   Criteria for choosing an agency

Before discussing the variety of agencies which exist today – there is no longer any such thing as 'an advertising agency' in a general sense – let us consider how agencies are selected by their clients.

First of all, should clients change agencies and how often should they do so? In theory an agency should be retained for as long as possible. It may take years to build up a thorough understanding and a good relationship. But such stability is rare, and too often agencies are changed too frequently. There are, as demonstrated in the previous section, reasons for this: competition and the clamour for new ideas; company mergers or change of client management and new broom approaches; agencies going stale; emergence of new kinds of agency. It can be a frenetic situation. New relationships can be full of promise, only to sour either because some clients are impossible or some agencies fail to achieve miracles.

How then and for what reasons are agencies sought? There are simple methods like finding out who produced a campaign that the client admires, or checking the names of agencies and their client lists in *Advertisers Annual*. A new advertiser with no knowledge of agencies could ask the IPA for a list of agencies likely to be interested in servicing the account.

A useful service is that of the *Advertising Agency Register*, which guarantees confidentiality. It works like this: The client gives AAR a brief of their agency requirements and AAR supplies a candidate list of agencies from which the client selects a 'screening' list. At the screening the client receives current background literature, including relevant category experience, and views the individually prepared video presentation and showreel of current press advertising. AAR personnel are present to answer questions. The client may spend three or four hours in the privacy of AAR's offices during which time some ten to twelve agencies will have been reviewed, enabling a short list of agencies to be visited.

AAR represents all the major multi-national agencies and many of the medium sized and specialist agencies. Founded in the UK in 1975, AAR has offices in New York, Paris, Dusseldorf, Milan, Brussels, Sydney and Toronto.

In its issue of February 3 1989, *Campaign* published a 'Report on Choosing An Agency', and Table 5.2 shows some of its findings.

Table 5.2   *How they rate agency disciplines*

Creativity	Over 40
Account management	Over 40
People chemistry	Over 30
Strategic direction	Over 20
Media buying	Over 20
Account planning	Over 20

Categories rating 8, 9, 10 out of 10. Total respondents: 50

The interesting thing about this list is that while creativity continues to head the list, media buying is now seen to be less important than the people factor in an agency. Is this because you can always hive off the media buying to a media independent but you still need the brains for the strategy, planning and direction?

In Table 5.3 are factors which, according to the Campaign Report, played an important part in drawing up a short list of agencies which would be invited to pitch for the account.

Table 5.3   *Influences on shortlisting agencies*

	Rating
Specific knowledge of agencies' previous work	43
Seeing some of their work generally	43
Personal knowledge of a person or people in an agency	41
Specific knowledge of an individual's work	26
A direct agency approach	26
Video showreels	20
Trade press comments	13
Mailings from an agency	11
Agency advertising in trade press	5

This is an interesting table because it shows the variety of ways in which a potential client may shop for a new agency. As was said in the previous chapter, the advertiser or whoever may represent the advertiser, must be a skilled buyer, and buying agency services is probably the client's most difficult assignment, for thousands and probably millions of pounds will rest on this judgement. Equally, the agency management has to be sure of both the integrity and the solvency of the new client.

5.7 Types of agency

As the years go by different types of agency emerge, only to settle down into certain recognized types. There was the 'hot shop' which became transformed into the *à la carte*; the 'third wave' which was a new sort of small *à la carte* agency when the original *à la carte* agency began to grow big; and the 'through the line' agencies which offered both the above-the-line and below-the-line services. Always, someone is trying to break away from the conventional and offer something different or special. In the 90s the following are the principal types of agency.

Full service agencies

They are the traditional advertising agencies, generally concentrating on above-the-line advertising but offering a full service including marketing and marketing research, and being equipped to handle radio and television advertising. They tend to handle the big multi-million pound campaigns for the largest advertisers, especially those which use networked television.

Media independents

As already mentioned at the beginning of this chapter, an innovation has been the arrival and development over the past decade of agencies which devote their skills to media planning and buying. They do not plan complete advertising campaigns, nor create or produce advertisements. They are recognized by the media owners but they do not rely entirely on commission for their remuneration. A number of payment systems are applied which reflect the complicated nature of modern media, particularly with the great variety of modern broadcasting media, to mention only independent local radio, Channel 4, breakfast time TV and Teleview teledata. Some media independents charge an agreed percentage of the media spend, some a share of agency commission and others a fee based on workload and volume (there can be combinations of commission and fee). This flexibility enables clients to buy the best media at the lowest cost.

Some of these media independents are quite large, and may even be used by the full service agencies, while Zenith was specially set up to handle media buying for Saatchi and Saatchi. Omnicon Group, holding company of BBDO and DDB Needham plus Ogilvy and Mather, formed The Media Partnership to pool media buying with a Paris office for global media operations. In the UK, the media independents handle more than £1 billion or about a quarter of all media buying.

Twenty years ago there were no media independents, but now more than one third of the top 500 advertised brands are using media independents.

Most media independents belong to the Association of Media Independents. The AMI applies the following four criteria to membership:

(i) Financial standing, and annual and interim accounts have to be filed with the AMI.

(ii) Open book policy. Copy invoices from media owners must be available to clients.

(iii) Members' companies must be recognized by ITVA, NPA and PPA and accept the BCAP.

(iv) Experience must cover all forms of media.

À la carte agencies

Once called 'hot shops', the *à la carte*, alternative or creative agencies, buy no media, do not therefore require recognition because creditworthiness in respect of media purchase does not apply, and concentrate on campaign planning and creativity for which they charge fees. Thus, a client can use a media independent and an *à la carte* agency, and get the best of both worlds.

Moreover, they are not agents of the media, and not necessarily concerned with media advertising. They may undertake *ad hoc* jobs such as pack design, a corporate identity campaign, production of TV commercials, or the design of an exhibition stand. But equally, they may create entire advertising campaigns, especially for new product launches, and use a media independent for media planning and buying purposes. The important thing is that they are independent creative agencies, free of the recognition restrictions which made it very difficult, for financial reasons, to set up new full service agencies.

In addition to the specifically creative agencies there are many other kinds which offer specialized services.

New product development agencies

Starting at the very birth of a new product, these agencies contribute to the whole process of new product development and its launch on the market. This can include product design, packaging, pricing, distribution, sales training, marketing research, test marketing, and the planning and creation of the sales promotion and advertising. A more thorough service is offered than when a general service agency is asked to prepare advertising for a new product, a big advantage being the experience gained from specializing in solving the problems of new product development.

Direct response agencies

Direct response marketing is the modern face of mail order trading and goes beyond the work of direct mail houses to embrace 'off-the-page' direct response advertising, inserts, direct mail and catalogue selling, mail drops, and new forms of direct response marketing such as offers on commercial TV with phone-in orders, use of credit and charge cards, and computerized recording of orders.

Sales promotion agencies

Sales promotion will be discussed in a separate chapter (Chapter 18), but here we have agencies which devise competitions, premium offers, High Street redemption schemes, in-store demonstrations, cross-couponing and charity promotions. The latter have become very popular, tokens printed on the pack having a charitable donation value. It is necessary to create original schemes which will boost sales, especially of fast moving consumer goods such as one finds in supermarkets. They also buy merchandise for offers from specialist suppliers, and arrange for handling of applications by a fulfilment house.

Sponsorship agencies

These fall half-way between creative advertising agencies and public relations consultancies, using the techniques of both. They work in collaboration with the representatives of interests seeking sponsors and companies willing to act as sponsors, bringing the two together in harmonious partnerships. Major sponsorships such as those of cricket, football, tennis, golf, motor sport, marathons, snooker and table tennis are organized in remarkable detail by these agencies. It is not just a case of awarding cash prizes and trophies, but of ensuring that the sponsor gains the greatest possible rewards in media coverage and achievement of specific advertising, public relations and marketing objectives. This can also include organizing hospitality for sports commentators, or for the sponsor's guests.

There are also other specialist agencies, often small or medium-sized, which may be recognized if they are involved in media purchase. Many of these may be recognized by only the Periodical Publishers Association if they do no newspaper advertising, or by the ITVA and AIRC if they buy airtime.

Poster agencies

Poster advertising may be used irregularly, and may not be handled by service agencies. Over the years various poster agencies have come and gone, but the object is to offer a site booking service coupled with the planning of economic campaigns to gain maximum coverage of required poster audiences.

Industrial and business-to-business agencies

These are usually medium-sized service agencies handling technical accounts and having copywriters and artists skilled in the creativity required by clients. They service companies which advertise goods such as raw materials, machinery, components, office furniture, business machines, and other products and services used by industry and commerce rather than by consumers. There is an Association of Business to Business Advertising Agencies.

Studio agencies

Again, these may handle mainly technical accounts, but the design and production of promotional print may predominate over even trade and technical press advertising. They will have little if any commission income, and will charge for time and creative work.

Overseas press agencies

As the name implies, these agencies specialize in the preparation of international advertising, including translations, and they are experts in the press of other countries. They handle export campaigns.

Recruitment agencies

Recession has reduced their number, but these agencies place both classified and displayed advertisements for clients seeking staff. It was with this type of advertising (for the Government) that the first agencies were set up in the early nineteenth century.

Financial agencies

These place advertisements such as those seen in the *Financial Times* and *The Times* for new share issues, and other financial advertisements announcing company results, or during take-over bids.

Radio and television agencies

These agencies specialize in the selling of airtime and/or writing scripts for radio commercials or producing TV commercials.

Telephone selling agencies

Yet another new development has been the setting up of agencies to provide campaign facilities for telephone selling and telemarketing, a form of direct response or retailing without shops distribution.

Many of the specialist agencies above are independent companies. However, a number are subsidiaries of the big full service agencies which have moved with the times by exploiting opportunities for new agency services for their existing clients, or for those who do not require the services of a large general agency conducting mainly above-the-line mass media advertising.

5.8 How do agencies work?

This question is best answered in two ways: how does the team operate and how do the individuals within the team operate?

When we speak of the agency as a team it is clear that various specialists must come together to plan, create and execute advertising campaigns. But this is done in different ways, with different nomenclature, mainly to suit the kind of accounts serviced by the particular agency. The role of the *account planner* is dealt with in the next section.

Some agencies operate the *plans board* system, the board being a committee of departmental heads. Typical members will be the account executive (or agency representative), the media planner, marketing manager and creative director. If TV is being used there may be separate representatives for press and TV planning, and there will be a TV producer. The PR manager or consultant may also be present. This board or committee will meet to review news of a new assignment, meet again with preliminary ideas, and gather to consider the final scheme for presentation to client. They may go on meeting as other needs arise. They may meet regularly. In some agencies these agency leaders will get together at four o'clock in the afternoon and go on talking until mid-evening, while in another agency the plans board may take a working lunch with beer and sandwiches.

Dependent on the closeness of relations with the client, and the calibre of the advertising manager, these plans board meetings may also be attended by the client who can guide the agency towards an acceptable scheme. It is ideal when agency representative and advertising manager can present client top management with a joint scheme, and even better if the managing director can be given a preview the night before!

Other agencies have a *review board* which works rather differently; a campaign being criticized by agency personnel who have had nothing to do with its planning and creation. It is possible to have a plans board for the first stages, and a review board for the last stage before client approval is sought. This is an excellent way of detecting flaws in a campaign before the presentation to client is made.

Some agencies have nothing so specific, and there are merely meetings or conferences of those involved at different stages. In a small agency, the principal will call together members of staff to report on the progress they have made so far.

Reverting to large agencies, it is also common for them to operate the *creative group system*, each group being responsible for one or more clients. The group will be led by either copywriter or visualizer according to which man or woman is the better all-round planner. This system is ideal when a new product – a new motor-car is a very typical example – requires the concentrated effort of a small team over a period of several months, and usually in great secrecy.

How the plans board and the creative group systems work can be illustrated by their handling of a TV campaign.

In the first case, some three meetings of the plans board will be held over a matter of four to six weeks. Present will be a director, the account executive, creative director and air-time planner. At the first meeting, the available finance will be discussed, at the second meeting the individual agency specialists will present documents setting out their ideas, and at the third meeting schedules will be ready spelling out number, frequency and timing of commercials together with a proposed shooting script and storyboard. The storyboard resembles a strip cartoon, sketches showing the sequence of action. Once client approval of expenditure and ideas has been gained, the creative group head discusses the scheme with one of the agency TV producers, The producer, perhaps guided by client wishes, will appoint the production company and film director and become involved in approving the casting of artistes and choice of music. There are therefore two stages, the plans board being responsible for the creative strategy and the producer for translating this into actual film or video-tape.

Under the *creative group system*, a more intimate team of specialists will produce ideas which, when approved, will be given to the producer to execute. The reader may see small difference between the two methods, but it is this: the plans board operates for the whole agency and all accounts in that same agency heads will be present, whereas with the creative group method there can be many of these groups operating independently and simultaneously. The plans board suits the medium-sized agency, the creative group is really a development of the plans board and suits the big agency.

Already a number of job titles have been mentioned, and a description of the roles and functions of agency personnel will explain the division of labour in agencies. Obviously, the smaller the agency the more individuals have to be jack-of-all-trades, the larger the agency the greater the specialization. In a very small agency, one person may write and design advertisements, mark up the type faces and buy the settings and organize litho and gravure artwork, but in a big agency a copywriter, visualizer, layout artist, typographer and production manager will handle each stage of the work.

5.9 Agency personnel

A characteristic feature of an advertising agency is its division of labour and use of many specialists. The client has the benefit of enjoying a share of this blend of talents, and it would usually be uneconomical to employ so many people full-time in-house. This is one of the ways in which advertising agencies and public relations consultancies differ: the latter have little or no division of labour and consultancy staff have to be jacks-of-all-trades. The two cannot be compared, and that is why most public relations people are employed in-house where division of labour is possible because public relations, unlike advertising, is an on-going job which justifies the employment of specialists such as press officers, house journal editors or photographers. Thus, while a single advertising campaign for a client may be completed in a short time, or worked on simultaneously with others, it is handling campaigns for different clients at different times and can justify the full-time employment of expensive specialist personnel.

In this section we shall describe the work of many people in advertising agencies, but first let us consider *account planning*. A few years ago account planning, headed by a planning director, was the 'in' creed, being introduced by BMPDDB Needham. At that agency and at others such as Abbott Mead Vickers SMS, Bartle Bogle Hegarty, GCT and KHBB, the planning function remains important, but McCann-Erickson, WCRS Mathews Marcantonio and BSB Dorland abolished planning operations.

Was it only a fad to be sacrificed as internal economics were hastened by cut-backs in advertising, or is it, as its supporters contend, an integral part of an agency? One of the problems has been that while plenty of lip service was given to the concept of account planning there was a dearth of trained, skilled planners.

It is a very senior job. An account planner integrates the work of agency departments and personnel, preparing a creative brief, and collaborating with the account executive or controller. The planner's responsibilities cover research, marketing and day-to-day direction of the campaign. Such an all-round expert commands a high salary and is unlikely to be found outside a large agency. He belongs to that top list of priorities that were seen in the way clients rate agency disciplines in section 5.6.

Now let us look at the general array of agency personnel (Figure 5.1).

The *directors* may be responsible for certain functions such as finance or the creative side. Most agencies are partnerships or private companies although some are members of international organizations, and a number are quoted public companies. Directors are usually specialists with working roles. *Account directors* control groups of *accounts* – the agency name for clients. This agency use of the word accounts should not be confused with accountancy. Under each account director will

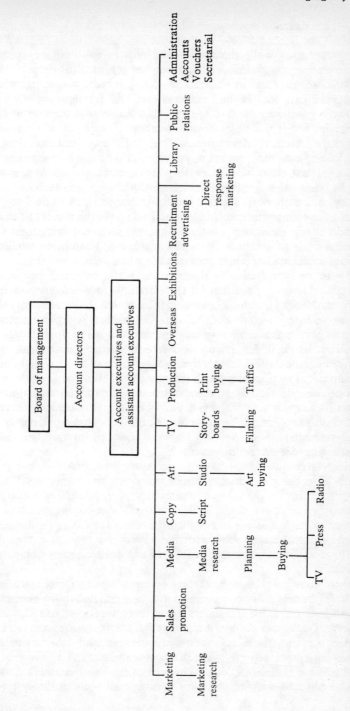

Figure. 5.1 Departments of a large full service advertising agency

serve a number of *account executives*.

Before the Second World War the account executive was known as the *contact man*, while the tendency is now to call him the agency *representative*, maintaining liaison between client and agency. The account executive has to understand what the client wants and what the agency can do. The best account executive (or representative) is usually a graduate who has been given an all-round training in the agency for about two years before specializing. This job is not unlike that of the technical sales representative, and it may not be concerned with seeking new business but more with servicing and keeping clients.

The account executive is the person the client will see most frequently, and by whom the agency will be judged. Although employed by the agency, it is important for this person to act as an extension of the client's advertising department. Trying to ride two horses at the same time is the real measure of ability. Not surprisingly, account executives often gravitate to the client side of the business and become advertising managers, although it is also true that industrial and technical agencies tend to be made up of ex-advertising managers who have set up agencies. The efficient account executive is therefore able to win the acceptance and confidence of the client, and is also able to win the regard of agency colleagues so that they produce the campaigns that will please the client.

In the 1950s the *marketing manager* became an important agency executive, but as clients set up their own marketing departments this service became less necessary and some agencies rationalized their organizations by dispensing with their own marketing managers. While it is necessary for all agency personnel to be marketing-conscious – bright ideas must sell – the agency marketing manager tends to fulfil one of two purposes, either providing an opposite number to the client's marketing manager or providing an extra service for the client who does not have a marketing manager.

Most large advertisers have a marketing manager or director to whom advertising, product or brand managers, and sometimes PROs or press officers, report. The marketing manager's role in the agency, and on behalf of the client, is to study and make recommendations about the market segment to which the advertising is to be directed, about new markets, or about distribution methods, packaging, pricing and product presentation, and to recommend marketing research where necessary.

There may also be a *marketing research manager* who will buy research services from companies which specialize in different classes and techniques of research, interpret reports produced in this way, and study and make use of the vast quantity of statistics which are produced by Government, trade associations, universities and other sources – this being known as desk research.

The *media planner* and *media buyer* (combined as *space buyer* in the smaller agency) evaluate and plan or haggle and buy accordingly. In big agencies, separate sections will deal with the press and TV. Media planning has become very sophisticated with the provision of statistical data about readers and audiences, social grades, programme ratings and cost per thousand (net sales, readers, housewives, etc). Campaigns can nowadays be calculated on a slide-rule or by computer. The media sales representative has to present agencies with statistical arguments for buying space, not a buttonhole, a smile and a free drink.

Skill in gaining maximum impact with costly television advertising can depend on just when and where the commercials appear. The contracting companies supply agencies with advance information about forthcoming shows. The sharp-witted media planner or air-time buyer will search for opportunities for the client's advertisements to appear in advantageous breaks. The media planner may have *carte blanche* to get the highest possible audience ratings. This is how a lively agency gets the greatest mileage out of the appropriation, and supported by good media intelligence (which is the responsibility of the sales offices of the TV companies) the agency can make advertising work extra hard for its clients.

Advertisement rates vary according to the regional audience size, and only a large national advertiser can afford to network throughout the UK. But cost is relative to the size of market and volume of business sought. What may seem expensive could be economical.

The *copywriter* may work under a *copy chief*, but the copywriter may be a member of a creative group or be a freelance who is commissioned by the copy chief. Copy has two meanings in printing, publishing and advertising. All material for printing may be called *copy*, as with the *copy date* by which a publisher wants advertisements. In this sense copy may consist of complete camera ready artwork of the advertisement, or a layout accompanied by typewritten wording and artwork, or typewritten wording and artwork such as drawings. photographs or colour transparencies. All these combinations are copy to the printer. But in advertising a more precise meaning is that *the copy consists of the wording*. The copywriter writes the words. However, he will probably also think up the general theme and presentation of the advertisement which will be interpreted by artists. This is known as the copy platform. The old idea of the copywriter sitting in one room writing the words, and the layout artist or visualizer sitting in the studio and fitting them into the design, is almost extinct. In any worthwhile agency, it is realized that there must be fusion between copywriting and its presentation.

The copywriter has to be a very talented person able to work in the different media of, say, press, poster, television or radio. He or she has to be able to coin the slogan or jingle that has universal application, or write competition rules that meet the gambling laws.

The *creative director* will combine the talents of writing and art to produce complete advertisements, and this may mean bringing together or directing creative groups, or buying outside freelance and studio services. This person is the conductor of the advertising orchestra, and the partner of the more administrative and business like media planners and buyers. Under the creative director will come the copywriter already described, and those who design and possibly those who instruct printers.

The *visualizer* is an artist who can rapidly produce rough ideas which are variously called *scamps, scribbles* or *visuals*. With these roughs the visualizer is able to interpret the copywriter's ideas and show a variety of ways of presenting them.

The *layout artist* (who may be the visualizer) produces designs which closely resemble the printed advertisement. The copy and pictures are laid out, usually producing a drawing of exact measurement which typesetter, paste-up artist and printer can follow.

The *typographer* (who may also be the layout artist) is an artist in type who not only knows the hundreds of different type faces but knows for which sorts of work particular type faces are most suitable. Having selected the faces, their sizes and weights are specified, and the printer is also instructed about spacing, according to the printing process. A good typographer can make an advertisement not only attractive and original, but legible and a pleasure to read. It may be necessary to obey a typographical style prescribed in the advertiser's corporate identity manual.

The *finished artist* draws or paints the final artwork, and much of the artwork in advertisements is produced by famous artists who also undertake commercial work. The *scraper board artist* is a specialist in producing a drawing, often based on a photograph, which, by means of lines, dots, stipples and cross-hatchings will gain clear and bold reproduction in newspapers.

Progress chasing is essential if many separate jobs are to culminate in a complete, approved advertisement delivered on time. The *production manager* heads a department of *production assistants* who are responsible for buying typesetting, and for supplying text and artwork for photogravure, flexography, and offset-litho printed publications. It is also his job to organize the work-flow so that copy and artwork, proofs, corrections and final copy are achieved to a timetable which is established once the presentation to client has won approval for the campaign to be executed. For greater convenience in the larger agencies there is a *traffic controller* who directs this work-flow, much of which requires duplicate copies of instructions and orders being distributed among the departments which need to be informed.

Finally, the *finance director* or *accountant* will control the despatch of bills to clients, supported by vouchers issued by the *voucher clerk*. Vouchers are copies of journals containing the actual press advertisements, and sent to clients as proof of insertion. Sometimes 'tear sheets' rather than whole journals are supplied.

Reference was made earlier to the extended credit which agencies may have to offer while being responsible for quick payment of their own accounts to media and suppliers. To overcome cash-flow problems one or two special systems are used. If it is a small account, or one producing little or no commission income, the agency may ask the client to deposit funds in a pool held by the agency – which is not unlike the public relations consultancy which charges fees a month or quarter in advance – while other agencies invoice clients with space accounts at the time of insertion and not after accounts have been received from the publishers.

Again, if an advertiser makes large regular expenditures, the agency may be so cautious as to book not more than one week ahead and demand payment before making further bookings. Even so, in the case of one direct response trader, this proved ruinous for an advertising agency since one week the trader went bankrupt and left the agency liable for payment of several whole page advertisements in the national press. The agency failed too.

Money problems are heightened by credit squeezes and the inability of banks to permit large overdrafts; the result being that firms simply borrow off their suppliers by extending credit. For businesses like advertising agencies this behaviour means one of two things: drop the slow-paying client or go out of business. In taking on new business, agencies need to be as strict about the credit-worthiness of potential clients as are the media owners when granting agencies recognition.

5.10 Agency paperwork

Important to the efficient and profitable running of an agency is its paperwork system, and a few brief recommendations will now be stated. It will be seen that some of these are as helpful to clients as they are to agents.

Job number

Whenever fresh work is started for a client it should be given a job number prefixed by the code letters allotted to the client. Thus, if a photographic session is booked for Jones Brothers Ltd, the job may be identified as, say, JB101. This procedure is most important because several people in an agency may be responsible for ordering materials and supplies for a client. Sometimes it is done under pressure, by word of mouth, over the telephone, through a secretary or an assistant. Unless given a job number it will be impossible to identify the account when it comes in weeks later, the client will never be charged, and the agency will be the loser.

Job sheet

Details of the job, and the job number, should be entered on a job sheet produced with duplicate sheets, each sheet being a different colour for, say, creative, media, production and finance department. Traffic control can then distribute the job sheets to their respective departments. This raising of job sheets ties in with the ordering, which should be confirmed by letter of instruction or contract and bearing the job number. Ideally, suppliers should be told not to accept an order that does not bear a job number which they must then repeat on their invoices to the agency.

Agenda

The agenda for the agency–client meetings should be drawn up by the account executive, items being identified by their job numbers.

Contact report

After the meeting (or even after a telephone call or a casual meeting) a contact report should be written at once. The report should state who attended the meeting, when and where it was held and its purpose and the distribution list. The report should follow the pattern of the agenda and state as briefly as possible what happened or what decisions were taken concerning each job-numbered item. On the right-hand side of the sheet there should be a vertical rule, setting aside in the right-hand margin a column in which responsibilities can be set out against the initials of the person on either client or agency side who has to take agreed action. If this contact report is presented within 24–48 hours it is possible to clear up any misunderstandings and get agreements, decisions and responsibilities determined beyond doubt. This may be called a *call* or *progress* report.

Invoices

Invoices can be paid by the agency on the basis of job-numbered information and instructions, and invoices can be rendered by the agency which both recover job-numbered outlays and charge for job-numbered work with which the advertising manager is familiar. Thus, accounts are likely to be accurate and beyond challenge.

5.11 The Institute of Practitioners in Advertising

The Institute of Practitioners in Advertising, founded in 1927, is the industry body and professional institute for UK advertising agencies and those other companies concerned with creating and/or placing advertisements. Its 265 members handle more than 80 per cent of all advertising placed by UK agencies, and this amounts to some £3 billion of media purchases.

The IPA plays an important part in media research, being one of the tripartite members of JICNARS, BARB, JICRAR, JICPAR and JICCAR (cable television) plus PETAR (Pan European Television Audience Research).

A few years ago the IPA withdrew from CAM and has its own seven stage education and training programme, each stage related to level of experience.

Each year the IPA makes awards under its Advertising Effectiveness Awards scheme, and the winning case histories and a selection of the commended case histories are published in the annual volume of *Advertising Works*.

6
The media owner or promoter

6.1 Selling media

Our third member of the advertising trio is the media owner. Without media our sales message cannot be expressed to the multitude, and media make all the difference between selling and advertising. The arrival of the popular national daily newspaper at the end of the nineteenth century made it possible for factory owners to reach thousands of potential buyers; but, sometimes, advertising is banned. In the 1930s advertising, including signs which were designed to pick up the headlight beams of traffic, were erected beside our main roads including dual carriageways, but these were banned as being dangerous, especially with the provision of motorways. Trafalgar Square, London, used to have electric night signs on the surrounding buildings, but these were prohibited to protect the environment. Low flying single engine aircraft bearing advertisements such as towed banners are illegal over cities. In the press and on television it is illegal to advertise certain products or services, and it was only the AIDS scare that made it permissible to advertise contraceptives on British TV.

The advertisement or sales departments of the media do not wait hopefully for advertisers or advertising agencies to send them orders. The space, airtime or sites have to be sold like any other product and there is tremendous competition between rival sellers.

Selling media is unlike selling any other product or service. The saleability of this sort of product depends on its value to others in selling *their* products. Thus the media salesperson can sell space, time or sites only provided it is of value to the advertiser as a means of making a profit, and not because the advertiser likes the medium. The advertiser may hate *The Sun* but if it sells baked beans better than the *Times* (which may be preferred personal reading), money will not be wasted on the *Times*. A newspaper may publish the best news coverage, or a television station may make the best drama series, but if readers or viewers are too few to justify the advertisement rate the newspaper will fold or the show will be taken off.

Consequently, the advertisement selling side of the media has to find selling points of some kind which are attractive to some advertiser! This is very different from selling a soap which cleans most people's hands, or a drink which quenches most people's thirst. Identifying markets for media calls for great selling skill which is probably why space salesman are nowadays often called marketing executives.

6.2   Media owners, promoters and the range of media

For the sake of simplicity those in the media business have been referred to in this book as 'media owners', but to be strictly accurate we should also refer to 'media promoters', since a direct mail house does not own any media, poster contractors rent sites on buildings and vacant land, while exhibition organizers have to hire halls for events which they own in name only.

Media consist of almost anything which can be used to convey an advertising message. It may be a deck-chair on the beach, a cloud in the sky, or the side of a vehicle. In other words, it is often anything unused which could very well be utilized by an advertiser, if he can be shown the value of it and is willing to pay a price. Parking meters are such a medium and so are taxi-cab exteriors and interiors, while tethered and flying balloons and airships have become popular media. Yet another medium, sometimes associated with sales promotion, is body media or clothing used to promote products.

In most cases the media owner is concerned with two functions and sometimes, but not always, two sources of income. In the first place he does something that attracts an audience, and in the second he sells the presence of that audience to advertisers: a football club attracts a crowd, and the perimeter of the pitch is sold to advertisers; the cinema-goers, theatre-goers or concert-goers congregate as an audience and the screen, safety curtain or programme becomes an advertising medium; or a medium of information or entertainment – radio, television, press – can be offered cheaply or free to listeners, viewers and readers if the costs can be subsidized by advertisers interested in reaching these people .

The home-delivered free weekly newspaper is a splendid example of this, although most paid-for journals have high cover prices because they are not nowdays subsidized by advertisement revenue. Times have changed from the 1930s when a national daily was sold for an 'old' penny, cost sixpence to print and the difference came out of advertising revenue! Today it could be uneconomical to print more than a certain number of pages, and advertisements may have to be rejected because it would be too costly to print them. This applies mainly to big circulation tabloids.

Media owners are therefore very similar to advertisers in that they have something to sell and have to adopt normal selling methods with sales managers (advertisement managers), sales representatives and all the supporting advertising and sales promotional techniques. Their 'product' is empty space or future air time or vacant sites whose value is determined by their potential audience.

It is important to understand this because although media owners are very much part of the advertising scene, they are not of the advertising business like the planning and creating agencies. A media representative need not known anything about advertising, but he does have to know how to sell. The advertising value that he puts upon his commodity is that of the sales person, not the advertiser.

There is therefore a natural conflict of interest between the media owner and the other two main sides of this tripartite business of advertiser, agency and media owner. There is a simple buyer and seller situation.

It is also important that this be understood because it may be thought that advertisement managers and media representatives are merely order takers, waiting for the agencies to book space, air-time and rent sites. True, the media planner and the media buyer can plot a campaign without any help from the media owner, but to survive hard selling is still the task of the media owner's sales department.

6.3   How media are promoted

The sales department of most media organizations is headed by an executive known as an *advertisement manager*. To remember the distinction, it may be said that an *advertising manager* buys space and an *advertisement manager* sells it. In small publishing houses, editor and advertisement manager may be the same person, but in a large publishing house the two sides of editorial and space selling are often poles apart. Some editors scarcely admit that advertising exists, some advertisement managers regard the editorial as the space between the advertisements. In other publishing houses the two work very closely together. In some – newspapers which run special features to attract advertising – a special editorial section is run as part of the advertisement department.

In commercial television, advertisement managers are called sales managers, and normal sales management titles are used.

Display and classified advertising is usually handled by separate advertisement managers. Displayed classifieds – for staff recruitment, estate agents and various traders – come under the classified advertisement manager if they appear in the columns of 'smalls'.

Advertisement rates are related to sales, readership or audience figures and, of course, 'what the traffic will bear'. Generally speaking, a cheap rate means a low audience figure, as when newspapers offer bargain rates for insertions on bank holiday or television companies offer package deals including time on Sunday afternoons when one half of the audience is sleeping off Sunday lunch while most of the other are taking a 'constitutional'.

The media owner does not therefore have one rate for a column centimetre, a page or thirty seconds air-time no matter when and where it occurs. If more people read page one than page two, or if more people watch TV between 7 and 9 o'clock or listen to radio at 8.30am rather than at 3.30pm, then higher and lower rates will be charged accordingly.

The following are some of the terms used to depict varying value, just like theatre seats in the stalls, circle and gallery.

Special position means that the advertisement will occupy a position on a page of special interest such as the front page, leader page or women's page.

Run-of-paper on the other hand means that the advertisement may be placed anywhere at the publisher's discretion.

Solus position implies that there is no adjacent advertisement. Large supersite outdoor advertisements occupy isolated or solus sites often decorated with gardens and given extended visibility by means of floodlights. A single advertisement on the page likewise enjoys a solus position.

Bled-off means that the advertisement prints to the edge of the page and results from trimming. This occurs in magazines.

Spot colour applies to the printing of, say, the logo in a second colour.

Facing matter means that the ad is not buried in an advertising section but is next to editorial. *Next matter* means the same thing.

Series rate means that there is a discount for booking a given number of insertions simultaneously.

The *single column centimetre* (scc) has replaced the old single column inch (sci) as the unit of vertical measurement of advertisement space, although the sci may be retained in those countries where metrication has not been introduced.

An *island site* at an exhibition is one that is open to visitors on all sides, and clearly has advantages over more confined sites, commanding a higher rate.

All these details are set out on the media rate card, and current rates appear in *British Rate and Data (BRAD)* which is the space buyer's monthly bible.

The media owner also has to provide mechanical and copy date information, and in planning an advertising campaign it is essential to know the different requirements of journals printed by the three major printing processes, flexography, lithography and photogravure. While an advertisement may be inserted in some newspapers at a few hours' notice, it will be a few weeks, and perhaps months, in the case of women's magazines and weekend colour supplements which are printed by offset-litho or photogravure.

It is therefore an important aspect of media selling to keep advertisers and agencies aware of opportunities to reach readers and viewers, of production requirements and of deadlines.

While it may be thought that the statistical information used by the media planner in the choice of media is mainly to the media planner's advantage, it can also be exploited by the media owner. The advertisement manager will study circulation figures and readership and audience surveys and seek to attract advertising from firms which can benefit from, for instance, the fact that a journal has the largest number of A-B readers who might want to have a swimming pool constructed in the garden. Likewise, advantageous cost-per-thousand figures can be calculated. If the *Daily Moon* is able to offer the lowest cost-per-thousand spinsters under 22 years of age, this may be an ideal market for advertisers of engagement rings, transistor radios or cola drinks.

Service departments

Many media owners try to encourage and develop new advertisers by offering a service department. This may mean giving advice on how to produce a TV commercial, placing posters on the outside of a bus for the advertiser to see, or writing and designing press advertisements.

Supplements and features

Enterprising advertisement managers will naturally try to increase sales and one method is to organize special features and supplements, an editorial being published as an inducement to advertisers who wish to be associated with the theme. Some of these are excellent, others are a waste of advertisers' money. Some are blatant attempts to exploit a certain situation, others are respected annual reviews which are of great reader interest and therefore great advertisement value. The advertiser needs to pick his way carefully through this particular jungle. But no advertiser should feel obliged to take space, and if there is any element of blackmail the advertiser is advised to keep out. Obviously, it is well worth while for a fuel or appliance company to take space in an important feature on central heating, but quite unnecessary for a supplier to congratulate a trader on opening new premises. The first is an excellent bringing together of reader and advertiser, the latter is little short of a racket. Unfortunately, the trader is often too flattered to realize the imposition he is placing upon his suppliers.

A weakness with supplements, which may not be appreciated by the unwary advertiser, is that while the normal rates will apply the actual readership of the supplement may be only a small proportion of the total circulation or readership. Against this it is only fair to say that a really important supplement may attract additional readers.

6.4 How media promote sales

Having taken a general look at some of the ways in which media owners promote sales of space, time and sites, let us now examine more specifically the range of sales-promoting material and activities which may be used to create revenue.

The rate card

It will give full details of rates for various positions, series rates, and production data. This is reproduced in *BRAD*

Sales letters

They will announce special numbers, supplements and composite pages. The latter consist of market-place features which bring together like advertisers such as holiday resorts, horticultural firms, direct response traders, property or educational services. These sales letters may be accompanied by *dummy pages* showing the available advertisement spaces surrounding the editorial.

Promotional folders

Often lavishly produced, and sometimes designed as a wallet to carry a specimen copy of the publication, such packs will include the rate card, and details of circulation and readership figures which provide a profile of the publication.

Specimen copies

Specimen copies of special issues may be mailed to advertisers and agencies to demonstrate the success of the publication. Some mammoth issues have been sent out in specially made boxes, and the cost of postage has been a sizeable item in the promotion.

Maps of circulation areas

Combined with the extent of penetration into a region, such maps are favourites with regional newspapers.

Research material

Publishers may undertake their own research. The more elaborate surveys may be sold which tends to enhance their value.

Editorial mention

Any firm gaining an editorial mention may have a specimen copy of the journal mailed to the advertising manager by the advertisement manager. This is commonly done, and is somewhat self-defeating. *It indicates that the advertisement manager does not know the difference between public relations and advertising.* There is no reason why the advertising manager should feel favourably disposed towards a newspaper or magazine just because its editor prints a news story, picture or article about the company. In fact, it is quite likely that advertising will appear in one group of journals and public relations material in another.

Reader service enquiry schemes

With these schemes readers do not have to clip coupons but can make requests for literature on one coupon or card returned to the publisher, enabling the advertisement manager to prove the pulling power of his journal. There is a danger here that having been invited to fill in the application coupon or card some readers will greedily ask for many items. Is this wasteful or not, or does it give the advertiser an even better chance of getting his literature into more hands? In the holiday business, where full-colour brochures are expensive, requests are nowadays limited to four or six items.

However, while these reader service schemes may be very useful to the publisher as a means of proving the pulling power of a journal, there can be a delay before all the replies are assembled and passed on to the advertiser, whereas a coupon, clipped from an advertisement, can be received and handled more quickly.

Numbers of readers

Controlled circulation magazines supply breakdowns of the classes and numbers of readers to whom copies are distributed.

Exhibitions

These are not only profitable ventures in their own right but help to sell space in the sponsoring publication. Examples are: French Property Exhibition (*Daily Telegraph*); Ideal Home Exhibition (*Daily Mail*); Building Materials Exhibition (B&M Publications).

Stands

Media owners take stands at exhibitions, e.g. *Homefinder*, at the Ideal Home Exhibition.

Brochures

Television companies issue brochures to sell package deals, or holiday advertising at Christmas which is linked with press media, especially *TV Times*, or to convince advertisers that there is a summer audience.

Exhibition promoters issue *brochures* supported by *plans* of the exhibition site with stand spaces drawn out and numbered.

Catalogues

Direct mail houses and list brokers issue catalogues listing the categories for which they hold mailing lists, and stating the numbers of available addresses.

Advance programmes

Publishers issue advance programmes of special numbers, the *Financial Times* providing an annual list.

Novelties

Novelties such as miniature issues of newspapers or magazines, are occasionally used as special gimmicks.

Specimen campaigns

Specimen campaigns are planned and costed for advertisers, sometimes in combination with other media.

Transportation contractors

Brochures are issued illustrating the use by advertisers of different positions outside and inside vehicles and about premises. They also give specimen costs for using different quantities of posters or cards in each situation or position.

Statistics

Outdoor advertising contractors supply statistics about the poster audience, and the cost of gaining maximum coverage of marketing areas throughout the country.

Reprints of trade press articles

Articles about the medium are reprinted and mailed to advertisers and agencies.

Advertisements

These are placed in the trade and business press; transportation firms advertise on their own vehicles; and individual television companies show commercials on their own behalf. Similarly, billposters take their own medicine and advertise their services on their own sites.

Case studies

Media owners produce case studies which demonstrate the success advertisers have experienced with the medium.

From these twenty-two items alone it will be seen that there is very vigorous promotion of advertisement media, and that space, time or sites are sold just like any other product.

6.5   The television pre-emption system

A peculiarity of commercial television is the pre-emption system whereby a spot may be booked at one price in the pre-emption table but lost to another advertiser who is prepared to pay a higher rate. Table 6.1 shows peak segments on one television station followed by the details set out in the rate card. These figures are given as an example and are, of course, subject to change.

Table 6.1   *Peak segment rates for segment 2: 17 : 20–20 : 00*

Time(s)	10 £	20 £	30 £	40 £	50 £	60 £
T1	19000	30400	38000	50540	63460	66500
T2	17000	27200	34000	45220	56780	59500
T3	15000	24000	30000	39900	50100	52500
T4	13000	20800	26000	34580	43420	45500
T5	11500	18400	23000	30590	38410	40250
T6	10500	16800	21000	27930	35070	36750
T7	9500	15200	19000	25270	31730	33250
T8	8500	13600	17000	22610	28390	29750
T9	7500	12000	15000	19950	25050	26250
T10	6500	10400	13000	17290	21710	22750
T11	5500	8800	11000	14630	18370	19250
T12	4500	7200	9000	11970	15030	15750
T13	3500	5600	7000	9310	11690	12250
T14	2500	4000	5000	6650	8350	8750
T15	1500	2400	3000	3990	5010	5250
T16	250	400	500	665	835	875

Spot advertisement rates

Pre-emptible spot definitions
Subject to availability, pre-emptible TI to T16 rates may be purchased as specified below.

T1 Fixed spots may be purchased at all times in all segments. Such spots are pre-emptible only by T1 spots carrying special position status, save that the provisions of the special positions clause shall not apply after 12 noon two working days prior to the day of transmission.

T2 Fixed spots may be purchased in specific breaks in all segments and such spots will become non pre-emptible at 5.30pm one working day prior to the day of transmission.

T3–16 spots may be purchased in specific breaks in all segments. Such spots are fixed and pre-emptible.

Non pre-emptible spots
Subject to availability and at the company's discretion, spots purchased at T2–16 may be made non pre-emptible. Where this facility is required a surcharge of 15% is applicable to each spot booking.

Pre-emptible airtime packages
Subject to availability and at the company's discretion, P1 and P2 packages may be made available. Packages failing to achieve the required number of spots shall be charged pro-rata to the total package price. The full package price will be invoiced on transmission of the first spot.

6.6   The agency recognition system

Agency recognition is granted by the various bodies representing the media owners such as the Newspaper Publishers' Association (national newspapers), Newspaper Society (regional newspapers), Periodical Publishers Association (magazines and trade press), and the Independent Television Association (commercial television). Agencies are *not* recognized by the Advertising Association or the Institute of Practitioners in Advertising, as is sometimes mistakenly thought.

The agency recognition system was changed to comply with the Office of Fair Trading ruling of November 1978 that, under the *Restrictive Trade Practices Act 1976*, the old system (described in Chapter 5) of stipulating a fixed commission was monopolistic. The various media owners' organizations now recognize advertising agencies for their credit-worthiness and adherence to the British Code of Advertising Practice. To prove their credit-worthiness agencies have to submit detailed evidence of their financial strength, but recognition now means that agencies must negotiate their own discounts or commission from the media, and may seek remuneration from their clients in various and sometimes competitive ways. The new system differs from the old in the following respects. The ban was lifted on rebating commission, and on the granting of recognition to certain categories of agency only (with provisions regarding agency equipment, staffing and ownership). It was accepted by both the NPA and the NS that these areas concerned individual relationships between publisher and agency.

Details of the agency recognition systems will be found in Appendix 7, page 420.

Part Two
Planning Advertising Campaigns

7
Campaign development and execution

7.1 Campaign procedures

This topic was looked at briefly in Chapter 5, section 5.8, under the heading of How Do Agencies Work. Here we shall consider all the stages that occur from start to finish in developing and executing an advertising campaign. These procedures will apply whatever the size of the account or the size of the agency, except that the number of personnel involved may differ, while the media could consist of trade journals for an industrial client and networked television for the manufacturer of a fmcg. These are differences of degree.

7.2 Briefing

Two situations can operate at this stage. The agency may have been appointed, (or be preparing a renewal programme for a succeeding year), or it may be pitching for a new account in competition with other agencies. Either way, the initial briefing by the client is the crucial first step. This is a two-way operation with the account executive seeking all the information necessary to plan the campaign, and the advertising manager being forthcoming with this information, however sensitive it may be. Frankness and confidentiality go together at this stage, and certainly if it is a regular client. This is where the account executive has to be accepted as a professional adviser.

It is usual for the account executive to initiate proceedings by producing a questionnaire, and the more searching this is the better because it can look very inefficient to come back and ask further questions which should have been asked in the first place. Dependent on the nature of the client's business, the chief questions will be as follows.

1 In the case of new account

Details about the company: history, finances, directors, whether it is a subsidiary or part of a group, national parentage and so on. A copy of the annual report and accounts would be required, together with sales literature such as catalogues or brochures.

2 The budget

Ways of arriving at the budget are discussed in the next chapter, and responsibility for calculating the appropriation may lie with either the client or the agency. However, in most cases the appropriation will be determined by the client as part of the total marketing budget. It is important to agree the budget as soon as possible as everything depends on the size of the spend. For instance, it is no use thinking in terms of TV advertising if the budget is inadequate.

3 What is being advertised?

The account executive must know everything about the product or service which is to be advertised, even if it is only at a prototype stage. He or she may need to sample the product in some way in order to understand how it works, what it does, how it can benefit the consumer, or is superior to other products. This may mean tasting the tea, driving the power mower or wearing the clothes. In one case a woman account executive actually spent time in uniform with a women's forces unit to discover what it was like before planning a recruitment campaign.

The account executive should never take the client's word that the product or service is excellent for the client is bound to be prejudiced. There have been occasions when an account executive has been bold enough to tell a client that the product is unlikely to sell, or needs to be modified before it can be sold. The point is that to produce a first-class campaign the account executive must be convinced about the merits of the product or service, even if he or she would not buy it for personal reasons. The account executive might not fancy a holiday in Majorca, but thousands of other people would, which is different from being asked to produce a campaign for a run-down holiday camp which could not honestly be recommended.

4 Market

What is the market, or the market segment, and has this been researched? On this will depend the copy platform and the choice of media. Maybe some research is necessary.

5   Distribution

How will the product or service reach consumers or users? This could affect trade advertising, but could also require special techniques if the product or service is sold direct.

6   What is the name?

Is it just a code name or number at present, and is finding a suitable name part of the assignment? Or has a name been decided which may or may not be an advertising asset?

7   Price

The pricing policy will influence the style of the advertising. Is it being sold on price, is it a competitive price, or is it an expensive product where it is necessary to show how the customer can afford it or pay for it? Does the price have to be justified by evidence of quality or value?

8   Packaging

Is this an attribute that can contribute to the product, e.g. a very convenient container, or one of distinctive design like some drinks bottles, or has it a colour which lends itself to pack recognition in colour advertising? Or is the agency expected to advise on package design, or conduct packaging research? This is yet another element of the marketing mix which can concern the agency.

9   Competition

What is the extent and nature of the competition? Few products or services are unique. They usually have to compete with something, even if it is discretionary income which can buy only a limited number of luxuries. What, for instance, are the rival products in the same price bracket? How does it compare with rival lines?

10   The after-market

What happens after the customer has bought the product? Are there guarantees, warranties or promises; are there adequate instructions or a service manual; are there spare part and servicing facilities; are there ways of maintaining customer interest, loyalty and piggy-back (e.g. accessories) or repeat sales?

7.3   Account executive reports to account director or agency head

When the account executive returns to the agency he or she will discuss the briefing with his or her superior. In a large agency this will be an account director responsible for a group of accounts and a number of account executives. In a smaller agency, the report will be made to, say, the managing director or principal.   This initial report is essential, particularly where a new product or a new client is involved. A policy decision may be required, and there could be a conflict of interests to resolve. It is possible that the agency already services a company that has a subsidiary which makes a product which rivals that for which the account executive has been briefed. Rival accounts may be handled by an agency if the two companies have no objection, and this will need to be determined. But it could be that it is agency policy not to handle certain accounts, or the new one introduced by the account executive presents problems. These problems may not be ones of ethics or principles but of direct conflict between two products or services which are antagonistic to one another, e.g. butter and margarine, starch and slimming aids, or tobacco and a cancer charity.

7.4   Account executive reports to departmental heads

Once the go-ahead has been given to proceed with the preparation of a presentation to a client, the account executive issues a detailed report to the agency department heads who are immediately concerned, these being the marketing manager, art director, copy chief and media planner, and possibly the agency's public relations manager. If TV is to be used, the TV producer will also be briefed. These people will form the plans board, unless a creative group has been formed, or an account planner takes over. One way or another, those responsible for the different facets of the campaign are invited to consider the assignment and make their recommendations. To simplify the procedure it will be assumed here that the plans board system applies.

7.5   First plans board meeting

The account executive will chair the meeting, and each department head will make observations and recommendations. At this early stage there will be a mixture of ideas and opinions, some sceptical, others enthusiastic, about the product or service. The fact that one person would buy it but another would not is immaterial if it is capable of satisfying a particular market. The account executive will call the discussion to a close and ask for proposals to be presented at the next meeting, and this will call for co-operation between the different departmental chiefs.

7.6   Second plans board meeting

At this meeting the proposed campaign will be shaping up. The marketing manager will have done some desk research to assess the market. The copy chief will have evolved a copy platform and the art director will have interpreted this visually. The media planner will recommend the media to be used, and the TV producer may have ideas on how the commercial should be filmed. All these ideas will be discussed and refined. Ideally, the client's advertising manager will be present to comment on the proposals so far. There may be more than one way of presenting the sales argument, and it may be decided to carry out some copy-testing to see which treatment is most favoured.

7.7   Preparation of campaign

Now the campaign will be assembled. Final copy will be written, visuals will be prepared, photographic ideas may be produced with a Polaroid camera, and ads 'mocked up', while a TV storyboard will be presented in cartoon form, and a media schedule showing media, sizes and dates will be drawn up. All in all, a tentative campaign will be put together which will be sufficiently intelligible to the client without spending money on typesetting, artwork, photography or filming.

7.8   Presentation to client

This may take place at the agency or at the client's office, and according to the size of the campaign it could take half or a whole day. Very often, the client will invite a number of directors and executives to attend the presentation. While the agency may have spent weeks considering this and that idea, and the presentation is the result of much thought and probably copy-tests, the final scheme is received for the first time by the members of the client audience. Not surprisingly, some of them may hark back to earlier ideas which the agency has already discarded. There can be much argument because those present will have their own ideas. The account executive has to convince everyone that the proposed campaign will work giving, for example, statistical evidence in favour of the recommended media. In all this it will help if the client's advertising manager has sat in at plans board or other agency meetings and can also support the account executive.

This is reasonably straightforward when the presentation is to an existing client for a renewal of contract, but when more than one agency is competing for a new account the presentations are inevitably very competitive, and the competing agencies will be unaware of the schemes put up by their rivals. The client has to be very critical and perceptive in order to pick the proposed campaign most likely to be successful.

Large sums of money are involved, both in business for the agency and in expenditure by the client.

7.9 Executing the campaign

As a result of the presentation there may be amendments or deletions to the campaign, and the contract of service will be signed. This should make clear how accounts shall be rendered and paid, and also any arrangements for the assignments of copyright. An agency may insist that copyright of creative work produced by agency staff shall not be assigned until the final payment has been paid.

Now artwork and photography can be commissioned, and space and air-time can be booked or confirmed. (In the case of some magazines with long lead times, space may have been booked provisionally before the client had approved the schedule). Production of TV commercials can be put out to a production company, and director and performers or animation artists engaged. All this has to be controlled on a progress chasing basis by the production manager or traffic controller.

Work will have to be planned so that, for instance, copy and visuals are produced, artwork is finalized, typesetting is undertaken, proofs are submitted to client, client approval (or amendment) is received, and the final camera-ready copy is despatched to the publisher by the copy date. This procession of activities has to follow a strict timetable, and satisfactory stage-by-stage progress will be checked daily, otherwise the advertisement will never appear. In the case of TV commercials, they need to be approved (both script and film/video) by ITVA before being broadcast.

During this period the account executive will work closely with the advertising manager so that work in progress is approved quickly. This is a very critical time because many other campaigns will be progressing through the agency departments at the same time. The client has to understand that there are other clients. Some of the larger agencies actually work 24 hours a day to cope with the through-put of work. Production managers are sometimes regarded as agency sergeant majors who get things done on time.

7.10 When the campaign breaks

When ads and commercials appear both the advertising manager and the account executive will watch the press and the TV screen to see how well, and in accordance with booking instructions, they appear. Things do go wrong sometimes, colours come out badly, advertisements are wrongly or badly positioned, and it may be necessary to negotiate improvements for subsequent appearances. The account executive has to spot such things first, and not wait to be told by an irate client.

Research may be organized to test the response. This will be dealt with in a separate chapter, but next day recall tests may be conducted, or longer term tracking studies may be conducted.

If direct response is desired, either enquiries or orders, this response can be measured by means of keyed replies.

7.11   Vouchers and charging out

In Chapter 5 reference was made to agency paperwork and to vouchers and tear sheets. The latter are proof of the appearance of the advertisement.

An essential part of the agency work is the maintenance of cash flow, and it is significant that in November 1990 the media owners were concerned about the solvency of agencies. Recognition is granted on the basis of credit-worthiness but it was reported in *Campaign* on November 23, 1990 that 60 per-cent of recognized agencies probably did not meet the credit-worthiness or solvency agreement.

While this may be due to bad management, insufficient business, unrealistic overheads, or unwise investment in acquisitions, a very simple cause of insolvency is poor cash flow. In other words, monies are going out but remuneration is coming in too slowly. Creative people may not be the best business people.

Essentially, it comes down to charging clients as soon as suppliers submit their accounts and insisting on no more than 30 days credit. In the case of media purchases, when the media insist on immediate payment, the client can be charged simultaneously with booking the space or air-time. Thus, it becomes the responsibility of the agency accountant to invoice clients promptly, and for the account executive to act as debt collector if the situation warrants it. Otherwise a cash flow problem erupts, there can be an overdraft dilemma at the bank, and if the media are not paid promptly they can refuse commission and call for agency recognition to be withdrawn, in which case the agency will collapse.

7.12   Agency and client relations

In all these proceedings from initial briefing to payment of accounts it will be seen that agency–client relations can be a delicate matter, and the account executive has to be a diplomat. The client may be over-demanding, the agency may seem to be dragging its feet, and the account executive is the pig in the middle. Consequently, the closer the two can work together the more successful is likely to be the relationship.

As has been said earlier in this book, the agency should augment the company in-house department and be seen as an extension of it, and not as an outside service to be made a scapegoat when something goes wrong.

8
Advertising costs and budgets

WHAT INFLUENCES ADVERTISING COSTS?

8.1 Who pays for advertising?

Before discussing the cost of advertising and the factors which influence its cost, and before going on to discuss ways of arriving at a budget of advertising costs, let us face up quite frankly to the perennial question: *who pays for advertising*? The answer to this question is one of the keys to determining the expenditure on advertising.

In any business there are only three people, or three groups of people, who can pay for running a business and making a profit. They are the investors (and they include both the bank which permits an overdraft and the supplier who provides credit), the entrepreneur who may invest capital plus earned income, and those who buy the goods or services. If the business fails, the investors fail and in effect pay the bills through their own losses: if the business succeeds everyone profits and everyone is satisfied. Only if the entrepreneur sells at a price higher than costs is it possible for him to make a profit. Costs include selling effort, which may mean renting a shop, hiring a salesperson or advertising in the local newspaper (and these promotional expenses can be multiplied according to the size of the business). If these costs are to be recovered *and* a profit is to be made they can come from only one source, the customer who pays the price for the goods or services.

If the product sells easily, the cost of promoting each unit is slight. But if it is a new, a costly or a difficult product to sell, the advertising cost per unit will be high.

Assuming that products or services are sold, the cost of advertising is borne by the buyer. However, if the goods remain unsold in spite of monies spent on advertising, the cost of advertising reverts to the producer or distributor who has failed to make the necessary sales and so pass on or recover the costs plus a profit. Even if the goods are sold off at a reduced price and the profit is forfeited, the recovery of costs is still being sought.

This has to be said because a false idea exists that the cost of advertising is taken out of profits. There are even some business people who delude themselves to the extent that they speak of spending on advertising 'what they can afford', as if it were a sacrifice, donation or something they could avoid, when in fact, to make a profit, they cannot afford *not* to advertise, or at least adopt some form of persuasive sales-promoting action.

This is not to say that advertising is an unjustified part of the price. It is an old chestnut to say that a certain product costing a fraction of a penny to produce is sold at an exorbitant price, of say, ten pence. It costs a lot to distribute products, and advertising is a distribution cost. *The price of advertising may be the difference between enjoying a product and not having it at all.*

8.2 The advertising appropriation

An ideal advertising budget, called the *appropriation*, is one which produces the greatest result for the least expenditure. This is implied in the reference in the IPA definition to 'lowest possible cost' with the further implication that effective, economic expenditure calls for expert advice.

It is not easy to be either ideal or expert in this business of mass marketing communications. There are so many imponderables, and it would not be facetious to include the weather. A few years ago there was such a wet summer that posters on the hoardings were ruined. A vicious winter, making the transportation of fuel impossible, could lead to power cuts (as during the miners' strike of 1973) so that television advertising suffered small audiences and diminished effectiveness. Guinness once inserted an advertisement in Sunday newspapers with wording to the effect that Guinness was good for you when it was nice weather for ducks. Obligingly, that Sunday was a soaker! Strikes at newspaper plants have robbed advertisers of editions.

Textbooks on this subject usually offer a familiar set of methods for arriving at the appropriation, but these methods tend to be academic and it is doubtful whether many advertising people consciously debate which one to apply. They may well use one or the other method because it happened to be convenient to their type of business. They may be unaware of any other way except their own. It may be rule of thumb and hit or miss, but only to a degree as we shall see. In most methods there is a blend of common sense, experience, flair and statistical evaluation.

Thanks to the data available from JICNARS, BARB, JICPAR, ABC and other reliable sources, much of the one-time gamble can be taken out of mass consumer advertising. Advertisers can thank ISBA for much of this. It is, however, rather less possible to minimize wastage with industrial advertising if traditional media are used. And it is very difficult in the case of the small or local advertiser who may have to use a disproportionate amount of advertising to achieve his objective, but again this is a matter of trial and error, experiment and good judgement. A lot depends on what is being sold to whom, and also how cleverly the available resources are exploited. A local shopkeeper could send out a hundred tatty duplicated sales letters and get nowhere: a more enterprising person could make one significant announcement on local radio and sell out by lunchtime.

So, before launching into an analytical study of the ways of assessing the advertising appropriation – and we shall examine the largest variety of ways that have appeared in an advertising textbook – let us first of all think about a general assumption. Then let us consider an actual example. After that, let us face up to the imponderables which make budgeting far from being an infallible arithmetic exercise.

A general assumption

It is generally true that the cost of advertising per product unit is in proportion to price. The advertising per unit of, say, toothpaste is minute compared with that for a motor-car, and it costs more per unit to promote an unknown product than a well-known one. Profit margins, or 'marks ups', follow a similar pattern. All this is relative to turnover. This assumption should not be confused with the total sum spent on advertising: the toothpaste manufacturer will spend more *in total* than the motor-car manufacturer because of the difference in volume of sales represented by regular repeat purchases by a very large number of people over a long period.

An example of an actual appropriation

While the following example may be untypical it does have meaning for the new advertiser whose business can grow as a result of judicious advertising.

The company in our example retailed a certain do-it-yourself product and twenty years ago decided to market a service for those who could not do-it-themselves either because they did not want to or the job was beyond them. As a try-out, a modest advertisement was placed in a middle-class national newspaper, and it was repeated from time to time. The new servicing department consisted of only three people, who were kept fully occupied in response to this modest advertising. Gradually, the advertising was stepped up, work flowed in, more men were engaged and trained, and branches were set up in strategic parts of the country. The whole process was like a staircase, each step being an extension of advertising resulting in an extension of business. The original retail product lent goodwill to the service, and customer satisfaction with the service produced recommendations. There is a clear element of public relations here which was supported by educational activities about the nature of the work and its benefits.

Once this business was operating on a national basis, the advertising was reviewed very carefully; this was necessary, because a variety of newspapers and magazines was being used including many regional papers in support of local branches. It was possible to relate keyed replies to media and further to evaluate business against enquiries. By this means, publications which had failed to draw profitable business were eliminated from the schedule. Thus, the appropriation moved from *what was considered necessary* to attract business (a target or task method) to *that sum which could be shown to actually produce business* (a percentage of previous turnover method).

A short list of economic media was compiled, and sufficient insertions were booked each month to produce the volume of enquiries and resultant business necessary to augment recommendations and other sources of new business, and achieve the sales target for the year. The sales target itself was increased year by year, which in itself implies that it was achieved each time! The system was kept sufficiently flexible to permit deletions or additions as media also changed. To be fair, credit must be given to management for its attention to research and development, and to its financial policy of acquisitions of other companies with additional products, techniques or services. The sales graph of this company rose like steps of stairs. Eventually, in order to finance overseas expansion, the company went public and the new issue was generously oversubscribed during the late '60s when the stock market was severely depressed. In the '90s the company's share price reflects success and it has become one of the UK's most successful growth companies.

8.3   Seven imponderables concerning advertising appropriations

However prophetic the advertiser tries to be, some influences are bound to be beyond control. The following are some examples:

a   The variety of media
b   The variety of appeals
c   The variety of techniques
d   Imperfect knowledge of the market
e   Imperfect knowledge of the competition
f   Unpredictable rival promotions
g   Unpredictable politico-economic conditions such as inflation and unemployment, interest rates, social changes, new life styles and acts of God.

There are doubtless many more imponderables but these seven are sufficient to set us thinking realistically about the handicaps to fixing budgets. Can anything be done to reduce their detrimental effect, thus helping to justify the place of advertising in the marketing mix? This consideration matters whatever the size of business, and becomes more critical if the business is smaller, more specialized or localized. By this is meant that the larger business with the larger expenditure is likely to benefit from the snowball effect of mass advertising. Those with more specialist products and markets may be faced with the dilemma that even maximum advertising expenditure in certain media, say a whole page each month in the main trade journal, may be ineffectual. The latter is a common dilemma with 'secondary suppliers', that is with firms which supply components (as in the electronics and motor-car industries) whose advertising can be quite small yet extravagant if the wrong media or tactics are employed.

This problem is worth examining before proceeding to a detailed study of the seven imponderables. Some industrial advertisers, carefully relating advertising expenditure to potential sales, may arrive at a sum which will buy a certain number of insertions (plus production costs) in trade or technical journals. Yet that spread of advertising may be inadequate, lacking in *size* of space, or *regularity* of insertion and volume of *appearance* to have worthwhile *impact* and *result*. (With large consumer campaigns the media planner will seek at least 80 per cent coverage of the market, and this is often highly unlikely with the sums usually spent on industrial advertising using traditional media.)

What are the alternatives? Different media, say print and direct mail? Possibly. It may be that traditional above-the-line advertising is too expensive to be economic in this case, and other marketing techniques have to be explored. Perhaps it will be better to use technical sales people who can set up travelling exhibits, demonstrations and seminars for potential customers. Perhaps the more educational techniques of public relations, using technical feature articles, an external house journal for specifiers and users, or a documentary video-tape distributed to invited audiences of prospects, will be more economic and productive.

Looked at in this context, some (not all, of course) trade and technical press advertising may be doing no more than subsidizing these journals and ensuring their existence, which may be important to the industry. But it has to be said when expenditure versus results is under the microscope that some advertising agencies, confronted by a technical or industrial account, can see no farther than press advertising.

Not surprisingly, industrial advertising tends to be handled by advertising agents not over-inhibited by the commission system, conscious of the client's value-for-money problem, and relinquishing commission-paying media and operating on a time-sheet and consultancy fee basis. Alternatively, it is handled in its entirety by skilled industrial advertising managers or thirdly, if public relations approaches are adopted, the work is handled by a public relations consultancy. The commission system is explained in Chapter 6.

Such moves away from traditional media (press, TV, outdoor, radio and cinema) have also been made by firms selling to the mass consumer market as may be observed by the extensive use of premium offers, banded offers, free gifts, contests, money-off offers, sampling and other sales promotion schemes.

Now let us look at the seven imponderables.

1   The variety of media

Any advertiser is faced with an incredible choice of media. With their media planning and buying expertise, this is where advertising agents come into their own, and their services may be engaged for this reason alone, especially those of media independents. The UK is favoured by a large national and regional press with journals covering every specialist interest. More than that, the press is an ever-changing medium which has to be known and understood. But for the small trader, whose volume of advertising may not yet justify use of an agent, the variety of media may be bewildering. The proliferation of media, and advertising propositions put up by plausible salesmen, not only encourages profitless spending but the scattering of advertising over too many different media too thinly to be effective. *Benn's Media Directory* lists nearly 14,000 UK publications.

A common sense approach to media selection can be gained by noting that national campaigns are mostly restricted to a *small, carefully chosen group of complementary media*. The consumer may first see the product on TV, then see local stockists advertising in the local press, and finally spot point-of-sale material in a shop window. A media sequence is thus achieved, and an example of this particular sequence is the building society which advertises in the national press and on TV, promotes its branches in local newspapers, and makes good use of branch premises and window display material.

In the place of TV, another advertiser may use the press or posters; and choices may be made within the great variety of press media, say, between national newspapers, general magazines and women's magazines; or a combination of TV and poster (very popular with brewers) or press and poster (as with cigarette firms) may be used. Weight and concentration of advertising is preferable to placing advertisements here, there and everywhere. Some advertisers may not be permitted to use certain media, e.g. cigarettes are banned on TV.

The small trader, with a limited budget, will do better by placing an advertisement in the same place regularly so that maximum impact is achieved. This may be on the backs of local buses, or in the local newspaper, or on local broadcast media. Consistency pays. With this discipline, the temptation to indulge in useless and wasteful advertising is trounced.

There are rare exceptions when *saturation advertising* may be adopted by the very largest mass-consumer market advertisers, although it is more usual for them to alternate between primary media. It is interesting to watch the tactics of big advertising. Commercial TV has attracted a greater variety of advertisers in recent years including expensive rather than mass market items, for instance, perfumes, airlines, motor-cars and computers. With the banning of cigarette advertising from commercial TV, the hoardings have become a major medium in conjunction with whole-page full-colour ads in the national press.

The chapters on media will help to distinguish between the special values of each medium, but the small trader also has to contend with classes of media which seldom concern the big advertiser.

Media to be avoided by the small trader

i   Unknown directories of doubtful distribution, some of which are never published. It is necessary to beware of invoices for advertisements which have never been placed! Staff must be instructed not to sign any forms, not even to say that a *directory entry* is correct!

ii   Guide books and maps of doubtful distribution, especially those with contracts extending over several years or editions with no opportunity to change the copy.

iii   Blackmail requests to advertise in souvenir brochures or newspaper features as a supplier or subcontractor, unless such advertising support promises to be truly beneficial.

But having uttered these warnings, there is still a multiplicity of media which can be valuable to *some* traders, to mention only programmes, menu covers, telephone directories, litter-bins, display panels in Post Offices, local magazines, street maps, timetables, delivery vans, deck chairs, taxis – in fact, anything with a vacant space capable of being filled with advertising! Each needs to be approached on a strict cost-benefit analysis. A lot of penetrating questions need to be asked, for the innocent trader will be bombarded with wondrous advertising propositions.

As a quick guide, it is fair to say that one gets what one pays for. The dearest medium fetches its price because of the audience it commands. So, although we may be confronted by what appears to be a bewildering array of media, many of them are irrelevant if we have a specific market clearly in mind. London cinemas have used the London Underground in this way.

2 The variety of appeals

It is said that, if asked, six different advertising agencies could put up six different advertisements for the same product, and all would be good. This is true.

Let us take a central heating system and try to think of six different appeals.

i   The boiler is so well lagged that there is no heat loss and all the heat is transferred to the radiators.
ii   It uses the cheapest fuel.
iii Installation is easy, cheap and causes little disturbance.
iv   In the summer it can be converted into an air-cooling system.
v   There is a low-interest hire-purchase system of payment.
vi   The heating units in each room are unobtrusive e.g. underfloor or skirting.

Or an ice cream may be taken as another example.

i   Entirely new flavours.
ii   Does not melt so quickly in hot weather.
iii Special packs for table use as sweets.
iv   Premium offer.
v   Money-off offer.
vi   Big prize competition.

Which appeal shall we use, bearing in mind that we are in competition with other firms? We need to be different, original, compelling and competitive.

We may have to use some form of research to find out: a consumer panel, copy-testing or test marketing.

If we take some of the psychological appeals which can be introduced into copy and presentation, we can start with the instincts and the emotions, or the biological and social drives, and find a whole range of appeals. Those already discussed are in line with Rosser Reeves' *unique selling proposition* (USP) where the appeal is directed through some special quality in the product. The USP has been superseded by the concept of emotional buying triggers, the appeal being made to biological and social (inherited and learned) drives, the modern psychologist's version of McDougall's instincts, emotions and sentiments, Other appeals are based on the findings of motivational research which searches, usually, by means of clinical tests or group discussion techniques, for hidden, unknown buying motives.

From this brief sketch it is possible to see that choice of appeal is an imponderable at the outset of budgeting, since it can influence media choice, volume of advertising and its effectiveness. Some advertising appeals have seemed right to their creators, only to prove a costly flop in practice. *The appropriation may have to include the cost of research to discover the best appeal,* followed by copy-testing, and ultimately other research such as reading and noting tests to test the reaction after the advertisement has appeared. Dealer audit or consumer panel research may be used to test the share of the market achieved or the kind of people who are buying the product in what quantities and how often. Tracking studies may be adopted to test the long-term effects and endurance of advertising.

Selecting the right appeal can be a means of reducing the volume and therefore the cost of advertising necessary to achieve the sales target. Research to this end is therefore a good investment. Weight of advertising is not everything. Of course, it goes without saying that few things help cut the cost of advertising so much as a good product, or a good reputation. Rentokil spends remarkably little on advertising because 60 per cent of the business comes by way of recommendation. When goodwill is high, and that is public relations working at full throttle, little advertising expenditure may be necessary, Marks & Spencer being the supreme example of this even if their stores are colossal self-advertisements.

3   The variety of techniques

We are discussing a business which offers a truly amazing abundance of techniques. We can write, draw, print, photograph, film, act, speak, animate, sing, illuminate, reflect and, in the last resort, go so far as to subliminate our message. (Subliminal advertising – showing a few moving pictures which register on the mind without being accepted by the eye – is illegal in the UK.) The advertising practitioner is able to choose by elimination, or by ability to combine several techniques within one medium. For example:

Press – direct mail – poster: writing, drawing, photography, printing.
Radio: writing, acting, speech, sound effects, music.
TV/cinema: writing, acting, speech, sound effects, music, movement, cartoon, film/video.
Newscaster: writing, movement, illumination.

It may be decided that a particular technique is essential, and this will determine not only the medium but either the cost or what we get for a given sum of money. Some media achieve a purpose better than others. TV is clearly excellent if a product demands visual presentation, and more so if it is demonstrable. Detergents, foods and motor-cars score here.

4   Imperfect knowledge of the market

Marketing research, and test marketing, can reduce uncertainty about the market. But the majority of new products still fail to succeed and, even successful products suffer from the whims of fashion or are the victims of *product life-cycles*. (A motor-car, for example, usually has a life-cycle of ten years and large-scale production is generally based on that assumption.) There are few certainties about markets. The bottom can drop out of any market, as with fashionwear where production is necessarily on a cautious scale. No manufacturer can control a product's destiny absolutely. Conversely, products with no apparently exceptional merit can sometimes rocket to record sales because of a fad, as when it is taken up by a popular personality. The Anthony Eden hat was an example in the 1930s although no one seemed to copy Harold Wilson's raincoat in the 1960s! The Royal Family made corgi dogs popular, and the Beatle hair styles had their vogue. And when the Prince of Wales started going hatless in the 1930s, hat manufacturers got very worried. Today, Princess Diana inspires hairstyles, hats and fashions.

The business person has two alternatives:

i   There can be a cautious start, with profits being re-invested, and the firm growing steadily like the firm in our example of an actual appropriation.

ii Sales and production can be planned at an optimum level, with investment in the immediate conquest of a viable market.

The first method is suitable for a labour intensive service company where the greatest investment is in human skill, but where the investment has to be in capital intensive tooling, research, machinery and materials the business must begin with a certain take-up of production followed by a sustained demand. A variation on the first method is where the product is first of all sold in a *zoned market*, and is then extended to adjacent markets until eventually the national and later on export markets are developed. An example of this was St Ivel *Gold*, first launched in Wales and the West.

Imperfect knowledge of the market tends to invite a 'suck it and see' policy which seems oddly unbusiness-like in these days of computerized marketing techniques, yet it is astonishingly common in highly successful businesses as diverse as Cyprus sherry shippers, double-glazing manufacturers, unit trust managers and kitchen furniture makers.

The *zoning method*, mentioned above, is certainly one way in which a rational approach can be made to an unpredictable new market. Zoning, that is selling to a confined geographical or distribution area, and then gradually expanding to a larger area, has been made possible by the incidence of powerful regional media – press, outdoor, broadcasting – so that it is not necessary to launch products in national newspapers or weekly and monthly magazines. In this convenient fashion, a manufacturer can concentrate advertising sales, warehousing, delivery and distribution and gain from all the economies which must result if all his lines of communication are comparatively short and inexpensive.

5   Imperfect knowledge of the competition

Although it is possible to gauge the performance of competitors' products by subscribing to dealer audit surveys which give regular market share rankings for competing brands of popular commodities, and by studying the published analyses of the month-by-month advertising expenditures and promotional schemes of rival advertisers, much remains a mystery about competitive activities.

For instance, a campaign may be planned in total ignorance that one's chief competitor is planning a bigger and better one, or that a product is about to be launched that will make yours obsolete or redundant. The budget that seemed a perfect calculation could prove to be the miscalculation of all time.

But this is the gamble of the entrepreneur and the nature of capitalism. Knowledge of competition must be imperfect in a free economy, except where it has been eliminated by monopoly, and the only true monopoly is an industry like coal, gas or electricity, and even then these are rival fuels! In these circumstances one has to aim to capture a realistic proportion of the market. A new soft drink set out to gain 12.5 per cent of a zoned market. In an overcrowded market that objective seemed ambitious, but the firm justified its estimate of the quality appeal of the product. In the event, they took 15 per cent, and went on to become a national brand leader.

6 Unpredictable rival promotions

In the 'below-the-line' battle of premium offers and cross-couponing, sales promotion resembles all-in wrestling. Perhaps this is why some companies adopt one of the following tactics:

i They cut traditional advertising in favour of sales promotion.
ii They have permanent schemes such as picture cards, trading stamps, gift coupons or premium offers that call for long periods of collecting as with tableware and crockery.
iii They have a continuous series of six-weekly promotions.

Food producers are among the most consistent users of 'below-the-line' tactics, with teas and coffees not far behind. To these must be added the uses of regular devices such as reusable containers or returnable bottles which encourage repurchase, as with some drinks.

With sales promotion schemes care has to be taken to avoid either disappointment through delay in sending premium goods, or because demand exceeds supply and credit tokens are substituted. Some schemes have proved costly to advertisers who failed to forecast demand for an offer, and in honouring the response had to exceed their budget.

The problem here is how to evolve an outstanding promotion and to support it thoroughly, the classic example of this being the Esso Tiger campaign, which was a mixture of traditional advertising, point-of-sale display, gimmickry, give-aways and actual sales of 'tiger

tails', and there was even a book written about it. A tiger still features
in Esso advertising.

7 Unpredictable, politico-economic conditions and other events

Changes in taxation, or in Government, price increases of raw materials,
unfortunate climates of opinion, the results of an official investigation,
war or rebellion, a Suez, Vietnam, Rhodesia, Northern Ireland or Gulf
situation, devaluation or unemployment, a Post Office or miners' strike,
all such influences may be unthinkable and unpredictable when deciding
on an advertising appropriation. Often, they are so untoward that
allowance cannot be made for them. One just does not know where
fate or man's idiocy will strike next.

Examples have been the cancer reports, the thalidomide tragedy,
reports on cyclamates, reports on the Monopolies and Mergers
Commission and changing interest rates.

From being a negative sales appeal in the past – as expressed by
General Motors in the USA in the 1930s – safety factors have become
much bigger sales appeals in these days of motorway madness and the
efforts of Ralph Nader. From time to time there are varying political
attitudes to the products of Japan, Italy, Russia and South Africa which
may be unpredictable according to world events. Until fairly recently
we did not expect to find goods from China or Korea in UK shops.
Cheap holidays in the USA were unthinkable. The Far East and
Australia have become tourist venues.

It is a swings and roundabout guessing game that confounds the
most ardent marketing astrologist, and it is worsened by wars, civil
wars, epidemics, floods, pestilence, drought, crop failure, strikes and
unemployment. Faced with disasters and dilemmas as remotely uncon-
nected as simultaneous civil war in Ulster and Bangladesh, or the
simultaneous Rolls-Royce collapse and the Post Office strike, the poll
tax and a stagnant housing market, it is a wonder that business survives
the constant assault of external affairs. Yet it is in this very state of
doubt and chaos that the advertising manager has to sit down and
decide seriously the sum of money most likely to be sufficient to finance
the advertising ingredient of the marketing mix. It is not permissible
to complain that the task is impossible.

8.4 Uncertainties of the 'marketing mix'

Finally, and assuming that the advertiser's estimate is not far out, it is
still necessary to contend with the vagaries of the *marketing mix* itself,
for the planned expenditure will succeed only in so far as it is combined
with the other ingredients. Moreover, it has to be assumed that the

other ingredients in the marketing mix are as well budgeted, planned and executed as the advertising! As a reminder of these further elements here is a list of them:

i   The product must be right for the chosen market segment.
ii   The product must be correctly priced, named and packaged to appeal to this correctly judged market segment.
iii The field sales force must be efficient and in sufficient number to conduct the shortest necessary journey cycle and to service the trade as well.
iv   Distribution must be efficient, whether through wholesalers, own shops, appointed agents, all possible outlets, direct response traders or door-to-door sales people.
v   Instructions, guarantees, after-sales service, spares and replacement services must be efficient.
vi   At all levels of communication – staff and dealer relations, customer education and relations – there must be continuous public relations activity.

Thus, however thoroughly we budget the advertising money, the success of the expenditure will be enhanced or weakened by:

i   External forces over which we have little control and
ii   Other marketing influences which also need to be budgeted, planned and executed by other executives with equal rigour. The closer the advertising manager can work in concert with colleagues the better. In the smaller organization one person will, of course, be responsible for the lot.

We have not exhausted our preliminary considerations, and before turning to the choice of methods of fixing the appropriation we should next consider the extent and the limitations of its *coverage*. The appropriation is not just a sum of total media expenditures.

Items such as the following have also to be included:

i   Photography, retouching, prints; filming, video-taping, location expenses, actors, music, prints, distribution, artwork, models.
ii   Typesetting, camera-ready copy.
iii Sales literature.
iv   Sales promotion schemes.
v   Competition prizes, administration, judging.
vi   Postage, stationery and other direct mail costs.
vii Advertising agency fees.
viii Public relations consultancy fees.

To be utterly realistic, an advertising manager should also cost departmental staff salaries and a proportion of office overheads, although this is not always done. It is necessary if any comparison with agency or consultancy cost is to be made.

The appropriation should include all forms of advertising which, in this discussion, can be sub-divided into:

i   *trade* or distributor advertising and
ii   *user or consumer* advertising.

This again may be divided into *above-the-line* and *below-the-line*.

8.5   The public relations budget

It is a mistake – frequently made due to misunderstandings about public relations – to include this in the advertising budget. The further error is sometimes committed of counting public relations as a below-the-line expense. This often happens in advertising agency budgets when anything below-the-line is regarded as of secondary importance, if only that it is not commission paying! Of course, a percentage can always be added onto below-the-line activities, but this does not properly compensate for time.

When public relations is restricted to product publicity news releases, these confusions are understandable but not forgivable; but, as suggested in the sketch of the marketing mix, it can contribute to many stages of the marketing strategy. Moreover, as will be shown in the chapter devoted to public relations (Chapter 20), it is a management function which serves an entire organization, not only the marketing division.

The sensible way to budget public relations is to plan a complete programme for the whole organization, the public relations officer being directly responsible to the chief executive, and the allocations from this separate budget being made to the production (including staff), the financial and the marketing functions of the business. In those organizations where advertising is not a major marketing cost, the advertising may actually come within the public relations budget.

Unfortunately, there are a lot of 'chicken and egg' arguments about the respective roles and responsibilities of advertising and public relations. Provided it is properly understood that it is neither a form of nor a part of advertising there is really no problem for, as already shown, public relations can play a bigger and more varied part in the marketing mix than advertising, important though that is. Public relations concerns the total communications inside and outside an organization which are quite beyond the more specialist task of advertising.

In this book reference will be made to public relations because it has a close affinity with advertising. *The advertising appropriation can be a waste of money if the public relations has been neglected.* An advertising campaign can fail to produce enquiries or sales if:

i   the product is unknown or misunderstood; and
ii   the manufacturer lacks the goodwill of distributors, and/or prospective customers.

The classic example of i was the abortive launch of New Smoking Mixture (NSM) cigarettes containing a substitute for tobacco so that smokers would not risk suffering from cancer. The product failed, in spite of massive advertising, and millions of packs had to be withdrawn from the market. Among other mistakes, the manufacturers had assumed that because there was such a substantial anti-smoking lobby the product would sell, forgetting that non-smokers would not smoke even NSM! This disaster could have been averted had the smoking market been educated about the product so that it would have been welcomed when launched at the right time.

Understanding and goodwill are prerogatives of public relations

In budgeting public relations costs in relation to the advertising campaign, one vital difference must be clearly understood if outside consultancy services are being used. The consultancy, since it is not buying space or air-time, is not paid by media as is the case with the advertising agency. This means that the income of the consultancy is derived from the sale of professional labour or time. Every minute spent on the client's account has to be paid for by the client, and that is the basis of the fee. After that, materials and expenses are also charged, but *the prime cost of a consultancy service is the expenditure of time*. This time is usually charged at an hourly or daily rate which recompenses the consultancy for salaries and overheads and provides for profit. To operate at a profit a consultancy has to have an income roughly treble its expenditure on all kinds of salaries from the office junior to the managing director. One of the first charges is therefore the cost of talking to the client, and the client has to understand this, because when dealing with an advertising agent he does not have to pay for the time spent on his behalf by the account executive, media planners and buyers, production staff and others. Buying public relations consultancy services is similar to buying those of any other professional adviser be he lawyer, doctor, architect or accountant.

HOW TO BUDGET ADVERTISING EXPENDITURE

8.6   Seventeen ways of assessing the appropriation

Having surveyed some of the problems which beset the advertising manager when trying to determine how much to spend on advertising we now move on to study and compare some of the possible methods of assessing the appropriation. The following 17 methods (with variations of title) will be discussed:

i   Arbitrary, rule of thumb or intuitive
ii   Percentage of previous turnover or 'historic'
iii   Residual of previous year's surplus
iv   Gross margin
v   Percentage of anticipated turnover
vi   Unit, case, sales ratio, sales volume or standard cost
vii   Competitors and competitive advertising
viii Comparison with total product group advertising
ix   Elasticity
x   Target sum, cost of exposure, task approach, objective
xi   Corporate evaluation
xii   Ideal campaign
xiii Marketing model or operational research
xiv   Cost per head of population
xv   New product investment or pay-out plan
xvi   Build-up
xvii Composite or eclectic.

1 The arbitrary rule of thumb or intuitive method

By 'arbitrary' is meant that the sum is not based on any exact calculation but is what the advertiser is prepared to spend, 'what the advertiser can afford', or what is thought to be adequate for the job. Perhaps it is a rough guess based on past experience – a blend of hunch and experience. It is a vague and unbusiness-like way of spending money, and it is more common than it should be. All too often one hears, usually at client–agency meetings, the words of amateur wisdom 'we have looked at the figures and we can afford to spend only so much on advertising', as if advertising was an afterthought, some sort of ill-afforded and regrettable luxury. What sort of figures have they been looking at – their bank overdraft? Such crystal ball methods are not worth taking seriously.

The fact that there are sixteen more methods need not depress the reader after such a poor start, nor make the right choice appear to be impossible. Two things will emerge: first that some methods suit some organizations better than others; and second that in practice it may be sensible to combine several methods. That is the final composite method which is worth keeping in mind as we proceed.

2 Percentage of previous turnover or historic method

If the appropriation is based on previous turnover at least the aim is to do as well as before, but it is not very ambitious or forward-looking.

It is virtually medieval in its lack of enterprise, but there is the further danger that if trade was bad during the previous year this unfortunate trend can be worsened by reduced expenditure in the following year.

A reasonable variation, however, is the *historic method*. The advertiser spends the same amount from year to year – not a higher or lesser sum according to the previous year's results – making adjustments to cover changing costs. This suits a business such as a hotel, motor-coach company or retail shop which is unlikely to expand its trade, has a limited capacity, and repeats much the same volume of trade year after year. It follows the same pattern as expenditure on other items such as redecoration.

3 Residual of previous year's surplus

Hardly worth taking seriously, this is nevertheless a method adopted in all seriousness by 'business people' with less than necessary faith in advertising. Moreover, it makes nonsense of the fact that it is the purchaser and not the manufacturer or distributor who pays for advertising. Advertising is not paid for out of profits but out of price. It is an on-cost. This economic fact escapes those who pretend to spend on advertising 'what they can afford'. Yet in this method the appropriation is based on what remains after profits have been taken from the previous year's turnover.

At first glance it looks ridiculous and one dreads to think of the firm's prospects following a lean year, But there is some merit in the idea of ploughing back profits in the form of future advertising. This is no different from any other investment of increased income. It can be applied to a growth industry, and it can be mellowed by judicious calculation of how much of the residual should be applied to advertising. It does follow that cautious principle of only spending what is in the kitty, and its avoidance of speculation or application to a sales target does not promise much growth.

Alternatively, the 'residuum' may be assessed from the *anticipated surplus*, cost and profits being forecast. This is better and more flexible, and is favoured by some large advertisers. Nevertheless, it still suggests an appalling attitude of mind towards the job of advertising. Surely, as only one of many distribution costs, advertising should take its rightful place as one of *the calculated contributors to the gaining of gross profits?* This method is discussed more fully in the name of the gross margin method.

4 Gross margin method

The gross margin method takes advertising as a percentage of the residuum *after* production and distribution costs have been deducted from income. Thus, if total sales = £A and production and distribution costs = £B, £A − £B = £C, the latter representing the balance or gross margin. Advertising is taken as a percentage of £C, and so is directly related to gross profit. As sales increase, the fixed costs are spread more economically, leaving a larger proportion for division between advertising and net profits, the opposite applying as sales fall. However, the percentage of £C-overheads may be adjusted if the sum available for advertising falls below the effective optimum. That is to say, profits may be invested in promotion to bolster up declining sales.

The fallacy of this method is that it makes a special thing of advertising, making it dependent on a residuum actually existing. In other words, if the gross margin holds nothing to cover fixed costs there will be no fund for either profits or advertising! It is therefore fallacious to divorce advertising from other expenses included in the distribution costs accepted under £B. Advertising does not belong to the gross margin any more than do the costs of warehousing, delivery services, field salesmen and trade terms. The method is back to front, and overlooks the primary contribution which advertising has to make to the total sales effort. It seems to regard advertising as a luxury to be indulged in only if there is money to spare. It belongs to the irrational 'what we can afford' philosophy which cannot be taken seriously as business-like budgetry. Its frequent use suggests either a poor understanding of the value of advertising in the marketing strategy or, which is by no means impossible with some industrial advertisers, that advertising is the wrong means of communicating with the market.

The gross margin method is clearly useless for a new product requiring a heavy investment in advertising. For such a product the break-even may not occur in the first, second or even third year of trading, and eventual success will depend on investment in advertising. Promotion of a freshly styled newspaper by a new owner would require the sort of investment which fell within the target or task method.

5   Percentage of anticipated turnover method

Looking ahead at anticipated sales is more progressive, and so our fifth method is rather more realistic, provided the sales target is a good forecast. But if the forecast is wrong – maybe thwarted by one or more of those imponderables such as a strike or war – the advertising appropriation will also be wrong. It may be too late to recover or adjust, as UK motor-car manufacturers found after Japanese makes had earned reputations for reliability, and had won a substantial percentage of the UK market. This method also invites increased expenditure in good times and less in bad times, a contradiction since it should be easier and less expensive to sell in good times and vice versa.

6 Unit, case, sales ratio, sales volume or standard cost method

Various names are given to what is best known as the *unit percentage* method, which is usually applied to repeat purchase consumer goods. The price per unit totals percentages representing every production and distribution cost plus profit. It can be applied to a bag of flour, a tin of paint or a litre of petrol, or even to a complete saleable item such as a motor-car. If the manufacturer then plans to produce and sell a given quantity of units the available fund for advertising is easily calculated. Should sales exceed the planned production, and it is economic to extend production and distribution, the advertising expenditure is spread over additional units. Conversely, if the take-up of a limited production capacity occurs before the conclusion of the campaign, it may be possible to contract the campaign, thus reducing the advertising cost per unit.

There are weaknesses in this seemingly ideal system since it rashly assumes stability in the economy and presumes that proportionate costs, including advertising, will remain constant. It makes no allowance for the need to increase advertising expenditure to meet rising costs, increased competition or a diminishing market. The direct response trader, for example, has had to raise his prices to recover the continually increasing cost of postage. The retailer has to recover increases in taxes and electricity. And so it goes on. Such a method can work only if budgets are short term or seasonal, but an annual budget could be underestimated.

The unit volume or sales volume method implies cutting advertising expenditure as sales fall, and while it may sound correct to spend less on selling less there are optimum levels at which advertising expenditure can be too low to be effective to sell even a reduced volume. This can be illustrated by the example of a theatre deciding to advertise only one week in four because the show is playing to 25 per cent capacity. Apart from the qualities of the show, a cause could be *insufficient advertising* and the result of applying the sales volume method could be to deprive the theatre of business in three out of four weeks. Here, the 'unit' is a seat at a performance.

7 Competitors and competitive advertising methods

Here are two somewhat similar methods used for different reasons.

When we are uncertain about the weight of advertising necessary to promote a product it may be useful to study the Media Expenditure Analysis Ltd (MEAL) statistics on current advertising expenditure. In so doing we must remember that rivals may have had the advantage of build-up of advertising impact over a number of years. How do we catch up? Greater expenditure, a novel appeal, different media, or a novel marketing tactic? We *may* have to spend more than an established rival if we seek to gain a similar impact, unless our new product is so superior that it is an instant winner. *What competitors are spending* will at least be an indication of the probable minimum expenditure necessary to sell that kind of product. But it must not be taken for granted that rival firms are efficient spenders.

While it is sensible for a newcomer to take cognizance of the sums which other firms appear to find necessary to spend to maintain their existing shares of the market, there is also the situation where rivals attempt to match each other's spending. This 'pound-for-pound' *competitive advertising*, like war, is pointless and uneconomic. In the end its futility leads to trade association disagreements to desist, or amalgamations to eliminate uneconomic competition.

In this oligopolistic situation, forecasting becomes warped by circumstances because of the essential interdependence of a few very big companies upon each other. They can be so mutually interdependent that, as in the case of the Society of Motor Manufacturers and Traders, membership is dependent upon support for certain society-sponsored exhibitions only, other events being proscribed under penalty of fine. Or the competition can be so intense that there is an escalation of promotional costs, rather like an armaments race, which defies sensible budgeting; but even alleged business rivals tend to meet at golf courses, West End Clubs or round the trade association table and, as with wars, peace terms and economic stability are sought and eventually found by sworn enemies.

This is interesting because the lay consumer is apt to criticize the heavy expenditure on advertising by rivals (which is obvious on TV), and to imagine that such competition and such expenditure inflates retail prices. (There is a difference between advertising being part of the price and being a disproportionate part which inflates the price.) There are, as shown above, economic forces at work. If there is insufficient advertising the product will fail to sell and the consumer's choice will be reduced, and if there is excessive advertising the manufacturers will club together to minimize costs when they threaten to get out of hand and eat into profits. Equilibrium results in a maximum variety of choice, and for this privilege (and the privilege of entrepreneurs to profit by the supply of choices), the cost has to be met in the price. But the cost is not only advertising: it is every distribution cost once the product is made.

8   Comparison with total product group advertising method

Using the *comparison method*, an advertiser in a product group assesses the total expenditure of all firms in that group, probably using the estimates published by MEAL, and also those of Nielsen or other dealer audit units. Such a product group might be all makers of toothpaste or razor blades, typewriters or pickles. This total figure of product group advertising expenditure per year is then divided by the number of producers according to their market shares, the calculation suggesting what each firm should be spending. (It will be found, no doubt, that actual expenditures do not agree with calculated proportional expenditures, but it must be remembered that the product group total is not necessarily an ideal figure. Probably, it will be too high as in a saturated market where advertisers can only take sales from one another and not expand the market.) However, by this process, a member of the product group, and especially a newcomer to it, can work out what should be spent to achieve a particular share of the market, or perhaps a larger share of it. Again, this process can reveal whether the extra advertising cost required to increase sales is in fact worth while.

This comparison method is a sophistication of the previous study of competitors' advertising, relating competitors' advertising to market shares and the average cost of gaining a certain share. It goes beyond taking competitive advertising as a yardstick since it looks at the *total* expenditure of all members of the product group, rather than that of a firm doing a comparable volume of trade.

9   Elasticity method

This method follows the influences of supply and demand curves. The profit is compared with previous advertising expenditure to give a ratio between profit and expenditure. The ratio of the average cost of the extra unit of expenditure on advertising is compared with the average return in increased profit. This calculation will reveal the limit beyond which advertising expenditure is uneconomic.

Such a method is feasible only when advertising is the chief form of promotion, as with retail store or direct response trading, and is an over-simplified form of budgeting when there are the numerous distribution and promotional costs normally experienced by a manufacturer of consumer goods.

10   Target sum, cost of exposure, task approach, objective method

Here we have four variations of the *target method* which is fairly popular. The objective is determined and the cost of advertising to achieve it is then estimated. However, the slightly different names given to the method have to do with the kind of objective sought. Is it a volume of sales, number of prospects, or weight of media coverage?

The business person may say to the agency: 'What will it cost to use advertising to sell two thousand computers?' The agency plans board will consider the project, and the account executive will be given figures so that the client can be told that if such-and-such a campaign is mounted the cost will be £X,000. Meanwhile, the computer manufacturer may have sought quotations for achieving the sales objective by some other means. The agency scheme may be rejected and a sales promotion scheme substituted. If it is this sort of industrial product, the manufacturer may prefer to spend the same or maybe a smaller sum on industrial videos and technical seminars for prospective buyers.

A quite different use of the target method may be to ask the agency what will it cost to reach the national mass housewife market. Usually, 80 per cent coverage is the accepted target, and achievement of this target is the media planner's objective, aided by the statistics available from JICNARS and BARB.

Slight differences in the target and task methods are that the first method may mean planning an appropriation against cost of media to achieve the sales target, while the second method may refer to the cost of completing a given task.

The principle of these methods is the reverse of those already discussed. We have an objective – a sales volume, a stated number of desired enquiries, a specific number of presentations of an offer to the same prospects – and with such a target or task we set out to discover what will be the advertising cost. We can examine and compare this or that form of advertising campaign, or sales promotion or perhaps public relations. The merit of the method is its soundness in obeying the management precept that action must be preceded by definition of objectives. It is also flexible, and expenditure can be adjusted to meet events.

Mention was made above of public relations, although this is not an alternative to advertising. However, there are times when the target is more likely to be reached using public relations tactics. A good example of this is the charity appeal. And if, strictly speaking, that is not commercial, a different example is an exhibition which can be difficult to advertise because of the want of continuity over a short period of time. With exhibitions, public relations can be most effective if, as happens with the Motor Show, Boat Show and Chelsea Flower Show, the opening day is highly newsworthy, meriting coverage on, say, *News at Ten*. Cornhill and others have adopted sponsorship.

The *task approach* offers a slight modification of the more long-term target method, although the two terms are often interchangeable. A task can be something very specific such as launching a new product or boosting sales in a slack sales area, meeting exceptional competition, or overcoming something which is inhibiting sales. The task method may be applied to regions, a very big advertiser planning regional TV and outdoor advertising according to the task involved.

For this *special task* a sum of money has to be estimated which is believed capable of doing the job. Instead of saying we are prepared to spend so much for this special purpose we ask what will it cost? This is a positive approach, *assuming that a successful result is possible*. The more arbitrary method discussed in i could be a forlorn hope. But if the sum needed to win success was prohibitive it would be wise to forego the attempt. There would be no point in literally buying sales, unless sheer brutal domination of the market was the objective. With the task method there can be a 'go/no go' point of decision.

11 Corporate evaluation method

Almost identical to the target method is the *corporate evaluation* way of reviewing marketing research and corporate planning when determining what to spend on advertising. Taken to its logical conclusion, this method follows the *marginal utility theory*. Overall corporate objectives are achieved if marketing objectives are also achieved, the marginal expenditure of an extra £1 on advertising being matched by an equal or less than proportionate increase in profit.

12 Ideal campaign method

Not unlike the task method this is one which firmly places the initiative with the agency. Using its campaign and media planning skill, the agency produces a fully costed scheme which it offers to the client as the most effective advertising mix for a given purpose. The obvious snag is that unless the agency has an inkling of the client's budgetary ceiling, it can produce a wonderful scheme at a prohibitive price. Although it is often said that agencies, and not clients, should propose appropriations, it is better if this is a joint affair with full and frank disclosure of costs on both sides.

13 Marketing model or operational research method

This is an excellent method for the advertiser who wants to see the value of larger or smaller investments in advertising. It lends itself to the needs of the direct response trader who wishes to cost promotions in relation to prospects and market share for each commodity handled. This will also influence buying, which in turn may involve quantity discounts. Thus, a scale can be created showing the different buying, advertising, packing and posting and overhead costs for different quantities resulting in a certain net profit. This begins to look like the unit method except that it is really the other way round since advertising costs do not go up or down according to sales but sales are related to the injection of advertising.

There is no guarantee that the model will give precise results. It is only an abstraction. Meanwhile, the method is subject to the variables already remarked upon earlier. Nevertheless, on a probability basis of past experience, the figure on the scale can be adjusted from past knowledge and continuous current experience. This has to be said because the same advertisement can produce different results when placed in different issues and/or different positions in the same publication. The cause of the varying results may be utterly unpredictable and, as said before, it may be nothing more than a change in the weather. It is difficult to sell swimsuits on a wet day and umbrellas when the sun is shining. Fortuitous circumstances affect advertising results just as they do share prices or votes in an election.

The model under discussion may look like this:

Expenditure on advertising	£50,000	Sales £$\frac{1}{2}$ m
Expenditure on advertising	£75,000	Sales £$\frac{2}{3}$ m
Expenditure on advertising	£100,000	Sales £$\frac{3}{4}$ m
Expenditure on advertising	£125,000	Sales £$\frac{7}{8}$ m
Expenditure on advertising	£150,000	Sales £1 m

The figures can be any that the advertiser cares to project according to business experiences and needs. The marketing model method may be useful to the user of frequent, short, isolated campaigns, such as entertainment promotions or store events, seasonal holidays or direct response sales, which make swift adjustment possible from one requirement to the next. It lends itself very well to direct mail advertising, as used for book and record clubs, and the cost of sales letters, sales literature, envelopes and postage can be reckoned according to the size of the mailing list and the size of the mailing calculated to produce a given quantity of enquiries or value of sales.

Models are fashionable in the social sciences, and it may be thought that advertising is too imprecise for the building of models to forecast expenditure; but models are rather like algebra, a shorthand to rationalize thinking by abstracting the essentials. Just as a London Underground map is not geographically accurate, but is a stylised presentation of routes (or a model) it is helpful in giving the traveller information and directions. A marketing model can therefore inspire more methodical planning of advertising appropriations, and this sort of charting should not therefore be discarded as being pseudo-scientific. Models also make possible the use of computers so that answers, and alternative schemes, can be produced rapidly and accurately.

One particular model, using a computer, is known as the simulation linear programming model. Data are fed in about media and consumer characteristics and the desired market share to produce a linear relationship between the variables. It requires, as with all computer practice, absolutely accurate input information, which may be hard or costly to obtain quite apart from the expense of programming. The result will be as scientific as it can be – a computer is no master mind, only an electronic calculator of given input – and can take no account of such refinements as creativity or imponderables, such as external influences, except in so far as anticipated influences may be given values which can be fed in. The computer may be better kept for calculating reasonably known factors such as media costs, circulations, readerships, readership duplications and so on, where answers are valuable because the time consumption may be impractical if the sums had to be performed manually. The computer is used by agencies for this aspect of campaign planning.

The distinction may be made between *empirical* and *theoretical* models. The former is based on market intelligence, the latter on historical data. In a saturated market an empirical model takes account of competitive activity and advertising expenditure can be flexible to maintain market shares. The theoretical method is a more deliberate form of the percentage of past sales (historical model) already discussed, the percentage being calculated rather than declared in an arbitrary fashion.

14 Cost per head of population method

This refers to the 'population served by the advertiser'. If it is wished to increase the market share, the advertising cost is worked out on the basis of the cost per customer to be gained. If the entire market is, say, one million of which the present market share is 50 per cent (half million) and if the present appropriation is $£\frac{1}{2}$ m, the cost per head is £1. To gain another 10 per cent means increasing the appropriation by £100,000.

This sounds simple but is specious if purchases per individual are unequal. But if purchases can only be a single unit, say a lawn mower or a refrigerator, this method can be realistic. In other words, while it does not satisfy the demands of the manufacturer of repeat purchase goods, it does suit the advertiser of consumer durables and other products or services which are mostly limited to a solitary purchase which may or may not be repeated or replaced. Customers may only ever buy one central heating system in a lifetime whereas even some expensive products – cars, hi-fi sets, houses, small boats or cameras – may be replaced. But having made the distinction, it is still possible that the marketing aim may be to convert more people to taking photographs and making their first camera purchase, and a firm like Kodak could expand film sales in this way, using the formula for costing an advertising programme to that end.

In a sense the cost per head of population method is another kind of target method, except that it is specifically related to prospects. This means that it can be applied to a market of potential students for, say, a correspondence school, or enrolments for a book or record club, or donors to a charity. It is a very personal system. It can also be applied by the producers of a specialized line such as a slimming aid who aims to sell to more overweight people.

15   New product investment or pay-out plan

This is another product investment scheme whereby advertising is related to initial development and subsequent growth in succeeding and, hopefully, successful years. It is best explained with a table of figures (Table 8.1).

Table 8.1   *New product investment*

	Year 1	Year 2	Year 3	Total
Sales (£000)	100	110	120	330
Advertising (£000)	20	15	15	50
Advertising/ sales ratio (%)	20	13.6	12.5	15

Such a scheme is suitable for the launch of a new product when heavy initial expenditure is necessary in the first, and sometimes in the second, year.

16   Build-up method

Yet another variation upon the target method is this one which begins with allocations to various media and then compiles these sums into a total appropriation. The method is useful when specific media service precise purposes. A direct response trader may use the press to attract new customers, direct mail to gain further sales from previous customers, and catalogues, price lists, samples, order forms, sales letters, Freepost envelopes and other print to complete sales. The appropriation or total budget is a balanced collation of these related costs, the size of the mailing list and placing of press advertising controlling the print quantities and costs.

There is nothing hit or miss about such a plan, but flexibility lies only in injecting further funds into press advertising (or mailing to an extra prospect list) if response is disappointing, but this will erode profits if prices have been fixed to cover the original advertising budget.

Again, the allocations may be by products or departments, or possibly divisions or companies in a group. Perhaps some of the previously described methods may have to be adopted in certain cases. Here, the importance of the method lies in giving proper weight to special items or sections, rather than taking an overall sum and then parcelling it out to various claimants for advertising support. It is not unlike the departments of a local authority or the central Government presenting their estimates to the treasurer or Chancellor of the Exchequer who then produces the final budget.

17 Composite or eclectic method

Fixing the appropriation has been discussed at length, not to suggest that it is complicated but to emphasize that *while it pays to advertise it also pays to make a painstaking study of spending.* That is why probably the largest collection of methods ever to have been brought together in print before are presented here. In the end we may decide that the best way to arrive at the appropriation is to make an eclectic approach. This, our seventeenth method, may be termed the *composite* or *eclectic* method. It calls for consideration of a blend of calculable influences and recognition of some of the imponderables. All these factors can be compiled to form a model such as the following:

a   Past sales
b   Anticipated sales
c   Production capacity
d   Market conditions: economic, political, sociological
e   Selling problems of product, e.g. high price, unfamiliarity,
f   Efficiency and strength of the sales force
g   Efficiency and adequacy of distributor network
h   Seasonal fluctuations and seasonal campaigns
i   Regional fluctuations: including effect of local competition
j   Appropriate and available media, and comparative costs of reaching the market with effective impact and continuity to match possible demand with optimum productive capacity
k   Trends revealed by market, media, advertisement research and any other data.

An analysis of these eleven factors (which may vary slightly from one organization to another) will give the most thorough approach to determining the appropriation. Working backwards now it will also be possible to discover the percentage of turnover that is devoted to the single distributive cost of advertising, and the following year this 'percentage of previous turnover' is available for repetition or adjustment in the light of the previous year's results and consideration of the other items.

Forecasting the advertising budget resembles any other form of economic forecasting. The shorter the term the more readily can allowance be made for the influences over which one has no control. In a world of unpredictable disaster and strife, it is obviously foolish to have obstinate ideas, and even more irresponsible to adopt a haphazard attitude to this subject.

Cost effectiveness has become as important to the one-man business as it is to the big concern which can afford to take advice from management and other professional consultants. The small business is by no means an uneconomic unit, the supreme example being the housewife and her house-keeping money and shopping list who can be thoroughly economic, for unless she buys things 'on tick' or by credit card she balances her budget every week. The small, or smaller business person needs to plan spending against the greatest expectation of the greatest reward. The problem is no different from that of the giant corporation or the conscientious housewife. This chapter has therefore taken a very keen look at advertising expenditure because budgeting is the first thing to get right before tackling any other aspect of advertising or, for that matter, marketing in general.

It is possible to arrive at conclusions that the cost of advertising is so great that the inflated price will inhibit sales: conversely, advertising may be unproductive at any price and some other means of communicating with the market may be more profitable.

To take two final examples: encyclopaedias have met the first difficulty, resulting in the adoption of high-pressure sales gimmicks which have provoked justifiable criticism; while press advertising for services used by the majority of industries has proved both prohibitive and unproductive compared with the public relations techniques of feature articles and seminars with speakers and videos. In between these extremes advertising has time and again proved to be the cheapest and most successful means of making known goods or services in order to sell them.

Advertising is not a cure-all, but well used it can, as so many successful companies have proved, be irreplaceable.

8.7   Special departmental and seasonal or feature appropriations

Some classes of advertiser make good use of advertising by sub-dividing their total appropriation according to products, departments, weeks, months or seasons. Or, by adopting a task-method approach to each sub-division, they can arrive at a total expenditure, rather like the build-up method. However, a manufacturer of a range of products must be careful that his subdivisions do not result in individual budgets each of which is too small to be effectual. A *composite* advertisement for several allied products can gain greater impact, and such advertisements are likely to be *larger and will command better positions.*

Department stores apportion their appropriations between departments, e.g. soft furnishings, drapery, menswear, hardware, china and glass and so on. They also allocate for seasonal and shopping events such as Christmas gifts, January sale, spring fashions, summer sale and autumn fashions.

Supermarkets divide their expenditure between different classes of merchandise, e.g. cereals, drinks, biscuits, dairy produce, confectionery or toiletries.

Holiday trade advertisers concentrate their expenditure at the turn of the year and first weeks of the New Year. This is because package tour operators require deposits, and these are available out of Christmas bonuses.

UK holiday resorts are able to make minute budgets work like big advertising by taking small spaces together in holiday features, the collective effect having such impact that a mere three centimetre single-column advertisment in a January holiday feature is the equivalent of a larger isolated display advertisement.

Similarly, direct response traders can make tiny weekend bargain square advertisements do the work of much larger and more expensive spaces, because they too appear in a collective marketplace of lots of small display advertisements all making bargain offers.

This shows that the small advertiser can make money go further or do a 'big advertiser' job if the appropriation, timing and media selection is well thought out. He can really make advertising work for him. And nowadays with broadcasting as well as press, outdoor, transportation, cinema and direct mail, his advertising can be technically on a par with that of the national advertiser.

Many a High Street shopkeeper, with just one shop or a string of branches, can boost business if he plans along these lines. As one example of this, let us take a hardware trader and see how use can be made of consistent hard-selling advertisements in the locally available media. A regular month-by-month campaign can be devised like this:

January	New Year sale
February	Garden seeds
March	Spring-cleaning aids, curtain systems
April	Decorating materials, garden tools, crockery
May	Insecticides, fertilizers
June	Lawn tools, weedkillers
July	Holiday goods, picnic baskets
August	Deck chairs, garden furniture
September	Rose bushes, spring bulbs, bulb bowls
October	Alarm clocks, clothes driers, heat units
November	Electrical goods, Christmas gifts
December	Christmas decorations, Christmas flowering bulbs in pots, last-minute gift ideas

This is just a rough guide, and other ideas will be suggested by the range of stock carried and the trader's own experience of month-by-month demand which can vary from one locality to another. But the list set out above does imply that many traders can conduct profitable advertising if a regular series of topical customer-oriented advertisements is planned and costed against skilful buying and desired turnover and profits. After all, this is exactly what big city stores do with their combined personal shopper and direct response trade. The same system can be adopted by Bill Smith with his men's outfitters or Mary Jones with her fancy goods shop in any High Street in any town.

9
Assessment of results

9.1 Feasibility of assessing results

In Chapter 5 reference was made to advertising agencies being remunerated on the basis of payment by results, and it was pointed out that except in the case of direct response it was difficult to credit advertising with the achievement of specific results. This was not because advertising was intangible but because advertising was only one element in the marketing strategy, the whole of which was responsible for the ultimate results, good or bad.

Nevertheless, it is possible to gauge something of the effectiveness of advertising even if we cannot say it was responsible for a precise percentage increase in profits. Marketing research in a general sense will be discussed in fuller detail in a later chapter, but here let us examine how certain research techniques can be applied to the particular task of assessing the results of advertising. None of this may be precise but it could be helpful.

9.2 Discussion groups

Some advertisers use discussion groups to discuss their current advertising. The weakness of discussion groups is their small number of participants, and the extent of their representativeness. On the other hand if, say, 25 people can be assembled who (a) are likely buyers of the product and (b) have definitely seen the advertising, such a discussion group could be an inexpensive way of generating attitudes to the advertising. Recruitment would have to be conducted very carefully.

9.3 Field surveys

Conducted in the street or on the doorstep in the quota sample style of interviewing people of various social grades, age groups and other demographic distinctions, the field survey requires an interviewer and a questionnaire. People may be asked about the subject in general, then asked what publications they read, whether they saw the advertisement and what they remembered of it.

The aim of the survey may be to test the effectiveness of the advertising, or this could be just one facet of a more generalized field survey. The danger with the latter is that the time lapse between carrying out the survey and the appearance of the advertising could be too long for respondents to recall the advertisement in detail.

The field survey method can also be conducted very cheaply by telephone interviewing, but it has its drawbacks. For instance, a sample of subscribers to a magazine could be telephoned and questioned about an advertisement in the current issue. The only problem with this is that the calls would probably have to be made in the evening, and such enquiries could be resented as much as those calls from home improvement sales girls.

Another version is the postal questionnaire which is less likely to be resented, but capable of being the victim of inertia. Posted questionnaires may be returned if they are of sufficiently interesting appeal to the recipient, or if there is a modest gift such as a ball-point pen.

9.4   Dealer audits

This is one of the best forms of advertising research because the results are self-revealing (not requiring any effort on the part of a respondent), and they make comparisons with rival advertisers. In fact, the effectiveness of other people's promotions could be the purpose of the study.

Dealer (retail or shop) audits use a sample of different classes of retailer (nationwide and usually broken down into television regions). These retailers are visited by a researcher who records invoices and stocks of brands by name and pack size. When this is done regularly, e.g. every one or two months, the shares of the market for each brand can be shown graphically over time. The results are given in product groups such as teas, coffees, biscuits, cigarettes, cigars, toothpastes, detergents. Thus, the published findings (to which one can subscribe) can relate rises in brand share to associated advertising or sales promotion campaigns. (Advertising expenditure for the same period can be gleaned from the MEAL Quarterly Digest.)

9.5   Questionnaires with products

This is a method often used with consumer durables for which it is necessary to forward a guarantee card to the manufacturer. The card carries a brief questionnaire about the purchase – was it a gift, was it bought for oneself, where was it seen advertised and so on. This not only produces useful information about purchasing behaviour but also about the source of interest.

Similarly, questions about the source which provoked either an enquiry or a purchase can be included in order forms. This is not always reliable because people forget or make mistakes, but if a certain medium is quoted repeatedly this is a useful pointer to the pulling power of that medium.

9.6   Keyed replies

Keys, applied to coupon requests or order forms or even in addresses for enquiries, are the most reliable form of measuring response. If the key is unobtrusive and self-revealing, so much the better. If the respondent has to include the key in a written address it could be quoted wrongly. However, different methods suit different advertisers. Some of the methods which may be adopted are:

i A change in the address for each publication, e.g. 12a High Street, 12b High Street, or Room 1, Room 2.

ii A change in the initial of a person to be addressed, e.g. A. Smith, B. Smith.

iii A different person's name in the address, e.g. Mary Smith, Betty Jones, or Henry Smith, Ronald Jones.

iv A key printed in a corner of the coupon which distinguishes the newspaper and the number of the insertion, such as DEI for the first insertion in the *Daily Express*.

When the post arrives the envelopes can be sorted according to keys, and the number of replies can be counted for each key. Response can be drawn graphically to show the accumulated results from a series of advertisements. The life of an advertisement can be measured by the period during which replies continue to come in. Cost effectiveness can be measured by dividing the cost of the space by the number of enquiries received (both by post and telephone). Cost-per-order can be calculated in the same way. This can be taken further to measure the popularity of different offers, or the best time to advertise, quite apart from the comparative pulling power of different media.

9.7   Split-run research

Sometimes called the A/B split method, the idea is to run a control and a test advertisement in different editions of a journal on the same day and in the same position to test which draws the greater response. This lends itself particularly to direct response advertising. Split runs can also be applied to other media such as radio, television and posters to test different commercials or posters, or even whether or not advertising is effective, there being no advertising in the control area and advertising in the test area.

9.8   Testing sales promotion offers

Similarly, by the control and test town method it is possible to assess the results of either making one offer or another, or of making an offer against ordinary sales. Thus, in one town there could be a premium offer of a bath towel, but in another a premium offer of a cushion cover. In the second case, sales would be conducted in the normal way, but in the test area there could be a special offer. If both were run for the same period it would be possible to measure the difference in sales between the control and the test town.

9.9   Day-after recall

This is a popular form of advertisement research, especially with television commercials, and is usually based on street interviews. People are stopped and asked if they read the newspaper in which the advertisement appeared, and, if they did, they are then asked if they saw the advertisement. Or they are asked if they watched television the previous evening and if so which channel they watched, and whether they saw the commercial. In either case they are asked to recall some significant feature of the advertisement or the commercial. However, this does little more than record whether people actually noticed and remembered the advertisement.

9.10   Reading and noting test

Here we have an impact test, evolved by Gallup poll, and it is not merely one of recall. Once it is established that the respondent not only read the newspaper but saw the advertisement, a detailed questioning follows regarding what is remembered of every element of the advertisement such as headline, picture, slogan, copy, sales points, price, product or advertiser's name. This really analyses the effectiveness of an advertisement, and it is usual to award percentage figures for both male and female recall of the various elements.

Reading and noting tests are also used in copy-testing when an actual advertisement is run in a regional edition of a London newspaper, and as a result of the test the advertisement may be modified before it appears nationally.

9.11 Tracking studies

This is an expression that is sometimes very loosely used, but a popular tracking study is a very elaborate form of continuous study of advertising campaigns. The TABS system of tracking study is described in detail in Chapter 20 on Marketing Research. Here, a short summary is offered.

The TABS method tests brand strength, the creative performance of advertising and the media performance. Its econometric analysis shows what occurs when there is no advertising, 'decay rates' (i.e. deterioration of impact after the campaign has concluded), the advertising activity of competitors, and marketing factors which can change the marketing situation at any time such as rival promotions.

TABS has also split markets into four vital sub-categories: committed users; cool customers; hot prospects; and no hopers, with ratios between these categories. The media are also analysed according to their readership or audience strength.

From the above brief introduction it will be seen that a tracking study can be a very sophisticated examination of what happens when and after an advertisement has appeared. This is particularly valuable when there is no measurable direct response. It also shows how long an advertising appeal can survive, either in competition with other advertising, or after it has ceased to appear. Some advertisements have an extraordinary after-life. For instance, the slogan 'Guinness Is Good For You' has not been used in the UK for decades (and would offend against the BCAP), yet there are many people who would swear that the slogan was still being used.

9.12 Conclusion

From this analysis of various ways of assessing results it will be seen that much can be learned from these forms of research. They may not always give an exact measure of the profitableness of advertising, but they can indicate the strengths and weaknesses of particular campaigns. They can help to avoid wasteful expenditure, and they can provide guidance for future campaigns. It is one thing to believe than an advertising campaign will work, and another to know what consumers think about it.

There are two other aspects to consider here. First there is the indirect effect of advertising on a company's corporate image. If people like the advertising it could create good relations with shareholders, distributors, employees and potential employees and many others. This is a public relations aspect embracing reputation and goodwill, assets which may be difficult to quantify in book value although they contribute to the overall success of a company. The endurance of companies like

Cadbury, Heinz, Ford, Unilever, ICI, Procter and Gamble, Kodak and Coca-Cola owe something to this.

Second, there is tremendous sales value in brand names which have been established over the years, and these brands do have a book value. Take-overs occur in order to acquire famous brands worth fortunes, and they are one of the most assessible results of advertising.

Part Three
Media of Advertising

10
Media evaluation and media mix

10.1 Vehicles for advertising

The most brilliant and original advertising ideas will be wasted if they are not presented in the right place at the right time to the right people. The football pool advertisements on the sports page early in the week, the holiday advertisements in the Sunday newspaper in January, the detergent commercial on peak-hour commercial TV, the Underground carriage card offering jobs to secretaries, and the poster on the back of a bus for windscreen wipers – all these are examples of carefully planned use of media.

Media supply the vehicles for advertising messages, carrying them to the right readers, viewers, listeners or passers-by. They are a study on their own, and in advertising agencies there are media planners and media buyers who are highly experienced experts. Conversely, the media owners exploit the advantages of their media in order to sell air-time, space or sites. Media are subject to intensive buying and selling activity.

Advertising would not exist if there were no media, and many media could not survive without being subsidized by revenue from advertising. Media are the mother and father of advertising. The importance of skilled media evaluation, planning and buying is exemplified by the arrival and success of the media independents. As will be explained at the end of this chapter, there have been revolutionary changes in media ranging from the exodus from Fleet Street to satellite television and, of course, the effects of the *Broadcasting Act 1990*.

10.2 Relative costs of media

A frequent error is to misunderstand the cost and value of media, maintaining that one 'cannot afford', say, television advertising. It is really a question of *need*, not *cost*. Media costs are relative to the size and penetration required of a particular market. The widow with a room to let may find that a card placed in her front window will produce an acceptable lodger; but if few people walk down the street, and there is inadequate penetration of her market, she will need to place a small classified advertisement in a local newspaper, or put a card in a shop window. But she does not need a 16-sheet poster in the High Street, nor even a spot on radio, let alone a colour commercial on TV.

It is therefore nonsense for an advertiser to say, 'I can't afford TV. It's too expensive'. What the advertiser really means is that TV is the wrong medium, and it appeals to the wrong market, or that TV would attract excessive business. Even so, some firms have found that with inexpensive slides and use of less popular viewing times it is possible for TV to work for smaller, regional advertisers. Many a big advertiser has started in a small way: Mosaic Cyprus Sherry began with a modest campaign on one-half of the Southern Television region: eventually it became so successful that it was acquired by a large group.

Similarly, a cigarette manufacturer may spend thousands of pounds on a whole-page advertisement in full colour in national morning newspapers, whereas a Scottish holiday resort may get a record demand for guide books from a number of 3 cm single-column advertisements in several newspapers, the whole campaign costing a fraction of the rate for only one of the cigarette advertisements.

The weekend bargain square advertisements are another case where a relatively modest expenditure in big media produces a very profitable return, but this sort of small space advertising would be useless for a beer, detergent, margarine, hair shampoo or a small cigar.

Media buying is not only a matter of negotiating for the best positions or spots at the best prices, but is enhanced by astute media planning in the first place. It is necessary not only to compare circulation, readership and audience figures, but also the demographic characteristics of these figures, and whenever possible to eliminate wasteful duplication.

10.3 Above-the-line media

The expressions above- and below-the-line are used in advertising to distinguish between two classes of advertising. They are quite artificial divisions which may not occur to the advertising manager who has to decide which media will best carry the sales message to the market. In the agency world, the distinctions are meaningful even to the extent of adopting a superior attitude towards below-the-line advertising.

Above-the-line is also known as media advertising, and this refers to the five traditional media of press, TV, radio, outdoor and transportation (mostly posters), and cinema. These are the media for which agencies have to be 'recognized' and from which they receive commission on the purchase of space, air-time and sites. These media represent the typical advertising agency world and the bulk of their income.

Although associated here with the agency world the expression was originally conceived by Procter and Gamble.

10.4 Below-the-line media

These are the media which normally do not allow commission, and the advertising agency has either to add a percentage as a handling and profit charge, or charge a service fee for the time spent on making use of the medium. Consequently, agencies may farm out such work to specialists such as direct mail houses, producers of display material and printers. Or the advertiser may deal directly with these specialists, including printers and exhibition stand designers, film and video makers and package designers.

Four principal media come under the heading of below-the-line: direct mail: point-of-sale; exhibitions; and sales literature, but as detailed in Chapter 12 there can be many more.

Mistakenly, public relations may be listed under below-the-line, but this occurs only when an agency may be referring to product publicity support, although this can be complementary to an advertising campaign.

10.5 Media: six general considerations

In succeeding chapters each of the media will be discussed and in this introduction it is necessary to consider the overall evaluation of media in general so that the most successful choice can be made. Then, within the chosen media, it becomes necessary to make more specific decisions concerning individual publications, sites or regions; timing; volume and frequency; and such value-for-money considerations as rate versus coverage. The six most essential general considerations are likely to be the following:

1 Frequency

How often does the medium appear, or how frequently can changes be made? Newspapers are printed daily – morning and evening – and weekly – Sundays and weeklies. Magazines are published weekly, fortnightly, monthly, bi-monthly and quarterly. The frequency with which an advertisement can be repeated or the copy can be changed will affect different advertisers according to what they are selling. A cinema proprietor has to promote changes of programme so that monthly publication is useless, but a monthly magazine may be suitable for a motor-car which is constantly on sale. Posters are usually changed every 13 weeks, so that this medium is best suited to popular repeat purchase goods, the poster acting as a reminder on the way to the point-of-purchase. Posters can also be rotated so that different posters appear on different sites for a period. An exhibition may be held annually or biannually. Direct mail is very flexible and can be targeted at certain recipients.

Thus media selection becomes a fascinating exercise, a medium being picked because of its precise value or rejected because of its limitations. It is no use wishing to use a certain medium just because we happen to like it. We may wish to make our flight to New York on Concorde but if the flight times are inconvenient or the fare is too high, we shall have to choose another aircraft, perhaps another airline. So with the choice of media.

2 Penetration

How can we penetrate the market most thoroughly, or how can we reach the greatest number of potential customers? Shall we use the morning, evening, weekly or Sunday newspaper? Shall we use a magazine that is bought by readers or one that is sent to them free? Shall we reach housewives at the kitchen sink by means of radio or in the armchair with TV, and which is likely to have the greatest impact and so penetrate the home market for washing-up liquid? Shall we reach more doctors, and appeal to them more effectively, by a direct mail shot in their morning post or though an advertisement in the *Lancet* which they may read at their leisure?

Here we can truly see the importance of correct decision-making, and that the success of a campaign will depend on a blend of creativity and media planning. The two are inseparable and weakness in either department can destroy the other.

Penetration also concerns the percentage of the market reached by rival media. For instance, a controlled circulation trade journal may reach more architects than one to which architects subscribe. This will be reflected in the advertisement rate, but it will be more economical to pay more to penetrate the market more thoroughly.

3 Circulation

This applies to the press, and a publication may be judged on two counts, whether it has an audited net sale at all, and what that net sale is in comparison with its advertisement rates and in further comparison with the net sale and rates of rival publications. There is no honest reason why a publisher will not submit to the auditing of his sales, except that he is ashamed of them, which means he may be charging an excessive rate for space.

Attendance at exhibitions can be placed under this heading, too, and certified attendance figures are given by many promoters. However, this is a controversial topic, because it may be more important to know the calibre of the visitors rather than their numbers, this being especially true of business and trade exhibitions where admission is by invitation ticket rather than turnstile ticket purchase.

Circulation should not be confused with *readership*. Circulation means the number of copies sold after deduction of free copies, returns and other differences between the total number of printed copies and the total number sold at the full price. The circulation of controlled circulation journals is audited on the basis of requests for copies.

Circulation is often identified as an 'ABC figure'. This figure is certified at regular intervals (usually six months) by the Audit Bureau of Circulations who certify the figures of average net sales produced by the publishers' own auditors. A more detailed profile of a magazine can be obtained in the form of a *media data form*. This comes in four parts: details about the publisher; reproduction of the most recent ABC Certificate of Net circulation; geographical analysis of circulation; and the editorial policy.

4 Readership

One person may buy a copy but there is likely to be a secondary readership by others. A magazine is passed round the office, read by the family, or given to the neighbours. A newspaper may be read by all the family. Small circulation newspapers like *The Times, Financial Times* or *Lloyd's List International* may have substantial readerships in offices, clubs, waiting-rooms and other places frequented by likely readers. This is the *quantity* or *secondary* aspect of readership which will usually show that the readership figure is anything from three to fifteen times greater than the circulation figure. Readership is not guessed by multiplying the circulation figure by a certain number.

There is also the *quality* aspect. What kind of people read the publication? What sex, age, income, social grading statistics are available? For most large circulation newspapers and magazines such data can be obtained from the National Readership Survey conducted by JICNARS, but we have to rely on publishers' statements if we want to know who reads some of the more specialist and technical press. In the latter case there may be a discrepancy between the readers aimed at by the editor and those who actually read the journal. Nevertheless, it is possible to differentiate between the readers of say the *Chemist and Druggist, Manufacturing Chemist* and *Chemical Engineering Communications* in that they are aimed at retail chemists, industrial chemists and research chemists respectively. The *Benn's Media Directory* gives this kind of information, but only an impartial readership survey will give a breakdown of the *profile* of a journal.

5   Profile

The profile of a newspaper or magazine is the proportional breakdown of its readers into the social grades known as A,B,C1,C2,D and E as described more fully in the chapter on Marketing Research and as revealed in the JICNARS readership survey mentioned above. Having selected the market segment for the product or service which is to be advertised it then follows that media must be selected which will reach the largest number of people in the segment to produce the greatest response at the lowest cost.

The profile can also be the breakdown of the readership into, say, architects, civil engineers, town planners and builders for a construction industry magazine, or into university, polytechnic, secondary and primary school teachers for an education journal.

6   Primary or secondary media: the media mix

Media selection implies narrowing down the choice, and the art of media planning is often to produce a schedule or media mix containing the fewest necessary media to reach the market most effectively. The advertising is not scattered hither and thither, impact being achieved by concentration and repetition provided this can be directed at the maximum number of potential buyers. It may be more economic to exploit the largest section of the market than to attempt to reach pockets of possible buyers on the periphery of the main market. Thus, a clock campaign was aimed at C1–C2 women who, research showed, bought clocks as gifts, although clocks are bought by men and by both men and women from other social grades.

The choice will be narrowed down to primary media which will gain the initial and most powerful impact. This may be women's magazines or TV for one product, the *Economist* and the *Sunday Times* for another, and may be radio for another. Different media suit different products or services. One medium may be taken as primary, or two or more which are complementary to one another, such as TV and *TV Times*, may be combined as first-choice media.

Secondary or support media will then be used to perpetuate the message and help to continue the campaign to the point-of-purchase. Typical media mixes may be TV, posters, and point-of-sale display for a food product, or trade press advertising and direct mail for a technical one, or local press, bus advertising and window-bills for a retailer's campaign.

Here it will be seen that each medium has a specific job. One medium on its own may prove a failure because it needs the support of other media at different stages of the advertising approach.

If we take the food product once again, the housewife may see the TV commercial at home, during the evening, sitting relaxed with her feet up. She is not going anywhere and in any case the shops are closed. Next morning she does not jump out of bed intent on rushing to the grocer's to buy the new soup. She has the family breakfast to see to and, because she shops only once or twice a week, it may be a day or two before she does enter the grocer's shop. This is even more critical when large volumes of shopping are undertaken at long intervals at supermarkets and superstores.

But each night she sees the commercial again, reinforcing her interest, desire and intent. On the day she does go shopping, and probably on other journeys on previous days, she sees posters for the new soup. Finally, at the shop she sees window-bills, display outers, special offers, sales promotion or other support media which clinch her intention to try the product. Throughout there is a progressive use of media from the moment of original awareness to that of actual sale, and there may be yet another inducement on the pack in the larder to encourage repeat purchase.

Primary and secondary media are both important, but they should not be confused with above-the-line and below-the-line media. The opposite could be the case as with direct response media when below-the-line media, and off-the-page press advertising (producing new prospects and enlarging the mailing list) could be a secondary medium.

10.6   Changes in the media

In recent years there have been great changes in the media which have to be reckoned with when evaluating media and deciding on the most effective mix. Some of the major changes are now summarized.

1   Viable small circulations

Either because the reading public will pay high cover prices for journals of minority interest – a newspaper like the *Independent* has a high cover price compared with the popular daily tabloids costing half the price – or, because of the replacement of labour intensive letterpress printing by more economical web-offset printing, it has become financially viable to publish journals with relatively small circulations. Previously, it was difficult to launch a new newspaper unless it could achieve a circulation of two million and so attract sufficient advertising revenue. Today it is possible to make a profit with a circulation of only 400,000. This has not been without its perils as was seen when the *Sunday Correspondent* was launched, followed by the *Independent on Sunday*, both appealing to intellectual readerships. The latter had the advantage of an established readership of its Monday to Saturday daily, whereas the *Sunday Correspondent*, although first on the scene, had no sister paper.

The slump in advertising revenue in 1990 made it difficult for both new Sundays to survive. The *Independent on Sunday* was losing money, but the *Sunday Correspondent* actually folded with sales of only 209,000. The *Sunday Correspondent* existed for little more than 14 months in spite of an injection of £10m by the late Robert Maxwell, the *Chicago Tribune* and a Saudi Arabian businessman, and its conversion to a tabloid in September 1990. It folded in November after the failure of talks to merge it with *Today* as a seven-day newspaper.

2   Better reproduction plus colour

Using either web-offset-litho or flexography (e.g. *Daily Mail*), reproduction of half-tone pictures has been greatly improved, and many newspapers now offer full-colour so that they compete with colour magazines.

3   Family readership of Saturday editions

Saturday circulations used to be less than Monday to Friday circulations because dailies were not bought on the way to work. The inclusion of features of family interest means that many dailies are bought six days a week.

4   Weekend magazines

At one time there were only three colour supplements supplied with national newspapers (*Sunday Times, The Observer* and *Sunday Telegraph*). Now, most newspapers have a Saturday or Sunday magazine. This has been a growth area with these magazines taking a large slice of magazine advertising.

5   Broadcasting Act 1990

In the 1990s there are new opportunities for both television advertising (with the new Channel Five), and national commercial radio stations. Even before the new Act, split-frequency radio and new radio stations were reaching different audiences, while on both BBC and ITV new forms of sponsorship had been introduced. The ban on religious advertising has now been removed from commercial television. An innovation is BBC Select, providing direct marketing on TV.

6   Foreign-owned magazines

A number of continental European publishing houses, especially in France and Germany, are producing English language editions, of which women's magazines and *TV Quick* have been very successful.

7 Pan-European journals

Both British and continental European publishers are producing journals with cross-frontier circulations, to mention only *The European*, while Verlays Gruppe Bauer have UK, German and French magazines with pan-European rate cards. This group alone claims a total circulation of 4m or 10m readerships for their four women's magazines.

8 Overseas circulations

A number of newspapers and magazines have international circulations, and have editions printed at overseas locations, for instance the *Financial Times, Wall Street Journal, USA Today, International Herald Tribune, The Economist* and *The Guardian Weekly*. Conversely, there are Japanese and Chinese newspapers published in Europe and the USA.

9 Satellite television plus cable television

Cross-frontier media are also offered in Europe by Sky television and through the various cable TV networks. There are also satellite TV systems in the Gulf States, and in the Far East.

In Britain, BSkyB attracted many new viewers when it covered World Cup Cricket. BBC Enterprises and Thames TV formed a new satellite channel using Astra satellite.

10 Outdoor advertising

New forms of outdoor advertising are to be seen such as sites which revolve to show a succession of advertisements. Aerial advertising has grown with flying airships, and tethered airships and balloons.

10.7 The media register

Finally, the study of media can be enhanced by using the facilities of the *Media Register*. The organizers can provide reviews of the use of media by advertising during the previous year. Subscribers may view a TV (plus cinema) commercials review tape; international commercials review tape (covering USA, Canada, Brazil, Australia, France, Germany, Italy, Spain, Holland and Belgium); a press advertisement review file covering 500 publications; a review of international press advertising from more than 200 French, German, Spanish, Italian and Dutch publications; a poster review; a radio review of radio commercial tapes from Capital, LBC and Piccadilly Radio; and media expenditure reports are also available.

11
Above-the-line media analysed

11.1 Introduction

The distinctions between above- and below-the-line advertising (expressions which were originally used by Procter and Gamble) were explained in the previous chapter (10.3 and 10.4). In many cases an advertiser will use an agency to create and place above-the-line advertising, but handle below-the-line in-house or through specialist agencies such as direct mail houses. In this chapter we shall consider the characteristics, merits and demerits of press, TV, radio, cinema and outdoor (including transportation) advertising.

11.2 The press

The press has developed over the past four hundred years (*see* 2.2) to become the most versatile and most successful advertising medium. Television advertising, in spite of its realism, even in countries such as the UK where the quality of commercials is unsurpassed, cannot equal press advertising. Instead, television has encouraged popular newspaper features and special interest magazines dealing with topics introduced by television. People like to read about television shows and personalities. In fact, the publishing of such features has helped evening newspapers to survive because they are taken home, while some people will buy the Saturday edition of *The Sun* because it contains a TV listing guide for the week ahead. Far from harming the press, television has made it prosperous in sales and advertisement revenue.

To give some idea of what is involved in producing a mass-circulation national newspaper, *The Sun* uses every night for six nights a week 3000 miles of paper weighing 360 tonnes, and 1,800 gallons of ink. Rupert Murdoch bought it for a mere £600,000 in 1969 when its circulation was only 850,000, compared with four million today, or a readership of more than 12 million. *The Sun*'s readers are predominantly under 24 and come from the C2 social grade.

Nevertheless, in the period December 1985–February 1991 there was an 8 per cent fall in the sale of mass market national tabloids, and a 7 per cent fall in the sale of mass market Sunday tabloids. *The Daily Record* (Scotland), *The Sun, Daily Mirror, News of the World, People* and *Sunday Mirror* all slumped. Why was this? According to Michael Leapman writing on the media page of *The Independent* on April 17 1991, the reasons were: 'For the tabloids, a combination of the slump in advertising, higher cover prices and an increasingly literate population have combined to produce a decline in sales that is unlikely to be reversed. It is significant that full-colour printing, now universal among the tabloids, has failed to attract new readers'. The latter point is a curious factor in modern publishing. The new world of colour newspapers envisaged by the enterprising Eddie Shah when he shook Fleet Street with his printing techniques, has been the all-time flop of British publishing. Readers do not like it, perhaps because it is often cheap and nasty compared with the lush realistic colour of the magazines.

Some of the reasons for the importance of the British press as an advertising medium, and for the existence of a national press are worth consideration. While some of these reasons apply to some large industrialized countries, there are economic, historical and geographic reasons why the UK enjoys a national press and is unique in so doing.

i   In the UK many millions of people exist in a compact geographical area with an elaborate network of road, rail, sea and air communications.

ii   This large population consists mainly of big urban populations, many in huge conurbations.

iii   Production is highly industrialized and has been so for more than a century in most cases. This has required mass markets, again made possible by urbanization and communications. Mass production calls for mass distribution and mass media.

iv   A high standard of living has resulted, justifying the proliferation of press media to cover every possible subject. This further assists distribution of goods and services.

v   The standard of literacy is high and there is virtually none of the lost-literacy found in developing countries. The demand for reading matter is nation-wide.

vi   The UK has a single language, Welsh and Gaelic being of minor importance, but an immigrant press has emerged. Publications, therefore, can be printed in large quantities in one language common to all.

vii   Traditionally, London has been the capital and centre of the UK, making London a national press centre.

No other country in the world enjoys this combination of advantages. Moreover, English is understood in a very large part of the world, including a great deal of Northern Europe, so that British publications have international circulations. This is probably the greatest single asset that British manufacturers have in the Single European Market. There are more than 12,000 British publications, according to *Benn's Media Directory*.

However, this is not to overlook the importance of European press media, and *British Rate and Data* (BRAD), which is a monthly record of British rate card information, also has associate publications in Austria, Belgium, France, Germany, Italy, the Netherlands, Scandinavia, Spain and Switzerland.

Moreover, the press has certain specific advantages over all other media. It is still by far the cheapest way of reaching a very large number of people, and it is the most effective and economic means of reaching large numbers of scattered and unidentified prospects. At little or no extra cost, copy can be changed at short notice, and different copy (e.g. branch address) can be inserted in regional editions. A major advantage is that press media offer the opportunity to include coupons so that immediate response can be stimulated. This makes the press a primary medium for direct response marketers, book clubs, music clubs, insurance companies, horticultural suppliers, unit trusts, football pool promoters and others who have no comparable means of reaching their market. For some, radio may be an alternative, but preferably national or networked radio, not local. For others, direct mail can provide similar, often better, spread of sales information, but direct mail requires known prospects. Answers to press advertisements may provide mailing lists of enquirers and customers for future direct mail shots.

The intelligent user of press advertising can exploit the reader's selectivity, accepting that readers are unlikely to read every word of every advertisement. Nevertheless, the newspaper or magazine with its wide-ranging readership is likely to attract response from a sufficient number of people to make the expenditure worthwhile. To take another instance, a Sunday newspaper may have a circulation of some millions, but a thousand requests for a brochure will be a wonderful success for an advertiser who has spent only a few pence on each enquiry. To achieve this kind of economic return it is necessary to take only the minimum amount of space and, if the advertisement is small, to see that it is included in a market place of advertisements for like products or services.

An analysis of the UK press will help to show the variety of press media that are available to all kinds of advertiser, large or small, national or local.

11.3　Newspapers

National daily morning newspapers

The *Daily Express, Daily Mail, Daily Mirror, Daily Star, The Sun,*

Daily Telegraph, Financial Times, Guardian, The Independent, The Times and *Today*, together with the sporting dailies *The Racing Post* and *The Sporting Life*, the shipping journal *Lloyds List International*, and the licensed victuallers' daily, the *Morning Advertiser*.

London evening newspaper

The *Evening Standard*. Its circulation area covers the Home Counties with fringe circulation some distance farther off, but a number of regional evening papers compete for the peripheral circulation areas. Its circulation is about 500,000.

Weekly colour magazines/supplements

The *Sunday Telegraph, Sunday Times, Scotsman, Mail on Sunday, Observer, People, News of the World*, and other Sunday newspapers have photogravure or offset-litho printed colour magazines which supplement the normal newspaper. *The Independent* has a Saturday magazine and there is the *Telegraph Weekend* and the *Independent on Sunday* magazine.

National Sunday newspapers

News of the World, Observer, Sunday Express, Independent on Sunday, Mail on Sunday, Sunday Mirror, People, Sunday Telegraph and *Sunday Times. (The Independent on Sunday, Mail on Sunday* and the *Sunday Telegraph* are the rare exceptions of new post-war national newspapers.) Several Sunday newspapers have been closed in the past 20 years, and two have changed titles.

 N.B.   National dailies and Sundays are divided into two categories, 'popular' and 'quality'. The former have circulations in the millions, the latter mostly around 400,000.

English regional morning newspapers

Their dwindling number includes famous papers, for instance the *Liverpool Daily Post, Birmingham Post, Western Morning News* and *Yorkshire Post*.

English regional evening newspapers

Some 70 provincial evening papers remain, but no English region outside London can now boast of more than one title. Whereas the regional mornings tend to have a business readership, the evenings are popular family reading. By the introduction of women's interest features, these papers have achieved a take-home readership which has in turn increased their value as advertising media. Many of these papers are among the very best produced newspapers in the UK, enjoying circulations in excess of 200,000 nightly. It should be remembered, however, that the expression 'evening newspaper' is something of a misnomer, since racing editions appear in mid-morning, followed by lunchtime editions. They might better be called all-day newspapers!

Table 11.1 *Approximate figures for British National Daily and Sunday Newspapers*. NB These figures vary from time to time as reported in the trade press and published in *British Rate and Data* and *The Media Pocket Book*

Social Grade	National daily	Page rate mono	Page rate colour	Circulation
A	The Times	£14,000	£26,000	425,000
	Financial Times (UK)	£22,400	£28,500	200,000
B	Daily Telegraph	£32,000	£39,000	1,000,000
	Guardian	£15,500	£17,000	425,000
	The Independent	£12,500	£17,000	400,000
C1	Daily Express	£20,825	£27,000	1,500,000
	Daily Mail	£27,500	£30,000	1,600,000
	Today	£6,200	£6,750	560,000
C2DE	Daily Mirror	£28,300	£32,800	3,100,000
	Daily Star	£9,432	£13,000	915,000
	The Sun	£28,000	£32,500	4,000,000

Social Grade	National Sundays	Page rate mono	Page rate colour	Circulation
A–B	Sunday Times	£36,000	£69,000	1,200,000
	Sunday Telegraph	£23,000	£30,000	600,000
	The Observer	£22,000	£26,000	550,000
	Independent on Sunday	£12,000	£16,500	350,000
C1	Mail on Sunday	£26,000	£39,900	1,900,000
	Sunday Express	£51,968*	£67,558*	1,700,000
C2DE	News of the World	£31,500	£36,000	5,000,000
	Sunday Mirror	£25,900	£34,500	3,000,000
	The People	£20,550	£27,300	2,500,000
	Sunday Sport	£12,303	£14,245	427,000

* *Sunday Express* is broadsheet, hence higher rate than *Mail on Sunday*.

English regional weeklies including bi-weeklies

There are three classes of weekly newspaper, the suburban paper to be found in large cities such as London and Manchester; the town weekly with a circulation fairly restricted to an urban area; and the truly regional weekly which is read in towns and villages in a geographical area which may contain two or three counties. These regional weeklies may have localized editions, as with the *Kent Messenger, Chester Chronicle, Warrington Guardian* and other series.

English regional Sundays

Four exist, *Bedfordshire on Sunday* in Bedford, *Sunday Independent* in Plymouth, the *Sunday Mercury* in Birmingham and the *Sunday Sun* in Newcastle.

Scottish, Welsh, Northern Ireland, Channel Islands and Isle of Man newspapers (Table 11.2)

Scotland has four important newspaper publishing centres producing morning, evening and Sunday newspapers, these being Glasgow, Edinburgh, Dundee and Aberdeen and there are also numerous Scottish weeklies. Welsh dailies – one morning and three evenings – are to be found in the three principal cities of South Wales, Cardiff, Newport and Swansea plus one evening in North Wales. In the north, North Wales editions of Liverpool and Manchester papers cover the area. Belfast is the publishing centre of morning, evening and Sunday newspapers in Northern Ireland. The Isle of Man has no daily newspapers but does have three weeklies, but Jersey and Guernsey have their evenings and weeklies, one of each in each island. Most national campaigns will include at least one Scottish daily and one Northern Ireland daily in their newspaper schedule. Scotland, Wales and Northern Ireland may be regarded as having their own national presses, even though the London papers also circulate there.

Business supplements and magazines

With millions of people now owning shares, either directly through purchases of shares in privatized industries or indirectly through unit shares, many newspapers now cater for this new reader interest by publishing separate business or financial supplements and magazines. For example, the *Independent on Sunday* has its tabloid *Business*, the *Evening Standard* has its *Business Today* printed on pink paper like the *Financial Times*, and the *Daily Mail* has its weekly *Money Mail*.

Free newspapers

There are more than 1000 free newspapers distributed door-to-door in the UK. In large towns there may be three if not four titles. They offer the advertiser penetration coverage of urban populations, and adver-

Table 11.2   Scottish, Welsh, Northern Ireland and Channel Islands newspapers

Scottish dailies

Aberdeen	*The Press & Journal*
Dundee:	*The Courier & Advertiser*
Edinburgh:	*The Scotsman*
Glasgow:	*Daily Record*
	Glasgow Herald
Greenock:	*Greenock Telegraph*
Paisley:	*Paisley Daily Express*

Scottish Evenings

Aberdeen:	*Evening Express*
Dundee:	*Evening Telegraph*
Edinburgh:	*Evening News*
Glasgow:	*Evening Times*

Scottish Sundays

Edinburgh:	*Scotland on Sunday*
Glasgow:	*Sunday Mail*
	Sunday Post

There is also the *Scottish Daily Express* published in London

Welsh Daily

Cardiff	*Western Mail*

Welsh Evenings

Cardiff:	*South Wales Echo*
Mold:	*Evening Leader*
Newport:	*South Wales Argus*
Swansea:	*South Wales Evening Post*

Welsh Sunday

Cardiff:	*Wales on Sunday*

Northern Ireland Dailies

Belfast	*Belfast Newsletter*
	Irish News
	Ulster New Letter

Northern Ireland Evening

Belfast:	*Belfast Telegraph*

Northern Ireland Sunday

Belfast:	*Sunday Life*
	Sunday News

Channel Islands Evenings

Guernsey:	*Guernsey Evening Press & Star*
Jersey:	*Jersey Evening Post*

tisers consist mainly of retailers, car dealers, estate agents and restaurants plus large numbers of small, private classified advertisments. In recent years the editorial content has been greatly improved. Some are published by regular newspaper proprietors, and in some cases (rather like controlled circulation magazines) it has been possible to attract more advertising (because of the guaranteed circulation) than was possible with newspapers which readers purchased.

11.4 Magazines

These are best broken down into five groups. If the reader wishes to become more familiar with titles and readerships covered he or she is advised to study works of reference such as the *British Rate and Data, Benn's Media Directory*, the *Media Pocket Book* the *PR Planner* or *Advertisers Annual*. The five groups are: (a) consumer and special interest; (b) trade; (c) technical; (d) professional; and (e) regional.

Consumer and special interest magazines

The remarkable thing about the UK periodical press is that almost every conceivable interest has its own journal. This makes it possible for advertisers to direct advertising at very precise markets such as bee-keepers, electronic engineers or gatherers at the nineteenth hole. However, recession saw many titles fold in the late 1980s and early 1990s.

Women's magazines, both weekly and monthly, form the largest single group of special interest magazines. There are some 16 weeklies, two fortnightlies, 42 monthlies and eight bi-monthlies. They represent different age groups, social grades and special women's interests.

A medley of not-so-specialized magazines may be lumped together under the heading of 'general interest' magazines and these include such diverse titles as *Country Life, Men Only, Private Eye, The Spectator* and *What's On In London*. Really specialized titles cover angling, boating, gardening, hi-fi, motoring, photography, pop music, retirement, and TV listings.

A major change has occurred with TV and radio programme or 'listing' magazines. At one time BBC programmes were the monopoly of the *Radio Times*, ITV programmes that of *TV Times*, both of which had vast circulations. With the end of the monopolies, publishers could pay a licence fee to publish any listing. This led to fierce competition between the two original magazines, a short-lived rival *TV Plus*, and the emergence of the IPC's low-price *What's On TV* and of *TV Quick* on whose launch the German publishers H. Bauer Publishing spent millions. *TV Quick* is printed in Cologne. Circulations of the listings are around 2,700,000 with the *Radio Times* leading. They cover terrestrial TV (ITV), satellite TV and BBC radio.

Originally, it was thought that deregulation would expand the market for mass-market programme magazines, perhaps to nine million sales a week. But the tabloids gave so much space to listings that the magazines suffered. *TV Quick*, with a launch cover price of only 10 pence in March 1991, initially won 3.1 million sales, but when the real price of 40 pence was introduced in May 1991 sales plummeted to 1.2 million. Bauer had already spent £17 million on promoting *TV Quick*; but Bauer had the advantage of 62 per cent corporation tax in Germany against which its extravagant advertising spend could be set. Bauer had already moved into the UK three years earlier with the women's magazine *Bella* (1.2 million sales), and the puzzles magazine *Take A Break* (1 million).

The French publishers Hachette invaded the British market in 1985 with *Elle* which now sells in 15 other countries, even in China! Another German publisher, Gruhner & Jahr, sells *Best* in Britain and other countries. British publishers no longer command the home magazine market.

In some appraisals of the magazine press it has become common to list the weekend magazines (newspaper colour supplements) together with consumer magazines, showing that advertisement spend on magazines is dominated by that in the weekend magazines to the detriment of the more traditional magazines.

Trade magazines

While 'the trade press' is a common expression, it is better to be more explicit and refer to trade, technical and professional magazines which have specific readerships. Trade magazines are read by distributors – wholesalers, retailers, direct response marketers, agents, franchisers, importers and exporters. Examples are *British Baker, The Grocer* and *Retail Newsagent Tobacconist and Confectioner*. They carry news of interest to the trade such as new products or packaging, price changes, new legislation and forthcoming advertising campaigns. For manufacturers, they provide an advertising medium for the announcement of new products, sales promotion schemes, dealer offers, co-operative promotional schemes, and advertising campaigns.

Technical magazines

These magazines are read by manufacturers and skilled workers including those in service industries such as heating and lighting, refrigeration, air conditioning and electronics. Typical journals are *Electronics Weekly* and *The Engineer*. Editorial will consist mainly of technical articles and new product news, and advertisements will be for equipment, materials, components and services. A number of technical magazines have controlled circulations, that is they are distributed free of charge to selected and requested readerships which give the journal greater penetration of its market than is usual with paid-for magazines. This greater or guaranteed circulation enables the publisher to charge advertisement rates which reflect this circulation and market penetration.

Professional magazines

Teachers, doctors, lawyers and other professionals are the readers of these journals which differ yet again from trade and technical ones, and included are *The Times Higher Education Supplement, The Lancet* and the *New Law Journal.*

There are some broad-based journals that cover two if not all three interests, such as *Campaign, Marketing Week* and *PR Week.*

Regional magazines

These fall into three groups: glossy magazines that have revived the style of the *Tatler*; county magazines that devote themselves to historical and environmental, cultural and development interests; and trade, commercial and industrial magazines published by Chambers of Trade, business organizations and similar local bodies, a good example being *Midlands Industry and Commerce.* To this group may be added the localized farming journals such as those of the NFU county committees.

11.5 Directories, year books and timetables

A large number of reference works such as *Kelly's Directories*, the *Rose Society Annual* and *ABC transport guides* form another press medium. *Advertisers Annual* is a valuable desk aid, but lesser annuals may serve as little more than mailing lists for direct mail campaigns. It depends who you are and what you are selling. If your prospects are likely to be frequent thumbers-through of a certain book it could be a first-class medium for your kind of advertising. The important thing about a directory is that it should be as complete as possible in its infomation and this means that initially all entries must be free, paid entries being quite additional. A directory consisting only of paid entries is likely to be very unrepresentative. *Yellow Pages* (owned by BT) and Thomson local telephone directories attract much advertising from local businesses.

11.6 House magazines

These are private journals, 85 per cent being published internally and 15 per cent externally. There are about 1000 titles published in Britain.

Those with very big circulations, e.g. *Ford News*, are useful media for popular consumer products. Among the externals there are those like the *Port of London* which circulates round the world and provide useful media for those whose prospects lie within that kind of circulation.

11.7   Some basic terminology

All media have their special nomenclature, and the following terms are peculiar to the press.

Bleed: to print to the extreme edge of the page, achieved by having the artwork large enough so that the paper can be trimmed to give the bled-off effect. Advertisements that bleed are charged at a higher rate.

Camera-ready copy: those printed by offset-litho or web-offset require artwork or camera-ready copy which can be photographed for platemaking. This artwork will usually consist of pasted-down typesetting and Letraset display lines. Illustrations will be supplied separately if half-tone screens are to be applied. Colour separation will be necessary for full-colour pictures.

Classified: advertisements that appear under classified headings, and usually in words run on, not displayed. The 'smalls'.

Copy date: date the advertisement, whether paper set or camera-ready copy must be delivered.

Cover price: the retail price.

CPT: cost per thousand (circulation or readership).

Display: advertisements that are laid out with a variety of type faces and sizes, usually illustrated.

Displayed classified, or *semi-display*: advertisements in the classified section which are not merely run on, but set out and possibly illustrated, e.g. recruitment advertising.

Ears or title corners: small spaces on either side of the title or masthead at the top of the front page of a newspaper.

Mechanical data: page type area, and advertisement space measurement.

Next matter or facing matter: advertisement position next to editorial or reading matter for which a premium is charged, and making it a kind of special position.

OTS: opportunity to see, another way of expressing readership figures, one OTS being one reader.

Press date: the date of publication and not to be confused with copy date – the date of going to press.

Rate card: a postcard-size price list of space rates together with every kind of information required by the advertiser or his agent. Rate cards are reproduced in *British Rate and Data*, the monthly Bible of the media planner and buyer.

Run-of-paper: advertisement inserted at the discretion of the advertisement manager and charged at the basic rate.

scc: single column centimetre, the standard unit of measurement for advertisement space in newspapers, the minimum space being three single column centimetres. Magazines sell space by the page and pro rata. Newspapers also sell by the whole or full page, and half page.

Solus position: the only advertisement on the page.

Special position: advertisement position which earns a premium because it attracts a higher or a special readership.

Spot colour: a single second colour as when the brand name is picked out in, say, red.

Type area: the area of the page occupied by printing matter whether editorial or advertisement.

Voucher: copy of the publication containing the advertisement as proof of insertion.

11.8 Advantages of press advertising

1 Morning and Sunday newspapers, and most magazines including trade, technical and professional, are available nationally, either through bookstall (plus home delivery) sales, or by postal subscription and postal controlled circulation (free distribution).

2 Provincial morning, all evening newspapers, many county and other weekly newspapers, and county and district magazines (including Chamber of Trade and Commerce journals) are distributed over large regions and are not limited to towns of origin. Thus advertisements can be addressed to readers in areas such as the West Country, South Wales, Merseyside, the Midlands and so on. Advertisements are also accepted in the regional editions of certain national publications, and local addresses can be inserted in advertisements of regional editions of newspapers and magazines.

3 Local or town newspapers are available. These are used by local advertisers, and a national advertiser can support stockists by encouraging them to advertise national brands in the local press. This can be done by co-operative schemes, the manufacturer offering to pay a proportion of the cost of space, or by the supply of stock advertisements with a space for the stockist's name, logo and illustration for inclusion in the stockist's own advertising.

4 The press excels with its variety of specialized circulations, with big groups of journals appealing to, say, women, juveniles, investors, church-goers, gardeners, motorists, or do-it-yourself enthusiasts, and much more specialized journals appealing to categories of tradesmen, technicians, and professional groups. These very specialized circulations may be comparatively small but they must be seen in relation to the extent of their penetration of the particular

market. The controlled circulation magazine offers a high degree of penetration.

5 Readership surveys of the larger circulation journals are conducted by JICNARS (see Chapter 21), analysing readership (including 'secondary' readership).

6 Advertisements can be placed at short notice, in some cases the previous day or only a few hours before printing. Many newpapers operate telephone selling services.

7 It is the cheapest means of reaching large numbers of potential buyers, classifieds being extremely inexpensive.

8 Newspapers, especially, provide an excellent means of reaching the broadscale market of unidentified prospects in all locations.

9 Sufficient space can be taken to tell the story. The 'reader' advertisement can give in-depth editorial style content.

10 The message can be re-read, retained and is intransient. Some publications are filed or bound and become permanent literature. Advertisements can be cut out and kept for later reference. Magazines are often kept for a long time or passed on to other readers so that advertisements live for months, sometimes years. The *Radio Times* and *TV Times* are on sale before the weekend, and are about the house for some ten days.

11 Orders and enquiries can be encouraged and coupons can be used including the fold-up-and-post postage paid kind. Freepost coupon offers induce reader action. Bingo cards provide a tear-out reader service in some controlled circulation magazines.

12 Because replies can be keyed with codes (e.g. SN29/3 printed on coupon, meaning *Sun* March 29), response can be measured, and cost-per-reply and cost-per-conversion to sales, can be calculated to assess pulling power and cost effectiveness of media. This is important in direct response marketing and the use of off-the-page offers.

13 The reading public places great faith, rightly or wrongly, in the integrity of the press. Publishers guard the reputations of their journals by vetting advertisers, operating protection schemes for readers, and by supporting the British Code of Advertising Practice.

14 Advertisements can be illustrated.

15 In an increasing number of publications colour may be used providing extra attention value and realism. Even in daily news-papers, colour reproduction is possible. The weekend colour magazines in the *Mail On Sunday, Sunday Telegraph, Sunday Times, Observer* and other newspapers, the women's magazines, *TV Times* and the *Radio Times* and other journals make colour advertising available for every class of commodity and service from cake mixes to holidays and travel. This has helped the press either to compete with or support colour TV advertising.

16 Different copy, such as changes of address and telephone number, may be placed in regional editions of some publications.

17 In some publications it is possible to advertise in certain editions only. *The Economist* offers different international editions.

18 Because some publications are still subsidized by advertising their cover price is low and purchase is encouraged, although the inflationary cost of paper and production has reversed this tradition in many cases, the reader subsidizing the advertiser!

19 Most publications are well distributed and marketed, using national and international networks of wholesalers, retailers and news-vendors, promoting large national and even international circulations and market penetrations of benefit to advertisers. The building of motorways has encouraged the use of road transport, thus avoiding the delays that used to occur with rail strikes and other causes of delay.

20 The British trade, technical and professional press (especially the technical) is, like the American, of authoritative international consequence.

21 Many publications are bought regularly, home delivered, bought on the way to work, office delivered, bought on the way home from work, subscribed to or received by controlled circulation or free newspaper delivery. Advertising can benefit from this consistency. Readers know where to find their favourite topics, and appropriate advertising can be placed selectively on these pages, often in special positions. Series of advertisements can thus gain from repetitive and accumulative impact.

22 The mobility of a newspaper or magazine is an important characteristic and advantage for it can be carried about and read at almost anytime almost anywhere.

11.9 Disadvantages of press advertising

1 Newspapers and weekly magazines are fairly short-lived. The daily (especially the evening) newspaper may have a life no longer than a train journey or lunch hour. It is dead next day and there is another issue to supersede it. The content of a popular British daily can be absorbed very quickly.

2 Newspapers, and some magazines even when printed by web-offset-litho, are poorly printed on low quality paper. Photographs reproduce badly. Pale pictures can be ruined by show through from the reverse side. Advertisements that look well on block-pull paper can be very disappointing when they finally appear in print. This applies particularly to big circulation papers like *The Sun*.

3 There are many advertisements, and unless extra payment is made for large solus or special positions, an advertisement can be lost among so many others.

4   The vast circulation and readership figures quoted by media owners can be deceptive; only a proportion of readers are likely to be interested in any one advertisement. Consequently, waste circulation is inevitable.

5   There are rarely any special inducements to read advertisements in the press. Unlike radio, cinema and TV advertising, the reader has to make a voluntary effort to study the advertisements. Noticeably, press advertising has had to borrow from TV and modern advertisements have displayed sentences, even paragraphs, which are so visual they are absorbed rather than consciously read.

6   A press advertisement is static, lacking the movement, sound, realism and ability to demonstrate which some other media can offer.

7   Colour is available only in a limited way. Even so, colour advertising is expensive, and the standard of quality varies.

8   Some magazines group all advertisements at the front and back of the book so that they are divorced from the main reading interest of the editorial pages. This increases the amount of effort required by the reader to take notice of the advertisements.

9   Many newspapers are taken out of the home or are not delivered to the home and, being discarded in the course of the day, are never brought into the home at all. The housewife readership of morning newspapers is of dubious merit and suggests a very serious defect in readership surveying. Generally speaking, working class readers leave home before newspapers are delivered and have to buy their copies on the way to work. In fact, charges for home deliveries nowadays deter people from having newspapers delivered by the newsagent.

10   Some press advertising, especially in regional newspapers and trade journals, is crude and amateurish, and this detracts from the advertising value of the medium. Sometimes the more professionally produced advertisement can look out of place, too sophisticated, among the paper-set local or trade announcements.

11   High cover prices have encouraged some people to reduce their purchase of newspapers and magazines. Total sales of popular national dailies fell by two million between 1984 and 1990, although there was a slight increase in the overall sales of quality newspapers since the arrival of *The Independent*. National Sundays have generally lost circulation. Many magazine titles have failed to sell either enough copies or enough advertisement space and have folded.

11.10   Advertising features, supplements and special numbers

Features, supplements and special numbers are devices for increasing advertisement revenue. They range from supplements in eminent papers like *The Times* and *Financial Times* to features in the *Baddington Bugle* to commemorate the centenary of Biggs the butchers, father and son, The trouble – from the advertiser's point of view – is that they occur too often, are superfluous and, despite the full advertisement rate being charged, they appeal to only a minority of an already comparatively small readership. Even those in *The Times* and *Financial Times* have been criticized by the Incorporated Society of British Advertisers, and these are at least quite competently written. The worst, the blackmail type, are those when suppliers or contractors are solicited, on the client's recommendation, to take space in the feature which is to celebrate his great event, official opening, inauguration or whatever may be the occasion which has been exploited by the advertisement manager. However, not all these special advertising opportunities are worthless, and the following is a brief analysis of the various kinds of feature, supplement and special number which flourish in the imaginations of advertisement managers. Potential advertisers must judge their advertising value on their merits. Occasionally they may originate as the editor's brainchild, but usually (in spite of editorial content) they have nothing to do with the editorial side of a publication.

1 Features on topical subjects, e.g. an exhibition, opening of a university, cathedral, bridge, dock, or tunnel.
2 Features on a major subject, a foreign country, an industry or a profession. Among the most exploited have been the anniversaries of the independence of former colonies, or the official visits by foreign rulers, most of which have been of very limited reader interest and negligible advertising value.
3 Features on the opening of a new hotel, shop, etc., (usually in a local newspaper). Wise suppliers spurn these useless features by stating quite honestly that their advertising is fully allocated according to an agreed plan. Sometimes there is a blackmail element when the supplier or contractor is afraid of damaging goodwill with the customer or client if space is not bought, but if a positive policy is adopted for this type of feature the advertising manager should be able to give a frank and acceptable explanation. Some of the advertisements which appear are banal with messages like 'congratulations from XYZ Company on your 25th anniversary'. Who cares – except the advertisement manager!
4 Features on a seasonal subject, e.g. holidays, spring cleaning, gardening, home decorating, heating and lighting, Christmas gifts. These more naturally fall into the editorial topic planning of the journal, and this means that there is genuine editorial with which seasonal advertisers will wish to be associated. This point needs to be emphasized: the supplements and features inspired by advertisement managers are usually produced by separate journalists working in special departments. In fact, regular journalists have objected

to having to write for advertisement departments.

Included in this section are *special numbers*, when most if not all of an issue is devoted to a certain topic such as the Motor Show, Heating and Lighting, or Spring Bulb Planting. These are bumper issues with extra pages and higher sales, supported by 'boom' issue advertising to attract retail stocking and reader purchase. They can be well worth supporting by advertisers. The editorial is usually independent of advertising except that its volume will depend on the quantity of advertisement space sold. An excellent guide to forthcoming features is the monthly loose-leaf *Advance* published by Themetree Ltd of Aylesbury.

5   Purely advertising features when advertisements for certain products or services are congregated in a market place of competitive advertising. These features, or groupings of like advertisements are welcomed by advertisers because they focus attention on the subject which might be direct response bargains, holidays and travel, entertainments, houses for sale and so on. Moreover, even a tiny advertisement such as a 3 scc will have enhanced value when placed with others, as occurs with advertisements for holiday resorts which have small budgets.

All such inducements to buy space, no matter how great the reputation of the journal and how well produced the feature or supplement (and those in *The Financial Times* and *Times* are well done), should be judged solely on potential advertising value. One way of judging the advertising value is to attempt to estimate the proportion of regular readers who will be interested in reading the supplements. One on, say, Nigeria, Zambia or Kenya, will interest a great many readers of *African Business*, fewer readers of *The Times* or *Financial Times*. This is only a rough guide, but the advertiser needs to study the readership profile of journals running features and supplements to assess the proportion of readers likely to be interested in the special topic. The proportion may be small!

It is usually bad policy to ask for a write-up – often worse policy to accept one. Public relations and advertising do not mix, expecially on a 'sprat to catch a mackerel' basis, and truly independent editorial will refer to products, services, companies or people irrespective of advertisers. Public relations material should always merit publication, that is it should be of interest and value to the reader and therefore a service to the editor.

Editors and advertisement managers play different roles – sometimes hostile ones with editors regretting the intrusion of advertisements and advertisement managers regarding the editorial as the stuff that fills the empty space between advertisements. Consequently, offers of 'free write-ups' generally come from advertisement managers who are 'trying it on' and have no power to influence their editors, or from those working for small circulation journals anxious to sell space at any price.

There is also the *special article racket*. It works like this: the chairman or managing director of a company receives a letter offering to publish an article about his organization. Flattered, the chief executive agrees to the idea, probably without even mentioning it to the PRO. Then comes another letter from the publisher asking how much supporting advertisement space will be bought, this decision being necessary before a quantity of space can be determined for the editorial and before the 'reporter' makes his visit. It is perhaps only now that the chief executive recognizes that he is corresponding with the advertisement and not the editorial department. Depending on his ego and gullibility, the CEO either commits the company to expenditure on probably useless advertising, or confesses to the PRO and appeals to the PRO to get him off the hook. This racket has been perpetuated for many years and it relies on the top level approach. The publications mostly have imposing titles that appeal to managing directors.

11.11 Commercial television

Note that this section is headed 'commercial television', for this is where British television differs from that in many other countries. Commercial television, in the British sense, means that the programmes are put on by the contractors, e.g. Granada or Anglia TV and independently of the advertisers. Sponsored television usually means that the advertiser provides the programme in which he inserts his commercials. However, as detailed in 23.10, there is now a new kind of sponsorship which is covered by the ITC Code of Programme Sponsorship. This permits the sponsorship of a programme produced by the contractors, e.g. Croft Port sponsorship of the *Rumpole* series. This Code was introduced in 1991. Further comment on this is made in 11.13.

First, let us dispose of one point. Some critics object to television advertising as such, disliking the breaks in programmes (especially films) which they would not otherwise suffer in a theatre or cinema. They also object to the repetitiveness of some of the advertising and to the persistence of the appeals. To these criticisms three answers can be given:

1 Without the commercials there would be no other channels providing an alternative choice of programmes. This extra choice of viewing is not paid for out of licence fees even though it is illegal to watch the commercial channels without having paid the licence fee.
2 As explained in Chapter 23, where the control system is detailed in the section about the Independent Television Commission (23.9), there is very strict control over what is shown. Scripts and storyboards are vetted at an early stage, before shooting, and many commercials are checked at the double-head stage before sound and

vision are joined in the married print. All commercials are viewed by the ITVA for approval prior to transmission.

3   The medium is one of popular entertainment and information. Products advertised, especially in the peak viewing hours of mid-evening, are bound to be those which are likely to be bought by the mass public, particularly housewives. This tends to reduce the number of products or services suitable for TV advertising, and to concentrate the medium on those products or services (e.g. repeat purchase small unit items such as foods, drinks and toiletries) which either require or justify frequent presentation. However, there are other TV advertisers such as banks, building societies, car manufacturers, and the promoters of privatization share offers. Production of commercials is costly, and not every advertiser will be justified in making more than one. Moreover, much depends on the geographical location of the viewer and the extent to which he is watching the commercials of local or national advertisers. In the London area, very few local advertisers use the medium, whereas the reverse is the case in the regions. Obviously, the larger advertiser will invest in more sophisticated commercials than the local firms with more limited resources.

11.12   The background story

Television advertising was well established in the USA long before it was permitted in the UK by the *Television Act 1954*. Although there was a limited amount of TV in the UK in the late 1930s, its development was impeded by the Second World War. After the war the BBC introduced TV programmes for those who could afford to buy receivers. Audiences were large enough by 1953 for the Amalgamated Press to launch *TV Mirror* which failed to secure the programme publishing or 'listing' right and eventually ceased publication. The break-up of the listings monopolies was described in 11.4.

TV was popularized by the coronation of Queen Elizabeth II in June 1953, and from then on TV became less of a luxury for those who could afford it and increasingly the major form of entertainment for the mass of the population. Council housing estates became jungles of TV aerials. Today, this western enjoyment of TV contrasts greatly with that in developing countries where TV is often an elitist medium, sometimes limited by the availability of electricity.

The growth of the medium, aided by the renting of receivers, raised a clamour for additional channels to be made available by the Post Office for programmes subsidized by advertising. These proposals were fiercely resisted by the press, especially by the *Daily Express*, because loss of advertisement revenue was feared. The Advertising Association found itself in a difficult position, and having so many large publishers among its subscribing members it was obliged to adopt a neutral role in the controversy. Consequently, the industry's advisers to the Government were the Institute of Practitioners in Advertising, representing the advertising agencies, and the Incorporated Society of British Advertisers, representing the advertisers, both of whom had a vested interest in the new medium.

It was decided that advertisers should not produce the present programmes, but that programme contractors should supply the programmes and sell time for advertisements that would appear in 'natural breaks'. Thus, in 1955, the UK had 'commercial' and not 'sponsored' TV. Although only six minutes advertising per hour is permitted, and the breaks do not usually exceed two minutes, the commercials imposed a new styling of programmes. Plays had to be written with acts of a length which permitted the appearance of the commercials. Symphony concerts were almost impossible. Unlike the cinema, films that were normally continuous became, on ITV, subject to breaks. However it has to be remembered that ITV (meaning independent television, there is no organization of those initials apart from the ITV Association which represents the contractors), comes to us by courtesy of the advertisers. The annual TV licence pays only for the BBC TV, although one cannot opt out of the licence payments on the grounds that one will never watch BBC. The next major development was the introduction of colour transmissions in November 1969.

The original TV contractors had their licences renewed for a further three years in July 1964, but in other years when new six-year contracts were awarded there were some changes. Under the *Broadcasting Act 1990* the Independent Television Commission (ITC) replaced the Independent Broadcasting Authority (IBA), with commercial radio now coming under the Radio Authority. The ITC took over in 1991 and its remit consisted of new methods, based on quality standards and an auction, for the issuing of franchises. This was highly controversial and generally considered to be unfair. Some former contractors, e.g. TV-am, Thames TV and TVS, lost to competitors.

There are 16 contractors covering England, Scotland, Wales, Northern Ireland and the Channel Islands with two London companies, one providing weekday and the other weekend programmes and breakfast time TV. These companies frequently combine to network programmes, and buy and sell programmes among each other so that, for instance, Londoners may see a programme produced by, say, Anglia, Granada or Yorkshire Television. Meanwhile the BBC and ITV compete to buy the rights to televise major outdoor events, although some items such as political broadcasts appear simultaneously on all channels. The contractors own between them Independent Television News (ITN) which produces networked programmes such as *News At Ten*.

It is therefore a *regional* medium, attracting local advertisers but being available to larger advertisers who wish to use part or all of the network. Rates are therefore based on the different-size audiences in each region, and even when running a networked campaign it is more like buying space in a number of regional newspapers than the whole circulation of a national daily or Sunday. Rates are also based on time segments since the size of audiences varies at different times of the day and on different days.

Special techniques are applied to TV such as the 'break through repetition factor' or 'rate of strike'. It depends on the commercial, but it may be possible to reach 86 per cent of the total audience with four exposures and 90 per cent of that audience may be likely to see the advertisements a second time with ten exposures.

In February 1983, the BBC introduced breakfast television, followed a fortnight later by the commercial TV-am. As the latecomer, TV-am had to struggle for audiences, and a dispute over repeat fees for actors in commercials since advertisers thought smaller audiences justified lower repeat fees. The quarrel also concerned Channel Four, introduced in November 1982, as an alternative commercial channel with smaller audiences than the established ITV. Television generally had to compete with forms of alternative viewing, such as video games and home computers, and 'time-switching' with VCRs, plus satellite television and cable television. TV-am also lost its contract in 1991.

11.13   ITV contractors as licensed in 1991

The contractors awarded contracts in October 1991 and these are listed in Table 11.3.

Table 11.3   *Regional TV contractors*

Contractor	Region
Anglia Television	East of England
Border Television	Scottish/English borders and Isle of Man
Carlton Television	London: Monday–Friday 5.15pm
Central Television	East and West Midlands
Channel Television	Guernsey and Jersey etc.
Grampian Television	North Scotland
Granada Television	North West England
HTV	Wales and West
LWT (London Weekend Television)	London: Friday 5.15pm – Sunday
Meridian Broadcasting	South and South East England
Scottish Television	Central Scotland
Tyne Tees Television	North East England
Ulster Television	Northern Ireland

Westcountry TV	South West England
Yorkshire Television	Yorkshire
plus	
Sunrise Television	National Breakfast television
Channel 4	National
Channel 5	Semi-national (1994)

According to BARB (1990) the total number of ITV households is 21,257,000.

At the time of writing Channel 5 is an enigma. It is another of the Thatcher legacies resulting from the ill-conceived *Broadcasting Act 1990* that proposed an additional commercial channel which would become operative in 1993. This has been postponed to 1994, bids being invited in January 1992 for a 10-year franchise to be awarded in mid-1992. While the ITC does not make it obligatory to broadcast regional or local programes, the semi-national nature of its coverage suggests this. In order to compete with other popular channels it will need to be a mass appeal channel. This new network suffers from vagaries of transmission capabilities.

Michael Grade, chief executive of Channel 4, described Channel 5 as 'the biggest dead duck in history'. It does have three major handicaps. Thirty per cent of viewers will not be able to view the new channel due to frequency interference from France, thus eliminating many south coast and north London viewers (unless watching by cable at extra cost). Moreover, it will be broadcast on frequencies usually used by airport radar systems and radio microphones. New aerials will be required by most of the people living in the 70 per cent of the UK covered by Channel 5, and half of these people would need to retune their VCRs because of interference from Channel 5. This retuning is likely to cost the franchise holder up to £100m. These details were contained in an article by Steve Clarke on the media page of *The Independent* of December 11 1991.

The new channel will use two spare frequency bands, channels 35 and 37, but cover only about 70 per cent of the population because of the limited frequencies available. In contrast, BBC and ITV and Channel 4 use some 51 main sites with 900 relay systems. Using only about 32 local transmitters it may be attractive to local advertisers. Areas unable to receive Channel 5 will include parts of the South East outside London, parts of the South Coast, parts of East Anglia around Cambridge, and mountainous areas such as Wales and Scotland.

11.14 Sponsorship

As described, together with the ITC Sponsorship Code in Chapter 23 a new form of sponsorship has evolved ranging from PowerGen's support for ITV weather reports to Croft Port's sponsorship of the *Rumpole* series and Barclaycard's sponsorship of the long-running holiday programme *Wish You Were Here*. *Campaign* (April 26 1991) was caustic about this kind of sponsorship, especially regarding PowerGen. Mark Edwards said: 'The logo is subtle and hard to find. It just wafts across the opening title sequence. You could easily miss it. In other words, it bears no relation at all to conventional notions of good advertising. What it does bear at least is a passing relationship to something that sells so well that it is usually legislated against – subliminal advertising'.

11.15 TV artistes, presenters and soap operas

A feature of commercial television has been its use and in some cases creation of star performers. Many famous artistes have lent their voices to voice-overs, and over the past thirty years many famous voices have made the chimps vocal in the Brooke Bond PG Tips chimp commercials, for instance Valentine Dyall, Peter Sellers and Bob Monkhouse.

A popular series consisted of 25 episodes of 'Beattie', a Jewish mother and hen-pecked family, played delightfully by Maureen Lipman. It was so realistic that many viewers grew to believe Maureen Lipman was as old as the character she played, which was somewhat inhibiting for her acting career.

However, the Lipman example is also representative of recognition of growth of the grey market with a combination of early retirement on the one hand and an ageing population on the other. Many of the characters in modern commercials are frequently middle-aged and less young and romantic, perhaps recognizing that a facet of recession is that young people are no longer the big spenders. Another example of this was the use of the actress Liz Smith playing a jolly granny in the *TV Quick* commercials.

11.16 Nineteen advantages of television advertising

1   Advertisements are presented in the home to a receptive family audience. The products are often those whose advertising will benefit from the home atmosphere in which the message is received, e.g. breakfast cereals.
2   Pictures can often tell more than words, and the TV advertisement can show and demonstrate the product. This is very true of motor-car commercials.
3   Movement attracts attention, and TV has the fascination of the movie. This action scores over the static picture on posters, in the press, or in direct mail or sales literature. It can be achieved by a variety of film, video, computer graphics and animation techniques.

4 Moving pictures of actual scenes, people and products have a realism with which only the cinema can compete.

5 There is sound, too, of voices, music or of noises characteristic of the product. This sound can be made memorable as with jingles, cartoon character voices, and the voices of presenters who become associated with the product.

6 Little effort is necessary to absorb commercials. Although not exactly the captive audience of the cinema, the more voluntary TV audience is nevertheless cooperative, taking in the two minutes of advertising in order to enjoy the continuation of the programme. This effortless viewing means that provided the advertisement does not bore or irritate, there is hardly any resistance: the advertisement it is almost hypnotic. The buying public can quickly be made familiar with a new product, thus overcoming one of the biggest handicaps in marketing a new brand.

7 A TV advertisement can be timed to appear in the segment when the right sort (or quantity) of audience is likely to be viewing, sports fans, children, housewives, families or adults after children have gone to bed.

8 The advertisement can be repeated with full impact on the same day, whereas a newspaper advertisement may be seen only once during its few hour's existence. The newspapers cannot present advertisements again and again, but advertisements can return to the screen perhaps three times in an evening, and be absorbed yet again in their entirety. Even if one reads a newpaper advertisement from beginning to end in the first instance one is unlikely to repeat this every time one sees the advertisement, whereas almost involuntarily the viewer takes in an entire 15, 30 or 60-second TV commercial each time it is screened. The repeated showing may also reach viewers who were not watching when the commercial appeared earlier, something which can be achieved only in the next issue of a newspaper.

Repetition is a particular phenomenon of TV advertising and serves a basic need of advertising. It is possible to seek a given number of audience ratings (TVRs) and to withdraw the commercial when these have been gained as revealed by the weekly BARB rating for programmes. After a rest, the commercial can be shown again until the required quantity of audience has been achieved. It has been one of the reasons for the success of the Brooke Bond PG Tips chimp ads. The furniture shifter one even made the Guinness Book of Records for its record number of showings. This spreads the cost of making the commercial and avoids boring viewers with prolonged repetitiveness. Again, some commercials are brought back and made to work after an absence of a year or more. The strategic re-showing of commercials is known as cyclical advertising.

9   Campaigns can be zoned according to TV areas which are also recognized marketing areas.

10   Zoned campaigns can be linked with other media such as direct mail regional press point-of-sale, posters and sales promotion schemes.

11   The medium lends itself to test marketing because the advertising can be extended realistically on a wider or national basis using the same techniques. Although some newpapers and magazines have regional editions, it is less easy to simulate national conditions with the press than it is with television. TV has thus removed certain objections to testing in a miniature market.

For test marketing purposes the Nielsen areas are useful since they approximate ITV areas or combination of areas and are not confined to ITV areas. These areas are: London, Anglia, Southern, Wales, West and Westward, Midlands, Lancashire, Yorkshire, Tyne-Tees and Scotland. Population figures for each Nielsen area are based on those of the Office of Population Censuses and Surveys (OPCS).

12   Sales promotion facilities are usually available. (The old expression 'merchandising' is still used by some ITV sales departments.) Most contractors try to make the advertiser's use of the medium as effective as possible by offering tie-ups in the form of 'as advertised on TV' display cards, postcards and giant telegrams sent to stockists to tell them about forthcoming commercials while studio receptions can be arranged when stockists can be shown previews of forthcoming commercials. There are two strong reasons for keeping stockists aware of TV advertising plans. Some retailers will stock only those products which are supported by TV advertising, or are more likely to stock up if there is promise of TV support. Retailers are themselves viewers as developed in **14**.

13   Audience figures are available through BARB. Contractors publish case studies of research conducted to prove the pulling power of particular TV campaigns.

14   Retailers also see TV. Because there is, in most areas, only one commercial channel (apart from Channel 4) and assuming that they are not watching BBC, cable or satellite, large numbers of stockists will also be aware of the advertising campaign and it can, therefore, serve a double purpose. They can also be influenced by members of the family who see the commercials.

15   Economical in relation to audience size. If penetration of the mass consumer market is required, TV offers immense multi-million coverage. It is the ideal medium for small unit repeat purchase goods bought by the majority of families. Even so, some remarkable successes have been achieved by advertisers of products as specialized as women's wigs and investments, and some large employers like Ford have found it an economical medium for staff recruitment.

16 Colour gives added realism. While it is true that colour is available in other media it is particularly effective in a medium so 'live' as TV. It makes the advertising look more natural and the product more appealing.

17 Colour aids pack recognition. This can help to overcome the time lag between seeing the advertisement and going shopping, colour helping to register the pack very clearly in the viewer's mind. It can also help to establish the corporate identity.

18 Colour brings out the attributes of the products as with paints, carpet patterns, wallpaper designs, styling of cars, and particularly with products that benefit from the choice of colours being offered. Foods such as cakes, soups and biscuits are made to look appetizing.

19 Less expensive spots are usually available to local advertisers. In recent years new advertisers have appeared on British TV screens. Led by Woolworth, retail stores have adopted the medium, while more expensive products such as motor-cars, video games, VCRs, television sets, computers, air travel and cruises have replaced some fast-moving consumer goods which have moved to sales promotion. Records, discs and tapes are sold on TV, orders being phoned in and handled by computer. Noticeable has been the greater variety of TV advertisers.

11.17 Nineteen disadvantages of television advertising

1 Television is an expensive medium, even on a regional scale, and this tends to limit it to those products likely to be bought by a majority of viewers, or where the repeated take-up of factory production is necessay as with detergents or even motor-cars, unless cheaper segments with smaller audience – the 'light' viewers – can be used economically.

2 Television production costs are high because the programme contractors very rightly insist that advertisements must be of the same technical standards as the programmes themselves. Shooting on location and the use of famous artistes can be costly.

3 Television advertising can be more irritating than other kinds. Because the commercials break up the programmes some annoyance may be caused unless the advertisements are amusing or interesting. Unfortunately the most frequent users of the medium can be the worst offenders, mainly because their products depend upon economies of scale and constant reminder advertising is necessary in order to induce the volume of sales required for optimum profitable output. In other words, the commercials have to be frequent and insistent if the price is to remain as low as it is.

Another problem is that the TV commercial has to be short if it is not to outstay its welcome on the domestic TV screen. This results in a lot of action being compressed into a short time so that it is very swiftly absorbed. One can see a cinema, documentary film or video more than once and see new things in it, but the truncated commercial tells its story so rapidly that repeat viewings can be tiresome. The commercial that can be seen time and time again without boring is a masterpiece of TV creativity. Some have a sequence of shots so rapid they are almost subliminal.

4   ITV programmes tend to be ones which can be broken into. Because of the necessity to show advertisements at prescribed intervals, many programmes (with the exception of old films) tend to be quiz shows, variety shows, chat shows and three-act plays which can be conveniently interrupted.

5   Impact is so great it can pall. A distinct weakness of the medium is that because of its transient nature it is necessary to repeat advertisements. Some advertisers cannot afford to produce a number of different commercials (like Guinness), and repetition of the same commercial can kill the initial novelty of even a very good one. The weary viewer is apt to complain, 'Oh, no, not again!' Passers-by seldom get bored with seeing the same poster despite its exhibition for maybe three months. It may be that the sound of TV is in some ways its undoing, especially when there is a particularly high-pressure presenter.

6   It is a transient medium, and the fleeting message cannot be retained for future reference. This may be overcome by advertising simultaneously in *TV Times*, as with holiday advertising, but this only points again to the inadequacy of the medium.

7   It is very difficult to attract enquiries and this can limit the exponents of the medium to those who do not wish to attract postal enquiries. However, telephone facilities are offered.

8   There is a long time-gap before purchase is possible. There is at least an overnight, and perhaps a weekend, time-gap before purchase can be made of advertised products.

9   Television cannot be watched while doing something else apart from a few things like eating, drinking or knitting. The required concentration limits the value of the medium to those times when people are prepared to sit in one room and watch.

10   The smallness of the screen does not permit the more dramatic effect of the large wide cinema screen, where the advertisements are strikingly superior to TV commercials.

11   It is an insidious type of advertising which sells by almost brain-washing, semi-subliminal repetitive sound techniques which make viewers brand conscious through their memorizing of jingles and sayings. When shopping, the housewife is apt to mentally hear the jingle when she recognizes the brand on the shelf. This is an

advantage so far as the advertiser is concerned, but TV advertising invites the social criticism of those who are worried about the manipulative powers of advertisers.

12 Catchphrases can work against the advertiser. There is the danger that a catchprhrase may became so popular that it is no longer credited to the advertiser. *'Nice one, Cyril!'* is a typical example.

13 TV lacks mobility, and there are physical limitations on viewing. There are portable TV sets, but generally speaking TV cannot be watched while travelling, eating out, or working about the house.

14 Too strong a presenter can attract more attention than the advertised product or service, as happened with the use of Joan Collins to promote a building society. In fact the use of famous performers may strain credibility.

15 TV screen time will be less and less available to audiences as video cassette receivers become more commonplace and viewers can play back recorded programmes, ones hired from video cassette libraries, or their own camcorder movies, while the Ceefax and Teleview systems of information broadcasting and receiving the written word at the touch of a button, can also reduce the time available for watching standard studio programmes. There will also be competition from interactive multi-media systems like Philips CD-I, now that these are being retailed to the general public. In the future it may be very difficult to know precisely what viewers are watching, and audiences may be less able and willing to watch commercials. According to BARB there are over 14,000,000 households with VCRs, representing 40 per cent of all TV households.

16 Zapping may occur, the viewer of ITV switching temporarily to BBC when the commercials appear. This is encouraged by the use of a remote control pad.

17 Research has shown that younger and more intellectual people watch less television than older people. While the 'over-50s' grey market is not insignificant, with an ageing population the viewing public is bound to include a large number of much older people with minimal pension incomes.

18 At a time when there is so much talk about diets and healthy eating it can be irritating to see one food after another being promoted on television. One sees breakfast cereals loaded with sugar, chocolate, meats, fast food restaurants and so on following one another on the screen even though we are constantly advised that they are bad for us. They can be as bad an influence as cigarette advertising which is banned from television.

19 The television viewer is less selective than the press reader because the viewer is usually a passive observer of all the advertisements in a commercial break. Their brevity invites this, but the newspaper ads reader chooses which, if any advertisements he or she wishes to read. Indeed, the advertisements may be a particular reason for

buying the journal, but no-one buys a TV licence to watch the advertisements on ITV. Thus, whether or not one has a pet one is subjected to cat and dog food advertisements, irrespective of the likelihood of ever flying to distant parts one has to sit through airline advertisements, and those who would never buy a popular tabloid newspaper are exposed to their advertisements. The alternative, of course, is to zap. With the press the teetotaller can turn the page advertising whisky, or at least any reader can read the editorial instead of the advertisements. Lord Leverhulme's famous remark that half his advertising expenditure was a waste of money but he did not know which half, is truer of television advertising where the wasteful half is obvious.

11.18   Future of television advertising

With the new ITC finding its feet in 1991, new franchises coming into effect in 1992, the introduction of new forms of sponsorship, the possible value of satellite television to British advertisers in the Single European Market, the growth of the grey market and the end of the yuppie market, and the long drawn-out effects of recession, a stagnant housing and house goods market, and large-scale unemployment, what is the likely fate of television advertising at the end of the 20th century? The future of television advertising is not very promising. It may have had its hey-day like the 3000-seater Odeon cinemas and cinema advertising. When TVS bid to renew its franchise in 1991, it put in an enormous offer based on extravagant predictions about future advertising revenue. In rejecting TVS the ITC obviously did not share its optimism.

The latest development in 1992 was BBC Select, offering a direct marketing service on television. Programmes are screened at night and the viewer can record selected programmes on a VCR for future viewing. The service accepts advertising and sponsorships, and appeals to niche markets. These are in-clear programmes which anyone can tape, and scrambled programmes which require an encoder, and for which a subscription is charged to select programmes for taping.

11.19   Satellite and cable television

Satellite television scores when it can provide better programmes than the terrestrial broadcasters and also (as in the USA) when it can offer programmes free of advertising. Sky television has been successful in continental Europe where it has been able to offer programmes superior to those put out by national stations, but it has failed to compete with the quality of BBC/ITV programmes in the UK, in spite of so many repeats. Its lack of success is shown by the small take-up since the introduction of Sky Channel in 1982, when the British-based British

Satellite Broadcasting (BSB), launched in 1990, survived only a few months and became merged with Sky as BSkyB. The BSB disaster cost its backers £1.3m and left a couple of unwanted satellites stranded 23,300 miles up in the sky.

Although satellite programmes were listed in the Murdoch-owned newspapers, and since BBC/ITV listings lost their monopolies, are listed in the TV/radio listing magazines e.g. *Radio Times, TV Times, TV Quick, What's On TV* and *TV Guide*), all this daily and weekly publicity has failed to popularize satellite TV in the UK. The main satellite programmes are Sky One, Sky News, Sky Sports, Comedy, Screensport, Eurosport, Children's Lifestyle and MTV Europe, Sky Movies and Movie Channel. However, BSkyB's attention to sport has succeeded.

In December 1991 ITC released viewing figures which showed that cable and satellite TV had fallen from 42.1 per cent in 1990 to 35.3 per cent in 1991.

Receipt of satellite television requires the fixing of a circular disc to the exterior of the premises. No fee has to be paid to watch the programmes.

It has been argued that colour TV and VCRs took five years to become popular, but they suffered the disadvantage of being expensive and unaffordable items until prices fell. By contrast satellite dishes are cheap and affordable but remain unpopular. They account for less than 4 per cent of total British TV viewing, which is not encouraging when TV generally is experiencing a decline.

Thousands of miles of British streets have been dug and cable laid ready to connect 14.5 million houses with cable television. Cable offers the advantages of first class reception of a large variety of programmes, BBC, ITV, cable and satellite. A monthly fee has to be paid for various packages of programmes, it costing most to watch Sky Movies and Movie Channel which are sometimes called pay movies. Cable, although available for many years, has not won popularity in the UK, probably because so many of its programmes are inferior to BBC/ITV programmes for which a licence fee is already being paid. This is demonstrated by the inducements offered by cable operators whose salesmen seem to have soul-destroying jobs like those trying to sell timeshare rackets or double glazing.

The channels available on cable television are:

All terrestrial channels	*Satellite channels*
BBC 1 and 2	Sky One
Channel 3 (ITV)	Sky News
Channel 4	Eurosport
Channel 5	Sky Movies
	The Movie Channel
Cable only channels	The Sports Channel

Discovery Channel
Cable Network News (CNN)
Super Channel
Bravo
Home Video Channel
Indra Dhush (Hindi)
Cable Juke Box

The Power Sation
Screensports
TV Europe
Lifestyle
Children's Channel
Japan Satellite TV (Europe)
TV5 (French)
Sat-1 (German)
VOA Europe
Worldnet

By means of cable (or 'Broadband' cable) many homes can actually receive up to 40 channels of television without use of a dish. Significantly, the hundreds of thousands of Japanese living or working in Europe can watch their own programme, Japan Satellite TV (Europe).

New satellite developments in 1992 ranged from TV Asia, broadcasting Indian films in Hindustani but with English subtitles to UK Asians, mostly women and children, to the Financial Times Television pan-European media show produced in conjunction with Super Channel. BBC Enterprises linked with Thames TV to launch a joint satellite screening repeat programmes by means of the Astra satellite.

11.20   Television world-wide

It has already been noted above that satellite TV now brings television advertising (and more viewing hours) to viewers in continental Europe. There are also satellite systems elsewhere in the world (apart from the USA) such as in the Gulf and the Far East. Cable Network News (CNN) has brought on-the-spot news of events (including wars and disasters) as they happen, and these news programmes are screened world-wide. Thus television of all kinds is reaching larger audiences world-wide. Only a few of the poorest Third World countries have no television, and even in some of these countries (e.g. Botswana) it is possible to watch programmes from neighbouring countries. Systems vary: there may be more sponsored programmes, more government control, advertisers may demand prime time so that commercials are clustered at peak viewing times, or they may be confined to certain segments. Imported foreign commercials may not be permitted, and commercials will have to be produced locally. Anyone contemplating television advertising in other countries, say, for export purposes, should check local conditions which are likely to be wholly different from those available in the UK.

11.21 Commercial and sponsored radio

History and development

Radio advertising is the most universal of all advertising media, and first came into prominence in the 1920s. Among the earliest commercials heard by British radio audiences were the Sunday lunch-time programmes from Radio Paris when Christopher Stone broadcast his programme of British gramophone records complete with sales information. In the pre-war 30s, when popular programmes on the BBC were limited to a Saturday night variety show and Arthur Askey's *Bandwagon*, Radio Luxembourg, Radio Paris, Radio Lyons, Radio Toulouse, Hilversum and other continental stations were presenting sponsored shows not unlike the American 'soap operas'. The late John Slater, of *Z Cars* TV fame, was an early radio performer when shows were recorded in London studios and flown over to the French transmitter.

However, the Second World War put an end to these broadcasts, the BBC Light Programme and Forces programmes adopted more popular entertainment, and after the war only Radio Luxembourg resumed sponsored programmes beamed on the UK. The attempt to run 'pirate' commercial stations on ships and forts off the British coast was quashed by the *Marine Broadcasting Offences Act, 1967*. One of these was operated by ex-advertising agent Ted Albeury, now the author of best selling spy thrillers. Once again, the BBC learned a lesson, realized the popularity of disc jockey pop music programmes, and created Radio 1 and Radio 2.

While radio advertising is commonplace in most other countries of the world it took 50 years for the novelty to reach the UK through the *Sound Broadcasting Act, 1972*, the *Independent Broadcasting Acts, 1973, 1974*, to the more recent *Broadcasting Act 1990*, the promotion of the Independent Television Authority to its dual status of Independent Broadcasting Authority and finally the separate Radio Authority of today. Perhaps the greatest novelty for British audiences was daytime commercial radio, since most of the overseas and off-shore broadcasting was at peak listening hours such as breakfast-time and Sunday afternoons, or late evening.

In 1969 the Conservative Party made an election promise that, if returned to power, it would create 100 commercial broadcasting stations. A curious thing about British politics is that the Conservative Party tends to be pro-advertising and anti-public relations, whereas the Labour Party adopts opposite policies. The Conservatives kept their promise, the first five being announced by Chris Chataway in 1971, and by 1984 there were 69 approved locations for ILR stations.

Four-and-a-half years after Capital Radio and the London Broadcasting Company first went on the air, John Thompson, director of radio for the Independent Broadcasting Authority, was able to tell a meeting of the Broadcasting Press Guild on February 22, 1977, that the total turnover of the the 19 commercial stations was £14.5m He reported that 14 million adults, about one-third of the adult population, listened to commercial radio each week, and that more than a million young people under 15 listened to commercial radio. Radio audiences tend to be most significant at times when the businessman is unlikely to be listening!

In recent years some stations have closed down through lack of advertising revenue; some have introduced split frequencies to reach different social grades or groups with different kinds of music; and specialist stations have emerged such as Jazz FM, Kiss FM and Melody Radio. Since radio tends to be town or city based rather than regional, its stations have smaller, more localized audiences then television.

More air-time is available to advertisers on radio than on television, up to nine minutes per hour compared with a maximum of seven minutes on television.

While sponsorship of whole programmes is common in many parts of the world, not forgetting the original soap operas of American radio, British radio has for several years permitted the discreet sponsorships now being accepted by ITV (*see* 19.9). Thus, the announcer will credit a sponsor for supporting, say, a traffic or City prices report. This was approved under the former IBA.

A report by Carat International into radio audiences in 16 countries in 1990 showed that the Greeks devoted 3.8 hours a day to radio listening, the Swiss 2.9 hours, and the Dutch 2.8 hours with the British coming fourth with 2.65 hours. Audiences were generally biased towards the male, younger and more up-market listener, this being the opposite to TV audiences which are biased towards female, older and lower social grades. The cost of radio advertising is about one fifth that of TV advertising.

11.22   Independent local radio stations

London has many ILR stations, the original ones Capital and LBC having split frequencies, Capital Gold and Capital Radio, and LBC News Talk and London Talk Back Radio. In London there is also Choice FM, Jazz FM, Kiss FM, London Greek Radio, Spectrum Radio, Sunrise Radio, and WNK Radio. Radio Luxembourg, after 58 years ceased beaming programmes on the UK at the end of 1991. Outside London the following groups operate:

Chiltern Radio Network: Chiltern Radio (FM), Northants Radio (FM), Supergold AM, Horizon Radio (FM).
Radio Clyde: Radio Clyde 2 (AM), Radio Clyde 1 (FM), NorthSound radio (FM/AM).

County Sound Radio: First Gold Radio (AM), Premier Radio (FM)
East Anglia Radio: Radio Broadland (FM/AM); Suffolk Radio Group:
Radio Orwell (FM/AM), Saxon Radio (FM/AM).
Radio Forth Group: Radio Forth RFM (FM), Max AM, Radio Borders
(FM), Radio Tay (FM/AM).
GWR Radio Group: GWR FM(West), GWR FM (East), Brunel Classic
Gold (AM), Plymouth Sound (FM/AM), 2CR FM, 2CR Classic Gold
(A), 210 FM, 210 Classic Gold (AM).
Midlands Radio Group: CER: BRMB-FM, Mercia-FM, Xtra-AM;
Radio Trent Group: Trent-FM (Nottingham), Trent-FM (Derby),
Sound-FM, GEM-AM.
Mid-Anglia Group: Hereward Radio (FM/AM), CN-FM (FM).
Metro Radio Group: Metro FM, TFM, GNR.
Southern Radio Holdings: Ocean Sound Group: Ocean Sound (FM),
The Light FM, The Gold FM, Power FM, Southern Sound Radio:
Southern Sound West, Southern Sound East.
Trans World Communications: Aire FM, Magic 828, Piccadilly Gold,
Piccadilly Key 103 (FM), Red Rose Rock (FM), Red Rose Gold (AM),
Red Dragon FM, Touch FM.
Yorkshire Radio Network: Hallam FM, Pennine FM, Viking FM and
Classic Gold (AM).

There is also Downtown Radio and Cool FM and Classic Trax BCR
in Northern Ireland, Marcher Sound, Red Dragon Radio and Swansea
Sound in Wales, Manx Radio in the Isle of Man, and Contact 94 in
the Channel Islands. In addition to the Radio Clyde and Radio Forth
Groups there are several other Scottish ILR stations. Within the British
Isles there are about 80 ILR stations.

11.23 National commercial radio

The nearest thing to national radio which used to exist was Radio
Luxembourg, which once had an audience as large as a popular daily
newspaper, but this has been splintered by the intervention of so many
local ILR stations, not forgetting that BBC Radio 1, 2, 3, 4 and 5 plus
numerous BBC local stations are also competing for listeners. Radio
Luxembourg re-emerged in 1992 by Astra satellite radio.

However, the *Broadcasting Act 1990* proposed two national commercial radio stations, presumably the political move to abolish the
BBC's monopoly of national radio. (This may be as regretted as the
auctioning of ITV franchises.) The first contract was announced by the
Radio Authority in 1991, but soon collapsed as funds were not
forthcoming, and another company was licensed with effect in 1992. At
the time of writing it is too early to make further comment. The Radio
Authority was obliged under the Act to award the first INR1
(Independent National Radio One) licence to the highest bidder which

was a consortium called Showtime, but the franchise was finally awarded to Classic FM, broadcasting to commence in the Autumn of 1992. In February 1992 the second franchise for a national commercial radio station was awarded to Independent National Broadcasting.

A weakness of ILR has always been that from the advertiser's point of view it was merely *local* radio and could not be compared with national newspapers, TV or posters. A national radio station can have greater credibility with potential advertisers.

11.24   Sixteen advantages of radio advertising

1   It is possible for the small advertiser to participate, compared with regional TV which can be too costly and wasteful because it covers too large an area.
2   Transmission is longer than TV. Radio broadcasts occupy a greater number of hours than BBC TV so that more people and more categories of people at different times of the day may be reached.
3   The use of the human voice is a big advantage over all silent media such as press, outdoor and direct mail. The copy can be spoken or treated dramatically, requiring little effort on the part of the listener to absorb the message. Radio voices have acquired characters of their own and broadcasters are recognized by their voices.
4   London Broadcasting (LBC) (news programmes) enjoys concentrated listening since its bulletins, phone-ins and interviews cannot be used for background effect. Advertising messages are likely to receive the same attention.
5   Other sounds can be used such as music or sound effects, adding to the impact or authenticity and realism.
6   Thanks to the transistor and car radio, radio advertising can be listened to almost anywhere. This creates an extensive range of possibilities for listening, large audiences and many categories of listener.
7   Radio can be listened to while doing something else. This is a major strength of commercial radio. Women in factories assemble equipment while listening to pop programmes, craftsmen on building sites or in workshops have their sets tuned in to all kinds of programmes, motorists enjoy the radio as they drive along, and perhaps most important of all housewives working about the house can take the radio from room to room, giving themselves company and entertainment to break the loneliness and monotony. This is not possible with any other medium. With radio it is literally possible to do two things at once.
8   The message can be quite detailed. Because it is not visual it is necessary for the commentator to give convincing word-picture detail, rather like a direct response advertisement except that the

      script-writing can be more catchy, alliterative and memorable.

9   Being associated with entertainment there is a connotation of pleasure, whether it be a sponsored programme where listeners are consciously attracted by a show presented by a named advertiser, or a spot in the break-in station programme. For many people, radio is a form of companionship.

10   Radio advertisements are inexpensive to produce, unless big star fees have to be paid.

11   According to the time of broadcast, the medium can be useful for appealing to specific types of listener, such as the 'drive time' commuter.

12   It is versatile in geographical coverage, national audiences being reached by either networking ILR or using the new national stations, while local areas and social grades/age groups in these areas can be reached through an individual station. The 'Gold' stations play more traditional light music or 'oldies' while the others play pop music.

13   It is a good medium for reaching young people, whether by means of Walkman radios or at home when young people prefer to listen to radio in their rooms rather than watch TV with their parents. Many young people living away from home have no TV set, but do have a radio.

14   Bonus coverage: commercial radio has the unusual bonus of additional audiences in neighbouring countries. Many people in the UK receive Radio Telefis Eireann and Manx Radio, while many Irish listeners tune in to British stations.

15   Commercial radio complements TV in several ways. Radio is mostly listened to outside the peak TV viewing hours, or at times of the day or in places where it is not possible or convenient to watch TV.

16   Young audiences tend to be equally divided between males and females like cinema audiences.

11.25 Six disadvantages of radio advertising

1   Unlike all other media there is no visual effect, neither static illustration nor moving picture.

2   Some presenters have irritating voices, tending to over-sell.

3   It is a transient medium. The message cannot be retained or returned to. It may be easier to write down an address given on radio than it is in the cinema, but it is less easy than when watching TV. It is probably impossible to note down information when mobile.

4   In developing countries where there are several language groups, radio may be limited to certain languages, whereas visual media such as posters and films can overcome language and literacy

difficulties by their use of pictures, cartoons and diagrams.

5 Advertisers often find it difficult to evaluate and appreciate radio advertising because it is intangible and they cannot see it or imagine people listening to it.

6 There is less temptation to switch stations with radio than there is with TV and a remote control handset. Most radios are pre-set to a limited number of desired stations so that there is reluctance to sample new or different stations. This inertia is one of the problems experienced by the newer specialized stations in their search for audiences. It is perhaps even more difficult than trying to sell a new magazine. This makes it all the harder to sell air-time to sceptical advertisers. These stations have no licence fee income like the BBC and rely on advertising revenue.

11.26 Cinema screen advertising

The cinema has a fascinating history. The silent films of the '20s were accompanied by a pianist who sat in the pit below the screen and improvised music to match the action above his or her head. Some cinemas introduced orchestras which played in the intervals when talkies arrived. When the huge 3000 seater Odeons and Gaumonts were built in many towns a new attraction was the Wurlitzer organ which rose out of the pit in the intervals. Some of the organists became famous and gave radio recitals.

By this time Hollywood was booming and cinemas were running three programmes a week, Monday to Wednesday, Thursday to Saturday, plus Sunday evening, from which grew the saying 'twice a week and once on Sunday' which was the pattern of many people's lives. A cinema seat cost only a few pence – for a three-hour show! The very big cinemas ran an A picture, a B picture (like the ones in which Ronald Reagan starred), and a half-hour stage show consisting of a big band, a variety show or even a circus. In these circumstances, when people queued up outside for hours to see a film like *King Kong* or *Hell's Angels*, cinema screen advertising excelled. It had a large captive audience.

During the immediate post-Second World War years (when rationing ended and food and clothing coupons ceased) cinema advertising flourished in hundreds of cinemas throughout the UK, and there were large family audiences interested in buying foods, drinks, clothes, washing powders and other consumer goods. Newsprint rationing continued for some years after the war and national press advertising space was still scarce in the 1950s. The regional dailies, poster and cinema screen advertising filled the gap. There was no commercial television and only a little radio advertising on Radio Luxembourg.

The death of the big cinemas and with them mass consumer cinema screen advertising came with the arrival of ITV in the late 1950s. Films and plays could now be seen at home. It was only the young people who 'went to the pictures'. To some extent the cinema has retaliated by converting some large cinemas into three small ones.

There are now more than 400 screens in the UK's multiplexes which consist of small cinemas with shops and cafes. The multiplex has revolutionized both audience figures and the prosperity of the cinema industry. Having several screens of different auditorium capacity it is possible for a multiplex to show a popular film to maximum audiences for perhaps up to 18 weeks while showing a less popular film to a screen with a smaller audience. Multiplex income is boosted by confectionery and food concessions from on-site shops and restaurants.

But, whereas a town like Croydon, with a population of 320,000, once had 15 cinemas and two theatres it now has only one cinema with three screens. The largest cinema-going age-group now consists of the 18–24s. However, although the number of screens now showing advertisements (other than multiplex) is down to about 50 compared with some 1600 in 1981, multiplex cinemas have created an increase of about a quarter of a million a year admissions since 1987, bringing total annual admissions up to nearly 90 million. The greatest frequency of cinema-going is among 15–24-year-olds, closely followed by 7–14-year-olds. Most cinema attenders do not attend on their own.

Studies of cinema-going are conducted annually by Cinema and Video Industry Audience Research (CAVIAR), which is run by Carrick James Market Research on behalf of the Cinema Advertising Association. Tables from this research are reproduced in *The Media Pocket Book*.

11.27 Buying cinema advertising

Cinema advertising time may be bought in minimum units of one week's advertising in one cinema. Commercials are screened within one reel which is shown in all performances during the week, after the interval, when house lights are down, and before the major film. Unlike television there are no commercial breaks while the film is showing.

Screentime varies between 10 and 60 seconds and in multiples of five seconds. Most campaigns run for several weeks. To avoid monotony an 'alternative week campaign' or 'one week in – one week out' pattern for each cinema is recommended. For regular campaigns two prints of the commercial are required for each cinema, and 10 per cent extra prints is advisable to cover breakages.

A number of screen selling agencies are listed in *Advertisers Annual*. Apart from public cinema screens there are screens on cruise ships, in Forces cinemas and in hotels which take adertisements. Two of the largest are Pearl and Dean Cinema Ltd who operate internationally, and Rank Screen Advertising. Rank, for instance, offer cinema advertising in 1,311 screens in England, Scotland, Wales and Northern Ireland, organized in 13 corresponding TV areas. To network a 30-second screen advertisement costs about £80,000 a week. Alternatively, showings can be based on the eight conurbation areas with 487 screens at a weekly cost of about £36,000 for a 30-second commercial.

Screentime may be bought subject to availability, at basic individual cinema rates (known as *line-by-line*), the minimum *one* week's advertising on any *one* cinema screen. Each cinema (screen) has its own individual rate geared to the level of admissions it attracts.

Advertisers wishing to target mass audiences may buy Rank's Audience Discount Passage (ADP) (Table 11.4), which offers substantial discounts for bookings which span an entire ISBA region (or group of such areas). An ISBA area is a net ITV area. Gallup supply an independent audit of UK admissions from which Rank supply advertisers with a specific campaign admissions statement, monthly in arrears.

Table 11.4 *ADP rate structure*

Time length (secs)	Index	London/TVS CPT	All other regions
10	50	£16.50	£12.50
20	80	£26.40	£19.40
30	100	£33.00	£24.20
40	133	£43.90	£32.20
50	167	£55.10	£40.40
60	200	£66.00	£48.40

The weekly cost is calculated by applying the percentage share of the candidate ISBA areas to the current all-screen weekly network admission average and multiplying this figure by the relevant cost per thousand rate.

Total screen advertising revenue rose from £16m in 1984 (representing 0.5 per cent of UK display advertising revenue) to £39m in 1990 (representing 0.6 per cent of UK display advertising revenue).

Screen advertising uses 35 mm film and most TV commercials which use this format can be readily adapted for cinema. If videotape has been used, the contractors can transfer this onto 35 mm film with excellent results. To give some idea of the number of prints required, 800 would be necessary for a networked Disney/U package.

Rank offer a number of packages to target specific niche audiences, such as the children's audience across the 18 school holiday weeks (primarily when the majority of Children's films are released) and the Art Screen package of classical film showings. Typical rates are shown in Table 11.5.

All advertisements submitted for cinema exhibitions must conform to the BCAP, and must be approved by the Cinema Advertising Association Copy Panel, preferably at script stage before prints can be released to cinemas. Commercials of 30 seconds or longer must also be submitted on VHS cassette or 35 mm film to the British Board of Film Classifications.

Table 11.5 *Disney/ U package*

Time period	No of weeks	Networked 30 second costs
February	2	£20,500
Easter	3	£28,000
May	2	£13,500
Summer	6	£57,000
October	2	£20,500
Christmas	3	£43,500
Total	18	£183,000

The Art Screen Package

London	25 screens	£2,824 per week, 30 seconds
Outside London	26 screens	£1,095 per week 30 seconds
Total Art Package	51 screens	£3,919 per week 30 seconds

11.28 Cinema advertising internationally

Although, for the reasons given in 11.25, cinema advertising has lost the power and popularity it used to enjoy, it thrives in other parts of the world or may be presented by means of different kinds of cinema. In some warmer climates the drive-in outdoor cinema replaces the roofed theatre of colder countries. There are also mobile cinemas in Third World countries which take film shows, including advertising films or videos – from village to village. Advertising videos are also shown with in-flight movies on many airlines flying international flights.

11.29 Twenty-two advantages of cinema screen advertising

1 There is a captive audience, better described as a 100 per cent medium concept. Apart from a tiny minority of cinema-goers who

may be arriving or leaving, buying ices and confectionery, or visiting cloakrooms, practically everyone in the audience must see the advertisements unless they deliberately shut their eyes. No other medium offers such concentration of attention, except possibly LBC with its news and talkback programmes.

2   The cinema screen wins greater concentration than the TV screen because the audience is confined to a darkened hall with no distractions, whereas TV is watched in ordinary home surroundings with domestic distractions. In a cinema even conversation is minimal.

3   There is a very large wide screen so that advertisements are dominating and impactive.

4   Whether live action or cartoon, there is movement, the great attraction of 'the movies'.

5   With music, jingles, commentary, and sound effects, or the actual sounds corresponding to the action, there is sound.

6   The subject of the advertisement can be demonstrated, whether it be a hairspray or a holiday camp.

7   Advertisements are usually in full colour and therefore look realistic.

8   Unlike commercial television, cinema advertising does not interrupt the entertainment. The completely isolated intermission with screen advertisements is far less irritating than the so-called natural commercial breaks on TV. In the cinema, advertising is deliberately restricted to what the contractors call the *peak point*. Commercials are shown the same number of times as the feature film so that they are seen by each audience.

9   Cooperative advertising is possible, a national advertiser inserting local stockists' names rather like cooperative advertising schemes in the local press.

10   Purely local advertising is possible, making this a useful medium for restaurants, estate agents, car-hire services and retail traders.

11   The contractors will provide stock material to minimize production costs for local advertisers whose names and addresses and voice-over effects can be added.

12   Zoned advertising is possible, but more precisely localized than if a single area were used. A campaign could be limited to a town or suburb or at least to a small area. This would be useful for backing up a weak sales area, and could be excellent for test marketing purposes since the medium could be used more expansively without altering its characteristics other than the social grade classification of the audience which would be different in, say, Brighton and Bournemouth.

13   As with TV, only more so, there is effortless acceptance of the pictorial message, which is quickly impressed on the mind.

14   The advertisement is seen in a pleasant atmosphere of entertain-

ment, and the medium uses the same techniques as the entertainment being enjoyed.

15 There is mild repetition so far as regular or frequent cinema-goers are concerned, which can have a powerful accumulative effect since cinema advertisements are usually run for a period of thirteen weeks.

16 Research has shown that this is a popular form of advertising with a high recall value. Seven days later, 50 per cent of cinema-goers interviewed have correctly recalled a screen advertisement.

17 The audience is subject to only a small number of different advertisements in the period of attendance which aids attention and ability to remember.

18 Cinema and TV advertising can complement one another, using the same basic film material, shorter on TV and longer on the cinema screen. This economic use of filmed material means that the costs of producing a cinema commercial are low.

19 Since competing products or services are not shown in the same set of commercials, the medium can be dominated by a single advertiser.

20 The medium lends itself to exporters whose products are widely sold overseas, and Pearl & Dean offer an international service that can reach some three hundred million people.

21 Since cinema-goers visit the cinema only from time to time they are less likely to be bored by repetitive advertisements as is possible with TV commercials which may be seen more than once on the same day, and again on successive days.

22 It can be a means of promoting brands on sale on, say, a cruise ship, in a Forces canteen, or as duty free items on an airliner.

11.30   Eight disadvantages of cinema screen advertising

1 Because the advertisements run for a period of time the same advertisements can suffer from the monotony of repetition and become boring to regular patrons who may even give them an ironic reception. This can happen with the more static slide-on-film or stock film type of local advertisement. Some local trademen's ads can be very crude.

2 Because of the audience characteristics, the things advertised tend to be limited in range of subject.

3 There is a lack of family audience, making the medium less suitable for mass-market consumer products than TV.

4 As with TV, this is a transient medium, incapable of using a long and detailed script. To be memorable, the message depends on catchy slogans, jingles and visual impact, yet unlike TV it lacks repetition during the same period of viewing. This latter point can be both a strength and a weakness.

5 Being transient, the audience cannot keep or refer back to the message. In the darkness of the cinema, and with even less likelihood of having pen and paper handy, it is virtually impossible to write down an address which might be done in the home following a TV commercial.
6 There is no guarantee of consistent audience figures which are dependent on the popularity of the film, time of year and even the weather. Available statistics tend to be either old or annual ones unlike the previous week's audience figures for TV.
7 With the small modern cinema, either purpose built or a large cinema converted into two or three theatres, the audience is small.
8 It is a medium which is deliberately limited to those who visit the cinema, and is isolated from the home or the street and from casual observers.

11.31 Outdoor and transportation advertising

How old is advertising? You might say as old as outdoor advertising because some of the earliest examples date back to Biblical, Greek and Roman times when advertisements for the sale of slaves or about events in arenas and amphitheatres were daubed on walls. Because of the beautiful pictorial designs used for posters, those on the street hoardings once bore the nickname 'the poor man's art gallery'.

Because this section will deal with many variants of outdoor and transportation media, two points will be clarified at the onset. First, these media are sometimes described rather generally in the UK as '*poster*' and in the USA as '*billboard*' advertising, although they are by no means limited to paper posters pasted on hoardings. In the UK, billboard refers, as explained later, to special kinds of *small* poster. In India posters are often referred to as 'postals' which is a confusion of terms. Postal advertising is direct mail. Second, although both outdoor and transportation advertising may use similar advertisement forms, e.g. posters, they are likely to be of different size, shape, content and audience, while the sites are mostly completely different. About the only absolute similarities are poster sites outside railway, airport, seaport, bus and coach premises which resemble poster sites in the street. The chief difference, however, is in the manner in which outdoor and transportation advertisements are seen and absorbed.

11.32 Differences between outdoor and transportation media

Although outdoor and transportation are dealt with separately in this section, it is important that the differences between the two be defined.

The main differences are as follows:

i   Outdoor sites themselves are mostly static, except for special vehicles which take advertisements from place to place such as those described in 12.7 Promotional Vehicles and Admobiles.
ii Transportation sites are often moving ones which carry advertisements over routes where they may be seen by a continually changing and accumulative audience. These sites include public service vehicles (buses and trams), minicabs and goods delivery vehicles, overland and underground trains, ferries and passenger ships. Airliners do not usually have displayed advertisements but they may be included in airline magazines issued to passengers or during in-flight movies.
iii The outdoor audience tends to be a passer-by one which cannot absorb much detail so that the content of outdoor advertisements needs to be brief. Exceptions are the smaller billboard (the British version being a small board as used for cinema advertisements) and the information panel as seen at bus stops.
iv The transportation audience, especially inside vehicles and transportation premises – stations, waiting rooms, forecourts, booking offices – is one willing to be interested, diverted and informed while waiting or travelling. Consequently, it can absorb more detailed messages, and accept them on smaller posters, cards or signs.
v   In the London area (and also in other large cities such as Paris with its famous Metro and the exceptionally attractive advertisements on the Champs-Elysees and other central stations and the Hong Kong MTR system) the Underground provides a very special medium with a large audience of commuters (especially young women), shoppers, cinema/theatre goers, and tourists (both UK and overseas). This is a unique medium.

From the above remarks it will be seen that by transportation advertising we mean all kinds of advertising on or in public transport, passenger or goods, and on or in transportation land or premises.

Outdoor advertising was defined in the *Town and Country Planning (Control of Advertisements) Regulations, 1948* as 'any word, letter, model, sign, placard, board, notice, device or representation, whether illuminated or not, used for the purposes of advertisement, announcement or direction'. It includes any hoarding or similar structure used or adapted for the display of advertisements. It also includes such forms of advertisement as a doctor's nameplate. The siting of outdoor advertisements must conform with the 1948 Regulations with their re-enactment in 1962.

Like radio, outdoor advertising is a universal medium and one of great value in developing countries where there are problems of many languages or illiteracy. Posters can be pictorial, conveying messages more effectively than words which have to be few in any case with this medium. In West African towns the poster is therefore an important medium for beers, cigarettes, detergents and aspirins.

In Asia, the poster has been a major medium in nation-wide family planning campaigns, the message being presented in various styles to cover local languages, customs and religions.

Slogans and cartoon drawings have been used on posters to create awareness and stimulate interest in family planning in India, so that whether the slogan was comprehensible or not the point was made by the child in the small family looking happy while his counterpart in the large family looked miserable. The Western world might learn much to its advantage from these techniques. Some of the Indian family planning slogans have been these:

> Two or three children – stop
> A small family is a happy family
> Three or two – that will do
> Next child not now – after three, Never

These positive appeals also had long-term value in that they sensitized schoolchildren to the idea that a two-child family was normal and beneficial.

This example is interesting because it demonstrates the qualities of the medium which we shall now examine more specifically.

The pictorially detailed posters in Malaysia demonstrate how super-sites can be used to convey sales messages to people who speak different languages.

A particularly eye-catching kind is the spangled or 'flutter' poster which appears to be constantly moving. Mostly seen in places like Indonesia, *flutter signs* have appeared occasionally in London such as in Piccadilly Circus.

On the continent, and especially in France, uni-poles, which are tubular-shaped poster sites on pavements or in shopping precincts, may be seen. These, too may be found in pedestrianised shopping areas in the UK.

A novel innovation in recent years has been the *ultravision* site consisting of a number of different advertisements produced on slats which revolve to present a succession of advertisements, thus giving movement to an otherwise static medium.

11.33 Poster sizes

Posters are mostly based on the minimum crown size, with multiples of this size resulting in terms such as 16-sheet meaning the size of 16 crown poster units. Posters are usually printed on larger sheets than normal paper sizes and trimmed to the actual poster size. However, a 16-sheet or other large poster is not printed on many crown size sheets but on a few sheets which the billposter pastes up to assemble as a whole poster. The standard sizes for both outdoor and transportation are given in Table 11.6.

Table 11.6 Posters (finished trim sizes)

	Millimetres	*Feet/inches*
Crown	500 × 381	20″ × 15″
Double Crown	762 × 508	30″ × 20″
Quad Crown	1016 × 762	40″ × 30″
Double Quad Crown	1524 × 1016	60″ × 40″
6 Sheets	1790 × 1190	$70\frac{1}{2}$″ × $46\frac{3}{4}$″
16 Sheets	3048 × 2032	10″ × 6′8″
32 Sheets	3048 × 4064	10′ × 13.4″
48 Sheets	3048 × 6096	10′ × 20″
City Information Panels	1750 × 1185	69″ × $46\frac{1}{2}$″
Adshel Superlites	1800 × 1200	71″ × 47″
Tube Car Panels	280 × 609	11″ × 24″
Escalator Panels	572 × 419	$22\frac{1}{2}$″ × $16\frac{1}{2}$″
Double Royals	1016 × 635	40″ × 25″

Posters are usually printed by litho or silk screen, and the latter process has become very popular with its modern ability to print full-colour posters with excellent reproductions of colour photographs and other artwork such as bus sides.

11.34 Types of outdoor advertising

The following are some of the most important forms of outdoor advertisements. Some of the more unconventional or fringe outdoor media are included in the following chapter on Below-the-Line, e.g. Aerial Advertising (12.6), Directional Maps (12.25) and Flags (12.28).

1 Hoardings

Mostly 16-sheet or larger, these are the large sites flanking the pavement which may be permanent or temporary in the case of building operations. *Gable ends* are similar sites on the corner walls of houses or shops.

2 Pedestrian housewife posters

This is the name given to the 4-sheet posters, often on vandal-proof vinyl material, on sites which architects have introduced into shopping precincts. The sites are either flat or circular (uni-pole) and some revolve.

3   Bulletin boards or supersites

These are large solus sites consisting of painted panels, specially built and usually well set out with gardens and floodlights. Special versions are those which are animated or given a three-dimensional effect with a cut-out figure or replica of the product, or made to glow by means of a backlighted translucent surface, while the *rotary system* allows a set of designs to be shown in rotation among the selected sites. Bulletin boards should not be confused with the little bulletins or notices pinned up outside public places, as when a member of the Royal Family is ill, or when there used to be an execution at a gaol. Bulletin boards are about the same depth as a 16-sheet poster but may extend for 27 ft, 36 ft or even 45 ft and make very impressive advertising sites.

4   Public information panels

These are also found in shopping precincts and on pavements, and the panels carry the smaller double-crown posters. Similar panels are available on bus shelters.

5   Billboards

Small portable or fixed boards for double-crown or quad crown posters as used by cinemas, they are sometimes used for temporary announcements.

6   Signs

These are almost a medium on their own. They range from moving, coloured, lighted signs like the famous ones of Piccadilly Circus, to metal plates, glass boxes and advertisements painted on walls, bridges or any other publicly situated flat surface. They also have special uses as when contractors announce the work they are doing, e.g. landscape gardeners, heating engineers, painters and decorators, scaffolding contractors, steeplejacks, builders and civil engineers. Architects, having to follow a professional code regarding advertising, are permitted to use only a stylized announcement which may be observed whenever building work is in progress. In post-war years, with so many new estates, high-rise flats, office blocks, motorways, bridges, tunnels and docks under construction, the contractors' sign has become an important advertising medium, and where numerous sub-contractors are involved very large 'credit' signs are erected. Tower cranes often carry a sign in the form of the contractor's name, or logo, positioned at the rear end of the arm and usually illuminated at night.

7   Flutter sign

(*See* 11.31.)

8   Newscasters

Placed on high buildings in city centres or at main-line stations, these electronic signs spell out news flashes in lighted strips, interspersed with advertisements. They are not to be confused with sound broadcasting systems on railway stations – the ones used to apologize for the late arrival of your train!

9   Meter Ads

An innovation is parking meter advertisements, a medium conceived by Tamlint Promotional Services Ltd of Manchester. Their appeal is that people passing a line of meters see a message repeated every 15 seconds. However, with the removal of many meters and their replacement by pay-and-display ticket dispensers, this is a diminishing medium.

10   Ultravision sites

(*See 11.31.*)

11   Uni-poles

(*See 11.31.*)

12   Giant billboards

Mention of overseas uses of outdoor media invites the inclusion of the huge, hand-painted portraits of Hollywood stars which have appeared on the Sunset Boulevard and elsewhere in the USA.

13   Projected advertisements

Very effective, these are slides projected from one building to a blank wall opposite, and flashed on and off. They are forbidden in UK streets, but may be seen in shopping precincts and inside buildings. In other countries, where they are not deemed a traffic hazard, they may be seen in the street.

14   Litter bins

These can be seen attached to lamp-posts. They combine usefulness with advertisements which serve a double role in attracting attention to both message and bin. Or companies may donate bins which stand on the pavement and bear the name of the donor.

15   Puppet shows

This is an Indian medium which provides entertainment while conveying a message, and is yet another method used in the family planning campaign. One such show tells how the rich man of the village has a large family, rejects the family planning campaign, but when his wife has twins and there are complications he calls in the midwife who tells him that his wife will not survive more births. He accepts the family planning advice, and so becomes the innovator in his village. These are a form of oramedia.

16   Arena boards and banners

Arena boards occupy the perimeter of a football pitch or other sportsfield, that is between the arena and the spectators. These boards may be seen by spectators but will also be picked up by the camera if the event is being televised. They may be displayed regularly or for a season, or for a special occasion only. Boards may also be erected beside race courses and motor racing tracks, especially by sponsors of events or participants, and advertising banners may also be displayed.

11.35   Twenty-one advantages of outdoor advertising

1   The size and dominance of posters, bulletin boards and signs is a great advantage. It is difficult not to see and even subconsciously receive the larger than life sales message.

2   The position of outdoor advertisements is also very often dominant. Hoardings are placed beside main roads, in shopping centres, on the gable ends at street corners, and bulletin boards and the slatted revolving Ultravision sites occupy exceptionally prominent positions such as at crossroads and roundabouts.

3   Outdoor advertisements are nearly always in colour which apart from its attractiveness, impact and realism, makes possible pack recognition which is important in either reminder advertising or when posters are linked with a TV campaign. It also means highly attractive advertisements in otherwise drab surroundings.

4   Long life and exposure. Signs make the most of coloured lights, whether those of, say, Piccadilly Circus or at a local filling station. A feature of Hong Kong are the posters on bamboo structures which project above the street and are lit up at night. Posters can be exhibited for a week, a month or two or three months. 'Rotary' bulletin boards consist of painted panels which can last for a year simply by changing sites every three months. Many signs are

permanent or are seldom changed. An outdoor advertisement therefore works very hard and it is there all day and all night, a continuous saturation medium. Moreover, large sites are floodlit, and there are four-sheet sites in shopping precincts which are back-lit. There is nothing transient about this medium nor is it short-lived like a newspaper.

5   There is a great repetition value because posters are distributed at numerous vantage points so that there are many 'adult passages' and members of all social grades, ages and both sexes have repeated opportunities to view the same advertisement. In this way, a poster campaign is likely to be seen by all people who are able to leave their homes. Electric signs and newscasters, being in well visited locations such as city centres or railway termini, are likely to be seen repeatedly. Since one of the secrets of successful advertising is reiteration, outdoor advertising obeys this criterion supremely well.

6   There is high coverage. With 80 per cent of the population in the UK living in urban areas, posters and signs are seen by almost everyone. It is a universal medium without peer in its ability to be seen. Moreover, outdoor advertisements will be seen by people who might never see announcements for the same product in the press media chosen for a campaign. In developing countries, where either illiteracy or language problems may mean small circulations of newspapers and magazines or lack of television, the pictorial poster can convey its message to all and so gain wide coverage. Even illiterates can 'read' pictures. In Malaysia, posters are exceptionally pictorial. Posters are successful in countries like Nigeria where there are some 62 languages.

7   Geographical flexibility can be organized. Nowadays poster advertising is based on marketing areas which become campaign planning units. These marketing areas define the normal weekly limits of the movements of people living within them and a poster campaign consists of a number of sites so placed to take account of movement of people. Each marketing area campaign is a complete unit, consisting of sites concentrated in the marketing area.

8   The availability of sites is quite good, over 50 per cent of all sites changing hands in the course of a normal year. This is worth remembering because it is sometimes thought that big advertisers monopolize the best sites, and this is not always true. Moreover, new sites are always forthcoming as when hoardings are erected to obscure a building site.

9   For the national fmcg advertiser – foods, confectionery, beers, detergents, petrol – the medium in all its forms lends itself to continuous all-the-year-round coverage. It has also been used in the shorter term to launch new motor-cars.

10   It is also a medium which lends itself as a secondary medium, complementing primary media such as the national press, TV or radio, providing a link between them and the point-of-purchase.

11   By judicious use of sites through marketing centres, a modest national campaign can be provided for a small or medium-sized advertiser.

12   For advertising agencies it places their creative work on public show in a manner which demonstrates their artistic abilities. Equally, it means that the agency must be capable of producing work worthy of such a public showcase. Few advertisements are likely to be judged more critically for artistry and originality. The Guinness posters, for example, have a history of ingenuity. Many posters are collectors' pieces and some advertisers even sell copies.

13   It is a useful medium for launching a new product on a national scale at low cost. Dreft, the washing powder for woollens, was launched by means of posters when newspaper space was scarce in the 1950s, owing to the continuation of wartime newsprint rationing.

14   Zoned campaigns are possible to support test marketing schemes, a national campaign being easily simulated, or to give sales boosts in certain areas.

15   Posters are also excellent for short-term campaigns such as for entertainments, sports meetings, exhibitions and concerts. It is possible to buy colourful double crown poster blanks which can be overprinted with details of the event. Companies which conduct sponsorships often gain reciprocal publicity by supplying posters naming themselves as the sponsors.

16   Compared with other media, much can be done for a small expenditure so that advertising appropriations can be stretched a long way.

17   Lighted signs, including newscasters, have the extra attention value of movement and novelty so that people are encouraged to stop and watch the advertisement. In Paris, the combination of several advertisers within one neon sign, offers an interesting variety. There are also three-dimensional supersites which have added interest.

18   Because of their brevity, messages are easily memorized and many poster slogans are remembered for a long time, e.g. 'Guinness Is Good For You' which the company has not used in the UK for many years.

Guinness Is Good For You originated in 1929 and is said to have emerged from research when people were asked why they drank Guinness. In the 1930s it was actually recommended by doctors – hardly likely today when patients are warned not to drink!

19   When other media (e.g. press or TV) are used for seasonal campaigns outdoor advertisements can be used to maintain an

all-the-year round continuous link so that the brand is not withdrawn from the public mind.

20 In spite of the long life and exposure of outdoor advertisements they seldom bore, and probably it is the one form of advertising which does not provoke public criticism or resentment.

21 The medium is excellent for pan-European advertising campaigns because the poster message is simple and visual and overcomes linguistic and cultural misunderstandings. It is simpler to mount a pan-European poster campaign than a TV campaign with its fragmented audience. The French media giant Avenir Havas Media (AHM) offers pan-European poster packages covering the capital cities of eleven countries.

11.36   Ten disadvantages of outdoor advertising

1 The biggest disadvantage of outdoor advertising is that the message – the copy – has to be short if it is to be big enough to be read at a distance. Usually it is confined to three elements, a slogan or statement, a picture, and the advertiser's name. The exception to this is the double crown or quad crown on a billboard or public information panel, advertising an auction or an entertainment, and more copy is possible on the four-sheets in shopping precincts.

2 The poster audience is a moving one, hurrying about its business, and taking in outdoor advertising in a very casual and secondary fashion. Very little concentration can be expected, and although research can show the journeys people make and ability people have shown to recall poster messages, it is not a positive medium which can produce enquiries or directly related sales.

3 Posters are subject to the vagaries and effects of the weather. When posters become soaked the print of the covered-up poster shows through. Inks can fade under intense sun. Bad weather can dirty posters, although the contractors do provide a replacement service and extra posters are always supplied for this purpose. Moreover, on wet days people carrying umbrellas cannot see posters.

4 Posters are liable to mutilation, damage and alteration. Vandals will rip posters, young comedians will add moustaches to faces, and protesters have been known to deliberately overlap wording with political slogans in matching lettering. For the four-sheet sites in shopping precincts, vandal proof posters can be supplied printed on vinyl.

In 1991 *The Economist* displayed 50 three-dimensional posters in London, each one bearing a large plastic fly – a fly on the wall – but within a few days more than half of these flies were removed by hooligans who cut through the steel bolts by which the flies were fixed. Meanwhile, another controversial Benetton poster showing a priest kissing a nun was vandalized in France.

5 Colours may not only fade as a result of the weather but become temporarily distorted under certain kinds of street lighting, a nuisance when the colour of the pack is an important recognition factor.

6 Such advertisements are best for products which can benefit from name plugging and pack recognition – to habit purchases – and this minimizes the range of products which can effectively use the medium. It is of little use to services, with perhaps the exception of banking.

7 It is suitable only for long-term campaigns (except perhaps for local showings of double crown bills). It takes a fairly long time to prepare an outdoor campaign. First the designs have to be drawn, approved and artwork finished up. Then it may take up to eight weeks from artwork to delivery, and the contractors require delivery five working days prior to either the start or the change of the displays. All this can take three months. If sites are booked for long periods, long cancellation periods are required, generally three months' notice. However, some contractors have introduced 14-day campaigns.

8 There are censorship restrictions, in addition to the BCAP, and the contractors may refuse any poster which it considers unsuitable or they prefer not to show, such as advertisements which are hostile to others – for example anti-smoking posters!

9 Another problem with outdoor advertising is that sites are scattered throughout the country and the value of such advertising is even less easy to evaluate than, say, local newspaper advertising.

10 Unless illuminated, posters can be effective only in daylight, and few people may be about after dark.

11.37 OSCAR

The acronym OSCAR stands for Outdoor Site Classification and Audience Research. This includes all four-sheet or larger poster panels at roadside sites or pedestrian areas, a total of some 120,000 panels. The research is based on a 100 per cent census by National Opinion Poll (NOP) under the tripartite Joint Industry Committee for Poster Advertising Research (JICPAR). It provides Cover and Frequency data for roadside poster panels, the audiences of panels being measured, care being taken that panels are reasonably well spread to avoid audience duplication.

An example of the OSCAR service is coverage and frequency data for more than 200 sociodemographic groups which can be calculated for size or length of a roadside poster campaign through the on-line computerized OSCAR system. Thus the advertiser can get the campaign he wants to suit his objectives.

11.38 Transportation advertising

Although the same 16-sheet poster, seen on a street hoarding, may also be seen on hoardings in a railway station forecourt or across the tracks on all Underground railway station, it is displayed through the medium of transportation advertising, not outdoor advertising. Much of it would be better described as *indoor* advertising. The distinction is necessary because with transportation advertising we are addressing the travelling public, not just any passer-by in the street whether on foot or using a vehicle. This distinction can be taken even further: travellers are temporarily in a different environment which inevitably contains periods of time spent waiting for the train to arrive or, once aboard, for it to travel to its destination. This means that advertising can present sales messages to audiences willing to be interested, amused or informed, audiences which for the time being are not concentrating on something else and which are mentally disposed to pass the time reading the advertisements. Not every advertising medium possesses this appeal.

There are, of course, exceptions. Some people read newspapers or books while travelling. Others study papers to do with their work. Some talk to companions or other travellers, but the British are not eager to converse with strangers. Some sleep. Others are morbidly worried about missing connections and getting stranded. But all these people are more likely to notice, read and remember at least some of the advertising displayed during their journeys, especially as the advertisements are usually displayed for anything between one and thirteen weeks and will be seen repeatedly. Many people, such as commuters, travel daily by public transport. Only the blind are immune to transportation advertising.

One curious paradox does exist concerning this medium, and it is one that defies the statistics of the contractors. There is sometimes least opportunity to study advertisements when the audience is most numerous! When the contractors claim that millions of people travel by Underground every day, this could be a disadvantage! It is well nigh impossible to read advertisements on the Underground in the rush hours, when commuters are packed tightly into compartments and pressed densely on platforms, in lifts and on escalators. Some advertisers have met this problem by using *spectaculars*, the huge posters built over the escalators and thus over the heads of travellers. However, the travelling public is not confined to rush hours, while advertisements on the exteriors of buses confront large audiences in busy streets.

Transportation advertising includes:

1   Buses: all advertisements inside and outside vehicles, in waiting rooms, bus stations and yards.
2   Trains: in compartments, on station platforms, in booking halls, forecourts, station approaches, and on land owned by the railway company such as beside tracks or facing roads.
3   Underground: in booking halls, concourses, lifts, corridors, on escalators, on platforms and across the tracks, and in compartments.
4   Airports and seaports: outside and inside buildings.
5   Goods vehicles: posters on sides of vans.
6   Taxicabs: externally and internally.
7   Ships and ferries: display panels.
8   Tickets, e.g. recycled plastic tickets on Hong Kong MTR.

11.39   Nineteen advantages of transportation advertising

These remarks are not limited to the UK. Public transport is universal. There are trams in continental European cities, and Hong Kong's trams are world famous. Underground railways operate outside London in the UK, in places like Paris, Rotterdam, Hong Kong and Singapore.

1   The message on a public service vehicle is carried to an ever-changing audience over many miles and is constantly moving among people. Bus routes take mostly main roads well frequented by people. Certain routes can be chosen. Underground trains traverse the metropolis and suburbs and overground trains travel the country. Taxis travel everywhere.
2   People are attracted by moving objects. Buses and trams are big and attract attention so that advertisements on them are noticed. People wait for and watch out for public transport vehicles, and advertising on them is looked at.
3   Passengers in buses, trams and the trains are provided by advertisements with something to do and to occupy their minds. There are opportunities for amusing advertisements as may be seen with the 16-sheet posters 'across the tracks' on the London Underground. Many travellers are temporarily unoccupied, perhaps bored. Advertisements are, therefore, favourably received.
4   Because people are waiting, whether standing or sitting, and have time to pass a more detailed advertisement can be used because people can stop and read it. This presents a major difference between outdoor and transportation posters. Whereas outdoor posters are seen at a distance and cannot, therefore, carry copy in small lettering, the posters on a platform wall can resemble a newspaper advertisement in quantity of wording which can be read at a short distance. Thus we have informative, sometimes quite subtle copy, in contrast to the necessarily brief slogans on posters on the hoardings in the street.

5   There are more than 250 London Underground stations and sites can be selected according to traffic. There are A, B and C gradings of stations at different rates and in both the A and C classes there are some 100 stations. The stations nearer to and in the centre of London have traffic throughout the day.

6   On road vehicles advertisements can be placed on certain routes – ideal for recruitment by employers on the route, to advertise local newspapers, or to attract shoppers to stores passed by the bus.

7   British Rail stations can be selected according to the local or regional needs of a campaign.

8   Bus companies, routes, trains and stations can be selected to coincide with TV regions so that transportation advertising can be used as a secondary and complementary medium.

9   National campaigns are possible on buses and railway stations, using the combined services of the various contractors.

10 New ideas are making this medium increasingly attractive. Four-sheet lightboxes combine the twin attractions of colour and illumination, giving extra impact to posters in poorly lit places or forming part of the architectural design of modern station concourses. Illuminated bus sides extend viewership, and extra impact is gained with illuminated bulkhead advertisements in the lower deck saloons of buses. Spectaculars have been mentioned already, but they are not confined to the Underground and dominant 48-sheet illuminated sites are available on other stations. The painted bus or tram is a familiar sight in many parts of the world, and there is also the bus on which all the normal advertisement positions are monopolized by one advertiser. Streamer lightboxes have been incorporated into redesigned stations. A very old device, the banner, is used as a striking advertisement on rail station concourses, platforms and facades, and at bus stations.

11 It is a flexible medium, equally valuable to national, regional or local advertisers who can choose sizes, positions and quantities of displays according to their needs. A national advertiser might take giant illuminated sites at rail, sea and air terminals, or bus sides throughout the country, or on the tables of Intercity dining cars, while advertisers operating in more limited areas can determine stations and routes to suit their campaigns. Some very successful campaigns have been conducted solely on the London Underground, using no other media, e.g. swimwear.

12 Advertisements can be directed at particular markets by the skilful use of particular sites, for example:

Escalator cards: appeal to thousands of young women using the London Underground.
Posters on bus windows nearest entry: appeal to shoppers, including those on bus stops. Small double-sided posters can be used.

Roof cards in Underground carriages: appeal to secretaries and other young women, advertising employment agencies, secretarial courses, engagement rings, building societies.

Upper-deck bus advertisements: appeal to men.

Double-crown/quad crown posters on stations: appeal to cinema, theatre and concert-goers.

Lower rears on buses: interest motorists travelling behind and are useful for advertising car accessories, such as sparking plugs, batteries and brake pads.

Pullman car material: businessmen can be appealed to by means of bookmatches, leaflets, menu cards and cut-outs.

Bridge spans: appeal to motorists and are more dominant than bus lower rears and rear waistbands.

Timetable frames on bus stops: useful for local traders who can appeal to waiting passengers.

Bus sides: good for reminder; outdoor-type campaigns, such as for teas and coffees. The double deck T-sides are used by such advertisers.

Bus fronts: good for newsy announcements because of their dramatic position. But posters with small print which are suitable for station walls should not be put in high-up positions on fronts and backs of buses. Some 'teaser' campaigns have used bus fronts.

Banners: excellent for dramatic announcements.

Spectaculars: very suitable when the advertiser wishes to be noticed by hurrying commuters. They can hardly be missed by users of escalators.

13   Short-term campaigns are possible. Some retail traders command attention and interest by having regular weekly changes of poster. For example, a supermarket could make special weekly offers on the backs of buses, while an exhibition promoter might use the sides of buses for a month. It is usually the smaller size posters that are changed frequently.

14   Static road sites owned by the transportation authorities can be used to augment an outdoor advertising scheme, especially the giant bulletin boards or supersites. Some of these are beside the tracks of overland trains.

15   The ability to offer isolated, solus advertisements is a strong characteristic of the medium. Buses and trams can be large, dominant and solitary advertisement sites.

16   Transportation advertising is a fairly effortless medium in that it can be absorbed by a more or less captive audience, but unlike some media which have to compete for the effort to be noticed and studied, this medium is capable of attracting both involuntary and voluntary attention. The voluntary attention is that of people who deliberately study the advertisements in search of information, as with posters for entertainments and events.

17 The advertisements work hard for they are on show for a great many hours and may be seen for days, weeks or months.

18 The travelling public has changed in recent years. No longer are passengers concentrated on 'rush' hours, but thousands of people are on the move all day. The UK has an ageing population, and some old-age pensioners have free travel passes. Many people have been made redundant, or have taken early retirement in their fifties, and there is a new and growing 'grey' market which is better off than most young people. No longer do the trains run empty between the 'rush' hours.

19 Although the medium is not subject to continuous research as with press and TV, there have been significant surveys which have indicated public awareness of transportation advertising. One such survey was the '*See You in Barking*' tracking study in 1987. A poster picturing barking dogs with a caption 'See You in Barking' was placed on 750 bus T-sides for a month. After two weeks interviews showed that 32 per cent recalled the poster, and after four weeks 37 per cent.

Perhaps the biggest proof of the public awareness of posters occurred when Benetton, the trendy Italian clothing company, put up posters showing a new-born baby which brought protests flooding in to the Advertising Standards Authority, and the poster had to be withdrawn. It was part of a pan-European campaign and only the British were squeamish about it.

11.40   Eight disadvantages of transportation advertising

1 The principal disadvantage is that in some cases (where there is either overcrowding of vehicles or rush-hour anxiety) passenger traffic is so great that the advertisements tend to be obscured or ignored by the hurrying, scurrying commuters wanting to get either to work or back home..

2 Public transport is subject to big fluctuations in numbers of passengers. There may be very few travellers at night.

3 Unless one places sufficient numbers of posters on a station there is little chance that all the thousands of passengers quoted by the contractors will in fact have a reasonable chance of seeing the advertisement. If an advertiser has only one poster on each station it could be on a very slightly used platform. We do not know from the figures supplied how passengers are distributed over the various parts of a station which may have many platforms, tunnels, passages and bridges. Placing adequate numbers of posters can mean that the apparent low cost of the medium is contradicted by the print order and rent bill.

4 Travelling posters can rapidly become dirty during bad weather, reducing their attractiveness and legibility. This applies especially to buses, and particularly to lower rears which can become so dirt-spattered by following traffic as to be unrecognizable.
5 The medium is limited to those who use public transport. For instance, most Underground passengers tend to be young and in the lower income brackets, while motorists seldom use trains.
6 Most of the interior advertisements (bulkhead posters and roof cards) are small which means that in spite of the illusionary huge number of passengers these advertisements are readable only by those very close to them. Again, this could mean higher than expected costs in having to repeat the advertisements. They can be repeated quite usefully in Underground trains but less so in the saloons of buses when the advertisements are seen only by those sitting opposite and not by the entire busload of passengers.
7 The advertisements on tip-up seats in taxis disappear when there are more than two passengers, which again means that the greater the traffic the weaker the effectiveness of the advertising. In fact, this medium is most effective when there is only one fare, so that knowing the minimum number of fares is a better way of evaluating than knowing the maximum number of passengers.
8 It is not an entirely captive audience like that of the cinema. Although pasengers have to wait for trains, or sit in buses and trains until their destination is reached, they are not obliged to read advertisements, and they could be otherwise occupied.

However, the popularity of the medium can be judged if one studies old pictures of public transport and railway stations: a surprising number of famous names will be spotted and some like Whitbread, Heinz, Wallace Heaton and Ovaltine have been using various forms of transportation advertising for many decades, even for as long as a hundred years.

11.41 Taxi-cab advertising

For many years taxis have carried advertisements in the passenger section, and for a time there were mini-cabs covered with advertisements (which were not allowed to travel through London's Royal Parks). During the 1980s external taxi-cab advertising became popular, with panels attached to the nearside front door. Leaflet dispenser facilities are also available. In recent years taxi-cabs have become more numerous in cities like London where public transport may be unreliable, and traffic jams deter motorists from driving in city centres. Taxi Media, one of the contractors, claim that 9.2 million people see taxi advertisements in London repeatedly.

11.42 The overall painted bus or tram

The first painted bus in the UK was for Silexine paint in 1972, although the idea is said to have originated in San Francisco. In Hong Kong there are both painted buses and trams. In Johannesburg almost every other bus seems to be a painted one and the novelty effect is destroyed. Fortunately, UK bus companies, after a period when painted buses were commonplace, decided to limit the number available to advertisers. Now, and to some extent because of de-regulation and the emergence of numerous bus companies, the medium has lost favour in the UK.

The advantage of the painted bus can vary according to the locality. Traditional red London buses are almost a tourist attraction like the pageantry of the Life Guards and the Beefeaters. Yet it is only forty years since London buses were of every colour imaginable – blue Public, brown City and green Birch. The red London bus is not all that traditional, although it was the colour of the old General Omnibus Company. With de-regulation we have reverted to buses in the colours of the various operators. Country buses have the disadvantage of travelling through thinly populated areas, and the cost of painting alone may be disproportionate to the advertising value.

These monster solus advertisements aroused several criticisms. A serious problem occurred in areas where different bus operators were distinguished by their colour and passengers looked out for the livery rather than a number or destination. The identity of a fully painted exclusive bus is lost to the waiting passenger who may literally miss the bus. This was a problem in the Midlands where there are bus liveries of blue, red and blue, and cream. Some designs included people or animals which were completed by the heads of the passengers sitting inside. Passengers objected to being either commercialized or made to look ridiculous. In spite of the proud claim of the bus owners and contractors, the consensus of opinion among young people was that some of the designs were crude and garish. Some people were offended that 'their' nice red buses had been messed about by advertisers, while one old lady saw the Bertorelli bus and exclaimed, 'Oh, the buses are now selling ice cream!' One advertiser offended the public with a message which said, 'You've missed the bus!' and after protests this wording was removed. There were also complaints that painted buses were a distraction to motorists and were therefore a road hazard. After four years London Transport Executive announced their withdrawal in October 1975. This brash advertising novelty had its vogue, and the modern counterpart is the bus on which one advertiser monopolizes all the poster space.

Painted buses seemed popular enough with their sponsors as Berni Inns were prepared to testify about their red bus covered with sporting figures and slogans such as 'Wrestlers eat at Berni Inns – they never get floored by the prices'. Berni reckoned that the medium had more than paid for itself in the first six to eight weeks of its year's run. Moreover, they took the bus to a Lord Mayor's Show in Liverpool, a car rally in Birmingham, and a golf tournament in Bristol.

No doubt the most popular painted public service vehicle is the Hong Kong tram, so popular that it has defied attempts to abolish it, while new ones have been built which are replicas of the original wooden ones. Each tram is painted to promote, say, Sony or an airline, and they are such tourist attractions that they are exploited in holiday brochures and travel agency posters to be found all over the world. Since they occupy the centre of the road over several miles of track on Hong Kong island, and are slow moving, they are remarkable advertising sites.

11.43   Transportation advertising contractors

There are several contractors specializing in this medium. Among the leading firms are British Transport Advertising (Adrail), British Transport Advertising (bus), London Transport Advertising (Underground and buses), and Primesight Bus Advertising (covering several regional sites). There are specialized contractors for taxi-cab advertising.

11.44   Some future trends

The last decade of the 20th century is something of a springboard for the 21st century. There have been remarkable changes in recent years which have made it necessary to re-write and not merely up-date this edition. Some current changes have been touched on such as the importance of the grey market and the need to think European. These call for entirely new attitudes of mind among marketing and advertising people.

Another change has occurred on our doorstep and that is the increasing size and affluence of ethnic markets. For example, there are 1.2 million Afro-Caribbeans of whom 43 per cent earn more than £15,000 a year. Many of the Asians who were obliged to come to the UK from African countries are professionals and business people, and have sizeable incomes.

Some are reached by specialized media such as *Black Britain, The Voice* and other journals and a black TV channel, Star TV, went on cable in 1992. Some of the ILR stations target ethnic minorities. Spectrum Radio appeals to listeners from Chinese, Greek, Kurdish, Hindu and other groups, but little, if any research has been conducted into the spending power of ethnic communities, and agency media planners are seldom able to advise their clients on the use of ethnic media. These people have their cultural pride and preferences.

12
Below-the-line media analysed

12.1 Introduction

Below-the-line advertising media consist of all media other than press, radio, TV, cinema and outdoor (including transportation), the traditional elements of commission-earning 'media advertising' or 'billable media' on which most advertising agencies concentrate. They are not necessarily inferior to above-the-line, and in some areas such as direct response marketing they may be the primary media.

There is much confusion over what constitutes below-the-line advertising media but it does not include sales promotion, direct response marketing or public relations for very definite reasons.

Sales promotion is a form of marketing which may *use* either or both above or below-the-line media to promote its schemes.

Direct response marketing (or direct marketing) is a form of distribution which may *use* either or both above or below-the-line to sell by post, or other form of delivery, that is, usually without shops.

Public relations is not a form of advertising, although it may help to make advertising effective. It applies to all types of organization, whether or not they advertise, and is consequently a much broader form of communication than advertising, its primary task being to create understanding.

The components of below-the-line media include:

1 Direct mail
2 Direct advertising
3 Exhibitions
4 Point-of-sale display media
5 Sales literature including catalogues
6 Aerial advertising
7 Promotional vehicles and admobiles
8 Body media and adbags
9 Sponsorship (*see Chapter 19*)
10 Give-aways, novelties and gimmicks

11   Incentive schemes
12   Business gifts
13   Book matches
14   Playing cards
15   Drip mats and coasters
16   Models and working models
17   Video presentations
18   Carrier bags and wrapping paper
19   Cassettes
20   Calendars and diaries
21   Extraneous advertising such as parking meters, supermarket and airport trolleys
22   Car and envelope stickers
23   Franking machine notices
24   First day covers
25   Directional maps
26   Tickets: bus, airline, parking, till-roll
27   Inserts
28   Flags
29   Paper clips
30   Milk bottles

From this remarkable list it will be seen that below-the-line media are numerous and versatile, may be sufficient in themselves, and be valuable additional media. Direct mail and exhibitions are substantial media, while sight of a shopping bag in a very striking shade of green will immediately remind people of Marks and Spencer. There may be times when something unusual may be needed to attract attention and this could be a tethered balloon in the shape of the pack. Some, like book matches and drip mats, become collectors' items.

12.2   Direct mail

Not to be confused with mail order, or direct response or direct marketing, which are forms of distribution by post or carrier, direct mail is *postal advertising*. Nor should it be confused with direct advertising which refers to mail-drop or door-to-door distribution of advertising material.

It has earned the unfortunate nickname of 'junk mail' because postal advertising is unsolicited, and recipients are likely to object if it is irrelevant to them. Some more about this problem will be found in Chapter 23, with special reference to the Mailing Preference Scheme (23.13) and the amended section VI(B) of the British Code of Advertising Practice (23.13). However, modern methods of de-duplicating mailing lists and the use of targeting systems such as ACORN (see later) can do much to eliminate junk mail.

Direct mail is largely used to sell by mail, but it can be used for purely informative purposes such as warning people to conserve water, for postal questionnaires, or to attract people to visit stores and showrooms where normal retail sales occur. So, while there is not always an immediate inducement to buy or make a further inquiry, there is usually some kind of pressure to act.

Twenty advantages of direct mail

1 If properly used, it is a *selective* medium compared with most other media which are broadcast to all who may or may not read, see or hear its advertising message. Because limited numbers of recipients can be chosen it is not a mass medium. It is a controlled medium.

2 It is a *personal* medium, a communication between one person and another. Salutations can be personalized rather than 'Dear Sir/Madam' which looks bad. However, it can be irritating if this personalizing is taken too far with insertions of the addressee's name within the body of a sales letter. This may look clever, and is possible with laser printing, but if overdone it can turn politeness into impertinence by a stranger.

3 It is an *individual* medium, gaining a solus position in the reader's hand or on the desk, commanding attention since only one letter can be read at a time.

4 It can be *timed* to arrive on certain days or weeks or at particular times of the year, lending itself to either urgent or seasonal appeals.

5 *Enclosures* can be included such as order forms, reply envelopes, leaflets, brochures, catalogues and sometimes samples or gimmicks. However, two warnings are necessary here. Enclosures can require a larger envelope, and by increasing weight enclosures may increase postage. If there are too may loose items they can confuse the recipient who does not know which one to look at first. Nevertheless, an enclosure may make it possible to include a lot more information than would be possible in a press advertisement.

6 It is a *secretive* medium since the campaign is, to a large extent, hidden from competitors, whereas other forms of advertising can be read, seen or heard by competitors. This is an advantage when making special offers such as when selling advertisement space, or announcing forthcoming campaigns to retailers.

7 It is a *speedy* medium. A mailing shot can be produced and envelopes or labels addressed very quickly, and put in the mail without delay. In fact mailing material may be prepared and stored in readiness for a quick mailing at any time. Material can be produced quickly by word processor, printer and copier.

8 It lends itself to *follow-up* campaigns, especially if enquiries received by post or telephone and handled by mail have not yet been converted into business.

9   By comparison with most other media, direct mail is inexpensive in spite of the high cost of postage, and the cost per reply is usually at least half of that of a couponed press advertisement. This is because so much of the press circulation can be wasteful, whereas direct mail can be targeted at identified prospects.

10   As mentioned in (1) above it is a *controlled* medium, and that means the number of shots, the timing and the cost can be controlled. Different appeals can be tailored for particular prospects, and recipients can be mailed for special reasons such as because they have been promoted or taken up new jobs, got married, or moved into a locality, are students or have started new businesses. Such controls do not apply to any other medium.

11   *Copy testing and research* is possible with test mailings to see which produce the best response, using a sample taken from a mailing list.

12   *Results* can be checked on a cost-per-reply and cost-per-conversion-to-sales and value-of-sales basis.

13   The mailing list can be *checked and updated.* Addresses change very rapidly, people die, and some respondents cease to be potential customers after a time. It may be necessary to compile fresh lists for each mailing, or to start again with the latest directory or membership list, or to mail people asking whether they wish to remain on the mailing list. Few lists are reliable after six months, which is one of the risks when hiring lists.

14   The medium lends itself to *colour* so that a mail-shot can be more realistic and compelling than a black-and-white newspaper advertisement. Colour can be achieved very simply with tinted paper, or laser printing effects, quite apart from full colour printing. Corporate house style and colour – as with stationery – can be used.

15   A direct mail shot is more *impactive* and *action-urging* than static press advertisements, The use of a pre-paid or post-free envelope or card makes it easy for the recipient to respond.

16   *Long life* is possible if a mailing, such as a catalogue, encourages retention. Some mailings, such as product information for architects, may consist of data sheets which can be filed in a supplied ring-binder. Gardeners will tend to keep horticultural suppliers' catalogues.

17   *Small businesses* without sales forces can use regular mailings instead of salesmen's calls, inviting orders by post or telephone. So can large firms like stationers who mail regular catalogues, offer free phone ordering services, and deliver next day by courier parcel service.

18   For *trade advertising*, direct mail is an excellent medium for advising retailers of new lines, price changes, cooperative advertising schemes, availability of display material and forthcoming advertising campaigns.

19   It is a useful medium for *introducing* new salesmen, or reminding

stockists of forthcoming calls by sales staff.

20 It is the simplest way of *reminding* customers of, say, the need to service equipment, or to make an appointment for a dental or optical check up.

From the above list it will be seen that direct mail is a medium with special strengths, and it is not surprising that some businesses rely on this medium alone. This, of course, refutes its denigration as 'junk mail' and why it has become the UK's third largest medium with a total annual expenditure of some £800 million.

However, as with any medium there are some drawbacks which should also be considered.

Twelve disadvantages of direct mail

1 It is limited to the *availability of mailing lists*. While an amazing variety of subjects are offered by list brokers, or by the database compilers, or as a result of 'life style' surveys which produce lists on numerous categories of people, or as advertised in the magazine *Direct Response*, and can be taken from published directories and membership lists, it is possible that no list may exist on certain specialized topics. It may, therefore, be necessary to use a rather generalized list with a high wastage factor, or a journal which may reach the target audience but only by buying a lot of waste circulation. Undoubtedly some of the junk mail comes because of inability to target precisely. A person who bought British Gas shares may not necessarily buy some other kind of investment.

2 It is subject to the *inaccuracy* of mailing lists. Most lists contain irrelevant or wrong addresses, and this wastage factor has to be borne in mind. This is a hazard rather than a fault of the system. There are many kinds of manager, engineer, farmer, or teacher who may be included in a list on that subject, and it is very difficult sometimes to eliminate the ones which are irrelevant. For example, a manufacturer of school equipment could mail 'schools' which would include a number which ran distance learning courses and did not use school room equipment. This might not be apparent from the names.

3 The *stigma* of 'circularizing' let alone that of junk mail still bedevils direct mail in spite of sophisticated techniques. British people in particular pretend not to be influenced by advertising and often resent being 'got at' by clever, gimmicky direct mail shots. A letter is a personal thing but a sales letter can appear insincere if it is dressed up too commercially. Some of the four-page, multi-coloured pictorial sales letters so loved by direct mail houses, and usually among the award winners in direct mail contests, are lacking in credibility. They suffer from overkill.

4 It may be subject to the vagaries of the *postal system*, making it

very difficult to time mailings. In some countries it is impossible to use direct mail because postal services are irregular.

5 Much depends on the *quantity* of direct mail a person receives. Doctors, for instance, have expressed resentment at the surfeit of elaborate mailings sent them by drug companies.

6 If recipients receive mailings with the *same style address*, perhaps with a computer number on it, they realize their name and address has been sold to others and they resent this exploitation. It happens in spite of the Data Protection regulations. An enquiry or purchase is made, or one is a member of an organization, and this results in the re-appearance of the same style of address in other people's mailings, especially when labels are used.

7 In the case of personal mail, it can be *disappointing* to the recipient if the letter turns out to be 'only a circular'. Attempts to pretend that a mail-shot is a personal letter, e.g. by a simulated hand-written address or letter is usually self-defeating.

8 Direct mail can be a very *expensive* medium if a shot contains too many items and the extra weight incurs heavy postage charges.

9 In spite of laws and codes, it is possible for *tricksters* to prey on gullible people by sending proposals or offers by mail. The directory racketeers have operated in this way, sending bills with attractive discounts if payment is made within, say, seven days. The entry has never been ordered and in many cases the directory is never published! Similarly a number of bogus operators, usually mailing from abroad, offer jewellery at bargain prices. Such schemes have been exposed on TV programmes, e.g. Esther Rantzen's *That's Life*.

10 While high professional standards are generally applied, it is a medium which is *open to anyone* so that some mailings are tatty, amateurish and liable to give direct mail a bad name.

11 The Post Office offers *special rates* to those who despatch large volumes of direct mail, but this has been criticized because the special Post Office franking, e.g. Mailsort, immediately identifies the nature of the mailing and so invites recipients to discard it unopened. The letter shown in Figure 12.1 appeared in the trade press in November 1990.

12 The mistake can be made of using *too large an envelope*. There is an odd psychology about this. Many people regard, say, a DL envelope as being one which contains normal correspondence, and these standard-size envelopes are likely to be opened first. Larger envelopes may well be direct mail shots, and so may be opened last or even ignored!

From this analysis of the strengths and weaknesses of direct mail two basic principles emerge. The contents of the mail shot should be credible and yet compelling, and the mailing list should be up-to-date and well targeted.

BURNETT ASSOCIATES
Publications: Direct Marketing

Dear Sir

THE COST OF THE MAILSORT SYMBOL - JUNK MAIL'S LOGO

I wonder if others in direct marketing share my dislike of the Mailsort symbol and suspect, like me, that it might not be worth the discounts that go with it. An increasingly familiar symbol coming through everyone's letterbox each day, the Mailsort 'M' has become junk mail's logo. It signals unwanted mail and whatever it's stuck to is treated accordingly.

To test readers' attitudes to the appearance of their mail we recently ran a split test across four lists using five different outer envelopes, all with identical enclosures, for one of our clients, the Muscular Dystrophy Group, a fundraising charity. The five envelopes were:

1. Closed face envelope, with typed address and postage stamp affixed (a normal, everyday letter).
2. Closed face envelope, laser-addressed with postage stamp affixed.
3. Closed face envelope, laser-addressed with Mailsort symbol.
4. Window envelope, label-carrying enclosure and postage stamp affixed.
5. Window envelope, label-carrying enclosure and Mailsort symbol (the conventional method for direct marketers).

Naturally, the stamped and typed envelopes were more expensive than direct marketing's conventional, systems-driven approach. But for a relationship-based proposition, such as a fundraising appeal, would the personal touch be worth the extra cost?

No prizes if you've guessed already, the personal mailing (hand typed and stamped) was <u>twice</u> as effective as the 'direct mail' approach (window envelope and that wretched Mailsort symbol). All other factors in the mailing were identical.

I read recently that organisations considered to be junk mailers could soon be penalised by losing their postage discounts. For fundraisers, the withdrawal of Mailsort could be just the boost their direct mail needs.

Yours faithfully

Ken Burnett
Managing Director
Burnett Associates
London N1 9PP

Figure 12.1 Letter of complaint concerning the Mailsort symbol

Targeting systems

A number of lifestyle systems are described in 21.10, but here are a number of geodemographic and other systems which apply particularly to direct mail.

ACORN (a classification of residential neighbourhoods) is conducted by CACI Market Analysis, and as Table 12.1 shows ACORN uses 38 neighbourhood types in 11 groups, based on their share of the 1990 census figures.

Table 12.1

ACORN types		% of 1990 population	ACORN groups	
A 1	Agricultural villages	2.6	3.4 Agricultural areas	A
A 2	Areas of farms and smallholdings	0.8		
B 3	Post-war functional private housing	4.4	17.5 Mod. fam. housing,	B
B 4	Modern private housing, young families	3.6	higher incomes	
B 5	Established private family housing	6.0		
B 6	New detached houses, young families	2.9		
B 7	Military bases	0.7		
C 8	Mixed owner-occ'd and council estates	3.5	17.9 Older housing of	C
C 9	Small town centres and flats above shops	4.1	intermed. status	
C 10	Villages with non-farm employment	4.8		
C 11	Older private housing, skilled workers	5.5		
D 12	Unmodernised terraces, older people	2.5	4.2 Older terraced	D
D 13	Older terraces, lower income families	1.4	housing	
D 14	Tenement flats lacking amenities	0.4		
E 15	Council estates, well-off older workers	3.4	13.2 Council estates -	E
E 16	Recent council estates	2.8	category I	
E 17	Better council estates, younger workers	5.0		
E 18	Small council houses, often Scottish	1.9		
F 19	Low rise estates in industrial towns	4.6	8.8 Council estates -	F
F 20	Inter-war council estates, older people	2.9	category II	
F 21	Council housing, elderly people	1.4		
G 22	New council estates in inner cities	2.0	7.0 Council estates -	G
G 23	Overspill estates, higher unemployment	3.0	category III	
G 24	Council estates with some overcrowding	1.5		
G 25	Council estates with greatest hardship	0.6		
H 26	Multi-occupied older housing	0.4	3.8 Mixed inner metro.	H
H 27	Cosmopolitan owner-occupied terraces	1.0	areas	
H 28	Multi-let housing in cosmopolitan areas	0.7		
H 29	Better-off cosmopolitan areas	1.7		
I 30	High status non-family areas	2.1	4.1 High status	I
I 31	Multi-let big old houses and flats	1.5	non-family areas	
I 32	Furnished flats, mostly single people	0.5		
J 33	Inter-war semis, white collar workers	5.7	15.8 Affluent suburban	J
J 34	Spacious inter-war semis, big gardens	5.0	housing	
J 35	Villages with wealthy commuters	2.9		
J 36	Detached houses, exclusive suburbs	2.3		
K 37	Private houses, well-off older residents	2.3	3.8 Better-off retirement	K
K 38	Private flats, older single people	1.5	areas	
U 39	Unclassified	0.5	0.5 Unclassified	U
		100.0		

Source: CACI Market Analysis, 1990. (CACI Copyright)

Mosaic is a classification system developed by CCN Systems Ltd which uses demographic and financial data, the Post Office Address File, and statistics from the 1981 census figures. Table 12.2 gives the 58 Mosaic types.

Table 12.2 *MOSAIC groups*

		% GB households
M1	High status retirement areas with many single pensioners	0.8
M2	High status retirement areas, married owner occupiers	0.4
M3	High status retirement areas with rented flats for elderly	0.2
M4	Boarding houses and lodgings, many in retirement areas	2.3
M5	Inter war owner occupied housing, commercial and managerial cadres	3.4
M6	Elite prof/educational suburbs, mostly inner metropolitan	2.5
M7	High status family enclaves in inner city areas	0.5
M8	Highest income and status areas, mostly outer metropolitan	0.9
M9	Inter war semis, white collar commuters to urban office jobs	5.2
M10	Inter war semis, owner occupied by well paid manual workers	4.9
M11	Areas of mixed tenure, many old people	3.2
M12	Lower income enclaves in high income suburbs	0.2
M13	Older suburbs, young families in Gov't and service emp.	5.3
M14	Older terraces, owner occupied by craft manual workers	3.5
M15	Lower income older terraced housing	1.4
M16	Overcrowded older houses, often in areas of housing shortage	1.6
M17	Older terraces, young families in very crowded conditions	0.5
M18	Tenements, caravans and other rented temporary accommodation	1.2
M19	Town centres and flats above shops	2.2
M20	Rented non-family inner city areas with financial problems	1.1
M21	Low status inner suburbs with subdivided older housing	0.9
M22	Older housing where owner occupiers often share with tenants	0.6
M23	Purpose built private flats, single people in service jobs	1.7
M24	Divided houses with mobile single people and few children	0.3
M25	Smart inner city flats, company lets, very few children	1.1
M26	Post 1981 housing in non family urban and city areas	1.1
M27	Post 1981 housing replacing older terraces	0.9
M28	Newly built council housing, mostly high density inner city	0.8
M29	Newly built inner cities estates with non family populations	0.9
M30	Post 1981 extensions to high stress inner city extensions	0.4
M31	High unemployment estates with worst financial problems	2.8
M32	Council estates with the highest levels of unemployment	0.4
M33	Council estates, often Scottish flats, with worst overcrowding	1.1
M34	Better council estates but with financial problems	3.3
M35	Low rise council housing, low incomes and serious deprivation	1.5
M36	Areas with some public housing for the elderly	1.7
M37	Council estates mostly Scottish, middle income small houses	2.1
M38	Council estates in factory towns with settled older workers	2.2
M39	Quality '30s and '50s overspill estates, now with old people	3.0
M40	Best quality council housing in areas of low unemployment	4.1
M41	New greenfield council estates with many young children	2.1
M42	Post 1981 council housing, higher incomes	0.6
M43	Post 1981 council housing, few families	1.0
M44	Post 1981 council housing with stable families	1.0

M45	Military accommodation	0.4
M46	Post-1981 housing in areas of highest income and status	0.3
M47	Highest income and status areas, newish family housing	1.1
M48	Post war private estates with children of school age	3.1
M49	Newly built private estates, high income young families	1.8
M50	Newly built private estates, factory workers, young families	2.9
M51	Post 1981 extensions to private estates	1.8
M52	Post 1981 housing in established older suburbs	2.8
M53	New commuter estates in rural areas	1.7
M54	Villages with some non-agricultural employment	1.9
M55	Pretty rural villages with wealthy long distance commuters	2.5
M56	Agricultural villages	1.7
M57	Hamlets and scattered farms	0.7
M58	Unclassified	0.4

Source: CCN Systems Ltd.

Personal Behaviourgraphics was developed by CCN Systems in conjunction with the National Shoppers Survey conducted by Computerised Marketing Technologies and is based on people's shopping and leisure behaviour (Table 12.3).

Table 12.3   *Personal behaviourgraphics groups*

		% GB households
1	**Golf clubs and Volvos:** Husband career orientated, materialistic	3.7
2	**The got set:** Higher income, well-educated, interested in arts	1.8
3	**Bon viveurs:** Winers and diners, articulate conversationalists	4.3
4	**Fast trackers:** Young, middle income, interest in active sports, leisure	3.6
5	**The high techs:** Motivated by technology, not necessarily high earners	6.2
6	**Faith, hope and charity:** Churchgoers and charity donators, generally with older/grown up children, community minded	3.9
7	**Safe, steady and sensible:** Mostly self-employed with health and accident insurance, savings and pensions plans	3.9
8	**Craftsmen and homemakers:** Little education but useful craft skills	6.1
9	**Trinkets and treasures:** Older, middle income group, intellectual rather than physical	4.7
10	**Cultural travellers:** Often elderly, love foreign holidays/theatre/concerts	5.0
11	**Carry on camping:** Outdoor types, like camping, walking, often in industrial and white collar work, particularly public sector	3.8
12	**Health and humanities:** Has spiritual values, political/social change	4.2
13	**Wildlife trustees:** Older, better off with country pursuits, enjoy travelling	5.5
14	**Factories, fishing and football:** Active, outdoor, mostly blue-collar	4.6
15	**Lager, crisps and videos:** Sociable materialists, pleasure seekers, poorly paid with little education	5.3
16	**Instant chic:** Lower income young people, interested in modern styles, eager for new experiences	4.9
17	**Gardeners'question time:** Older, suburban/rural owner occupiers	5.9
18	**Pools, horses and pubs:** Poorer, less educated, few material comforts	5.5
19	**Survivors:** Very poor, little education or confidence	9.1
20	**Reading, religion and routine:** Low income elderly, 'respectable' folk, give to charity and like to read, usually in small towns	8.1

Source: CCN Systems Ltd.

Pinpoint identifies neighbourhoods as in Table 12.4.

Table 12.4 *PINPOINT groups*

12 level Pin types	%		25 level Pin types	% of households
A Rural	5.14	a	Farmers & agricultural workers	1.22
		b	Rural villages	3.92
B Armed forces	0.30	c	Armed forces	0.30
C Upwardly mobile young families	14.12	d	Country towns	0.79
		e	Families with growing children	8.96
		f	Young couples and small children	4.47
D Affluent households	10.03	g	Wealthy	7.37
		h	Very wealthy	2.69
E Older people in small houses	11.50	i	Council flats with pensioners	2.19
		j	Comfortable retirement areas	2.31
		k	Council housing with elderly	7.01
F Suburban middle aged or older	17.04	l	Owner occupied with elderly	9.15
		m	Large houses, some divided into flats	2.59
		n	Suburban commuters	5.29
G Working people with families	10.26	o	Working people with families	10.26
H Poor urban areas	6.14	p	Unmodernized private dwellings	5.87
		q	Deprived areas	0.27
I Low status areas with flats	5.82	r	Poor small dwellings	2.61
		s	Small urban flats	3.21
J Inner city bedsits	1.12	t	Inner city bedsits	1.12
K Poor multi-ethnic areas	2.19	u	Poor multi-ethnic areas	2.19
L Overcrowded council neighbourhoods	16.27	v	Overcrowded estates with young children	3.34
		w	Crowded estates	2.57
		x	Poor estates	6.90
		y	With growing up children	3.46

Source: PINPOINT Analysis Ltd.

Super Profiles links consumer lifestyle with postal geography, using counts of households rather than census figures. It takes ten lifestyles plus unclassifiable (as shown in Table 12.5 below) and breaks these down into 36 target markets plus a 37th unclassified. These groups are further divided into geodemographic groups such as religion, family, occupation, property and car ownership. There are also clusters, 150 neighbourhood groups being identified in fine detail. A Super Profile Directory is published by Credit and Data Marketing Services Ltd.

Table 12.5   *Super Profile groups*

		Adults('000s)	Men(%)	Women(%)
A	Affluent minority	3,889	9	9
B	Metro singles	1,599	3	4
C	Young married suburban	3,889	9	9
D	Country	3,879	9	8
E	Older suburbia	3,674	8	8
F	Aspiring	7,076	16	15
G	Multi-ethnic areas	3,003	7	7
H	Fading industrial	4,766	11	10
I	Council tenants	7,894	17	18
J	The underprivileged	4,408	10	10
K	Unclassifiable	1,122	2	3

Source: JICNARS/RSL Marketing Data Book 1990

Such classifications will differ in other countries and the following list shows the 40 clusters which analyse every US neighbourhood, over 500,000 in all, in the Claritas Corporation's PRIZM system. The acronym stands for Potential Rating Index Zip Markets.

Blue Blood Estates	Middle America
Money and Brains	Old Yankee Rows
Furs and Station Wagons	Coalburg and Corntown
Urban Gold Coast	Shotguns and Pickups
Pools and Patios	Golden Ponds
Two More Rungs	Agri-Business
Young Influentials	Emergent Minorities
Young Suburbia	Single City Blues
God's Country	Mines and Mills
Blue-Chip Blues	Black Country Folks
Bohemian Mix	Norma Rae-Ville
Levittown, USA	Smalltown Downtown
Gray Power	Grain Belt
Black Enterprise	Heavy Industry
New Beginnings	Share Croppers
Blue Collar Nursery	Downtown Dixie Style
New Homesteaders	Hispanic Mix
New Melting Pot	Tobacco Roads
Towns and Gowns	Hard Scrabble
Rank and File	Public Assistance

This colourful list may be characteristic of a large country like the USA with its great mixture of immigrants over decades, but it provides a strong hint of the diversity of geodemographic types which would emerge if the attempt was made to apply classifications to the Single European Market.

12.3 Direct advertising

Direct advertising, as distinct from direct mail, consists of the door-to-door distribution of advertising material known as mail-drops. Direct advertising pieces are sometimes called 'doorstoppers'. It is one of the oldest forms of advertising, being much used by local shopkeepers and tradesmen. National advertisers also use the medium and there are a number of national and regional firms which specialize in delivering advertising material house-to-house. There are two ways of using such services. One is to use the networks of free newspaper deliveries, items being delivered with the free newspapers, and the other is to use a firm which employs teams of distributors. The first method is about 50 per cent cheaper than the second. In addition, mail-drops can be arranged with the Post Office, but these are made over a two-week period.

It is illegal, however, to ask newsagents to insert leaflets in the newspapers which they are delivering on regular rounds since this deprives the publishers of the right to normal revenue from inserts.

Seven advantages of direct advertising

1 It is an inexpensive medium, costing about a tenth of a posted direct mail shot.
2 Being directed to the home it invites the curiosity of the recipient.
3 Distribution can be targeted to particular towns or particular residential areas in towns, using systems such as ACORN.
4 It can be timed for certain weeks of the year, or to coincide with selling in to retailers who have been advised that, say, money-off vouchers have been distributed in the locality.
5 There is usually good response to distribution of money-off vouchers and samples such as sachets of tea or coffee. Research by Circular Distributors in 1987 showed that 25 per cent of recipients redeemed detergent coupons.
6 Working housewives and younger housewives, according to the same survey, are the most responsive, making it a good medium for fmcgs.
7 It lends itself to campaigns aimed at boosting sales in certain areas.

Six disadvantages of direct advertising

1 Even with the targeting of specific areas, mail-drops are indiscriminant and can therefore be wasteful.
2 Large print orders are necessary, and this cost has to be added to delivery charges.

3   While it may be economical to accept shareplan distribution
    whereby a number of non-conflicting items are dropped at the same
    time, this does mean competition for interest in the various items.
4   Recipients may object to a litter of leaflets on the doormat.
5   Tatty-looking cards and leaflets from small local tradesmen may
    cause resentment which could prejudice more professionally pro-
    duced material.
6   It could offend environmentalists who regard mail-drops as waste
    paper.

12.4   Exhibitions

Exhibitions have an advantage over most other advertising media in
that a visit to an exhibition is usually a pleasant and even an entertaining
occasion, full of interesting sights, demonstrations and often entertainment, free samples and frequently making a day's outing for the family.
Some have proved to be historic affairs like the Great Exhibition at
the Crystal Palace in 1851 which even attracted Japanese princes to
Britain, the Paris Exhibition of 1889 for which the Eiffel Tower was
erected, and the Wembley Exhibition of 1924. There was the Festival
of Britain in 1951 where Guinness won a poster contest with one
showing Guinness poster characters which were so well-known that
the name of the product was unnecessary. The Farnborough Air Show,
the Paris Air Show, the Motor Show, the Boat Show and the Ideal
Home Exhibition are famous regular events. It is sometimes mistakenly
thought that exhibitions are either a form of sales promotion or even
a public relations medium, but they belong to the realm of advertising
media. There are many different kinds of exhibition as now described:

1   Public indoor

In the UK, national and international events are held at venues such
as Earl's Court and Olympia in London, and at the National Exhibition
Centre, Birmingham, while smaller, more local events may be held in
local halls, hotels and marquees. Probably the most famous is the *Daily
Mail* Ideal Home Exhibition which runs for a month in the spring and
is usually opened by a member of the Royal Family. It has spawned
many regional imitators.

2   Trade and business indoor

These appeal to more selective, high-calibre, usually ticket-only visitors
(so that irrelevant visitors such as local school children are deterred in
the interests of exhibitors). Some of these events are sponsored by trade
associations or trade journals. Most of them take place in the three

venues mentioned in (i), but others are held in towns such as Brighton, Glasgow, Harrogate or Manchester where there are exhibition facilities.

3 Joint public and trade fairs

These are mostly large national shows of interest to both retailers and consumers, usually with separate trade and public days, but some, like philatelic and antiques exhibitions, will be patronized by collectors, dealers and professionals. Motor shows serve both trade and public.

4 Private indoor

Held in hotels, ballrooms, local halls, public libraries, schools, building centres, and perhaps on customer premises or in large retail premises, private shows are usually sponsored by one organization or by two or three non-competing or complementary firms. Attendance is usually by invitation, but a more general attendance may be encouraged by local advertising.

5 Outdoor

There are two kinds of outdoor exhibition, those where the exhibits demand outdoor showing such as aircraft or large construction equipment, but also camping and caravanning, and those in warmer countries where weather conditions permit uncovered shows.

6 Agricultural shows

County and national agricultural shows combine shows of livestock with exhibits of farm equipment and services. They usually have a number of features to attract members of farmers' families (such as cookery and flower shows) and also to attract the general public. A number of these have permanent showgrounds or, at least, venues.

7 Overseas trade fairs

These are international events with national pavilions and independent stands. The DTI organizes Joint Venture schemes, subsidizing the participation of British exhibitors who share a stand so that exporters can take part in low cost joint displays. There are generally a number of national pavilions to promote the exports of different countries. Joint ventures can be organized by local Chambers of Trade or national trade associations. Some countries maintain national exhibition centres at which importers can exhibit their goods.

8   Mobile

These are exhibitions, mostly for sole exhibitors, which are taken from place to place, making use of a remarkable range of transportation. The simplest kind are portable ones which can be packed in an estate wagon or small van and driven to any suitable venue such as an hotel, theatre foyer, public library or other site. Caravans, buses and specially constructed exhibition vehicles may be used. Even complete objects such as car ferries have been taken on exhibition trips, visiting ports to demonstrate their facilities. Ambassador exhibition trains can tour the country, stopping at up to 150 stations in the UK where customers can be invited to come on board to see an exhibition. Ship exhibitions are rare but an aircraft carrier was used during the Festival of Britain in 1951, and in 1964 and 1972 Japanese Floating Fair ships visited European ports. New motor-cars have gone on world tour, using specially designed aircraft to fly them from one venue to another.

9   Portable

The really portable exhibition is one that can be taken from site to site for display in, say, shop windows. Premises which tend to have rather dull window displays may accept the offer of such an exhibition to make their windows more attractive to passers-by. Ones which include some form of movement, such as working models, moving figures or lights are particularly suitable, e.g. model trains.

10   In store

This may also be an easily dismantled and transportable exhibit, but it will be erected within the store itself and perhaps have an attendant or demonstrator. Portable and in-store exhibits may be supplied if a retailer orders a large volume of stock.

11   Exhibition centres

Some organizations maintain a permanent exhibition centre to which visitors are invited to see their products which may range from wallpapers to motor-cars. A number of national centres are run by countries to exhibit their exports in world capitals. There are also PR exhibitions such as the Thames Barrier near Woolwich, and the Mary Rose in Portsmouth Harbour, and ones which tell the history of a business such as the Cadbury World of Chocolate Exhibition at Bournville.

12   Conference

A number of annual conferences have an associated exhibition in an adjoining hall, whereby delegates may see products and services related to their interests. In a smaller way, firms may set up private exhibitions in hotels or public rooms close to where conference delegates are staying.

Fourteen advantages of exhibitions

1 An exhibition is both a focus and a magnet, highlighting the topic of the event. It will be publicized before, during and after the show. A motor car show, for example, receives enormous coverage in the press and on TV. An exhibition can thus be a major news event, and individual exhibitors can attract the attention of not only visitors to the exhibition itself, but also those who will hear about it by other means. An exhibition may be held in Paris but may also be news in New York or Sydney.

2 It provides a means of supplying first-hand knowledge or experience of a product or service, by demonstration which is convenient and attractive to interested people. This is particularly true of large items that are not easily transported but which can be viewed by large numbers of people, e.g. many forms of machinery.

3 It allows people to sample a product, and sometimes to take samples home with them. Food exhibitions are typical of this.

4 Sales may be made from the stand, or orders may be taken. The exhibition can be a market place. Some traders deliberately travel from one exhibition to another for this purpose. It is also possible for exhibitors to sell to one another on a business-to-business basis. For example, publishers attend events such as the Frankfurt Book Fair where they may sell translation rights to other exhibitors.

5 Personal confrontation occurs where retailers meet suppliers, or customers meet manufacturers. Good dealer and customer relations can be established. Confidence can be created by such face-to-face confrontation when questions can be asked, complaints can be made, and faceless monolithic companies become humanized.

6 Distributors can have previews of new products or models, test them and place orders for supplies. The toy industry, for instance, is organized early in the year so that orders can be taken for the following Christmas season. This allows production to be organized in the middle of the year so that deliveries can be made in the autumn and the shops are stocked up in time for Christmas.

7 If good use is made of exhibition press office services, the value of an exhibit can be enhanced by the national and international media coverage that can be obtained. The PR opportunities of exhibitions are often overlooked by exhibitors who never get beyond selling. The exhibition press officer should be contacted as soon as stand space has been booked so that opportunities for PR activities and media coverage can be discussed. This may lead to an exhibitor's stand being placed on the itinerary of the VIP who will officially open the event.

8   Addresses of new contacts can be obtained for follow-up by the sales force if visitors books are provided or, better still, boxes for business cards are placed on stands. Business cards eliminate problems of illegible handwriting and inadequate addresses.

9   It may be more economical to make oneself centrally available to prospects than to call on them individually. It is also quicker. This is likely to be increasingly important in European marketing since people on the continent are already as frequent frontier-crossers as British people are at moving from one county to another. The international exhibition can be more effective than a salesman spending months travelling from place to place.

10   Exhibitions have a great curiosity value, enticing people to come and see what is new, or even what is being offered free.

11   Similarly, exhibitions have great entertainment appeal, providing a day out, whether for the business person or the family. An exhibition is a very enjoyable advertising medium, quite unlike any other. Some have been major social events and have gone down in history as such to mention only the original Great Exhibition (Crystal Palace) in Hyde Park, the Wembley Exhibition and the Festival of Britain.

12   Exhibits can be morale boosters for field sales staff who have a talking point when meeting clients.

13   Prototypes of new products can be shown, opinions invited, and modifications made as a result of this form of product pre-testing. It may even be decided to abandon a project because of hostile reaction!

14   Finally, the exhibition – as no other medium can – provides the dramatic situation for the introduction of something original and surprising, whether it be an air, fashion, flower or motor show, striking a fascinating balance between the showmanship of the circus and the salesmanship of the market.

Sixteen disadvantages of exhibitions

1   An exhibit is costly to mount. The cost of space is only the start, unless a standard shell scheme is booked. Otherwise, a stand has to be designed, built, transported, set up, decorated, fitted with services such as electricity or water, furnished, made secure from thieves and staffed by people either removed from their normal duties or specially hired. Special products may have to be devised which can be demonstrated. Costs are discussed more fully at the end of this section.

2   There can be too many exhibitions on similar themes or with overlapping interests. This can lead to cancellations because of inadequate support, which can be costly to exhibitors who were making preparations to participate.

3 Hospitality is usually necessary, for distributors, consumers or journalists, and there can be a hefty bill for drinks and food.

4 Stands have to be staffed, and if salesmen are taken off their rounds or journey cycles sales can be sacrificed.

5 There can be security risks calling for either thief-resistant grilles or security guards. Even when stands are staffed, items disappear. Anything from ashtrays to carpets and refrigerators can vanish. Visitors to exhibitions can be great souvenir hunters!

6 Give-away sales literature can require a high print bill. Literature may be vital, but some visitors cannot resist taking everything in sight. That is why ticket-only admission at trade shows is necessary.

7 Attendance statistics are given by some promoters, but they can be very unreliable if based on turnstile admissions which do not identify entrants. Stand staff will come and go continuously.

8 The cost of hired demonstrators and linguists can be heavy, especially at international shows.

9 Unless well publicized, and held at a popular and accessible venue, attendances may be disappointing. It is sometimes difficult for a promoter to give adequate advertising to a short-lived event, especially if it lacks the follow-on publicity of an established event.

10 Some stands, with enclosed areas and where lavish hospitality is offered, can hog the visitors and deprive other exhibitors of visitors.

11 The preliminary build up period may be too short because the promoters, in hiring the premises, want to devote as much time as possible to the event itself. This may result in expensive overtime work by stand constructors and decorators, and the stand may be incomplete when the show opens.

12 Some of the smaller exhibitions have poor press office services. The promoters may not be big enough to employ full-time press officers, but rely on PR consultancies being hired in the short term. Such consultants may be paid too small a fee, or be too inexperienced in this special PR work, to give exhibitors the service they need.

13 There may be too few fellow exhibitors to make the event truly representative of the topic, and the disappointment of visitors may be vented on those who do take part.

14 There may be no supporting activities such as seminars, conferences, cinema shows, demonstration programmes, entertainments, contests and other devices to either augment attendances or keep visitors at the venue for a reasonable time.

15 The promoters may not have sufficient reputation to attract visitors. It often helps, for instance, if an exhibition is sponsored by a representative journal or trade association.

16 There may be no VIP official opener who will attract the interest of the media so that it is well reported. Such reports can swell attendance figures.

From the above analysis it will be seen that while exhibitions can be a fascinating and rewarding medium they are complicated exercises which require expert handling. They can be one of the most arduous duties of the in-house advertising manager, calling for close liaison with the marketing, sales and PR managers. The following is a breakdown of responsibilities when engaging in participation in exhibitions.

Stages in the preparation of an exhibit

1   Check with various sources of information such as trade journals, the DTI, local Chamber of Commerce or one's trade association to find out what exhibitions will be held during the 12 months for which advertising is being planned and budgeted. Several trade journals publish diaries of forthcoming events.

2   Obtain from the exhibition organizers their rates per square metre and for shell schemes together with a plan of the proposed layout of the event(s).

3   Having decided to take part, book the most suitable site bearing in mind special requirements such as proximity to some relevant part of the hall (e.g. main entrance or conference hall), ceiling space if the exhibit is tall, build-up time if the exhibit is complicated to erect, and access to aisles. Prepare a budget of total costs. (See *Costs* later.)

4   Engage a stand designer, unless a small stand is being used as provided by the promoters, and discuss the aims of the exhibit.

5   Simultaneously, plan with factory production manager what products will be shown.

6   Notify the PRO or PR consultants of participation so that contact can be made with the exhibition press officer, and advantage can be taken of all pre-event publicity.

7   Consider print, photographic, video, model and other supplies for the stand. Get quotations, designs and put work in hand as necessary, ideally with a timetable of operations.

8   Engage a stand constructor to follow agreed design.

9   Allocate and/or engage sales and demonstration staff, including kitchen/bar staff.

10   Submit entry for catalogue, taking advertisement space if required and preparing advertisement. Keep the exhibition press officer supplied with information.

11   Take out insurance and engage security services, as necessary.

12   In the case of an overseas exhibition, plan all shipping requirements, and ensure that personnel have passports, visas, inoculations, currency, custom form requirements, transportation and hotel bookings, special clothing, etc.

13   In the case of a UK event, plan all travel, accommodation, parking and other requirements for personnel.

14 Make sure that all supplies will be delivered on time; organize build-up schedule including provision of services such as gas, electricity, water, telephones, furnishings, cleaning, catering supplies, photography. For some events with awkward exhibits (e.g. The Boat Show) it will be necessary to follow an arrival timetable.

15 Maintain contact with press officer, supplying news releases and pictures (*not* press kits) to the press office in good time; attending press day or preview; inviting press to stand; making sure that any special publicity features are enjoyed such as providing a good reason why the official opener should visit the stand.

16 Place advertisements in newspaper and magazine features about the event, if this is considered valuable. Arrange this with advertising agent.

Costs of exhibition stands

The costs of exhibition stand space follow the pattern of other media. You get what you pay for. The fame and likely attendance is not unlike the value of circulation and readership figures. An island site with access on all four sides will be more expensive than a corner site with access from two sides only, while the cheapest site is likely to be one in a row like a terraced house. The promotors provide a site plan from which sites may be selected.

Site space is also charged according to area, with a price per square metre. Other costs depend on what is planned within the space. It could be a simple 'shell' stand with walls provided, or the exhibitor could construct the entire stand himself. He also has to pay for attending staff, security, services such as gas and electricity, hospitality, print and give-aways.

12.5 Point-of-sale display material

Point-of-sale (POS) or point-of-purchase material can include everything used in windows and on shelves, counters or floor space to promote merchandise. It may be produced by the store itself, or provided by the suppliers. A supermarket may display its own posters to announce special offers, but the manufacturers of these products may supply their own POS material. Either way, this medium can be the penultimate link in the chain of advertising messages leading to the final sale, the ultimate link being the package.

Two considerations concern the advertising manager who is responsible for producing and distributing POS material: how to avoid wastage by making sure that retailers want it and use it; and the problem that supermarkets offer restricted opportunities for the use of display material. Choice of material will depend on the nature of the retail outlet. A travel agent may welcome a model of an airliner or car ferry, but a supermarket may be unwilling to surrender window, shelf or floor space to POS material and the main display will have to be the package or, in the case of small items, a display outer from which, say, packets of soup may be dispensed. The life of the POS material will also depend on seasonal demand. What will happen to POS material when a product is out of season (like a garden aid): will it be stored or discarded?

Use of POS material depends on the willingness of the retailer to use it, and it is likely that dozens of manufacturers will want their material displayed. This cooperation can be achieved in the following ways:

1   Placing by representative

This is a sure way of getting POS material displayed, the sales representative taking the initiative in looking for opportunities to set up displays. He may carry display material in his car and set it up for the retailer, or merely stick a transfer on the glass of the door. It can, however, absorb a lot of selling time.

2   Placing by a merchandiser or display person

Specialist staff may be employed to follow up the sales representative and arrange displays.

3   Notify retailers of the availability of display material

This may be done by mailing retailers with a broadsheet or folder illustrating the available POS material and inviting requests for specific material. This method is more economical than the general mailing of display material to retailers in the hope that they will use it.

4   Special displays for large orders

Costly or elaborate display pieces may be offered if the retailer orders a substantial volume of stock.

Twenty-five kinds of point-of-sale material

1   *Posters*. Sometimes called bills, these are usually of crown or double-crown size (381 by 508 and 508 by 762mm respectively).
      Some of the best posters are the scenic ones distributed by airlines, and usable anywhere in the world served by the airline. News bills are another example of the use of the poster at the point-of-sale, and some of the most attractive are those issued by

the holiday and travel industry and used to decorate travel agencies. Less artistic perhaps but very effective are the silk-screened posters seen on department store windows to announce sales and on supermarket windows to advertise bargain buys.

2 *Showcards* made of card or metal, strutted or suspended, are one of the original forms of POS material and are being ousted by the increase in self-service stores where display space is limited. They remain major display pieces in the confectionery, pharmacy and tobacco trades where shops tend to be smaller and more traditional. Showcards can be made three-dimensional to carry specimen products – e.g. pipes, ballpoint pens – or as dispensers from which the product may be taken by the customer. The decision to produce showcards depends very much on the typical outlet. While they have the advantages of portability they may have a brief life (and therefore be uneconomic) since only a few can be used at any one time by the shopkeeper. They can be printed on metal, or ones made of card can be varnished or laminated to achieve durability.

3 *Mobiles.* Suspended displays, often made up of a number of items, are useful in supermarkets where the ceiling is about the only unoccupied space, and they attract attention by their movement and novelty.

4 *Pelmets* are a fairly permanent means of gaining window display, being pasted to the top edge of the window.

5 *Dumpers and dump bins* are tubs for containing packages, and the attempt is to thrust the product right under the nose of the customer and urge purchase. The fact that the goods are presented in a tumbled fashion is dramatic and usually implies a special offer. The advantage is that the line is isolated from rival brands. A disadvantage is that retailers may use them for other products!

6 *Wire, metal and plastic stands.* These range from 'beanstalks', comprising a stack of trays or shelves, to smaller dispensers not unlike filing trays. Like the bins, these stands isolate and identify the product but they are liable to abuse as when a mixture of brands is placed in one by the shopkeeper who likes the utility of the stand but does not reserve it for its original use. It pays the supplier to see that the stand itself is identified by the manufacturer or his brand.

7 *Dummy packs.* Packaged products should be for sale, not display, and for window-dressing purposes the manufacturer usually supplies dummy packs. However, dummy packs are again more suitable for products sold by non-self service shops such as the small grocer, tobacconist, confectioner, ironmonger or chemist. They are useful for perishable items such as drinks.

8 *Display outers and dispenser cards.* For small packaged units such as confectionery, razor blades, medicines or soups, the original

carton can form a useful dispenser, the lid folding back to make a display panel. Dispenser cards have small products attached to them which the customer can detach, e.g. packeted peanuts.

9 *Display stands* are useful when the product is not a mass packaged item and can stand to advantage by itself on a tasteful stand. Clocks, watches, jewellery and china models look well on display stands.

10 *Cash mats, open/closed door hangers, drip mats and dart match floor mats*, mostly made from plastic or rubber, can be good reminder advertisements at the point-of-sale, or in pubs and restaurants.

11 *Plastic shopping bags*, carrier bags and boxes for men's suits and ladies wear are striking means of conveying publicity from the point-of-sale. Marks and Spencer and various airport duty-free shopping centres provide extremely attractive bags for carrying purchases.

12 *Crowners* carry price tags or slogans and when slipped over the necks of bottles make ideal POS material where space is limited. They are useful for window displays.

13 *Models*, static or working, provide a means of miniaturizing items that would be impossible to display otherwise, the airliner or cruise ship being typical examples. The working or moving model is an attention-getter, often proving an attraction to window-shoppers when the shop is closed, especially if lit.

14 *Clocks*. These may be attached to the exterior of shop premises, carry the shopkeeper's name, and attract attention to his location.

15 *Illuminated displays*. Very suitable for window displays, and sometimes with flashing lights, they can be a permanent form of attraction, both day and night.

16 *Window stickers and transfers*. Smaller than posters, they can be used for permanent or semi-permanent displays on windows and doors.

17 *Wrapping paper/trays*. Placed on the counter of, say, a wine merchants they can occupy a prominent position.

18 *Ash trays* in glass or plastic can be used to promote cigarettes or drinks in pubs and restaurants, but can be used by other firms which seek publicity in public places.

19 *Menu cards*. These are very useful for promoting products in catering establishments.

20 *Shelf-edging*. Printed adhesive strips for sticking to shelf edges, they have become a favourite form of display material in pubs where the message can face customers at the bar.

21 *Sales literature*. Leaflets, brochures, price lists and other print are a very important POS item, and showrooms and stores need to be kept well stocked, typical examples being domestic appliances and motor-cars about which prospective customers expect to find take-home information.

22 *In-store advertising.* Here can be included a variety of devices for promoting products by audio or visual methods such as electronic newscasters, videos shown on TV screens, or broadcast audio cassettes.

23 *Samples* may be distributed at the point-of-sale, perhaps in sachets or miniature bottles, or as offered by demonstrators.

24 *Trolley advertisements.* Where trolleys are supplied for shoppers, advertisements can be attached to the tops of them.

25 *Labels and stampings.* Some products such as bananas, oranges, grapes and grapefruit can be identified by label, for instance Dole, Fyffes, and Outspan. New Zealand meat and Danish bacon carry identification stampings.

The chief advantages of POS material are that they draw customers' attention to products, identifying, distinguishing and promoting them which can be important where there is a large range of merchandise. The chief disadvantage is that there can be wastage if distribution and use of POS/POP material is not well controlled.

12.6 Sales literature

Already mentioned under point-of-sale material, sales literature may also be required for other advertising purposes such as to accompany direct mail shots and as aids in direct response marketing, or for supplying in response to coupon requests. It may take one of the following forms:

1 *Leaflets,* which are unfolded single sheets printed on one or both sides; *folders* which are folded in a variety of ways from a simple centre fold to provide four pages to concertina and map folds; *brochures* which are small, bound booklets, mostly wire stitched; and *broadsheets* which are large folders, often as large as a newspaper page when flat and folding down like a map.

2 *Catalogues, price lists, timetables and tariffs* are usually booklets or brochures describing a range of products or services as used by mail order (direct response) firms, horticultural suppliers, holiday and travel organizations.

3 *Wall charts* are information posters, sometimes laminated with plastic film to make them long-lasting. They may be used for educational purposes, explaining the production of say, tea, coffee, coal or steel, or how to use gas or electricity safely.

4 *Data or specification sheets,* usually A-4 size, and sometimes with a gatefold, and perhaps punched to fit a binder, such sheets are used to explain statistical information about components, materials and products of interest to architects, quantity surveyors, electronic engineers, designers, formulators, and others who have to specify

items. Binders are usually supplied by the manufacturers who then mail recipients with sheets to file.

12.7 Aerial advertising

Not strictly speaking 'outdoor' advertising, aerial advertising includes all flown media, whether tethered or moving, and may include:

1 *Sky writing*. Once made famous by Persil, an advertising message is emitted from an aircraft as a trail of smoke, a word being written in the sky. A clear sky and good weather is required.
2 *Sky shouting*. A medium experienced in Zimbabwe with messages shouted from low-flying helicopter by means of loud-hailers. Originated in the days of Rhodesian UDI when the army used this method to address villagers.
3 *Sky banners*. Towed by slow-flying aircraft, this is one of the oldest forms of serial advertising which is still used in the UK and various parts of the world, subject to restrictions on low-flying aircraft over urban areas. May be seen over the sea at holiday resorts and over sports arenas where such advertisements may be seen by large crowds.
4 *Lighted aeroplanes and airships*. Used on clear nights, aeroplanes may carry illuminated messages on their wings, while Goodyear airships in the USA and in Europe have carried illuminated public service messages on their sides. On the eve of the Royal Wedding in 1981, the Goodyear airship *Europa* carried the message 'Loyal Greetings' when it flew over London.
5 *Projected advertisements*. These have been produced with laser beams, or with a searchlight effect on low cloud.
6 *Tethered inflatables*. Balloons (often in the shape of packages such as bottles), and small airships with painted messages may be tethered, either as an advertising gimmick or to draw attention to a subject below them.
7 *Airships*. A number of firms have hired airships, had them specially painted, and flown them over cities. A striking example was one to promote Fuji film being painted in the easily recognizable red and green colours of the package. Airlines and banks have used airships in a similar way.

   Castlemaine XXXX beer and other products have been advertised on the sides of small airships. The whole airship can be decorated, or an advertising panel can be fixed on each side of the balloon, each one being larger than a 96 sheet poster. For short periods, banners can be placed on the sides of the airship, but for long periods the whole skin can be painted so that the airship is completely branded. The large airships were built by Airships Ltd, now wound up, and the smaller GA42 two-man ones operated by

Flying Pictures of Fairoaks Airport, Surrey and made by Thunder & Colt of Oswestry cost £90,000 a month compared with £250,000 for operating the larger type as used by Fuji which could also carry passengers. A new development has been Richard Branson's introduction of the night-sign airship from America, which can carry lighted signs on the side of the envelope rather like the large Goodyear airships. Such airships are also hired for civilian purposes such as traffic control, and by TV crews filming, say, the London Marathon or other events.

8 *Hot air balloons* are sponsored by a number of companies, and a hot air balloon race with each balloon painted in the colours of its sponsor is an impressive sight in the sky. Races are organized by The Balloon Club of Great Britain. These balloons are also available from Flying Pictures of Fairoaks Airport.

The advantages of aerial advertisements are that they are unusual and attract attention and curiosity. The disadvantages are that the message is inevitably brief, the use usually short term, and in some cases it is an expensive medium in which to indulge. It all depends on how, why and where this medium is used, and whether it is justified by circumstances. It may be a dramatic way of announcing an event to thousands of people on a holiday beach, or of directing motorists to a farm where produce may be picked.

12.8 Promotional vehicles and admobiles

Included under this heading are forms of motorized advertising which travel the streets. Some carry large painted boards and resemble a travelling hoarding, others are large vehicles which may also have hospitality facilities for road shows. Popular in some countries such as Nigeria are loudspeaker cars or vans which tour the city streets.

12.9 Body media and adbags

Often associated with sport, these are items which people are willing to wear or use in spite of their advertising intent and some, like Guinness shirts and other apparel, are actually sold. They include T-shirts, sweatshirts, caps, hats, visors, headbands, umbrellas, pullovers, jogging suits, track suits, ties, head squares, aprons, rally jackets, sportshirts, rain-suits, light-weight jackets, ski-wear, sashes, towels and bar towels. Various bags for carrying sports gear, and also cameras, plus cooler bags are also available bearing advertisers' names. Such media are often included in sponsorship schemes, or are worn by fans and supporters.

They provide advertising in all kinds of situations, are usually long-lasting and if sold can be self-liquidating. There is of course no control over if, when and how these media will be worn or used.

12.10   Sponsorship

This subject is big enough to have its own chapter (Chapter 19), but here it may be said that sponsorship may be used for advertising, marketing, or public relations purposes, or for a combination of these purposes. Sponsorship can come under the general heading of below-the-line.

12.11   Give-aways, novelties and gimmicks

There are countless examples of give-aways such as children's balloons, pens, key-rings, pencils, rulers, paper-knives, bottle and can openers, wallets, card-holders, calculators, drinking mugs, and paper weights and acrylic blocks containing souvenirs. There are also gimmicks such as pop-ups and other items which arrive flat in the post, but can be converted into desk tidies or, when placed in water, change into a car-cleaner sponge. They may be used for two purposes: as an expression of goodwill or as an advertising gimmick.

A lot of money can be spent on such items. They may have reminder value, or be a generous gesture, but in the end it is a budgetary question. Are give-aways necessary and do they serve a worthwhile purpose? Could the money be better spent, or are such gifts expected by customers?

Numerous give-aways and sources are given in *Ideas* the monthly journal published by Headline Promotions of Maidstone.

12.12   Incentive schemes

This has become big business, and incentive schemes include all sorts of holidays, Christmas hampers and shopping vouchers and many companies operate special incentive departments to promote additional sales of their products or services. They are usually aimed at two kinds of people – sales representatives and sometimes other members of staff, and also customers. They may be used as prizes in sales contests. Companies may, for instance, buy books of vouchers worth from 50p to £10 and redeemable at High Street stores. A wallet of vouchers can be made up to any value as a cash prize, or points may be awarded for special efforts, and these points can qualify for vouchers of certain value. Holiday schemes such as free accommodation at hotels, or free meals in restaurants, are operated by incentive operators. Incentives can also take the form of gifts such as clocks and cameras offered to those who take out insurance policies. Many manufacturers and retailers publish catalogues of incentives which are available at special prices for bulk orders.

12.13   Business gifts

Also promoted by many of the companies which sell bulk supplies of their products as incentives, business gifts are mostly items which firms give to their customers at Christmas or on other occasions. Unlike give-aways, these are usually substantial items such as wines and spirits, Wedgwood china, glassware, cutlery, sets of books and so on.

12.14   Book matches and matchbox advertising

Most hotels supply their clientele with book matches, and they are a popular give-away with many other firms. They come in a variety of shapes and designs, provide a genuine service and thereby create goodwill. They are also collectors items for phillumenists.

There are also other forms of matchbox advertising, as when space on the back of a box is sold to advertisers or when direct response marketing offers are made as has occurred with Swan Vestas. Some hotels use book matches to promote other hotels in the group.

12.15   Playing cards

They are an old favourite, produced by firms such as Carta Mundi and Waddington. Card playing is popular the world over and packs of cards, with the sponsor's message on the backs, are useful give-aways.

12.16   Drip mats and coasters

A well-established medium in the drinks trades, drip mats are usually made of cork or card, while coasters are usually made of paper. The former may be laid out on bar or restaurant tables, the latter placed beneath glasses when drinks are served. But they can be more substantial like the 'flying kite' symbol pewter ones sold to Malaysian Airline passengers.

12.17   Models and working models

Reference has already been made to these in 12.4, and they can take many ingenious forms ranging from trade characters such as the Michelin Man, Black and White whisky dogs, and the White Horse whisky horse to moving or working models which demonstrate products or have an amusing and eye-catching series of movements.

12.18   Video presentations

These can take one of three forms. A series of advertisements can be shown continuously on a TV set placed in a retail store or Post Office; a single product can be demonstrated on a TV screen as in some motor-car showrooms; or a video can be supplied on loan by travel agents to promote a tourist attraction, e.g. Cyprus or Bali. More than 70 holiday videos are available. Videos can also be used for a variety of other purposes such as to explain the annual report and accounts, to promote investments (offered in press advertisements), for recruiting staff, or for showing on exhibition stands. Video is a versatile medium which can be used for either advertising or PR purposes, and an educational video may serve both purposes.

12.19   Carrier bags and printed wrapping paper

Here are take-home media by means of which a retailer can continue to advertise after a purchase has been made, especially when it is reusable for a long time – like a carrier bag – and is in a distinctive colour such as Marks and Spencer green.

12.20   Audio cassettes

Audio cassettes can be used for a variety of purposes such as sampling a language course, or explaining an investment (e.g. unit trusts), and they have been used by radio stations to sell air-time and by PR consultancies to explain their services. They can be offered in press advertisements for playing on home or office tape recorder.

12.21   Calendars and diaries

Calendars are a very old advertising and PR medium, the corner grocer of decades ago giving his customers a calendar at Christmas. It is a permanent and useful piece of good publicity. Some large companies produce much sought after and famous calendars. Pirelli calendars have even been auctioned at Christies. Attempts have been made to issue calendars at different times of the year, and for short periods, but this can be a self-defeating gimmick. There are well-known companies such as Bemrose and Evershed which specialize in printing standard but high quality calendars which can be overprinted with the sponsor's name. Pocket and desk diaries are also valuable and appreciated by recipients, whether for personal or business use.

12.22 Extraneous advertising

Under this very general heading can be included a mixture of advertising media since there will always be someone who sees the chance to sell some vacant space for advertising purposes. Their value has to be judged accordingly but it could include charity programmes, parking meters, supermarket and airport trolleys, sports fixture lists, litter bins or deck chairs.

12.23 Car and envelope stickers

Sometimes tourists are quite happy to have their cars decorated with stickers promoting resorts, or other motorists may display stickers for good causes. Similarly, envelope stickers may be used to promote events or charities.

12.24 Franking machine notices

This is a device whereby slogans can be printed on envelopes alongside the franked postage rate, this making an advertising use of the envelope.

12.25 First day covers

Mainly used by charities, this is a method of converting a mailing shot into a free gift of a first day cover. But will it be appreciated if the recipient does not collect stamps?

12.26 Directional maps, year planners, etc

Whether it be a directional map located in a town centre, or a year planner for the office wall, these are permanent or semi-permanent media which carry surrounding advertisements. These, and similar media, will depend on the value they give in keeping an advertiser's name in a prominent position. Other versions, as sometimes seen in sub-Post Offices, carry a clock or a calendar.

12.27 Tickets

Various kinds of ticket or receipt such as till receipts, display parking tickets, bus and airline tickets often carry advertisements. They are fringe media which again must be judged according to their value to the advertiser.

12.28 Inserts

A fast-growing medium is the insert tipped into a newspaper or magazine, and frequently used by direct response marketers. It is claimed to be cheaper than direct mail, and if the journal reaches a well-defined targeted audience it could have its advantages. Some advertisers report great success with inserts. Inserts probably depend for success on a number of factors, the chief one being that if the insert is the same size as a page of the magazine it may well seem to be part of the magazine and yet be cheaper than buying two pages if printed both sides. It may also succeed if it is a substantial item such as a catalogue. But many inserts fit neither category and invite being tipped out and discarded. Moreover, the print order is likely to far exceed that of a direct mail campaign. A trade magazine may have a circulation of 30,000 copies, but would you mail 30,000 prospects? Nevertheless, inserts are big business and many publishers have installed special machines for tipping them in.

12.29 Flags

Whether they be national or company flags, they should not be overlooked as advertising media, whether to decorate premises and draw attention to them, or to be incorporated in retail external displays such as those for ice cream.

12.30 Paper clips

Various coloured plastic paper clips are available on which are printed the advertiser's name, address and telephone number. When attached to correspondence they are more noticeable than ordinary metal paper clips, and recipients are apt to keep them and even re-use them.

12.31 Milk bottles and cartons

Since glass milk bottles survive and have to make several journeys they can be appropriate media for drinks and confectionery associated with milk. These doorstopper advertisements are printed on the bottles by silk screen by the bottle manufacturers, short-necked bottles being used because of their higher survival rate. However, it is a medium which has not found great popularity, probably because of the high price of home delivered milk compared with large cartons available more cheaply at supermarkets so that home deliveries are dwindling.

The popularity of milk in cartons, as sold by supermarkets, has created a new 'milk' medium. The medium was tested out by Lean Cuisine and Flora Margarine in 1991 and in mid-1992 Colgate toothpaste launched a nationwide on-pack campaign through supermarkets and dairies.

12.32 Conclusion

We have deliberately described a great variety of below-the-line media. The advertiser needs to make his choice very carefully at the time of planning and budgeting the year's appropriation. To what extent do any of these media represent a cost-effective way of achieving the objectives of a campaign? The danger with a lot of the more trivial media is that tempting offers may be made throughout the year which, if accepted, will mean exceeding the budget. Alternatively, a contingency budget can be carried in case anything worthwhile turns up unexpectedly.

Costs will vary from time to time but anyone contemplating the use of the more specialized below-the-line media will find current prices given in the *BRAD Premium and Incentive Price Guide*. A summary of many of these is given in Appendix 1, Other Advertising Media, in *The Media Pocket Book*.

Part Four
Creative Advertising

13
Layout and typography

13.1 The purposes of advertisement design

Many of these remarks will apply to all printed advertising material ranging from leaflets to posters, but this chapter will concentrate on the press advertisement. Advertisements are designed for the following purposes:

i   *To attract attention* which may be achieved by shape, layout, typography, colour, illustrations and position in publication.
ii *To compete with others* using creative devices such as special copy platforms, offers, slogans and the devices mentioned in (i).
iii *To be distinctive*, helping to enhance the corporate image and exploit the corporate identity.
iv *To sell* as a result of (i), (ii) and (iii).

It follows then that although the major cost of advertising will be the purchase of media, that expenditure will be a total waste of money if the space, time or site is not exploited to achieve the four purposes stated above.

This chapter will deal with two basic aspects of creativity, layout and typography. This pair achieves the impact and seeks to get the message absorbed. If one merely reproduced a piece of typewritten copy and called that an advertisement it would not achieve very much. The advertisement has to be designed or made readable. This is because, except in special cases, people do not buy newspapers or magazines to read the advertisements. A powerful inertia factor has to be overcome.

The unusual advertisement shown in Figure 13.1 was very topical at a time when there were some 'green' objections to events in South America. It achieves the purposes set out in Section 13.1.

13.2 Eight essentials of a good layout

We can now repeat and build upon the first purpose stated above by analysing the essentials of a good layout.

These animals live in the rain forests of the Amazon.

Their existence is at risk because, as we all know, the rain forests are being destroyed.

And the rain forests are being destroyed partly to make grazing for cattle.

The rumour is that McDonald's use some of the beef to make hamburgers.

We have even seen it reported as fact.

But it's not a fact.

None of the beef we use, anywhere in the world, comes from the area of the rain forests.

It never has.

All of the beef we use in Britain comes from the E.C.

(While we're on the subject, our hamburgers are made with 100% beef. And we use only whole cuts of fore-quarter and flank, with no binders, fillers or additives.)

Nor do we use trees from the rain forests to make any of our packaging.

They are mostly hardwoods. We use mostly softwoods.

Our polystyrene packs are made with an inert gas which has no effect on the ozone layer.

We stopped using CFC gases two years ago.

In telling you this, at a time when many companies are only too eager to show how green they are, we are not claiming to be perfect.

It is not, after all, a perfect world.

We're just doing our best to preserve it.

Contrary to rumour, we do not kill them to make hamburgers.

Figure 13.1 Example of an unusual advertisement (courtesy McDonald's)

1 *It should attract attention*, otherwise it will be ignored. But more than that, the advertisement must attract attention away from whatever was already attracting the reader's attention such as the editorial or other advertisements.

2 *It should be original*, or made to seem to be original because there are obviously some standard formats for layouts just as there are standard plots for novels, e.g. the Cinderella theme. However, it should not be so clever that it defeats its own purpose.

3 *It should have contrasting elements*, being neither all emphasis or grey monotony. Generous use of white space, different sizes of type face, or use of pictures may achieve this.

4 *It should have a focal point*, that is a point of primary interest which engages the eye at once.

5 *It should be immediately comprehensible*. People do not usually go through a publication reading each advertisement meticulously in turn. They are selective. The advertisement should therefore appeal very quickly to its likely audience. Gimmicky advertisements may arouse curiosity, but if they are ambiguous they may elude the very people they are meant to interest.

6 *There should be a logical sequence of elements* so that readers proceed through the advertisement and are encouraged to take whatever is the required action such as going to a supplier, or sending off a coupon, or actually ordering the goods. One way of doing this is to break-up the copy with a series of sub-headings. Not all advertisements are read thoroughly the first time, and it may be necessary to gain initial attention by inducing a flow of interest by way of, say, headline, picture, sub-headings, price and advertiser's name or logo. This progression of interest is very important and can attract even the 'glancers'.

7 *There should be movement*. A press advertisement is static, but design elements can be used to carry the eye through it.

8 *The advertisement should have unity*, all the elements hanging together as one piece and not as isolated bits. Even a retail advertisement with many items of merchandise should be seen as an entity rather like a painting which is absorbed as a scene and not (like a Breugel or Lowry) full of separate characters.

At this point it will pay the reader to pause and look at some advertisements in the press. How do they match up to the eight points set out above? Looked at critically, they will be seen in a new light. But of course the reader does not analyse them in this critical way. Either they work, or they do not.

13.3 The eight laws or elements of design

1 The law of unity
The parts of a layout should be united. This repeats the eight essentials

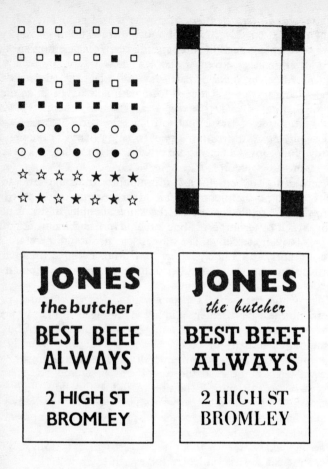

Figure 13.2   Four examples of variety

stated above, but applies to any design and not just an advertisement. Here, we should also consider the deterrents to unity. They could be attempts to be too clever. Cleverness should never be obvious. The design should look naturally attractive, not strive too obviously for attention. Certain things can spoil unity, such as an over-elaborate border, a conflicting mixture of type faces, patchy colour or what are known as 'busy' layouts because they have too many bits.

Unity calls for *emphasis* – something should stand out such as the headline, picture or maybe the price, and there should also be *contrast* otherwise everything would look grey and dull. But if there is over-emphasis, or too great a contrast, the effect is ruined. The wonderful use of light in a Rembrandt painting is a fine example of contrast which also creates a focal point.

2 The law of variety

Let there be change, perhaps represented by pleasant repetition. This can be expressed in a number of ways such as typographically with, say, display lines in one type-face (e.g. a sans face, that is one without serifs) and the text in a body type, or with some type in roman and other type in italics, or some type in bold face and other type in light face (Figure 13.2). This sort of variety introduces contrast without conflict. In the early days of press advertising everything was set in the same size type (as occurs with a typewritten letter) and there was no variety.

Variety can also be achieved with shapes. It would tend to look monotonous if all the pictures in an advertisement, or on an editorial page or in a catalogue, were all the same size like a set of postage stamps. Much better if there is one large picture and a number of other pictures of different but smaller shapes.

Patterns can also create variety as when two colours are intermixed at regular intervals, or there are black and white effects like a chess board.

3 The law of balance

A balanced layout pleases the eye, and is related to the law of gravity. In most print there is a *vertical* dimension so that the eye is attracted downwards, and there is also a *horizontal counter movement* carrying the eye from left to right. (At least, this is so in European print although it does not apply to Middle Eastern and Far Eastern print which is read differently but is still balanced.)

However, the optical centre – that is the downwards and crossways meeting point – is not the dead centre but is more like the hilt of a sword coming a third of the way down instead of half-way, as will be seen from Figure 13.3:

If the reader looks at a book, newspaper or magazine page it will be seen that the margins are of different widths to satisfy the optical centre. So, very often the brand name is placed at the optical centre on a label or package.

When designing print or an advertisement layout it is necessary to balance shapes or masses (pictures or type areas) to make a pleasing pattern. There are two kinds of balance: *symmetrical* or centrally balanced; and *occult* or *dynamic* based on the true optical centre described above. Each will now be explained in turn.

Symmetrical balance
This is the classical or traditional balance based on the mathematical centre. Two examples of a symmetrically balanced layout are shown in Figure 13.4.

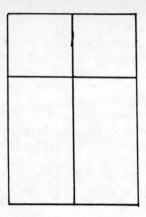

Figure 13.3   The optical centre

These are neat arrangements, but they lack the dramatic effect of the sword-hilt sort of dynamic balance as will be seen in the next section.

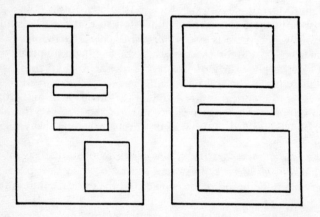

Figure 13.4   Symmetrical balance

Occult or dynamic balance
Here there is a balance between unequal masses set out at unequal distances from the mathematical centre, the optical centre being one third down. Thus the masses can be arranged as one-third or two-thirds shapes (often in the form of a headline or a picture). There is dramatic balance but also a sense of movement, as shown in Figure 13.5.

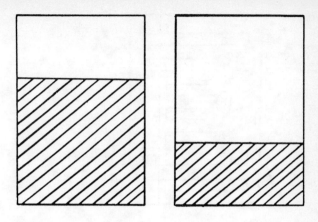

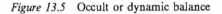

Figure 13.5   Occult or dynamic balance

4   The law of rhythm

The eye should be carried from point-to-point in the layout, making a natural but guided progression through the succeeding elements of the advertisement. All sorts of devices can be used to achieve this, such as headlines, sub-headings, different type sizes or weights of type, pictures, typographical signs like bold dots and asterisks, italic and roman type and so on. Here we begin to see how an imaginative visualizer and a skilled typographer can take a piece of typewritten copy and bring it to life. The physical presentation of the words can make them interesting, readable, legible and meaningful. We see this in the lengths of paragraphs. If modern authors were to write paragraphs like those of Henry James and Anthony Trollope no-one would publish their books today.

Once again the design principle is demonstrated by a simple arrangement of shapes (Figure 13.6).

5   The law of harmony

The various elements of an advertisement should be arranged in a harmonious fashion, again pleasing the eye. When there are no ugly contrasts and no undue emphasis there is a pleasing sense of harmony. This can be seen if the layout of a tabloid such as *The Sun* is compared with that of the *Independent*, or the front cover of a popular magazine is compared with that of, say, the *Independent* Saturday magazine. One is jazzy and the other sober.

However, in designing an advertisement it may be necessary to sacrifice harmony in order to attract attention.

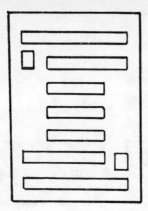

Figure 13.6   The law of rhythm

Nevertheless, even in a dramatic layout it is possible to use harmony to achieve legibility of text. Small type needs to be set to a narrow measure, large type to a correspondingly wider measure. If there is a lot of copy it may pay to set it in two or three columns of smaller type. If a half-page advertisement is placed in a magazine more wording can be put in a horizontal half page than in a vertical one because in the former two or three columns of text can be set in small type, whereas the long narrow space can only accept one column of larger type.

This is demonstrated in Figure 13.7.

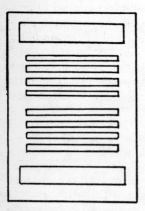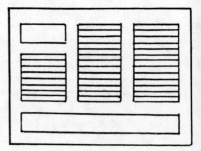

Figure 13.7   The law of harmony

6   The law of proportion

This applies particularly to the appearance of type areas, that is the blocks of typesetting, which should have a ratio of length to width – as already indicated in the examples of harmony. In print, a square is less attractive than a rectangle. An A4 sheet of paper follows this concept, as do the shapes of newspapers and magazines.

7   The law of scale

The extent of visibility depends on the scale or proportion of tones and colours. This can be taken to include shapes or masses (e.g. panels of text), and to solid areas such as headlines, pictures, brand and advertiser's names, symbols, logos and slogans. These bold, and either black or coloured, elements appear to come forward and look closer to the eye than items in small or light type or pale colours.

When colours are used it is as well to remember the colours of nature. Think of the tiger and the wasp – the most *legible* colour combination is black and yellow. Red and orange are advancing colours – and the ones missing from most scenes and coloured pictures. To make a colour picture (or a TV scene or personality) *colourful* there is need to include red or orange, and yellow is useful. Other colours, especially blue, are cold and retreating colours which are best used to create an illusion of distance, e.g. blue skies and mauve mountains.

8   The law of emphasis

Here we go a step further and achieve emphasis by variations of scale, such as by underlining, setting words in italics or bold type, or by the use of white space which throws up a grey, black or coloured area in contrast. Emphasis can brighten otherwise dull-looking areas of print and make the whole area more attractive to the eye. For example, if there is a large volume of text copy it can be relieved by typographical devices which emphasize and so achieve continuity of interest.

These devices could be sub-headings in bold type of a different face, drop initial capital letters at the beginning of separate passages, or the setting of the first two or three words of sections in capital letters, bold type or italics.

13.4   White space

Reference has been made several times to the use of white space, and this can be used to gain clarity, emphasis, contrast and attractiveness. A lot of copy set in small type and jammed together is offensive and tiresome to the eye. Some ways of using white space are as follows:

i   By *leading* or spacing lines of text type. With metal typesetting this is literally the placing of a strip of lead between lines of type to provide even space. But this can be achieved during typesetting by setting, say, '8 on 9' meaning that 8 point type is set on a 9 point body.

ii   By use of *margins*. If an advertisement is not framed in a border, the advertisement can be made to look larger by extending type and illustrations to the edge of the space (the type area), exploiting the page margins as surrounding white space.

iii   By *floating the headline* in white space, thus gaining extra boldness through contrast.

iv   By *indenting paragraphs* (as in publications) 'book style' meaning that the first paragraph after a heading or sub-heading is not indented (set 'full out'), but all succeeding paragraphs are indented. Thus the eye is automatically led into each paragraph, and easy readability is gained.

v   By *inserting space between paragraphs* if they are not indented. Unless this is done block paragraphs, with no clear paragraph beginnings or endings, become difficult to recognize. Paragraphing is important to the flow of reading, and it is lazy or illiterate typography which destroys paragraphs.

13.5   Illustrations

Pictures take two forms: open line, which consist of lines or dots separated by white space; and tonal which consist of tonal picture areas which have to be broken down by dot screens for printing purposes. Line illustrations consist of pen and ink drawings, diagrams, lettering, a signature or a tonal picture converted into dots and line such as scraper boards and quarter tones. All of these forms reproduce well on all qualities of paper, including newsprint. Tonal pictures, converted into half-tones, but being photographed through lined screens, may consist of black and white and full colour pictures, wash drawings and paintings. However, the screen has to be coarse or fine according to the quality of the paper. When newspapers were printed by letterpress, course screens of about 65 lines to the inch (metric 24–26 line) were used, but one of the advantages of offset-litho printing is that finer screens can be used, usually 100–120 line (metric 26–34 line).

13.6   Visuals and layouts

When experimenting with designs the visualizer will sketch an advertisement with pencil or marker pen. This will give a rough idea of the positioning of elements such as headline, illustrations, sub-heads, text, name, price, logo and coupon, if there is to be one. The only wording will be the bold display lines (Figures 13.8 and 13.9). The text will be indicated by lined boxes. The eventual layout will be drawn more carefully with measured areas for wording and pictures, making an accurate plan for camera-ready copy or paste-up, or for the printer to follow. In both visual and layout only display words will be drawn. The total wording or copy will be in typescript form, not written on the layout. (N.B. The mistake is often made in examinations of writing all the wording on the layout.)

13.7 Layout of headlines

Legibility and emphasis can be given to headlines if they are arranged to suit the shape of the space, and this is irrespective of whether the headline is long or short. If the space is broad, such as a half-page across, the headline could reach from side to side, but if it is a half-page down it is necessary to break up or step a long headline. However, if the shape of the space is known it is possible for the copywriter to use words of more than one syllable for a wide space and words of one syllable for a narrow space. How a stepped headline is divided up can help its readability as the following Atari example shows. Which is the most readable?

BEFORE BUYING
A PERSONAL ORGANISER,
CHECK WHICH
ONE IS BETTER ORGANISED

BEFORE BUYING A
PERSONAL ORGANISER,
CHECK WHICH ONE
IS BETTER ORGANISED

BEFORE BUYING
A PERSONAL ORGANISER,
CHECK WHICH ONE
IS BETTER ORGANISED

They all say the same thing and there is perhaps little difference in the three arrangements, but the second one helps the play on words by giving more emphasis to identification of the product 'personal organiser'.

13.8 Typography

Typography is the selection of type faces, sizes and weights. It is the means by which the plain-looking words of copy in typewritten form

Figure 13.8 Original rough visual for Timberland advertisement (courtesy Timberland)

WE STOLE THEIR LAND, THEIR BUFFALO AND THEIR WOMEN.

THEN WE WENT BACK FOR THEIR SHOES.

The Red Indians were an ungrateful lot. Far from thanking the whiteman for bringing them civilisation (guns, whisky, disease, that kind of thing), they spent years making very bad medicine.

Naturally, during the course of their disputes, the whiteman found it necessary to relieve the Red Indians of certain items.

Thousands of square miles of land, for instance, which they didn't seem to be using.

The odd buffalo, which provided some interesting culinary experiences for the folks heading West.

And of course the squaws, who were often invited along to soothe the fevered brows of conscience-stricken gun-runners and bounty hunters.

But perhaps the most lasting testament to this cultural exchange programme is the humble moccasin.

A shoe of quite ingenious construction. And remarkably comfortable to boot.

Even now, nearly two centuries after the first whiteman tried a pair on, they have yet to be bettered.

Which is why at Timberland, all of our loafers, boat shoes and walking shoes are based on the original Red Indian design.

How is this possible? Surely a shoemaker of our standing is capable of showing a clean pair of heels to a few pesky injuns?

Not really.

Although over the years, we have managed to make some modest improvements.

Rather than use any old buffalo hide, we always insist on premium full-grain leathers. And when we find a tannery that can supply them, we buy its entire output.

We then dye the leathers all the way through so you can't scuff the colour off and impregnate them with silicone oils to prevent the leather going dry.

It is at this point that we employ the wraparound construction of the moccasin to create the classic Timberland shoe.

Using a single piece of softened leather, our craftsmen mould and stretch the upper

around a specially-developed geometric last.

This has the effect of breaking the shoes in before you've even set foot in them.

It also extends the life of the shoe for many, many moons.

Our hand sewn shoes also hark back to the days before the whiteman came.

No machines. No mass production. No deadlines.

Just a pair of nimble hands making shoes in the time-honoured way.

With just a little help from the twentieth century.

Like the high-strength nylon thread, double-knotted and pearl stitched to prevent it coming undone even if it's cut or in the unlikely event that it breaks.

The two coats of latex sealant, added to stop even tiny droplets of water sneaking in through the needle holes.

And the patented process which permanently bonds the uppers to the soles.

(If the Indians had only known how to cobble soles onto their moccasins, we probably wouldn't be in business today.)

As you would expect, the result of all our

labours is a shoe which comes with a heap big price tag.

For which we make absolutely no excuses.

After all, who else uses solid brass eyelets? Or self-oiling rawhide laces? Or glove leather linings?

Come to that, what other shoemaker shows such concern for your feet when big rains come?

For example, as well as utilising all our traditional methods, our new Ultra Light range uses new technology to keep your feet dry.

They're lined with Gore-Tex to make them completely waterproof while allowing your feet to breathe. (Gore-Tex has 9 billion holes per square inch. We didn't believe it either but it works, so now we believe it.)

The soles are made from an incredibly lightweight and highly resistant, dual-density polyurethane.

And, in an uncharacteristic concession to fashion, some models even   sport tightly woven waxed cotton   cloth.

A far cry from the Red Indian moccasin? We certainly hope not.

Because if we ever   forget our origins, or change our old-fashioned way of making boots and shoes, one thing's for sure.

A lot of people are going to be on the warpath.

Timberland Shoes and Boots, 23 Pembridge Square, London W2 4DR. Telephone 01:727 2519.

Timberland

Figure 13.9   The final advertisement as it appeared in the press. Agency: The Leagas Delaney Partnership Ltd (courtesy Timberland)

can be brought to life, much as the script of dramatic dialogue is given reality by the actor's or actress's voice. Typography gives meaning, character, mood and verve to the static words.

It does so in three ways:

i   Good typography makes the copy legible.
ii   Good choice of type makes print attractive.
iii Right choice of faces creates style and character.

Settings may consist of metal characters produced by hot metal typesetting machines, but nowadays most settings are produced by computerized photo-typesetting units, and in advertising studios an increasing amount of work is produced in-house on Apple-Macintosh and other desk-top publishing input units.

The *face* is the design of the type. There are hundreds of type faces of which Rockwell, Bodoni, Times and Plantin are well-known names. The *fount* is the complete alphabet, including signs and figures, in one size and weight of one face. *Sizes* are given in *points*, 72 points to the inch. *Weight* refers to the thickness of the face, e.g. extra bold, bold, medium or light.

A family is a complete collection of all the variants of a face as described above, plus any special variant such as 'shadow'. With modern computerized typesetting, special effects can be achieved such as expanding or condensing type photographically which is physically impossible with metal type.

There are two main groups of type, the fancy display faces which can be used for headlines, and the neat text, book, or body faces which are used for the paragraphs of reading matter. A few faces are general purpose and can be used for both display and text, but most display faces become less readable if set small and in the mass.

Examples of different type faces will be found in Figure 13.10.

13.9   Typesetting

Typesetting has become highly sophisticated. It can be generated 'in-house' (in company, agency or studio), by the printer, or by a trade typesetter holding hundreds of faces for different systems.

For example, a trade typesetter, such as Typesetters (Birmingham) Ltd, has 400 Postscript typefaces with output on bromide or film produced by Linotronic 300 and 200P typesetters for Apple Macintosh and IBM keyboards supporting Postscript software. Using this software the customer supplies the copy for setting. The same firm has 1600 Kerned laser typefaces (250 with optional 'true cut' small caps and old style figures). Output is on the Linotronic 300 in bromide, positive or negative film, input by APL 230 keyboards. Sizes can be set up to 186 pt and up to 72 cm pica width. Also included are vertical and horizontal

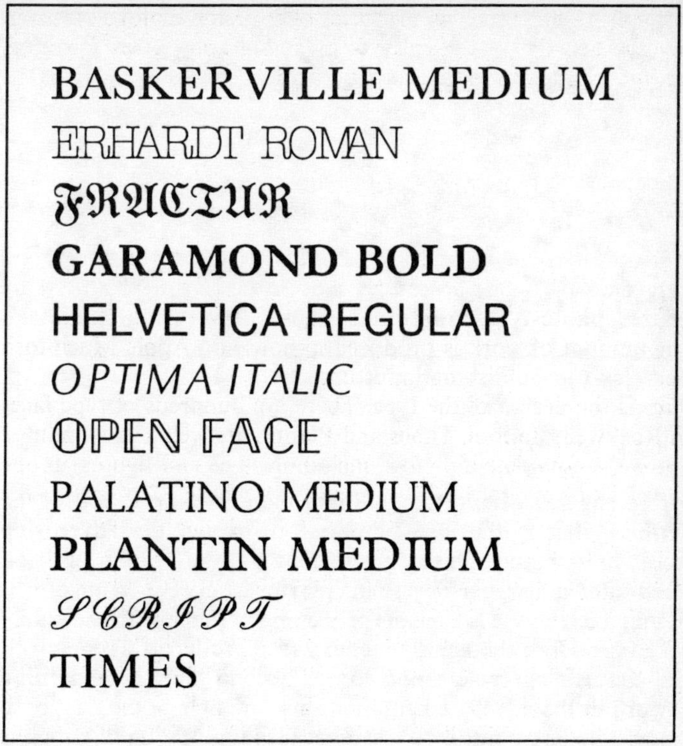

BASKERVILLE MEDIUM

ERHARDT ROMAN

𝔉𝔯𝔞𝔠𝔱𝔲𝔯

GARAMOND BOLD

HELVETICA REGULAR

OPTIMA ITALIC

OPEN FACE

PALATINO MEDIUM

PLANTIN MEDIUM

SCRIPT

TIMES

Figure 13.10   Examples of different typefaces

rules, boxes, tints, ruled forms, patterns and tick marks.

   This may seem very technical but it indicates the range of typo-graphical options that are now available thanks to computerized input of copy and output of typesetting, and customer and printer, or printer and trade typesetter, can operate 'on-line'. We see this in the advertising and house journal worlds, and also in the newspaper world where the central editorial can be in London but the printing plants are located strategically around the country, receiving made-up pages 'on-line'.

14
Copywriting

14.1 What is copywriting?

Copywriting consists of two things. First, there is the creation of the *copy platform*, that is the idea or theme on which the advertising campaign is to be based. This might be that a certain brand of drink is a reward after a summer day spent playing cricket or tennis; or it could be that a telephone is a means of keeping in touch with the family overseas. Eventually , the creative team will reproduce this in words, headlines, pictures, characters, and scenes. Second there is the writing of every word in the advertisement, and this can include the coupon if there is one. The last point is stressed because the writing of coupons (and order forms for off-the-page direct response advertisements) is a highly skilled business in order to achieve both response and correct information about the respondent and what he or she wants.

The writing of copy is a literary form different from any other. It is possible that no-one wants to read it, and yet the copywriter has to try to induce people to read his words. That is a challenge to the advertisement writer. How can he encourage people to read the sales message? In the previous chapter it was shown how the arts of layout and typography could be used to win the reader's attention and interest, but first we have to start with the cold still words of the original typescript. This may be termed the vocabulary and grammar of copywriting, or the special creative and communication style which makes the writing of copy different from any other kind of literature.

The AIDCA formula can be invoked to explain what copy has to do: it has to attract *attention*, stimulate *interest*, create *desire*, inspire *confidence*, and provoke *action*. This final action may be to return a coupon, send in an order, visit a retailer, telephone a supplier or simply remember the product or service when a purchase is being considered. Copy does not seek to entertain like a novel or play, report like a newspaper story, or inform and educate like a news release. It has to persuade and sell.

14.2 Ten forms of copywriting vocabulary and grammar

1 Advertising clichés

Normally, in good writing we try to avoid clichés or hackneyed expressions because they have not only become boring but often their meaning has become lost through overuse. This is not always the case in advertising where sometimes their very banality gives them strength. Here are some typical advertising clichés:

Free	Buy now	Order now
Here	Act now	Today
Now	At last	New
Look	Don't forget	Special offer

The word *free*, is the most commonly used and the most successful word in advertising, and it can even be incorporated in the admonition or the address, e.g. Freefone or Freepost. Few people can resist a free offer, even if it is only a leaflet, brochure or catalogue.

2 Action words or buzz words

If no-one wants to read your copy, and if you want to get your message across quickly, the most sensible thing to do is to use *short* words, and if they are active verbs they will give the impression that the copy is hurrying along. These words can give copy a sense of urgency and so carry the reader on through it. Typical action words are:

Buy	Ring	Go	Mail
Ask	Phone	Write	Use
Come	Call	Send	Try
Do	Clip	Look	Put
Pick	Cut	Test	Make
Watch	Save	Take	Pay
See	Let	Pop	Stay
Get	Post	Start	Add
Smell	Hear	Tell	Catch
Taste	Trust	Spend	Fly
Feel	Give	Gain	Pack

3 Colloquialisms

Copy can be personalized and given warmth by the use of familiar expressions which release it from pedantic and formal prose. Again, these words and word forms help move the copy along. There are two kinds of colloquialisms, that is forms of spoken language:

a Pronouns: we, you, us, our, your.
b Abbreviations: you'll, you're, we'll, what's, he's, she's, there's, don't, won't, shouldn't, now's.

4   Numbers

In literary work (and that includes news releases) strict publishing rules apply to the use of numbers. If a sentence begins with a number it must be in word form, e.g. 'One' not '1'. If numbers are used in sentences, we spell out one to nine and then use figures, e.g. 10, 100, 1,000. We may spell out unwieldy round numbers or abbreviate them, e.g. 1 m. But copywriting is a unique literary form in which almost anything can be done for effect. The normal rules may be broken if it makes the copy typographically more effective. In copy it is acceptable to write '50 people bought 5 kinds of Cheddar Cheese at Sainsbury's'.

5   Repetition

This is the essence of advertising. In fact, a hundred years ago some newspaper advertisements consisted of no more than the same words repeated line after line down a column. Advertising depends on the name, the slogan, the message, the logo or maybe the colour scheme being repeated in various forms over and over again. Sometimes this is called 'plugging', but the point is that memory requires the repetition of sights and sounds. This simple truth can be exploited in advertising. There are four chief ways in which repetition can be achieved to make advertising effective:

(i)   The company or brand name may be plugged throughout the copy.
(ii)   There can be repetition throughout the elements of the advertise-ment – in the headline, sub-headings, text, pictures, coupon and slogan.
(iii) There can be repetition of the advertisements themselves, there being accumulative impact as the advertisement is seen again in many media such as TV, press, posters, point-of-sale displays and the package or product itself.
(iv)   Repetition may also be used as a creative device to attract attention, emphasize or make an advertisement more original. The following examples appeared in a poignant Christian Aid Christmas appeal press advertisement, which was illustrated by a picture of a child from a poor third world country.

Like all small children
she wants lots of things for Christmas

She wants food.
She wants vaccinations.
She wants firewood.
She wants chickens to tend.
She wants a place to call home.
She wants to learn to read and write.
She wants your help to help herself.
She wants a life for Christmas.

This simple example demonstrates the skilful way in which the copywriter exploits words and sentence construction for effect, and this is strengthened by its typographical presentation. The Christian Aid copy was set in bold sans serif type enhanced by plenty of white space. You hardly had to read it, so clear and dominant was the message that it was visual rather than literary. The copywriter does have to write visually, not just produce a piece of typescript. He has to see in his mind's eye how his words will *look*.

6   Punctuation and sentence construction

One of the tricks of the copywriting trade is the use of punctuation, and the construction of sentences, not to please literary pundits or to pass an examination in English, but to put the AIDCA formula into practice. In other words, to make advertising work, and so to entice the reader to do the advertiser's bidding, within the law and codes of practice. We must not exaggerate, mislead or falsify, but like the actor on the stage we do have to be larger than life to be noticed and believed. Whatever devices may be used, credibility must prevail, otherwise we shall not go on being accepted like those who have been advertising from 50 to 100 years or more such as Cadbury, Guinness, Heinz and Whitbread.

Glance back at the Christian Aid advertisement. It looks very simple, but it uses short pithy sentences. It is not an essay, or even an article or a news release. The sentences contain the fewest number of words. Even the full stops at the end of each sentence are like drum beats.

Punctuation can be used instead of words, as in the *ellipsis* or omission of words, e.g. Come to Cyprus... now... this year.

Another popular method is to use dashes instead of dots: It's the taste – the smell – the colour – the price – which people love.

Or, there is the *emphatic full stop* deliberately placed at the end of a headline, not because it completes a sentence but because it adds power, as with:

The pen
is mightier than the
fire extinguisher.   (British Steel)

(Note also how the headline is broken up or stepped to make it very readable.)

A favourite device nowadays is to abbreviate the word 'and' so that we have snappy expressions such as chicken'n'chips, shop'n'park, pick'n'mix, fish'n'chips, free'n'easy or bright'n'breezy.

The use of the apostrophe, as was shown under colloquialisms, is another combination of punctuation and abbreviation.

The effect of these deliberate but unconventional uses of punctuation is to reduce the number of words, tighten up the copy, and convey the message speedily. This is called *pace*. In days gone by famous authors and poets were employed to write advertisements – to puff up products – but their languid styles would have no place today.

Other forms of punctuation can be used to bring copy alive. Subheadings or items in a list of selling points can be highlighted by the use of bold dots, or asterisks, thus attracting attention.

Another creative device, which may still be seen in many newspapers and magazines, is the drop capital at the beginning of the text. This is usually a capital initial letter of a size much larger than the following text. The drop capital derives from hand-written Bibles, when it was usually a very decorative and colourful letter. It may still be seen in illuminated hand-lettered work. In an advertisement it could give the text a very distinctive appearance.

Sentences themselves can be written not only concisely but incompletely. Taken to the extreme, it could be effective to have a one-word, one-sentence paragraph. Similarly, the rules of grammar can be ignored in order to write a paragraph such as:

> Port Royal. One-time wickedest city in the world. Buccaneer's ships groaned into harbour, near submerged with Spanish booty.
> The seadogs went party-party with rum, women and song. Didn't put to sea again until the galleons were high in the water and the last doubloon was gone.
> (Jamaica Tourist Board)

or

> Global Warming. The greenhouse effect. The melting polar ice caps. What on earth can the average man in the street do?
> (British Gas)

or

> We're Alcatel Alsthom. A major industrial group – present worldwide. We operate in over 100 different countries – on all continents – and we operate with an edge.
> (Alcatel Alsthom)

You're getting fit and feeling good.
What you won't feel are shock waves
blasting through your body.
Every time your foot hits the floor.
Bowing your legs. Compressing your spine.
Even bouncing the base of your brain
about half a millimetre. Very unhealthy.
It's called 'impact energy'.
The equivalent force on your body of
a 30 mph car crash. Every time your foot
hits the floor.
And no matter how fit you are, you're
just as susceptible to the same long-term
damage as the average couch potato.
Remedy?

(This was about the first half of the text copy of an advertisement for Sorbothane sports equipment.)

The Sorbothane copy does not waste a word, and it makes powerful use of the one-word, one-sentence paragraph, Remedy? Not all advertisement copy is written like this, and complete flowing sentences may be used, although still with precision. The art of copywriting is often called 'boiling it down', of using the fewest necessary words, of writing economically. The reader does not necessarily want to read advertisements, yet, if it has compelling brevity, the message is more likely to be absorbed.

Punctuation and sentence construction are writing tools which can be used to make copywriting a literary form different from any other.

7 Alliteration

Even though the advertisement may not be read aloud the *sound* of the words can still come across, just as one can mentally listen to music without there being any noise. Sound can be created by the repetition of letters, syllables or whole words. Some of the older slogans such as 'Guinness is good for you', 'Player's Please' and 'Don't be vague, ask for Haig', owed much of their memorability to alliteration. Sometimes such slogans are hard to forget. In fact, after an absence of seven years, Abbey National decided to revive its Abbey Habit slogan and jingle composed by Jeff Wayne. It had not been forgotten.

Alliteration can be achieved by using words with the same first letter as in 'Summer savings in Spain', or with a repeated syllable as in 'modernize, economize, revolutionize', or as in a one-time British Rail slogan 'Let the train take the strain'. A BASF advertisement used a clever piece of alliteration in its From Lips to Laps advertisement which referred to lipsticks and motor racing.

8 Special use of capital letters

In journalistic or publishing work, capital letters are used sparingly, being limited to proper nouns and geographical place names. But in advertising capital letters can be used for effect. Whole words, even sentences can be printed in 'caps', although this should be restricted to essential emphasis, otherwise a lot of copy in capital letters would be unreadable. All emphasis can be no emphasis.

9 Underlining or underscoring

Headlines, words, telephone numbers, and whole sentences may be underlined to give emphasis. This can look ugly if not handled carefully. In underlining words in copy it should be remembered that to a typesetter this means set in italics, so the copy should carry clear instructions. Underlining can also help to break up a mass of copy if sub-headings are underlined, thus helping to carry the eye through the copy. The following example appeared in bold sans type, occupying the top third of a Casio advertisement:

'DON'T FORGET OUR
FRIDAY APPOINTMENT'

'NO PROBLEM I'VE GOT
A BUILT-IN ALARM'

In this case there was triple emphasis: big black sans serif type, capital letters and underlining.

10 Superlatives

The copywriter has to draw word pictures, and create a mood or atmosphere, adopt a larger-than-life approach and very often be emotive rather than factual. The latter depends very much on the product, but the contrast between a piece of advertisement copy and a news release is that the former may be emotive but the latter must be factual. Few people can write both because utterly different literary styles are required. Bad news releases usually read like good advertisements!

The working vocabulary of the copywriter differs enormously from that of the public relations writer or journalist. He will be the master of the use of emotive generalizations such as attractive, beautiful, delightful, delicious, economical, fashionable, gorgeous, ideal, luxurious, money-saving, nutritious, outstanding, perfect, revolutionary, superb, tantalizing, unique, vivacious or wonderful. These words are the vocabulary of advertising, but they have no place in public relations writing. Most of them are unspecific and fairly meaningless, but they help to create an atmosphere of excitement, exuberance, pleasure, romance, satisfaction or whatever may be necessary with a mundane product such as a bar of soap or a lavatory cleaner, although sometimes they may suit an exotic holiday venue or a tasty foodstuff.

At a time when much advertisement copy is brash, bouncy or staccato, the literary quality of the following on behalf of Graham's Port, which appeared in the *Independent Magazine* on Saturday, November 16 1991, was a pleasure to read. It is reminiscent of the narrative style corporate advertisements which famous authors used to be commissioned to write thirty or forty years ago. Pity, though, that the expression 'port out, starboard home' is not explained as the origin of 'posh'.

PORT OUT,
PORT HOME.

IN THE GOLDEN AGE OF THE Ocean liner, anyone worth their salt would book a passage East 'port out, starboard home'.

Thus ensuring that both on the way to their destination, and on the way back, their cabin avoided the fierce glare of the sun.

The term 'port out, port home', however, is rather more apt (we're sure you'll agree) for those travelling West on the opulent leviathans that plied the Atlantic in the early 1900s.

The Olympic, as long as a sky-scraper was high, boasted 1,054 first class cabins.

The Aquitania weighed 45,647 tons yet exhibited such grace she was more popularly called the 'Ship Beautiful'.

And the Mauretania, sleek and straight stemmed, was the model of ocean liners for nearly three decades.

More exquisitely engineered than anything else on the horizon, she held the coveted Blue Riband almost continuously from 1907 until 1929.

A Queen of the seas that held court to reigning Kings, Royal Princesses, Heads of State and a host of loyal subjects straight from the pages of Debrett's.

As a passenger, you could join in the gaiety of the palm court and verandah cafe. Or, perhaps, withdraw to a smoking room that could have been lifted straight from the gentlemen's clubs of the day.

Then there was the flirtatious chatter of the elegant salons. The orchestral pieces of the music room.

And if you'd appreciate a small respite from this social whirl, the calm of the reading rooms.

Yet, beguiling as these rooms were, come evening all would be empty.

The only place to be was in the cathedral-like expanse of the two-tiered restaurant. (Evening dress *de rigueur*.) Here you could partake of Tortue Verte, Creme Chatrilion, Supreme de Sole, monumental sculptures in pastry and Beluga-filled swans of carved ice.

Could it *really* be pure coincidence that the port served on such occasions just had to be Graham's?

The sumptuous fare being an *essential* preliminary to raising the senses to a pitch where the rich, fruity flavour of this finest of ports could be most thoroughly savoured.

Sipping your glass of Graham's in such magnificent surroundings undeniably bestowed a feeling of well being.

And, whilst admiring its intense bouquet, you could also reflect that down below 25 boilers and 192 furnaces were powering you along at a previously unheard of 26.9 knots.

Perhaps you would also muse, as Graham's warmth gently soothed, that you were not actually in that much of a rush to get to America.

W & J,
GRAHAM'S
Established 1829

14.3 Three points to remember

In conclusion, three points to remember because it is easy for an over-zealous copywriter (or even a very competitive advertiser) to be too enthusiastic. Advertising is a tool, as has been said earlier, but it invites criticism and control when it is abused. The three points are these:

1 Exaggeration

Superlatives and puffery verge on exaggeration, and the dividing line can be ever so thin. If the reader, viewer or listener believes a claim in an advertisement is exaggerated doubt will be incurred and disbelief will make the advertisement ineffective and therefore a waste of money. Credibility should never be endangered.

2 Voluntary controls

As will be seen in the relevant chapter, there is, in most countries, a system of self-regulation in the form of a voluntary code of ethics and practice. In the UK there is the British Code of Advertising Practice as administered by the Advertising Standards Authority which regulates print advertising. Other media have their codes and a point made in the ITC's television advertising code is that motor-car advertisements must not exploit dangerous features such as high speed. The copywriter must therefore be thoroughly aware of the existing voluntary controls.

3 Statutory controls

More than 100 written laws concern advertising in the UK, some being fairly general such as the Consumer Protection Act, others relating more specifically to certain trades or practices. The copywriter should be familiar with the law concerning the product or service he is writing about, or certain aspects such as hire purchase or sales promotion schemes (e.g. free draws) which are covered by statute law.

15
Radio and TV commercials

15.1 Introduction

The production of radio commercials is far cheaper than that of TV commercials. Will the economy of national commercial radio appeal to advertisers whose budgets are slim? Shall we see a return to the use of big radio stars like Bing Crosby, Burns and Allen, Jack Benny and Gracie Fields as in the past? We have already seen the popularity of Michael Parkinson, who made his name on TV, as the anchor man on LBC.

While radio and TV are both broadcast media there are great differences which inevitably characterize the nature of the two as advertising media. While TV enjoys the impact of colour, movement and vision, radio has to depend on its impact on the ear. TV is restricted to wherever it may be viewed, but radio is mobile and can be listened to wherever one can take a radio, not forgetting car radios. These differences effect not only what is best advertised on each medium but also the kind of creativity required, bearing in mind that both are transient media. Retention of the message usually depends on repetition. To some extent advertising on both radio and TV are intrusive and there is risk of causing boredom or irritation. Thus the overall demands on creativity far exceed those of other media such as the press or posters.

15.2 Radio scripts

Writing a radio script is quite unlike writing advertisement copy. It resembles radio drama in which the actors read from scripts. The language is conversational. Variety can be introduced by the use of more than one voice, say, one young and one old or one male and one female. Sound effects and music can create realism and atmosphere.

Here are two contrasting radio scripts produced by Alliance International, one for Fruit of the Loom T-shirts and one for Air Call. There was a series of six Fruit of the Loom 50 second episodes in American accents, one of them being:

In a tiny town in the deep mid-West, a father takes his son aside on the day of his wedding.

(SFX cicadas, lone church bell and natural sounds throughout)

Pop: Well boy, it's the big day.

Son: Reckon it is Pop.

Pop: You're to be married to the prettiest girl in town.

Son: Pop, Mary-Lou's dang near the only girl in town.

Pop: Son, she's still mighty pretty.

Son: Pretty she ain't. Matter a' fact I thought she was a fellah until today.

Pop: Now boy. Don't worry 'bout nothin'.

Son: Why ever not?

Pop: See, her Daddy owns the general store.

Son: But I gotta love a girl before I can marry her.

Pop: ... and the general store's just taken in a nice big delivery of Fruit of the Loom T-shirts.

Son: No kiddin' ...

(pause)

Son: You know Papa, I look at Mary-Lou sittin' over yonder in her tractor with her purdy little hob-nail booties and shovel ... heck she don't look so bad after all.

Presenter: Fruit of the Loom. The original T-shirts since 1851.

As America's leading T-shirt brand the advertiser wanted to communicate its American heritage so all the advertisements were set in the USA. The theme was adopted that people treated their T-shirts as a valuable item they would not be parted from. Because the advertisements were aimed at a youth market humour was used.

The following was one of the three 40 second Air Call scripts:

John Sessions:

(in rude Cockney accent)

I'm rude me. I'm flippin' rude. I'm so rude I lean out of my taxi and say get outta the way you 'orrible little twits. But then I got Car Call the all in one mobile phone package. At £49.95 + VAT a month it's flamin' cheap. And since I got 30 minutes of inclusive air time, my Vodaphone subscription ...

(voice changes into polite home counties accent)

... and a car phone by Motorola in my hackney cab with insurance and repairs included, I've come over all polite. No more dreadful swearing for me, and no more for nice people when you get Car Call in your jolly old cars.

William Franklin:

To appreciate all the benefits of the Car Call package, visit Dixons or phone Air Call on 0800 200 200 ... whoever you are.

John Sessions:

Yes dears, you'll swear by it ... (voice changes) ... Woncha?

Here was a very different proposition for the scriptwriter to handle. A complicated carphone hire package called Car Call was not an easy brief given the information that had to be included. Because of the nature of the product it was decided to produce a clever advertisement with a bit of dry humour. The problem of changing accents mid-stream (without edits) meant finding someone who could do it, and John Sessions proved to be a good choice.

15.3   Stages in creation and production of a TV commercial

Producing a TV commercial is more complicated than making a radio advertisement because the idea will be conceived within the agency, where there is a TV producer, but the shooting will be done by an outside film or video unit with a TV director. Locations may also be involved. The following sequence of events is supplied by Alliance International who have produced commercials for clients such as the Woolwich Building Society.

i   Brief submitted to creative department of agency.
ii   Creative development.
iii   Possible research of anamatic or storyboard.
iv   ITVA script approval (mandatory).
v   Obtain a 'guide quotation' of production costs for likely outside production company.
vi   Prepare finalized script and storyboard and budget. (The storyboard is a series of drawings of the proposed commercial, in effect a cartoon consisting of oblong or TV-screen shape pictures mounted on board.) Investigate music copyright where relevant. Occasionally music may be specially written, but usually it will be hired from a music library.
vii   Client approval (or go back to ii).
viii   Appoint director.
ix   Brief casting director, wardrobe lady, make-up department, art department where sets/models may be needed.
x   Cast actors, actresses, presenter.
xi   Select wardrobe.
xii   Check set drawings, or check outside locations.
xiii   Pre-production meeting where cast, location/set, wardrobe, and ITVA approved script are all agreed.
xiv   Brief music composer/arranger.
xv   Shoot on 35 mm film.
xvi   Review rushes of footage shoot.
xvii   Edit on film or transfer to videotape and edit.
xviii   Record voices/sound effects/music. Dub together all these elements.
xix   Finished edit. Picture without any optical special effects. Sound track synchronized to visual.
xx   Client approval of rough cut.
xxi   Add optical effects to either film or videotape, e.g. titles, computer generated effects (i.e. Paintbox/'Harry' computer retouching).

xxii Double head (visual plus sound) if on film, or finished edit with sound dub approved by client.
xxiii ITVA shown finished film for approval if requested.
xxiv Duplication of commercial for ITV stations, either on film or videotape, with approval number, production details, and run up clock on the start.
xxv Distribute copies to ITV stations for them to assemble with other commercials to make up commercial breaks for transmission.
xxvi Appear on the air.

15.4 Cost of actors, actresses and presenters

Reference is made to artistes in TV commercials in 11.14. Large fees are paid to the actors and actresses who play in TV commercials. Nigel Havers and Jan Francis each received £70,000 for their appearance in Lloyds Bank commercials screened in 1992. David Jason earned £100,000 and Lenny Henry was paid £75,000 for work in Abbey National commercials. One-off payments are now common to avoid disputes over escalating fees and repeat fees when advertisements appear on other channels or are repeated in the future.

In November 1991 the squabble over repeat fees was partially settled in an agreement between the Institute of Practitioners in Advertising, the Incorporated Society of British Advertisers, and the independent producers group AFVPA and the actors' union Equity. The agreement provides for a method of calculating actors' fees for advertisements which treats all TV services in line with the audience figures measured by BARB. Advertisers can use terrestrial, cable or satellite airtime for advertisements irrespective of their fee loading. This replaced the old system which was based on separate use of scales for ITV, Channel 4, TV-am and satellite which was inflationary, stabilizing costs for advertisers and fees for performers.

16
Printing processes

16.1 Introduction

A great deal of advertising is printed so it is useful to have a basic knowledge of the different printing processes, whether an advertisement is being placed in the press or whether advertising materials such as brochures, catalogues or display items are being bought. Some forms of print are best suited to a particular process, others may be printed by more than one process. One printer may use one process, and another printer may use another.

The four main processes are letterpress (including flexography), lithography, photogravure and silk screen. The essential differences are that letterpress prints from a raised surface (like a typewriter key or a date stamp); lithography prints from a flat surface; photogravure prints from a recessed surface (like an etching); and silk screen prints through a stencil.

In most processes, printing may be either flat-bed with the printing material flat on the bed of the machine, or rotary with a curved printing plate clapped round a cylinder. Printing may be sheet-fed, using a stack of single sheets of paper, or web fed using a very large reel of paper as with newspaper printing. The basic principle of all printing is that ink is applied to the printing surface or plate and by the action of the machine this is impressed on the paper as it passes through, except that in off-set litho printing the print is received by an intervening blanket cylinder which then offsets it on to the paper.

16.2 Letterpress

Because this is a *relief* printing system everything which is to receive ink and be reproduced must be raised above the surface. All non-printing surfaces, such as the space round characters, must be below the surface so that it receives no ink.

Letterpress is a versatile process which can be used to print almost everything from a business card to full-colour brochures, from books to newspapers, having the advantage that it can print from any kind of paper or card. One reason for this is that pictures such as photographs or paintings – tonal pictures – can be reproduced by the half-tone system of dots. The screen – number of dots to the inch or centimetre – may be as fine or as coarse as the quality of paper will permit. Thus, when most newspapers were printed by letterpress a very coarse screen was used, but for a beautiful book of paintings printed on art paper the screen could be four times as fine. These dots are etched so that the surrounding area around each dot is not type-high and so cannot carry any ink to the paper. With a very coarse screen about 60 per cent of the surface area of the plate prints while the remaining 40 per cent leaves the paper unprinted, and this screen effect is easily visible to the eye.

The half-tone screen system is also used in lithographic and silk-screen printing, but not in photogravure as will be explained later.

The disadvantages of letterpress printing are that rotary machines are very big, a foundry department is required for setting metal type and making metal plates, and a great deal of labour is involved. Fleet Street in London used to be a 'factory' area when newspapers were printed by letterpress. The introduction of offset-litho produced an exodus from Fleet Street to smaller plants with fewer operatives, either on the fringes of London, or strategically placed throughout the country where contract printers (like Derby Daily Telegraph and Portsmouth Publishing and Printing) make it unnecessary for some London nationals to own their own presses.

However, letterpress is not entirely dead and there are still small jobbing and commercial printers who continue to set metal type by Linotype machines, and use line or halftone blocks to reproduce pictures.

16.3 Lithography

While letterpress was largely developed in Britain by people like Caxton in the fifteenth century who probably learned the process in Cologne, lithography is a more recent process attributed to the Austrian Aloys Senefelder at the end of the eighteenth century. His invention was due to the discovery of the absorption properties of stone quarried in the Jura mountains in Bavaria.

Lithography is a *planographic* method (Greek *lithos* a stone and *graphien* to write), and operates on the principle that grease and water will not mix. Thus, if the printing image is greasy, and ink is applied, it can be washed clear of the non-greasy non-printing areas. Originally, artists wrote or drew on slabs of Jura stone, and up until about 50 years ago poster artists drew their designs in *reverse* on the stone, using as many stones as the number of colours required.

Aluminium plates were first introduced by the Aluminium Co. of New York at the beginning of the 19th century, and the process has developed ever since, especially in the USA and Germany, but more slowly in the UK because of trade union protectionism which retained labour intensive letterpress newspaper printing until the mid 1980s.

However, just after the Second World War Woodrow Wyatt rescued provincial newspapers by bringing to the UK a number of American offset-litho presses, which were strategically located so that they could print newspapers for publishers who could not afford to buy new machines.

Offset-photo-litho receives the image from the plate cylinder on a blanket cylinder which then conveys it to the paper as the paper passes between the blanket and impression cylinders. For some years, offset was notable for its soft appearance and it was necessary to use hard cartridge papers. However, rapid improvements have seen the process benefit from a range of papers, highly-pigmented brilliant inks, computerized photo-typesetting, compact high speed machines, and economic labour use. In fact, in the change-over from letterpress to offset-litho we have seen a dramatic change from the craftsman printer to the electrician operator and computer keyboard operator.

One of the advantages of the process in publishing is that it has made viable the production of newspapers with circulations of only 300–400,000 (e.g. *The Independent* and *The Independent on Sunday*) and also magazines like *The European* with even smaller circulations. Because art work and copy is pasted up by the compositor all kinds of creative effects can be achieved, which was not possible with type and blocks. Moreover, even on newsprint, the half-tone screen is often twice as fine as it was with letterpress. This results in pictures being clearer and better defined, and good scenic pictures with tonal values can be printed instead of the old 'soot and whitewash' pictures of letterpress days. The photo-typesetting also means perfect unbroken and regular type compared with the irregularities of Linotype settings. In addition, it is more economical to print full colour, and to do so 'on the run' instead of having to pre-print colour by another process as used to occur with letterpress.

16.4 Photogravure

There are various forms of photogravure from the rotary presses which made the UK's big circulation women's weekly magazines possible in the 1930s to the presses for the superb quality printing of photographic prints or postage stamps. The former has also been used for the printing of full-colour catalogues and travel brochures, and also for packaging such as labels for cans and bottles.

It is an *intaglio* process, the ink being held in cells below the surface and their depth varies according to the intensity of colour required. The plate or sleeve is tubular, and its surface is a square grid or 'resist', from which excess ink is scraped by a steel doctor blade, the ink being a volatile spirit ink which is sucked out onto the paper, the solvent evaporating. Photogravure print is recognizable by the after-smell of the ink, the velvety rather than sharp appearance of pictures, and the effects of the square screen which is laid over the entire print area and can so cause imperfections to type. Its main advantage, as seen with big circulation magazines, is that it is a fast and economical way of printing in full-colour on comparatively cheap super-calendered paper. Newer magazines are mostly printed by offset-litho and have a superior appearance.

The sleeve is produced electronically by an engraving tool which cuts into the copper cylinder to produce the cells of different depth. This results in more accurate colour reproduction, a fault in the past being that sleeves had to be retouched by hand to achieve certain shades, and it was possible for the same advertisement in two gravure-printed magazines (e.g. *Woman* and *Woman's Own*) to appear in slightly different shades which infuriated advertisers.

There is another form of photogravure, the German Klischograph *hard-dot* cylinder system, which resembles litho by having the image on the surface instead of being recessed. Instead of cells of different depths, it has surface areas of various sizes according to the lightness or darkness of tone, these areas picking up the necessary quantities of ink.

16.5 Flexography

This is a variation of letterpress, using rubber plates and rapid drying inks, and was originally used for printing on delicate materials such as metallic papers for confectionery wrappers. Then it was developed in the USA for newspaper production, and adopted by the *Daily Mail* group when they moved to new plant in SE London.

Flexographic newspaper presses use photopolymer plates and special inks which are even brighter than litho inks, and they do not rub off on the fingers. There is very good picture and colour reproduction.

16.6 Silk screen (or screen printing)

Here is a process of great value in the printing of advertising items, and unlike other processes it can be applied to most materials and to any shape surface. It is commonly used for printing on T-shirts, balloons, bottles, ash-trays and for items like control panels, but can be used for printing book jackets, window bills, posters and point-of-sale displays. It is a *stencil* process.

Centuries ago the Chinese, who were among the first people to adopt printing, had a silk-screen system using a mesh of human hair. The process is based on the stencil, the design being cut out, a screen of silk, nylon, organdie or metal mesh separating the cut-out from the paper. A thick paint-like ink is then rolled or otherwise impressed so that it passes through the stencil and the mesh to the paper. Silk screen presses range from simple hand-made ones to sophisticated machines capable of producing half-tone effects in four colours.

The following examples of the versatility of the process are taken from an advertisement for Daytona Marketing Ltd of Tamworth.

Self adhesive panels for bus sides, line or four colour.
16 to 96 sheet posters, four colour/line and specials.
Hanging mobiles.
Membership and discount cards.
Door signs.
Mini flags in welded PVC, supplied with pole and bracket.
Window graphics and in-store promotion packs.
Posters such as four-sheets for shopping precincts.
Leaflet dispensers.
Corporate flags.
Car stickers.
Wobblers on PVC.
Shelf edging.
Cardboard engineering – point-of-sale cut-outs.
Outdoor banners on PVC, welded, eyeletted, roped any size.
Forecourt bunting to specific designs.
Computer cut vinyl graphics for vehicle livery, exhibition stands and
    other applications.

16.7   Four colour process

Full-colour work is produced by the use of four colours, yellow, magenta (beetroot red), cyan (blue) and black. These colours are extracted from the original by means of filters, and progressives pulled from each plate on transparent plastic are used to show the sequence and build-up of colours in the printing order as the order of colours stated above. These colours can also be used singly as is often seen in newspapers and house journals where one and two colour effects are achieved for, say, headlines.

16.8   Buying print

The print buyer not only has a choice of processes, but a choice of printers. There are printers who specialize in certain classes of work such as printing newspapers, books, calendars, packaging or promotional literature, and there are others who have particular kinds of presses and associated equipment such as folding, binding and laminating machines. The latter adhere a film coating to the surface of a cover. Some may do their own typesetting while others may buy in typesetting from a trade setting house (which could mean access to a very large variety of faces). Others may have laser printing facilities whereby items such as a person's name can be printed in the middle of a sales letter in a different type-face or a different colour, by means of a computer.

With so many facilities available it pays to shop around, collecting samples of print and getting quotations from at least three printers. When inviting quotations precise information should be given about size, quantity, colour work, volume of copy, number of pictures, quality of paper and delivery date. If possible this should be accompanied by a rough dummy of the job.

Prices quoted are likely to vary, either because some of the work has to be put out to trade houses, or because printers have different machines. It is always best not to be content with meeting a printer's representative, but if possible to visit the print shop. Printers are skilled people who are often willing and able to give the customer advice.

Part Five
Special Related Areas

17
Direct response marketing

17.1 Introduction

The mail order business has a long history, being pioneered in the USA as a means of supplying almost anything by mail to farmers scattered throughout the mid-west, this being helped by the spread of railways and the introduction of parcel post. The two leading firms were Montgomery Ward and Sears Roebuck of Chicago. In Britain, Empire Stores originated with the efforts of Antonio Fattorini in 1831, a pedlar selling jewellery and watches at rural markets and fairs.

For many years, mail order tended to be mainly of two types, the catalogue and mail order club business of Littlewoods, Empire Stores, Grattan, Kays and others whose advertisements appeared regularly in the women's press and in the *Radio Times* and *TV Times*, and the 'bargain square' advertisements in the weekend newspapers. In recent years it has grown into a major form of distribution, of shopping without shops, and has become known as direct or direct response marketing. The British Direct Mail Advertising Association was re-named the British Direct Marketing Association in 1976, and became the Direct Marketing Association in 1992. The magazine of direct marketing is called *Direct Response*.

In the 1980s, thanks to many aids such as databases and list brokers, and targeting systems such as ACORN, direct response has been adopted by some very big traders such as the Royal Mint, by many financial houses, and by department stores anxious to compete with catalogue firms. Insurance companies are now the largest users of direct response marketing.

It is conducted through a variety of media which include direct mail, catalogues, off-the-page advertisements, inserts, door-to-door distribution, and commercial TV.

The subject has also been introduced into the CAM Certificate syllabus, sharing an examination paper with sales promotion. The two are often closely related since a number of sales promotion devices are applied to direct response.

Direct response does have its precise meaning of producing sales by direct means with no retail intermediary. It does not mean the response generated by general advertising for goods sold by retailers.

The volume of expenditure on direct response marketing was revealed by a survey conducted by *Direct Response*, the results being published in the March 1991 issue. It showed that 50.75 per cent of all UK advertising expenditure was on direct response (compared with 67 per cent in the USA), this amounting to £4.2bn. Based on 1989 figures, as published in the Advertising Association's *Advertising Statistics Yearbook 1990*, and direct mail figures from the Direct Mail Sales Bureau, the media breakdown is shown in Table 15.1.

Table 15.1   UK direct response advertising expenditure 1989

Medium	£m	% of total
Television	222.8	5.2
Press		
display	773	18.3
classified	2038	48.3
Radio	102	2.4
Direct mail		
(inc. production)	758	17.9
Poster	1.9	—
Door-to-door	52	1.2
Telephone marketing	248	5.8
Total	4219	100

17.2   Reasons for success of direct response

Many of the reasons for the development and success of direct response marketing have been analysed in the section on direct mail in Chapter 12, but it should be remembered that direct marketers use both above-the-line and below-the-line media as primary media. As Table 15.1 shows, similar amounts are spent on direct mail and displayed press advertising. Press advertising may be used to achieve direct purchases, but those purchases can also produce database material for direct mail purposes. Specific reasons for the success of direct response are:

i   The impersonal services in self-service stores.

ii   The high cost of shopping by car, both in petrol and parking charges, or the inadequacies of public transport.

iii From the direct marketer's point-of-view, savings in cost of retail premises and sales staff.

iv   New media opportunities, with better targeting, such as weekend magazines.

v   Greater use of the telephone for buying purposes, assisted by acceptance of credit and charge cards.

vi   Facility of colour in many journals to give realism to illustrated goods.

vii   The pleasure of indulging in armchair buying.

viii Freedom from the hustle and bustle of crowded shops, and ability to choose and decide without the attentions of sales assistants.

ix   Exclusivity of merchandise.

x   Privacy or secrecy which may be desirable with personal products or services.

Stan Rapp, writing in *Direct Response* (October 1990), claimed, 'There are two socio-economic trends affecting the marketplace that ensure a bright future for direct marketing in the 90s ... The first trend is the mounting pressure on the personal time of the consumer. The other is the overcrowding caused by too many new products on the shelves'.

17.3   Media of direct response marketing

The following nine media are not ranked by their importance, and different direct marketers may find that one medium, or a certain combination of media, works best for them. It is a question of which medium achieves sales most economically, although creative tactics must also be considered. No medium will be successful if the offer lacks appeal and conviction, for while armchair shopping may have its attractions it does have to overcome the problem that the goods cannot be inspected or sampled.

1   Off-the-page

This is the kind of press advertisement which invites readers to order goods or services described. All manner of goods and services are sold in this way including fashion goods, collectibles, furniture, tableware, books, correspondence courses, car insurance, unit trusts and shares. These may be quite small advertisements, but many are full-colour whole page advertisements with realistic pictures.

Payment may be required with order, whether by cheque, postal order or credit/charge card, or the goods may be sent on approval and invoiced. The latter method may be an added inducement to buy, but there is risk of non-payment, although this may be covered by charging a price which covers average losses. Another inducement may be a discount for immediate payment. With high-priced items instalments may be paid, provided the order form states the total price of the instalments which is usually higher than the cash price.

The order form or coupon calls for skilful copywriting and design because it is vital to avoid unnecessary correspondence if the customer has failed to order correctly. This is particularly so when there are choices which may have to be indicated in boxes on the coupon. It is also wise to offer second choices in case the first choice has sold out as might happen with skirts or blouses of different colours. The space for the customer's address should be adequate, and to avoid wrong deliveries the county, postcode or country should be requested. Action can be encouraged by offering Freepost or Freefone services, and also by illustrating credit and charge cards.

Coupons can be keyed, e.g. by placing a code in the corner, so that the pulling power of the medium and the cost-per-reply or order can be assessed. The coupon should be positioned where it is easy to cut it out, and it may be edged with a dot line and perhaps illustrated with scissors. The address of the advertiser should appear in the remaining advertisement as well as on the coupon so that the customer has a record of the supplier.

An interesting device used in some off-the-page advertisements is a tip-on, a detachable item such as a reply card which is glued to the advertisement.

As Table 15.1 shows, a vast amount of direct response advertising in the press consists of *classified* advertising which clearly expects a response, usually by telephone or box number. These 'smalls' should not be forgotten, and they are the life-blood of local newspapers including free newspapers, but also appear in many national newspapers and magazines.

2   Inserts

These are advertisements tipped into publications, and there are varying opinions about their effectiveness. They are resented by some readers who tip them into the waste-bin before reading the journal! Nevertheless, some direct marketers prefer this medium as it enables them to say more than they can in an advertisement space. Some publishers have special equipment for inserting them. They may work best if they are the same size as the page size of the journal. Their success depends on how interesting they are to a sufficient number of readers, and also how well they are targeted to reach the right readers.

3   Direct mail

This is a very popular medium for direct marketers, and it is described more fully in Chapter 12. Its advantage is that direct mail can be targeted to selected prospects. Skill has to be applied to the careful use of appropriate mailing lists and to avoidance of duplication. The mailing shot can consist of sales letters, leaflets, catalogues and order forms but a proliferation of items can be irritating and counter-effective. Direct mail is a medium which can be very cost-effective, but its abuse has led to the unfortunate nickname of junk mail.

4 Piggy-backing

Here is a form of direct mail which consists of a direct mail shot, usually small, being inserted with other people's mail such as gas and electricity bills. It is, however, rather hit or miss because it is difficult to target if at all.

5 Mail drops

Sometimes called door-stoppers or door-to-door distribution, this is direct advertising delivered to homes. There are firms which carry out this work, or items can be delivered with free newspapers. Targeting is possible if the drops are made to certain areas or classes of housing. It is a comparatively cheap method, but householders may resent a litter of leaflets on the doormat. The greatest success has been with samples or cash vouchers redeemable at local shops.

6 Radio

As the *Direct Response* survey shows, some direct marketers use this medium, and it is possible to get response by giving telephone numbers. A number of business-to-business advertisers make good use of radio.

7 Television

Some firms have found this a successful way of selling, say, records, tapes and discs, coupled with a phone-in computerized ordering service, or use of 0800 telephone numbers, which are free calls.

In the USA, where there are 12 to 13 minutes of commercial air-time per hour, compared with six or seven minutes in the UK, direct response marketers are enthusiastic users of television. The 24-hour television service in the UK lends itself to direct response, in spite of the fall-off in audience figures, if the American system of payment per enquiry (PI) is accepted by the ITVA. (This was being investigated at the time of writing.) The PI method depends on the ITV contractors offering free commercials in return for a percentage of income from product sales, although in the UK a down payment would be required on PI advertising.

8 Catalogue selling

This continues to be a popular form of direct marketing and today there are many variations of the method. There are the well-known club catalogues whereby an agent enrols a circle of members, earning a commission on orders so obtained. But many other organizations sell by catalogues. Many charities have their seasonal catalogues of cards and gifts. A number of credit card firms insert catalogues with their monthly statements. Some are tipped in as inserts in magazines. Sellers of horticultural products, collectibles, wines, clothing and books, mail catalogues, especially to customers whose names and addresses they have compiled in mailing lists or databases.

9   Telephone selling or telemarketing

Very personalized, this is a method which works best when the subscriber is not plagued by unsolicited calls. For instance, advertisement space is frequently sold in this way. Some callers take the courteous precaution of writing first to say they intend to call.

Sugging is an abuse of telephone selling whereby the caller pretends to be conducting research as a means of capturing the subscriber's attention, and it is condemned by the Market Research Society.

17.4   Mail Order Protection Scheme

Known as MOPS, this is a scheme to protect readers from unscrupulous traders, and also to protect publishers from being criticized for carrying dubious advertisements. Advertisements appear in publications which support the schemes, and they state that, 'Mail order advertisements within this newspaper requiring payment to be sent in direct response are approved under the terms of the Mail Order Protection Scheme (MOPS). This means that you are fully protected from financial loss should the advertiser default and cease to trade'.

Such protection became necessary after some unfortunate experiences in the past when mail order traders either did not appreciate the power of press advertising and were swamped with orders or, worse still, they did not order stock until orders were received by which time the price had gone up and they went bankrupt in the attempt to satisfy demand.

17.5   Direct marketing agencies

The growth of direct response marketing, with its use of both above-the-line and below-the-line media, and its need for special creative techniques, has led to the creation of a number of specialist agencies, or specialist subsidiaries of full-service agencies. As already explained in 17.3, arrangements with ITV are different from normal airtime buying. They also satisfy clients who are in a business which requires 'accountable advertising' which enables response to be measured. Research may also be required such as the A/B split or split run system of placing different advertisements in certain copies of the same issue, or in different issues, to measure which advertisement produces the best response.

17.6 The Direct Marketing Agency Register

The Register holds portfolios and videos on some twenty five marketing agencies which, for a fee, may be inspected in confidence at the Register's London office. To help short list the companies to be studied, agency fact sheets can be supplied in advance. The service can also reveal client lists to avoid considering an agency which handles a rival account. In this way a potential client can review the work of direct marketing agencies without the knowledge of the agencies themselves. Then the client can invite the chosen agencies to put up propositions.

17.7 Database marketing

Computerized information about customers or prospects is the basis of database marketing. The megalist may comprise in-house data (which may be held by an outside computer company), or an outside database company may maintain and rent mailing lists. Some contain millions of names and addresses, such as those based on the share registers resulting from privatization flotations.

The in-house database may be a record of customer transactions which may be of value to several departments, and can be used by the marketing department. Such databases can be built up by requesting information when enquiries are made or goods are ordered so that names and addresses and particular categories of customer can be selected for particular marketing operations. Thomas Cook, for example, have a database which originated for accounting purposes, but has been adapted for direct response marketing campaigns. By means of the database, Thomas Cook are able to target particular types of traveller and holidaymaker. It is really a matter of exploiting customer information, much of which already exists in a company. It has been greatly developed by airlines, banks and insurance companies.

However, if such information does not exist, or new sources are required, it is possible to obtain lists either as printed labels or on disk from a database company such as Shalgate Publishing. They have a database of 6,000 senior managers and directors who have been appointed or promoted within the past year. They are coded according to company activity such as financial services, computers, transport, marketing or solicitors, and there are also position codes such as chairman, treasurer, personnel director, marketing director or purchasing manager.

Thus, instead of simply building lists of names and addresses a data base can hold details about job titles, number of employees, what people buy, and so on. Life style databases, produced from elaborate surveys, can supply lists of people of different age and income groups with identified interests. Computerized, all such information can be quickly cross-referenced or retrieved. This sorting process permits stored information to be chosen according to determined characteristics, e.g. name, within date, media code or region.

Some essentials of customized databases are:

i All addresses must be post-coded in accordance with the Royal Mail Postcode Address File. This not only enables mail to be delivered correctly, but makes possible use of economical Post Office services such as Mailsort. The sortation plan of Mailsort sorts direct mail shots on the basis of 1,520 direct selections of postcodes so that mail goes direct to delivery offices, and 80 are residue selections to post offices where mail is sorted to delivery offices.

ii Future uses of the database should be anticipated.

iii It should lend itself to particular kinds of targeting such as TV region and local radio areas, lifestyle analysis, or neighbourhood classifications. This is a process known as data fusion.

iv The proposal should be costed to see what various uses of the data base will cost, since this will be part of budgeting a direct response campaign.

17.8 BRAD Direct Marketing

This is one of the series of British Rate and Data Directories, published in March and September each year, which identifies more than 3,000 businesses, consumer and public sector mailing lists available for rental, plus 1000 direct marketing service companies of various kinds under 13 specialist headings.

17.9 Response handling

Finally, while direct response marketing – using any, some or all of the media described earlier – can be extremely successful, and it may seem to be very economical not to have to provide a retail store, it has to be asked whether the direct marketer is capable of handling response. This response may come by telephone or mail, and it may include both enquiries and orders. Is there staff to answer the telephone all day, or should calls be directed to a telephone answering service? How quickly can orders be turned round? What is the policy about personal cheques: is bank clearance required before dispatching, and does the advertising make it clear that, say, 21 or 28 days should be allowed for delivery? If it is an international business, is foreign currency or are credit cards accepted, or is there insistence upon sterling or another currency such as American dollars or Swiss Francs?

A clear policy and system should be devised, otherwise time and money will be lost on handling complaints. Not surprisingly, some direct response firms give only postal addresses. But some companies are bad response handlers, and delay or discourtesy immediately provokes bad public relations. This means that the volume of response should be estimated so that there is the quickest possible handling of orders, payment and delivery. For instance, one stationery firm mails a monthly catalogue, has a Freefone ordering service and delivers next day by courier service.

18
Sales promotion

18.1 Sales promotion and merchandising

The expression 'sales promotion' has replaced 'merchandising' which it better used in connection with the actual merchandise or goods for sale in a retail store. Sales promotion is not just the promotion of retail stock, but of special devices – mostly instigated by manufacturers – to achieve short-term results. These devices usually consist of special offers or inducements of some kind, and while they apply to all kinds of products and services, and are often associated with direct response marketing, they can be observed in abundance in most supermarkets where they are used to promote fmcgs.

Some argument persists as to whether sales promotion is a form of advertising or marketing, but since advertising is part of the marketing mix it would seem logical to include sales promotion in this book. Moreover, sales promotion is sometimes used as an alternative to media advertising, and the cost of a promotion is another way of spending the advertising budget.

18.2 Sales promotion defined

There are many elaborate definitions, but a simple one is that sales promotion is a below-the-line activity, usually at the point-of-sale but can be via media, whereby added value is given to a product or sale to obtain sales on a short-term basis.

The 'added value' distinction is significant, and it may be represented by a price reduction, bonus pack, premium or gift, on-pack offer, prize, cash token towards a future purchase and so on. In other words, customers are encouraged to buy because of the special inducement. Although the consumer may seem to be getting something for nothing, the cost (like that of advertising) is a promotional cost which is included in the price. The manufacturer spends his money on the 'extra value' instead of on, say, TV, press or poster advertising.

18.3 Current trends

Many forms of sales promotion are described in this chapter, but there have been some interesting changes – and some revivals! – in the forms currently used. Because of more competitive High Street trading in the 1980s and 1990s, it has become less attractive for consumers to collect tokens and send then with cash (postal orders being very expensive) for items such as household goods which can be bought just as cheaply in the shops. Consequently, although they have not disappeared entirely, there are fewer self-liquidating offers, and also fewer mail-ins which involve the customer in postage costs. The current trend is to organize schemes which can be redeemed at the point-of-sale. There has also been an increase in catalogue schemes with fairly expensive items being offered for tokens and cash. We have also seen numerous free draws, with no requirement to show proof of purchase but capable of attracting store traffic, these schemes being outside lottery legislation since everyone has a chance of winning a prize. Another move has been towards delayed-action projects, whereby the benefit is postponed by the need to collect sufficient tokens, not a new idea but one used by coffee and petrol companies.

18.4 Reasons for expansion of sales promotion

As recalled in Chapter 1, sales promotion has a long history, and some of the entrepreneurs of the past such as Beecham, Colman and Lipton were wizards of the craft. Some of the schemes in the 1920s and 1930s were directed at children. The travelling circus was promoted by colouring cards bearing outline drawings of circus scenes which were delivered door-to-door the week before the circus came to town. If a child presented a card which had been coloured it was allowed to see the show free-of-charge, but of course the accompanying parents had to pay. There was a popular cigarette called BDV (Best Dark Virginia), and press advertisements announced a free gauge 'O' clockwork railway engine. Schoolboys quickly converted their fathers to BDV smokers in order to collect the necessary coupons!

In recent years there has been a big increase in the use of sales promotion, supported by the Institute of Sales Promotion, awards for projects, a specialist magazine *Sales Promotion*, and British Code of Sales Promotion Practice, and inclusion of the subject in the CAM Certificate syllabuses, plus a CAM Diploma option in the subject. Why is this?

1   Because advertisers have found it a more cost-effective alternative to media advertising, especially TV where the increase in rates exceeds that of inflation, while air-times are being zapped or fragmented and made ineffectual for advertising purposes.

2   The growth of huge supermarket chains and out-of-town super-stores has made retail selling impersonal. Sales promotion schemes help products to sell themselves off the shelf.

3   The need for a national brand to remain 'listed' by a supermarket chain. There are many rival brands, plus the own labels of the supermarkets themselves, but limited shelf space even in huge stores. Tesco have even run sales promotion schemes for their own label brands. This situation is becoming increasingly difficult for national brands due to the import of foreign products which will be intensified by the Single European Market. Sales promotion schemes specifically designed for one retailer (e.g. Sainsbury or Tesco) help to keep the national brand (e.g. McDougalls flour and Nescafé) stocked. This is brought about when, say, a coffee firm offers a cash refund for labels representing several hundred grammes of purchases, which may take weeks to collect, and they must be bought from one named supermarket.

4   The need to create cash flow by creating stock-turn, either for the manufacturer or the retailer. Impulse buying helps here.

5   The availability of expert services by specialist agencies (see 18.8) which know how and why to buy offers (often from abroad), and who are able to create novel schemes and build brand strength.

6   The fact that sales promotion brings the consumer closer to the manufacturer and is free of the aloofness of traditional media advertising. This can create goodwill.

7   There is an entertainment aspect about sales promotion. People enjoy participating in schemes, collecting tokens or entering for prize draws. This, again, is much more personal then media advertising.

8   Impulse buying of small unit fmcgs is encouraged among first-time buyers.

9   The adoption of sales promotion by new users. For instance, insurance (which used to be sold quite seriously) is now promoted with sales promotion gimmicks like free calculators, clocks and cameras. Sales promotion is applied to all kinds of other products and services from package holidays to mortgages.

10 The rapid growth of direct response marketing has led to a combination of tactics, with free gifts, free draws, and offers based on promotional games such as scratch cards. This had led to some criticism as with certain time-share rackets when people are induced to attend sales presentations with promises of exotic prizes: one such prize was said to be a luxury yacht, but turned out to be a rubber one which had to be inflated. Some of these have been exposed by the Advertising Standards Authority. However, when used properly, sales promotion schemes can help to provoke response to direct response marketing, whether it uses direct mail or off-the-page press advertisements.

11   The setting up of fulfilment houses which relieve the manufacturer of the task of warehousing offers, receiving applications, and dispatching them.
12   The setting up of coupon redemption centres like Nielsen's whose address appears on many coupons instead of the manufacturer's, which also measure the retail sources of claims for cash refunds and help manufacturers to know not only sources of response but the possible extent of mis-redemption. The latter occurs when a shopkeeper allows customers cash refunds towards products other than those being promoted. Some supermarket chains are specific about this and will exchange any coupons for cash provided the promoted brand is stocked. The Nielsen system can detect any shortfall in sales as a result of this practice.
13   The imaginative print services of firms such as Don Marketing and Norpax Promotions who offer supplies of promotional materials including games such as scratch cards with bingo-style or fruit machine games. These are known as *bolt-on* promotions since they are ready made for the manufacturer to use.
14   Finally, many attractive new ideas, or rejuvenations of old ones, have made manufacturers consider the use of a sales promotion scheme.

18.5   The law and competitions

This is a good point to mention the law regarding competitions, lotteries, raffles or draws; free draws; and sweepstakes.

The law on this is laid down in the *Lotteries and Amusements Act, 1976* which added to the *Betting, Gaming and Lotteries Act, 1963*. Further guidance is given in the British Code of Sales Promotion Practice.

Briefly, to be legally accepted as a *competition* there must be an element of skill. As Lord Parker observed, 'If there is any degree of skill involved then there is no lottery'. For example, when it was stated in a newspaper competition that the winning entry must agree with the answer held in the editor's safe, this preconceived correct answer eliminated any element of skill.

A *lottery* is legal only if conducted by a non-commercial organization, as happens with charities and voluntary societies which run raffles and draws.

A *free draw* is legal if the entrant is not expected to show proof of purchase. A person can walk into a retail establishment, enter for a free draw, yet buy nothing. However, the object is usually to attract store traffic, but entries are not directly linked to particular purchases.

For example, *Radio Times* ran a Holiday competition in 1989. On the TV holiday show Desmond Lynam said a holiday prize could be won by viewers who correctly answered some questions and completed the entry form in the *Radio Times*. The first three correct entries drawn from the post bag on a certain date would win holidays. But since a copy of *Radio Times* had to be bought it was not a free draw and was illegal. It was a lottery.

A *sweepstake* is a lottery usually associated with an event such as a horse race when participants buy tickets and tickets are drawn in favour of each horse. Prizes are awarded to those whose horse comes first or is placed, and the remainder of those who have drawn horses may also receive consolation prizes. The most famous sweepstake is the Irish Sweep, proceeds from which help to fund Irish hospitals. Private 'sweeps' on big horse races such as the Derby and the Grand National are often held among office staff for example, although strictly speaking they are illegal.

The expression 'sweepstake' has been used loosely and unwisely for schemes such as delivering lucky numbers door-to-door with prizes if they match winning numbers held by a retailer. This is not really a sweepstake but comes within the category of free draws. Unfortunately, the word sweepstake appeared to the consternation of candidates in a CAM examination paper and, of course, the expression was unknown.

One such example of a promotional scheme which the promoters based on a 'sweepstake' principle was an Asda cash promotion which was distributed door-to-door, customers receiving a card containing a 'sweepstake' entry number unique to their household. During the promotion's two-month run customers had the chance to win between £5 and £50,000 each if their numbers agreed with those displayed in the supermarket. To control the promotion the numbers were changed every week, but it was not strictly speaking a sweepstake.

18.6 Forms of sales promotion

1 Gift coupons

One of the oldest devices to secure regular purchase, gift coupons have been used by cocoa, tea, cigarette and petrol companies, also by magazines and newspapers, and they appeal to the collecting or acquisitive instinct. A newer version is described under Collection schemes.

2 Picture cards

Again, the appeal is to the collecting habit. Cards have been given away with cigarettes, ice lollies, tea, children's magazines and petrol, but none has excelled the pre-war series of Players which are still available from collector's shops, or the Wills' series which could be exchanged for prints of the pictures formed by the complete set. Wills also issued miniature playing cards which could be exchanged for a full-size pack. The modern tendency, with collecting items, is to have shorter sets than the 50 or 52 cigarette cards, although sets of 50 cards are given with Brooke Bond tea bags. Goodwill is maintained by offering to supply cards not yet obtained when the scheme closes, thus avoiding disappointment among collectors who are often children, and albums are usually available. With most sales promotion schemes it is very necessary to observe the PR aspects.

3 Cash dividends

As with the former Brooke Bond's Dividend Tea, and Co-op trading stamps, cash dividends have a combination of gift and saving scheme not unlike the original Co-op 'divi'. It has both a bargain and a collecting appeal and once again has the merit of achieving regular sales and brand loyalty.

4 Putting halves of coupons or pictures together

This is another collecting scheme which seems to be a favourite with petrol companies, having been used by Shell and Texaco, the latter being linked with a competition. It can be irritating if one seems to get too many of the wrong halves!

5 Cash premium coupons or vouchers

Provided the retailers do not accept them in exchange for any goods, they are very effective in moving the promoted brand. There is some risk of irritating dealers who have to stock the brand demanded and are put to the trouble of claiming redemption, even if a handling charge is paid. Some retailers regard cash premiums as a nuisance, but manufacturers are often unsympathetic because, after all, the retailer is getting extra business.

There are several kinds of cash voucher: (i) they may be delivered house-to-house; (ii) published in the press; (iii) published in shopping magazines which contain collections of current offers; (iv) printed on the pack to encourage repeat purchase; (v) printed on the pack of another product (e.g. £1 off an automatic toaster at Currys on a large box of Ship matches).

6 Free gifts

This really is a method of inducing impulse purchases as with the free comb attached to the toothpaste package, or an ingenious offer on the label of Cadbury's drinking chocolate of a free bar of dairy milk chocolate to those who entered a £5,000 contest. Few people can resist a free gift, even if they have to buy something else to get it!

A frequently repeated offer is that for the various Nescafé blends, a free jar of coffee being offered for labels. For example, a full-colour whole page advertisement in weekend colour supplements carried the headline: *A free jar of Nescafé Blend 37 – delivered to your door*. The application form offered a 100g jar for 600g of labels, or a 200g jar for 1,000g of labels, and the free jars arrived safely packed in polystyrene boxes. Alternatively, for six ground coffee pack tops a free pack of Blend 37 was offered. The offer remained open for about two months. Nescafé have run several similar offers.

Free mail-ins are those where a gift is offered in return for the label or package, or for a number of tokens. It is important to limit such offers one to a family and to have a stated maximum number of gifts or a closing date, otherwise demand may outrun both supplies and the budget. Lyons tea have offered rubber gloves, tights and rose trees, indicating the variety of gifts that can be given in this way. The handling of these offers is simpler since there is no monetary transaction, and it is not necessary to seek self-liquidation of the cost.

7 Self liquidating premium offers

These are the non-profit-making offers of merchandise such as beach balls, coffee tables, fine art prints, towels, cutlery and other items offered for carton tops or labels and a cash payment. A criticism has been made that the quoted normal retail price may not be realistic if the item has been specially produced for the offer and is not otherwise available. Nevertheless, thousands of people have taken advantage of these offers and goodwill has been extended towards the supplier.

However, ill-will is easily provoked if the brand manager responsible for buying the offer does not make sure: (i) that the product can be supplied in sufficient quantities to meet the short-term demand; and (ii) that the product is well packed so that it is not damaged in transit. There have been instances where the manufacturer of the premium offer has been so swamped by demand that he has not been able to deliver, causing great resentment among customers; and some items such as gramophone records and picture frames have been sent out with poor protective packing that the item has arrived damaged, once again causing annoyance to customers. As demonstrated above, Nescafé go to some trouble in packing a heavy item such as a glass jar of coffee.

8 Free samples

This is surely one of the very best forms of sales promotion, customers being invited to try the product and decide whether or not they like it. If, in a store sampling booth, they express liking the demonstrator can move on to make a sale. If the sample is delivered to the house, another effort is necessary at the point-of-sale to remind people to purchase. Door-to-door sampling often consists of a sachet of the product, and instant tea has been launched by this method. Either way, it does invite goodwill for the manufacturer is obviously not afraid to let people try the product first before committing themselves to a purchase. Free trials and demonstrations of motor-cars, washing machines, sewing machines and other consumer durables are other versions of the same thing. Similarly, Butlin's have invited visitors to spend a trial day at their holiday camps, although this is not absolutely free.

9 Trade characters

Either in stores or calling door-to-door and using specially decorated vehicles, these are a dramatic form of sales promotion.

10 Cash awards for use of product

This is a very old one (e.g. the ten-shilling note to the man who provided the smoker with a light by producing a box of Blue Cross matches). This resulted in many men carrying a box of Blue Cross for years, just in case they were stopped in the street and asked for a light! Similarly, housewives are given cash awards by the caller if they have certain brands of goods in the larder.

11 Multiple packs

Sometimes called jumbo packs, these are used to encourage the sale of small items in multiples; bars of chocolate, chocolate biscuits, bars of soap, razor blades, paperback books and miniature packs of breakfast cereals are packed collectively in a single wrapper (or banded together), and usually offered at an advantageous price. Thus, instead of buying one bar of chocolate one buys a number which makes production and distribution much more economic. A typical example is the Oxo cube and the razor blade where single sales used to be quite normal. It is perhaps a sign of the times that people can afford to buy in larger quantities. But it is also an effective way of achieving repeat usage. Carry packs of canned beer are another example.

12 Flash packs

Provided they do not offend the *Trade Descriptions Act*, these are a method of making price-cut offers, and are used especially in the confectionery trade, the price cut being 'flashed' on the wrapper.

13   Children's contests

Contests such as painting and colouring competitions, have been used by circuses, soft drink manufacturers, publishers and confectionery firms. The method lends itself to the distribution of many small consolation prizes which make a lot of competitors happy.

14   Competitions

Competitions for adults need big prizes to make them seem worth entering after the extravagant football pool winnings, Premium Bond and Irish Sweep prizes. It is also necessary to avoid prize-winnings by doing all the possible permutations, and tie-breaking 'slogan writing' is one of the devices used to reduce the number of prize-winners, and so retain a big prize. A competition should be simple to enter, and should not be run over such a long period of time that contestants get bored or forget to enter. Today, competitors are usually protected by the Institute of Sales Promotion ISP Standard Competition Rules, and this will be stated on entry forms.

Free draws (see 18.5) have become an increasingly common form of sales promotion, and are more common than the competitions requiring skill. A variation on this was the Kit Kat offer on family seven packs. Twenty pounds could be won instantly if the wrapper bore an image of a £1 coin or a banknote. If the wrapper carried a value less than £1 it could be saved in order to claim £1 or any multiple of £s up to £50. There was the caveat that no purchase was necessary and single Cash Break wrappers were available on application.

15   Charity promotions

With these schemes the pack usually carries a token with a cash value which the manufacturer promises to redeem as a contribution to a charity or cause named in the promotion.

16   High Street redemption schemes

This is another on-pack scheme, and the premium coupon entitles consumers to discounts off goods bought from named retailers. One scheme offered discounts off rail tickets, another off the cost of dry cleaning. These schemes are welcomed by the associated retailers because purchases are usually made in excess of the value of the voucher.

17   Cross-couponing

An offer is printed on the wrapper or package, enabling the consumer to buy another product at a reduced price. It may be a sister product, or it may be a dual promotion with another manufacturer, e.g. a token on a bar of chocolate towards the price of a can of soft drink. These are known as third-party deals. Schemes work best if the two products are sold by the same retailer, but this is not always the case.

A good example of cross-couponing was the *Kids Eat Free*, a Little Chef offer on McDougall's flour bags and sister products such as Robertson's jams, Mother's Pride bread and McDougall's cake mixes. Tokens from these products could be exchanged for children's meals at 300 Little Chef restaurants nationwide. An accompanying adult had to spend £3 or more at one of these restaurants.

One of the biggest ever confectionery promotions was a joint scheme by Cadbury, Coca Cola and Schweppes, tokens from Cadbury's Dairy Milk, Wispa, Flake and Crunchie being redeemable for free cans of Coca Cola, Lilt, Schweppes Tonic and Fanta. With a £2m budget the scheme had a four-week introduction on network TV, and below-the-line support included a 10 million household voucher drop, point-of-sale displays and trade press advertising.

Another example was a tie-up between Kellogg's Crunchy Nut Cornflakes and the Automobile Association. Consumers were offered regionalized editions of the AA's *365 Days Out In Britain* for eight tokens from the eight million promotion packs.

18 Promotional games

A typical game is a scratch card with latex-covered symbols which are revealed to show whether they match, rather like a fruit machine, and a prize may be claimed according to the symbols revealed. These may be given with purchases such as petrol, but are also used extensively by direct response marketers.

There are also on-label games, such as the Cinzano Instant Roulette bottle label scratch-off game used as a pre-Christmas promotion, and produced by Don Marketing of Stowmarket. This firm has produced numerous scratch card games for Shell, McEwan's lager, Guinness and others.

However, promotional games are not without their problems. A Typhoo Tea promotion proved unexpectedly expensive in prize money because there were insufficient game variations, and the games code was broken. Too few permutations can prove disastrous, or if too many winning cards are produced as occurred in Esso's 'Noughts and Crosses' game. In one case there was a printing error when customers were able to see through the invisible ink on their cards. Cheating can also occur but preventive action is taken by security printers who can use special types of paper containing fibres which resist chemicals or solvents used to tamper with a game.

Disaster hit a Kraft cheese competition in the USA, costing them $3m instead of a budgeted $250,000, and a number of law suits, all because of a printing error which produced too many winners. Customers in Chicago and Houston were invited to buy packets of cheese slices and to match an enclosed puzzle piece with one in a newspaper advertisement. First prize was a Dodge van, with intended chances of 15.2m to one. There were further prizes of 100 bicycles, 500 skateboards and 8000 packs of sliced cheese, but at least 100 people found they could win the van! Kraft cancelled the contest and offered winners financial compensation, $250 to van claimants, $50 for bicycle winners, and $25 for skateboard winners. A lottery was also held among the winners for the original prize.

Not surprisingly firms like Norpax of Leeds, who produce promotional games, cover each client's game with an insurance policy written by Lloyds of London, with maximum cover for over-redemption of up to £1 million. Their service includes sourcing the prizes, verification and notification of prizes, distribution of prizes, redemption handling, and the handling of legalities. Norpax develop the concept, design the scratch card game, and print cards or tickets.

19   In-store demonstrations

These are usually set up in a large retail store, and products such as foods and drinks may be sampled, or kitchen and household equipment may be demonstrated. It has an entertainment atmosphere which makes it attractive to shoppers.

20   Advertorials

Quite an old idea, and one used to launch new products such as shampoos, lipsticks and cosmetics in the women's magazines, but also used for reader service offers of holidays and other services and goods, the method consists of an editorial provided by the publication and an introductory or special offer at an attractive price. An abuse is to buy editorial space for the same purpose.

21   On-pack direct marketing and coupon labels

This is not so much a premium offer as a method of using the pack to conduct direct response marketing.

On-pack coupon labels are attached to products, and are detached or peeled back by the customer in order to participate in an offer.

Research by Denny Brothers in the UK showed that 28 per cent of purchases are influenced by on-pack promotions; 56 per cent of unplanned purchases are influenced by on-pack promotions; while 61 per cent out of impulse purchases are so influenced. This applies to various on-pack schemes also described in this chapter.

22 Collection schemes

These are rather superior gift catalogue schemes, tokens being given with purchases such as petrol which are saved towards items shown in a catalogue, although the goods may be obtained partly for tokens and partly for cash. Shell had their Collect and Select programme, and Texaco Ltd had their Star Collection. These are usually referred to as 'forecourt collection schemes'.

Points-for-gifts schemes have also included the Ever Ready Power Collection, Barclaycard Profiles, Seagram UK Martell Collection and Imperial Tobacco Focus Collection. A number of charge card companies award points according to the value of charged purchases.

These schemes help to create habit buying and brand loyalty. Drivers, for instance, will always buy their petrol at a garage where they can get the particular tokens, and it is a more independently controlled operation than giving away trading stamps which may also be available from rivals.

A long-term commitment is necessary, repeat purchases being required over many months or even years, so it does not have the booster effect of short-term sales promotion schemes. It is also very complicated to close down a points-for-gifts scheme, otherwise disappointed customers are left stranded with useless tokens. Some form of final redemption has to be introduced.

It is a costly form of sales promotion since stocks of gifts have to be bought, large numbers of attractive catalogues have to be printed, and the scheme itself has to be promoted – perhaps with media advertising and certainly with point-of-sale displays. The scheme also has to be VAT efficient since the catalogue is a form of retailing. The gifts themselves need to be characteristic of the promoter, and this may require the selection of respected brands. Price rises of merchandise have to be watched in a long-running scheme, and it may be necessary to issue revised catalogues, although a customer could be annoyed if the number of tokens required was increased just when he thought he nearly had enough. Conversely, the promoter has to be careful not to carry too much stock, or run out of stock, and phased deliveries may have to be planned.

23 Co-promotion schemes

This is an interesting kind of promotion which involves no special offer. An agreement is made to give information about a product on another manufacturer's pack, this being of mutual value since it makes the pack more interesting.

An ingenious example of this was a joint promotion between Lego and Kellogg's in Germany. One whole side plus an end panel of the Kellogg's Snacks, Rice Crispies and Coco Pops box was devoted to a full-colour picture of Duplo bricks, a Fabuland environment, Legoland and Technic models of Lego trains and ships, and a tiny wooden duck who told the history of Lego. The designs were produced by Lego's advertising agency and appeared on 7.5 m packs. Since each box is reckoned to appear on the breakfast table eight times, and is seen by at least three family members, it was believed that there were 180m exposures of the Lego pictures and stories.

24   Bonus packs

This is a popular and instant sales puller which appeals to the bargain hunting 'cherry picker'. A larger than usual container offers 10 per cent – 25 per cent more detergent, hair-spray, deodorant, shaving cream, paint or some other product at the regular price, an opportunity not to be missed! This usually applies to goods packed in containers such as cartons, tins, bottles or aerosols, but two extra sausages to the pound or a miniature tube or tin attached to a toothpaste, hand cream or hair-spray are other forms of bonus pack. A clever one some years ago was an extra pack containing one cigarette which was stuck to a packet of Kensitas cigarettes with the message 'one for your friend'.

25   Buy-back promotions

This is an incentive guarantee which has been applied to high ticket goods such as cameras and electronic goods. The customer is offered repayment of the price of the product after from five to ten years of purchase.

Vivitar ran a buy-back promotion for their cameras, and the scheme operated from May 1990 to April 1991, pushing two Vivitar cameras up five places to become the fourth best selling make in the UK. Customers were offered a full refund in five years time, provided they returned the registration form with proof of purchase to a clearing house which supplied a buy-back refund certificate.

The Toshiba All Your Money Back offer was similar except that customers received a voucher equal to the original purchase price which could be redeemed for other Toshiba products redeemable in six years time. This scheme ran for one month only in September 1990, registrations had to be submitted within 21 days, and redemption had to be between October and December 1996. Registered redemptions amounted to 55 per cent of purchases.

The schemes are underwritten by well-known insurance companies. The number of likely redemptions is impossible to assess, but it is expected to be up to 10 per cent, but customers are taking such redemption promises seriously, and there could be some very high redemption bills. It can be a very risky promotion, and some insurers consider such schemes as being dangerous.

18.7 Sales promotion agencies

The sales promotion business has developed a great fund of expertise in recent years, and one has only to look at the number and variety of offers to be found every week in the shops to realize the skill and ingenuity that is put into sales promotion. We have already mentioned specialist suppliers such as Don Marketing and Norpax. Some large companies operate in-house sales promotion departments which create or buy-in bolt-on schemes or buy gifts from premium houses which specialize in sourcing supplies. Others use the services of specialist agencies.

Payment to sales promotion agencies may depend on whether there are occasional assignments which are serviced singly on a pay-as-you-go basis, or whether sales promotion is a regular feature of the marketing strategy in which case it is more sensible to engage an agency on an annual fee basis so that it can apply maximum advice and attention.

In an article in *Sales Promotion* (March 1991) David Moore, joint managing director of CBH & Partners was quoted as saying 'Sales promotion is as much concerned with long-term brand building as achieving short-term sales, consequently clients require longer-term relationships. Clients need an agency which understands brand plans and can work with agencies from other disciplines. A fee paid to cover the executive time for a year of various activities is a more workable arrangement than attempting to cost each project (consequently paying a number of small *ad hoc* fees)'.

Most clients operate on a fee basis, but there is some debate about whether schemes should be paid for on an *ad hoc* basis or whether an agency should be retained on an annual fee. The latter would seem to be the more professional method, but some clients are still dogged by their 'commission image' of an advertising agency and resent fees.

Matthew Hooper, author of the article, offered the solution of payment by results. 'If a client spends £1m on a project with the object of increasing sales by X% it would be reasonable for it to pay part of the fee upon achievement of this target plus, as a bonus for excellence, a percentage of an extra earnings above it'. The debate continues!

18.8 Sales promotion and the Single European Market

British expertise in sales promotion techniques is the most advanced in Europe, but there is such a quagmire of objections and contrary legislations, such as lotteries being legal in some countries, that harmonization is difficult. It is unlikely that UK firms will be able to operate cross-frontier schemes. In fact, different packs are necessary for different countries. What is permissible in the UK may or may not be permissible in France or Germany, and vice versa. The UK concept of adding 'extrinsic value' to a product by means of a free gift or price cut is held to be fraudulent in some countries since, one way or another, the customer pays for promotion whether it be media advertising or a special offer. Such logic is hard to dispute. The cost of sales promotion is part of the marketing budget and of the retail price. As the saying goes, there is no such thing as a free lunch.

18.9   British Code of Sales Promotion Practice

This is more fully discussed in the final chapter on voluntary or self-regulatory controls. The monthly *Case Report* issued free-of-charge by the Advertising Standards Authority contains a section on complaints relating to the BCSPP, some of which are upheld and others dismissed or modifications are required. It pays to read these reports because they indicate how even the most respectable of firms can, perhaps unintentionally, indulge in malpractices.

The following is an example of a case with quite complicated implications which had not been thought out by the promoter.

U Fix Double Glazing
Sugar Mill
Billacome Road
Plymstock

Complaint: Objection to a local press advertisement inviting entries to a 'Free Turtle Competition'. The advertisement requested that the entrant answer three questions and offered 'a great prize'. The complainant objected that the advertisement gave no indication of the prizes on offer and that its use of popular cartoon characters was likely to appeal to children. Further the request for a telephone number could lead children to disclose their telephone numbers without the prior permission of their parents (BCSPP 4.11; 5.2.1; 6.2.2(iv)).

Conclusion: Complaint upheld. The advertisers stated that the description of the prize, which was a mirror with stained-glass turtle heroes, was omitted accidentally from the original advertisement but a full description was later published. The advertisers offered no comment on the suitability of the promotion for children. The Authority did not consider that this promotional technique, by a double glazing company which required telephone numbers to be given, was suitable for direction at children. The advertisers' attention was drawn to the Code requirements on promotions to children, in particular that parental permission be obtained where the offer was likely to give rise to problems between child and parent. The advertisers were requested to ensure that future promotions are conducted within the requirements of the Code. *ASA Report 191* (March 1991).

19
Sponsorship

19.1 Sponsorship and patronage

There is nothing new about sponsorship or patronage as it used to be called. Many famous composers and artists would not have survived if they had not been financed by wealthy patrons such as royalty and aristocrats. One can still find old public library buildings bearing the name of Tate. Industrialists and business magnates such as Carnegie, Ford, Getty, Horniman, Kelvin, Nuffield, Rootes and Rockefeller have given their names as benefactors, funding institutes and foundations, University halls and hospital wings, art galleries and museums. They were the philanthropists, but philanthropy plays little, if any, part in the modern big business of sponsorship which in British sport alone amounts to some £200 million.

19.2 Different meanings of sponsorship

The word sponsorship in connection with broadcasting can have different meanings in different countries. In many parts of the world, probably originating from the soap operas of American radio 60 years ago, sponsorship means that an advertiser buys a period of programme time, perhaps half-an-hour or more, and puts on his own show. The advertiser who buys and fills such air-time is called the sponsor. For example, the Cup Final at Wembley may be seen on TV in, say, Singapore by courtesy of a cigarette firm.

In the UK there is both public service non-commercial broadcasting (BBC radio and TV) and commercial broadcasting (ILR and ITV) with commercial breaks, programmes being the responsibility of the stations. With commercial broadcasting, air-time (commercial breaks) may be sold by the stations to advertisers. However, as will be explained later in this chapter there was some relaxation in 1990 of the rules about sponsorship of whole programmes (e.g. weather forecasts), and certain forms of sponsorship of programmes became permissible in 1991 under the new Independent Television Commission and the Radio Authority. Even so, the majority of events are sponsored independently of the BBC and ITV, it being hoped that the sponsors will benefit from media coverage as when a golf or tennis tournament, a football or cricket match, or a horse or motor race is televised.

19.3   Sponsorship defined

For our purposes, sponsorship may be defined as the giving of monetary or other support to a beneficiary in order to make that beneficiary financially viable, sometimes for altruistic reasons, but generally to gain some advertising, public relations or marketing advantage.

Individuals, such as artists, mountaineers or athletes, may be supported; or prizes and trophies may be awarded; or whole events may be sponsored. Occasionally, the support may be purely philanthropic.

19.4   Why sponsor?

This is a question which must be answered. Numerous people and organizations would like to be sponsored, and most businesses receive requests for support, whether they be huge enterprises or local shopkeepers. There is sometimes a false idea that people in business are making fortunes and have money to give away. The reverse is truer: commercial concerns are likely to seek sponsorships which will benefit *them* in some way. They are not giving money away but investing it, and they expect a return.

Some of the practical reasons for sponsorship are:

i   To familiarize the market with a name. This is why the Japanese are among the world's leading sponsors, dominating British sports sponsorship.

ii   To create a favourable attitude towards a company and its products. Again, the Japanese can be quoted, especially as a means of overcoming hostility in Asiatic countries which they had occupied during the Second World War, but so can those such as banks which sponsor concerts, theatres, art shows and orchestras.

iii To position a product in the market, e.g. Coca Cola's sponsorship of young people's sports and other interests.

iv   As an alternative to, say, television advertising when a point is reached that it is no longer cost-effective. For example although Canon's three-year sponsorship of the Football League cost £3m it would have cost many times that sum to have bought TV air-time to achieve the same result which was literally that nearly every office in the UK had a Canon machine by the end of the three years.

v   To exploit other advertising opportunities such as the display of banners at events, arena advertising, advertisements in programmes and sometimes product displays at events.
vi   To establish corporate identity by the display of logos and colours.
vii To win the interest of journalists and photographers as with writing and photographic awards for those who cover the sponsor's subjects.
viii A good reason for supporting events may be the opportunity it provides the sponsor of playing host to invited business friends and customers.

As Andrew Marriott of CSS Promotions explained in an article in *Adline* (March 1991) corporate hospitality is an aspect of sponsorship which is prominent in the USA and could be more fully exploited in the UK. Marriott sees this kind of hospitality as more than providing strawberries and cream at Henley, but of guests having hands-on experience of sponsored events such as karting, laser shooting, dune buggies and off-the-road driving. 'Laser shooting, for those who do not know about it, uses real shot guns, but the trigger directs a laser beam to the moving target', Marriott explains. Getting the host's guests involved is certainly an interesting slant on hospitality.

ix   Dealer support may be another objective, as when products can be given special topical displays following their successful use, as with tyres and motor-racing.

In other words, there must be a good reason for spending money on sponsorship, whether it is a massive one like Canon's or a modest one such as a strip for the local football team. Costs are not just the prize or award but all the supporting activities, materials, advertising and hospitality. To support motor-racing means providing the cars, drivers, mechanics, transport, servicing and many other items, and this may have to be done on a world scale. Consequently, it suits only an international advertiser.

19.5 Sponsorship agencies

The organizing of sponsorships is a complex business which can rarely be handled by in-house staff, and most of this work is handled by specialist consultancies. They are able to bring together those seeking sponsors and those willing to sponsor, and to plan and execute the complex work of running a sponsorship, concluding with research to test its effectiveness.

Sponsorship consultants, an events register and other information about sponsorship in the UK occupies some 90 pages in *Hollis Press and Public Relations Annual*. In his introduction to the 1991 edition, Alan Pascoe wrote 'The high interest rates of the last 18 months have actually been a boon to sponsorship. I believe that many companies have had to look closely at their budgets in all areas. And sponsorship has been identified as a less expensive alternative to advertising'.

To attract sponsors, special efforts are made by the various bodies representing different sports. The Scottish Sports Council, for instance, distributes a monthly newsletter called *Leads* which details sponsorship opportunities. A calendar of Scottish sports events is published, including the costs of supporting each event.

19.6   What shall be sponsored?

What is the best thing to sponsor? What is likely to produce the best returns? What will reach our market best? The variety of choice is immense, and it is not a matter of pleasing the chairman's wife who happens to like protecting impoverished artists. It may be a case of what can be afforded. A great many subjects may be irrelevant or uncharacteristic. Why should a builder support power boat racing, or a soft drink firm put its money on snooker? Both would seem to be inappropriate. When a bank financed climbers of Mount Everest there was criticism of this as a waste of money, but when the mountaineers succeeded and became national heroes the bank suddenly found itself sharing in the glory. Making the choice is not therefore easy, and in this chapter a number of reasons and considerations have been set out. Here are some of the things that may appeal to a potential sponsor:

i   *Books and other publications*, examples being cookery books, road maps and sports annuals, some of which may be given away while others may have legitimate bookshop sales.

ii   *Exhibitions* may be sponsored as public or trade events by trade associations, societies, newspapers or magazines, or they may be sponsored by a single promoter and perhaps put on tour.

iii   *Education*, such as grants, bursaries and fellowships, or for educational buildings and teaching equipment.

iv   *Feats of endurance*, such as expeditions, explorations, mountain climbs, one-man voyages and so on.

v   *Sport*, by far the largest area of sponsorship covering almost every outdoor and indoor sport. In recent years, snooker, with a number of championships each year receiving coverage on BBC television on up to nine successive days, commands an audience of around 13 million viewers for each championship, ranking second only to the Grand National which occurs on one Saturday afternoon but claims about 14 million viewers.

Statistics on TV audiences for sports are published by AGB Sports Watch/BARB, and these figures provide a guide to those interested in sponsoring sports.

vi   *The arts*, including choirs, pop groups, concerts, recitals, competitions and recordings; art shows; literature; special shows at art galleries and museums and other cultural activities such as support for theatres or for plays, ballets and operas appearing there. This is an expanding area of sponsorship with more than 1,000 companies giving financial support.

Active in the promotion of arts sponsorship is the Association of Business Sponsorship of the Arts. Since 1987 ABSA in collaboration with the *Daily Telegraph* has made awards for the best sponsorships, winners including IBM, Digital Equipment Company, British Gas, Lloyds Bank and Sainsbury.

vii   *Causes and charities* as when companies donate to famine and disaster appeals, or contribute to education about diseases such as diabetes. Makers of treatments may supply videos which can be shown in clinics.

viii *Local events and organizations* such as sports meetings, flower shows, cycling clubs and carnivals can be supported as a form of community relations.

ix   *Professional awards* such as Businesswoman or Businessman of the year, and awards to architects, journalists, press photographers and others may be made.

In conjunction with *UK Press Gazette*, Canon runs a press picture of the year competition with £5,000 worth of prizes.

Some of these sponsorships may have special advertising, marketing or public relations benefits for the sponsor, but they also provide benefits to those sponsored. Moreover, some of the things sponsored might never survive but for commercial sponsorship, or they are encouraged to thrive. In the cultural sphere, sponsorship augments official grants.

19.7   Sponsorship by tobacco companies

The sponsorship by tobacco companies of televised events has been criticized on many occasions, and it is ironic that, although ITV companies banned coverage of tobacco-sponsored events in 1987 they have continued to appear on BBC television. These events permit exposure of brand names, logos and pack colours, because either the event or participants are sponsored. The BBC and the tobacco industry were accused of breaking the voluntary code aimed at regulating cigarette promotion on television in a report *Beating The Ban* published in November 1990 by the Health Education Authority in conjunction with Action on Smoking and Health (ASH). The report stated that in 1988 there were 76 seconds in every televised hour of Embassy's snooker tournament when the tobacco name or logo was visible. By 1989 this had increased to 176 seconds. Other sports in which such coverage contravened the voluntary agreement were bowls and motor-sport. So far as motor-sport, with its international Grand Prix racing, it is difficult to avoid coverage of sponsors like Marlboro' who sell internationally.

19.8 Liberalization of sponsorship

There have been two stages in the relaxation of the sponsorship of TV programmes, first during 1989–1990 and then in 1991 following the effects of the creation of the Independent Television Commission. There have also been sponsorships of radio programmes. These are departures from the original forms of sponsorships when the programme companies quite independently covered events which were themselves sponsored or had sponsored elements such as race horses, show jumpers, racing cars, football teams and individuals.

Mike Cobb, development director of MBS Media, explained in an article in *Campaign* (November 9, 1990) that the reason why some clients and agencies are 'increasingly flirting with sponsorship, barter and other newish-fangled devices when well-made commercials work so well' was cost. 'The cost of air-time in an era of fragmenting audiences and the cost to broadcasters of making decent programmes from their own financial resources'. He went on to say, 'Public and media reaction to the few high-profile sponsorships that have already graced our screens has been less than welcoming'. Cobb also commented acidly on National Power's inexplicable sponsorship of the World Cup in Italy, saying, 'the uninvolved observer certainly noted a significant amount of hostility to Peter Purves' constant appearance during Italia 90'.

During the same first stage, the ITV weather forecasts announced their sponsorship by PowerGen. One wonders what value for money could possibly be achieved by this label in the bottom right-hand corner of the screen. Even more puzzling have been the credits for charities on BBC weather forecasts, these being meaningless.

The PowerGen sponsorship of the ITV weather forecast began in September 1989, and towards the end of the forecast came a seven-second message, 'Produced in association with PowerGen'. The year's fee, renewable until the end of 1991 when the ITV franchise expired, was £2m. It followed the IBA decision to permit sponsorship for weather forecasts, instructional programmes, arts reviews and sport that was not already sponsored. Ed Wallis, chief executive of PowerGen, said that the motive behind the sponsorship was to get the name known to the public before privatization. When PowerGen and National Power (with less hype than the 'Frankenstein' electricity boards' privatization commercials) were privatized in March 1991, the shares were over-subscribed four times.

In his introduction to the sponsorship section of *Hollis Press and Public Relations Annual* (to which an earlier reference has been made), Alan Pascoe comments, 'Too many sponsors are merely putting their name to programmes without exploiting the sponsorship further'.

However, some worthwhile sponsorships were introduced prior to the new *Broadcasting Act* and the ITC which replaced the IBA. Let us look at three, the *Daily Telegraph* support for minority sports on Channel 4, which was commendable; British Gas sponsorship of Cathedral Classics which were beautifully done; and Lloyds Bank's BBC Young Musician of the Year contest which was most enjoyable and, as research showed, was well received by the right social grades.

The *Daily Telegraph* sponsorship was a bold one because it could expect no coverage from rival newspapers. *Today's* sponsorship of the Football League, following the great success of Canon's patronage, was a flop, and support was taken over by Barclays Bank. So the *Daily Telegraph's* £500,000 support for programme sponsorship, sponsoring Channel 4's coverage of the Tour de France cycle race, American football and the sport series Challenge to Sport was, in 1989, somewhat surprising. This was negotiated within the IBA guidelines effective at that time. The object was to emphasize that the *Daily Telegraph* carried very strong sports coverage across a wide range of sports, claimed the newspaper's marketing manager, David Pugh, in an interview with Torin Douglas in *Marketing Week* (April 21, 1989).

British Gas began its Cathedral Classics sponsorship in 1986 and the following details demonstrate how these concerts were organized. The cathedrals were often packed, audiences were appreciative, the musicians were pleased, guests were pleased to be invited, reviews were good and a number of charities benefited.

The British Gas sponsorship came within the BBC rules in that the London Festival Orchestra, on behalf of British Gas, stipulated that the sponsor be given both a verbal and an on-screen credit before agreeing to the broadcast. These credits made it clear that British Gas was sponsoring the event rather than the BBC. This was an ingenious development, and was rather different from conventional coverage of sponsored events unless the event itself had a name incorporating the sponsor's such as the Whitbread Gold Cup.

The British Gas sponsorship fee goes directly to the London Festival Orchestra who organize the concerts, and in 1989 there was a fee of about £150,000 for 22 concerts. No money was paid to the BBC, but there were additional hospitality costs and the cost of publicity for the concerts.

In 1989, in the fourth year of the sponsorship, the BBC broadcast recordings. Originally, British Gas had been approached by the Orchestra, but then the BBC noticed the advertising of the concerts, attended one of them and then asked the Orchestra and British Gas if they would agree to recordings. This of course was of greater value all round and, as a result of the concerts being televised, the sponsorship fee was increased.

Lloyds Bank's much publicized Young Musician of the Year competition on BBC 2 did not please the ITV companies, this being a BBC-created event which was developed by the sponsor. At the time, early 1990, it was regarded as a hybrid event which was banned by the IBA. There is an interesting situation here. It has always been easier to get coverage or publicity on BBC which is non-commercial, whereas the commercial ITV companies were always nervous of being accused by their advertisers of providing 'free advertising'. This was a hypocritical stance since sponsorship cannot persuade and sell as deliberately conceived commercials can. In fact, sponsorship is more nearly public relations than advertising, but like any public relations it can help to make advertising more effective through, say, familiarity with a name.

The Lloyds Bank sponsorship is a five-year one aimed at enhancing and developing Britain's premier musical event for young people. It was the first sponsorship collaboration of its kind for the BBC. In the run-up to the actual competition, there were five Masterclasses. Other elements of the deal were scholarships for competitors, international masterclasses, additional public performances and education packages. And of course there was listings coverage in the TV programme magazines.

It is believed that the sponsorship reaches a cumulative audience of more than 20 million people, nicely targeted through BBC 2. Audits of Great Britain carried out an evaluation study between February and May 1990, with very satisfactory awareness and attitude results. On the question of 'Young Musician of the Year is a suitable and worthwhile event for Lloyds Bank to sponsor', a sample of 1,000 said 'strongly agree' (53%), 'slightly agree' (29%), representing 82% ABs.

The second stage occurred in January 1991 when the ITC announced that anything but news and current affairs could be sponsored, provided that the sponsor did not interfere with the content of the programme, or use it surreptitiously to promote his brands. Brief acknowledgements were permissible during the opening titles and 15 seconds at the end. Not very generous, but a nice way of increasing revenue by the ITV companies.

In March 1991 a list of network and several regional programmes were offered to potential sponsors, these included *Rumpole of the Bailey*, *This Is Your Life*, *Survival*, *The South Bank Show*, *Surprise, Surprise*, *Poirot*, *London's Burning*, *Krypton Factor*, *Boon*, *Great Expectations*, and the *Cookson Dramas*. Expectations were that sponsors would pay about £500,000 for a programme.

However, there was no rush of sponsors and only *Rumpole* won a sponsor in Croft Port. This series appeared in November so may have provided a useful pre-Christmas boost since Croft were better known for sherry. The 1991–92 *Wish You Were Here* series was sponsored by Barclaycard, which may have been more appropriate than the Alan Whicker commercials. Another one in 1992 was the sponsorship by Beamish stout of the *Inspector Morse* series. True, he is often seen drinking a pint, but he never pays for it, and the actor, John Thaw is said to dislike beer.

How does this 'name in the credits' type of sponsorship compare with traditional sponsorship of something which may enjoy considerable coverage throughout a programme? Is it an answer to zapping and alternative television which are eating into commercial break time? Can it be exploited as Alan Pascoe has advised? Does this new kind of sponsorship offer 'aspirational benefits' because a company and its products are associated in viewers' minds with an exceptionally good programme? Are there opportunities for exploitation as with quiz shows which could have associated point-of-sale displays? Will it be beneficial to state in press advertisements or on posters that the advertiser is currently sponsoring a TV show?

Potential sponsors may need to be wary of this blind man's sponsorship. It is one thing to contribute to a worthy cause: quite another to make a free gift to the coffers of a commercial concern. The sponsor has no control: the programme could prove a disaster and have poor ratings. Unless there is considerable surrounding publicity, viewers could be little aware that they are watching *Poirot* by courtesy of, say, Sabena or *Great Expectations* by Equitable Life pension funds. It reminds one of the late Lord Thomson's boast when he bought Scottish Television, that it was a licence to print money. However, in spite of early misgivings, the first sponsored ITV programmes in 1991–2 showed considerable ingenuity in matching products to programmes and in exploiting the brief opportunities for credits before and during breaks (known as break-bumpers). In January 1992, ITVA published research findings on the Sony sponsorships of the Rugby World Cup, together with a number of case studies. The Sony sponsorship covered the seventy hours of broadcasting during the five weeks September 28 to November 3, 1991. There was massive TV coverage with a global audience of 1.5b. It far exceeded the earlier sponsorship of the Soccer World Cup by National Power. Its objectives were to reach the ABC1 market, maintain awareness in the Autumn, and reassure retailers of company support. It also sought to ensure that Sony would be identified with a supreme sporting occasion, have opportunities to boost all of its branded products, and marry its upmarket company image with quality television.

It succeeded in achieving all these things. It also applied some interesting creative techniques ranging from the Sony Music recording of Dame Kiri Te Kanawa's World Cup theme song, World in Ten, and of the England squad's *Swing Low Sweet Chariot*, to the inclusion of a trivia quiz during the break-bumper.

Very appropriately, Legal & General made good use of its new multi-coloured umbrella logo in its sponsorship of regional ITV weather reports, a more creatively superior exploitation than that of either PowerGen or National Power who have invested more heavily in weather forecast sponsorships.

Media Dimensions was responsible for imaginative credit sequences for Croft port, Beamish stout and Kronenbourg lager. In the Croft port credits during *Rumpole of the Bailey* one heard the bottle being uncorked and the wine being poured. An illuminated Kronenbourg sign was reflected in a puddle in breaks in *Maigret*, and the Beamish stout logo was dusted with a fingerprint brush in credits in *Inspector Morse*.

Most of the drama series sponsorships cost about £300,000–£500,000, but the Sony and the weather forecast sponsorships cost £1m–£4m because of the greater frequency and number of appearances. But for Croft port the expenditure produced ideal pre-Christmas networked coverage whereas the same sum would have bought air-time on a London TV station only. Sponsorships for products lend themselves to associated activities such as in-store promotions and special point-of-sale displays.

Yet another version of sponsorship is the American system of barter which has now crossed the Atlantic. An example of this is the Dallas-style soap opera *Riviera*, produced on behalf of Unilever by a subsidiary of the advertising group Interpublic. The idea is to barter such programmes to European channels, including British, in exchange for the surrounding commercial breaks. It seems to flout the ITC's rules about advertisers influencing the content of programmes, but many representatives of the advertising business are convinced that the only people capable of financing the production of major programmes will be the advertisers. In other words, back to the original soap opera days of American radio in the 1930s when the advertisers bought the air-time and produced the programme, often live with a studio audience. Eager listeners would switch on to hear their favourite actors, singers and comedians by courtesy of an advertiser.

The sponsorship code of Channel 4 is more stringent than that of the ITC code which covers ITV or Channel 3 stations. It not only bans sponsorship of news and current affairs programmes but also prohibits financial support for documentaries or consumer information programmes including topics such as gardening, cookery, travel and business. The Channel 4 code goes further than the ITC in another respect: programme-makers are distanced from sponsors and their money. 'No negotiation or agreement between a production house and sponsor will be acceptable by the Channel', and Channel 4's commissioning editors are not allowed to negotiate with sponsors, while their budgets will not benefit directly from sponsorship of programmes. As Torin Douglas said in an article 'Going Gets Tough for C4 sponsors' in *Marketing Week* (19 April, 1991), '... I think Channel 4 has got the balance right. If we have got to have sponsorship, this code provides the best guarantees of programme integrity.'

The new code upset the applecart for those sponsors who had succeeded in being accepted by Channel 4 under less harsh provisions.

For example, Spaceship Earth, a documentary series sponsored by Shell, became a casualty because it was a documentary and the sponsorship had been found by the executive producer. On both counts it was not eligible under the new code. Meanwhile, Channel 4 was seeking sponsors for American football, cycling, *Whose Line Is it Anyway?* and *Film on Four*.

19.9   Sponsorship of radio programmes

A number of forms of sponsorship have existed with radio for some years. Some of this consists of very short items such as traffic reports during rush-hours as reported by spotter plane, or sponsorship of stock market prices. A long-running sponsorship has been Nescafé's support for the weekly Network Chart Show.

Capital Radio, for instance, has about two dozen sponsors a year, usually on a minimum 12-week deal. London Car Telephone Co. have supported sports coverage, and Continental Airlines have sponsored 'flying eye' traffic reports. NatWest backed a concert series produced by Capital and syndicated to 22 other ILR stations.

Some of these deals are arranged by the network syndication company, PPM Radio Waves, others by radio sales agencies. Fees for sponsorship are around £600,000–£700,000. Usually there is no overt reference to sponsorship, and while relaxations are likely under the new Radio Authority the practice has been for presenters to state 'with' or 'in association with' a funder.

Independent local radio (ILR) got its first weekly rock magazine series in 1991, sponsored by the Rowntree Mackintosh brand Kit Kat. The 52-week series, hosted by Pat Sharp, was syndicated to more than 24 ILR stations. The £250,000 deal also included below-the-line promotions and eight night club events. The series was developed by Unique Broadcasting and J. Walter Thompson, Kit Kat's advertising agents, and was targeted at 15–24 years old.

20
Public relations

20.1 Public relations and advertising

Few subjects are more misunderstood than public relations, especially
by those engaged in advertising, which is a pity because it can be a
valuable ally of advertising. Misunderstanding occurs when it is thought
that public relations is a form of advertising.

The broad view is sometimes taken that any favourable commercial
reference is an advertisement. When, for example, a scene in a television
play occurs in, say, Sainsbury's viewers are apt to say, 'what a good
advertisement for Sainsbury's', but it is nothing of the sort. Similarly,
when it is reported that British Aerospace has sold aircraft to a foreign
airline, this is legitimate news, not advertising. It is publicity which,
being the inevitable good or bad outcome of publication, is hardly the
same thing. This was explained quite clearly in Chapter 1 when public
relations was defined. If a politician is exposed in a corruption scandal,
or a famous pop singer is reported to be suffering from AIDS, there
will be publicity in the media. But while each story may have maximum
impact, neither of these news reports will be an advertisement.

The distinction between an advertisement and a public relations news
item which may result from a news release is this: an advertisement is
a controlled announcement issued how, when and where the advertiser
wishes, provided payment is made for the space, time or site, and
provided it does not offend voluntary codes or the law. Moreover, the
advertiser has the right to be conceited and biased in favour of the
product or service, and can shout 'Bloggs Baked Beans are Best' with
impunity.

But the public relations news release depends on the whim of the
editor, and will be published only if the editor believes it to be of interest
and value to readers. The editor may re-write the story and print it at
any time. The sender has no control over its publication, and it will
need to be impartial and factual, otherwise the editor will discard it as
a 'puff'. The news release must not be biased in its own favour.
Unfortunately, many of them are and they are binned.

Public relations is not limited to press relations. Although it is relatively inexpensive compared to advertising, it is a far bigger activity than either advertising or marketing. This is because public relations concerns the total communications of the whole organization, of which marketing is but a part, while advertising is but a part of marketing. Moreover, public relations applies to any organization, commercial or non-commercial, in either the public or the private sector. Not every organization is engaged in marketing, let alone advertising, examples being the fire brigade and the ambulance services, but they are engaged in public relations.

20.2 Effect of public relations on advertising

There is an old-fashioned idea, and a very bad marketing one, as expressed in the Four Ps concept of 'publicity' of public relations being one of the promotional Ps. This saw public relations as no more than product publicity, a kind of 'free advertising' supplement.

It is interesting that Philip Kotler has modified his original view about the promotional P, preferring to call it C for communications. This is more in line with the modern concept of modern marketing communications which permits public relations more latitude within the overall marketing mix.

While it is certainly not free advertising – the editorial columns are priceless – there is of course a legitimate place for news about products and services. People do like to read about new motor-cars, lipsticks or investments. The Government's privatization schemes have contained a very large element of public relations for the millions of potential share owners had to be educated about both share buying and owning, and about the value of the investment.

There lies the fundamental difference: while advertising aims to persuade and sell, public relations aims to create knowledge and understanding, and the former will fail to succeed without the latter.

Eurotunnel is a very good example. The travelling public needs to understand the virtues of the Channel Tunnel, and one of the ways in which Eurotunnel has sought to achieve this is by means of its excellent exhibition at Folkestone. This exhibition centre seeks to educate the market. It also demonstrates the working of the PR transfer process since Eurotunnel is subject to the negative effects of hostility, prejudice, apathy and ignorance (Figure 20.1).

Many products and services may suffer from this invidious negative situation, analysis of which is the basis of preparing a public relations campaign. Advertising alone will not convert a bad situation into a good one, but public relations can contribute to a favourable marketing situation in which advertising can work successfully. It works on the elementary psychological principle that we prefer the things which we

Hostility	→	Sympathy
Prejudice	→	Acceptance
Apathy	→	Interest
Ignorance	→	Knowledge
Negative situation		Positive situation

Figure 20.1   The PR transfer process

like and know best, in other words, understand and trust.

Thus, while public relations has to do with many things apart from marketing and advertising it can have a powerful influence upon the effectiveness of both marketing and advertising.

The illusion that public relations is only to do with 'favourable' media mentions, 'favourable' climates of opinions, and 'favourable' images has also created mistaken ideas about it. Public relations also deals with unfavourable situations such as product failures and recalls, the tampering with products by activist groups, industrial disputes, disasters and other crises which endanger advertising.

Such unfavourable situations, and therefore bad public relations, occurs when an advertisement is criticized by the Advertising Standards Authority for a breach of the British Code of Advertising Practice, or a company is penalized under one of the consumer protection laws, or when a sales promotion offer fails to satisfy consumers.

In these cases reputation is at stake, and it is a public relations responsibility to see that products perform properly, that they are packaged safely, priced acceptably, enjoy good dealer relations, and that there are satisfactory after-sales services. This is very different from trying to supplement advertising with product publicity.

20.3   The organization of public relations

Public relations may be organized in one of two ways, although large companies often employ both methods. There may be an in-house public relations department, or an outside public relations consultancy may be engaged. Each has its own attributes and one is not necessarily better or worse than the other. However, there is a major difference between the organization and needs of advertising and public relations, in fact they have virtually opposite forms of organization.

The important role of the in-house advertising department and advertising manager was explained in detail in Chapter 4. But, in Chapter 5, it was shown that when the volume of advertising warranted this it paid to use the team of specialists found in an advertising agency. Except in a few cases it was not economical to employ such specialists full-time in-house.

The opposite occurs in public relations. When there is minimal public relations activity it pays to use a consultancy, but when there is maximum public relations activity it pays to have an internal public relations department with specialist staff. Very large companies may then find it necessary also to engage a public relations consultancy, either to augment the in-house department with *ad hoc* assignments, or to handle special work such as Parliamentary liaison, corporate and financial public relations, crisis management or perhaps house journal production using desktop editing techniques.

The reasons for this different kind of organization are that the in-house department is necessary because public relations deals with the day-to-day communications of the total organization, and the PRO has to have an intimate working knowledge of every facet of the organization. For this reason it is best if the PRO is not buried in the marketing department, but operates independently with direct access to all departmental heads and to top management. It is not surprising, therefore, that 60 per cent of public relations personnel are employed in-house, whereas probably 80 per cent of advertising personnel are employed in agencies. Only 37 per cent of PR personnel work in consultancies.

Figure 20.2 is taken from the report produced by the Cranfield School of Management and commissioned by the Institute of Public Relations in 1989. The report showed that 19,500 people are professional public relations practitioners, with 15,000 support staff. An analysis of the top 1000 companies indicated that expenditure on public relations was at least £500m, if not more, and predicted a £1b industry by 1992.

However, this is not to belittle public relations consultancies, especially those which are able to offer the newer and more specialized services mentioned above. But, even the more general consultancies have their advantages such as wide experience gained by servicing a variety of accounts, and the ability, as outsiders, to give professional advice on numerous topics which can range from solving communication problems to creating corporate identity schemes. The consultancy world has seen remarkable growth in recent years, and its professionalism is shown by the Professional Charter of the very efficient Public Relations Consultants Association. This is not to suggest that consultancies are a new development: the first consultancy was probably that of Ivy Ledbetter Lee, founded in 1906.

20.4 Public relations media

Another difference between public relations and advertising lies in the media used. While the mass media are used, e.g. the editorial columns of the press, and broadcast programmes, there are the private media which are created to reach particular publics. Again we have a difference:

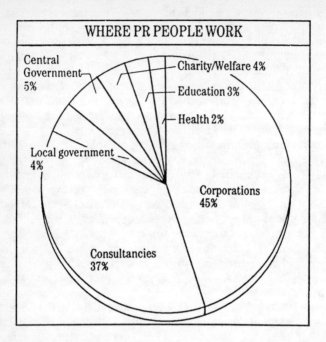

Figure 20.2   Where PR people work (Source: Report by Cranfield School of Management)

whereas advertising is aimed at large target audiences or market segments, public relations is aimed at numerous identified publics as varied as employees, politicians, and opinion leaders as well as distributors and consumers. The following are some of the special media which may be created for public relations purposes.

1   House Journal

This is the oldest form of organized public relations, and one of the first house journals was the *Lowell Offering* quoted by Charles Dickens in his book *American Notes* (1842). Another fallacy about public relations is that it is something new! There are two kinds of house journal, internal and external. The internal staff journal may be a newsletter, A4 magazine, tabloid newspaper, wall newspaper or in electronic mail form or electronic newscaster. Externals are addressed to certain publics such as users, consumers, dealers or suppliers. Some companies produce video house journals which are viewed at work-places or possibly in the home, and these resemble newsreels with a commentator, while corporate video news programmes are distributed nationally, continentally or internationally by satellite..

2   Videotapes

In addition to video house magazines, videotapes are made for showing to invited audiences, visitors, clients, employees, shareholders and other audiences. Videotapes have replaced documentary films. They may be produced for other purposes such as safety training, displays in showrooms, or to tell staff about venues to which companies are relocating.

3   Audio visuals and visual aids

Slide presentations, audio tapes and various methods of making presentations on screen or board.

4   Educational print

Different from sales literature, this can include recipe books and leaflets, home decorating guides or printed advice on gardening such as lawn treatment or control of pests.

5   Sponsored publications

These may be sold, such as road maps, cookery books, camera manuals, and sports year books.

6   Private exhibitions

Well-known permanent ones are Cadbury's World, the Thames Barrier, the Mary Rose, and Eurotunnel. Mobile exhibitions can be towed and shown, either on special vehicles such as buses and trains, or in premises such as hotels, libraries, public rooms or concourses of railway terminals.

7   Seminars, conferences and receptions

Guest audiences may be invited to events where there are speakers, video presentations and exhibits.

8   Works and other visits

Members of the public, distributors, journalists and others may be invited to visit all kinds of places associated with an organization, e.g. factories, shopping centres, sites, breweries, power stations, holiday venues or vineyards and wineries. Parties may also be taken on inaugural flights or voyages. The medium in this case is the facility to gain first-hand knowledge.

   The list could be extended to include calendars, posters and wall charts, postage stamps and first day covers, picture postcards, company histories, school project packs, induction material for new staff, and information kits for schools.

20.5   The image

This is an expression which has become somewhat hackneyed, especially when there is talk of a 'good image', 'image making' or 'polishing a tarnished image'. All these expressions are nonsensical and are best forgotten, although it is possible to *change* an image as when, say, a company which used to make railway trucks now makes containers for shipping.

An image is perceived as a result of knowledge and experience, and it is often gained as a result of an organization's behaviour and reputation. Everyone's image of an organization can be slightly different, as in cases of employees, distributors, shareholders or customers. The public relations task may be to provide information so that people have a *correct* image. Going back to the PR Transfer Process, hostility, prejudice, apathy and ignorance may affect the image, and all these attitudes may be unfair and undeserved, but exist because of lack of information, or because people are misinformed.

Two terms are often confused, these being *corporate image* and *corporate identity*, which are two different things. The corporate image is the perceived image of the organization, as explained above. The corporate identity is the way in which an organization is physically distinguished and may be recognized. It consists of such things as the logotype, colour scheme, typography, dress of employees and livery of transport. Airlines, for example, are very conspicuous by their corporate identity.

There are certain variations of the image. A *mirror* image is that held by people within the organization, but it may not coincide with the *current* image held by outsiders. When planning a public relations campaign, it is essential to discover the nature of the current image, and not accept management's wishful thinking. A *multiple* image can exist if different people working for a company create different images of it, as will happen with salesmen in the field who can each create personal images. Many companies, such as retailers, avoid this by giving all their shops a uniform appearance as do, for instance, Boots, Woolworth, Marks and Spencer and the banks. This may mean that High Streets all look alike, but the shopper has a clear image of each chain store or bank. Here we see the corporate identity (physical) contributing to the corporate image (mental).

20.6   Attributes of a public relations practitioner

In earlier chapters the qualities of the advertising man or woman were stressed, especially in the case of the advertising manager who required considerable technical knowledge and buying ability. The attributes of a public relations practitioner are similar in some respects and yet different in others, as the following six attributes suggest. He or she should:

i   be able to communicate
ii be able to organize
iii be able to get on with all kinds of people
iv have personal integrity
v   have imagination
vi be ever willing to learn.

20.7 Press relations

Press relations implies good relations with the press, and that means helping the press to publish material which sells papers. The managing director who says, 'I want this in the *Financial Times* tomorrow morning' is not practising press relations but press piracy. Press relations can succeed only when a service is provided for the press. This means supplying news, pictures, background information and features in a journalistic form in time and while it is still news. All communication media – press, radio and television – are included under this heading.

The reader may retort with some indignation that it is not their business to help the media make a profit – surely they do that well enough out of the company's advertising! The point is that *if* the reader wants the organization and its activities, policy, personnel, products or services reported, and reported accurately, trouble must be taken to understand the how, what and when of media requirements. When the media are served *first* the sender is also served. This is the elementary criterion of press relations.

Foolishly this criterion is generally ignored. Consequently, public relations is derided by the media. Consequently, 70 per cent of news releases, being obvious puffs or stale or misdirected news, are discarded practically unread. Consequently, the news agencies fill two huge plastic bins with useless news releases every morning because the authors will not confine themselves to the *hundred words* that news agencies require. The reason is that the majority of writers of news releases have never learned how to write a news release. Strangely, many of them are ex-journalists, but many more of them are business people and marketing, sales and advertising executives who do not know the difference between an advertisement and a news story.

The easiest may to learn how to write a news release is to read a newspaper and analyse how news reports are written. Two things should be obvious: the subject is in the first few words, and the first paragraph tells the whole story in a nutshell.

20.8   How to write a news release: seven point check list

First, collect all the relevant facts – try to prevent the editor's having to ring up for important details which are not in the story – and then check them to make sure that they are absolutely correct. The onus is on the writer to make sure that nothing is issued that is incorrect. Unlike the media, the PRO has the time and the opportunity to get the story right. This in itself is good press relations. The PRO will become trusted and his or her material will be sought after if a reputation is established for reliability. Having assembled the facts the news story should be written in the following way.

(i)   The *headline* should not be clever but should identify what the story is about. It is unlikely that the headline will be printed, editors preferring to be original or to write headlines that fit the space.

(ii)   The *subject* should be in the first three words, and preferably in the first. Many rejected news stories suffer from the defect that the subject is buried in the third or fourth paragraph. The writer must also decide what exactly *is* the subject. A story about an airline could have as its subject the name of the airline, the kind of aircraft or the route – which subject is news? If the company is the subject it should be presented as simply as possible – IBM rather than IBM (United Kingdom) Ltd. The full name can come later. And if the company is part of a group, do not drag in group references in the first sentence, no matter what the company secretary insists.

(iii)   The *opening paragraph* should summarize the main points of the whole story. It may be all that will be printed.

(iv)   The *development* should follow in paragraphs which give the facts in a logical sequence such as (a) advantages, (b) applications and (c) specifications.

(v)   The *final paragraph* should give the name and address of the organization, and the source of any additional information or material such as price lists, data sheets, samples or demonstrations.

(vi)   The story should bear the name of the *author,* and be *dated.*

(vii)   There is no need to use an *embargo* unless the media are privileged to receive the story in advance, as with an annual report, a copy of a speech that is to be made, or there is a time differential between two countries.

20.9   Presentation of a news release: ten point check list

(i)   The *heading paper* should be distinct from ordinary business letter-heading, but should not be so flamboyant that it looks like a sales letter. The best news release headings are neat and simple, possibly stating *News* or *Information* at the top, so that the story predominates, the name and address and telephone number of the sender being printed distinctly but discreetly at the foot of the sheet. A neat company logo may be used.

(ii) the first paragraph should *not be indented*. All succeeding paragraphs should be indented. This is followed by most newspapers and books such as this one. Other 'secretarial' styles should not be used.

(iii) Sub-headings should not be used – the editor will create them – unless the story refers to more than one item and sub-headings help to identify them. But it may be better to write separate stories about each item.

(iv) *Capital letters* should be restricted to proper names such as surnames, company names, geographical places and very important ranks such as the Queen, President, Prime Minister or Archbishop. Titles such as chairman and managing director do not need capital letters, nor do materials such as steel or polystyrene. Nothing should be completely in capitals.

(v) Nothing should be *underlined*. Underlining means set in italics.

(vi) *Figures* (except for dates, prices or measurements) should be spelt out one to nine, then set out in numbers, but to avoid confusion large numbers are best spelt out – twenty-one thousand – or clearly expressed such as one million or £1 million, or £1m.

(vii) *Abbreviations* should not be spattered with full points. A.B.C, B.Sc(Econ), I.P.R and P.R.C.A. should be presented as ABC, BSc(Econ), IPR and PRCA. At a glance, the reader will see that without the full points less space is occupied and the initials are more legible.

(viii) All copy for the press should be *typed* on a machine with upper and lower case characters – not italic or all capitals – and the work should be double spaced on one side of the sheet with equal margins of about 1.5 inches or 4 cm. If a word-processor is used words should not be typed in bold type for emphasis.

(ix) *Continuations* should be clearly stated at the foot of the incomplete copy and at the top of the following sheet. Write 'More'.

(x) The *length* of a news story should be the minimum necessary to present all the relevant facts. Ideally, the story should not exceed one sheet of A4 paper. Obviously, stories which set out to supply journalists with important background information will tend to be longer, but the average *product publicity story* need not exceed 200 or 300 words. If written as recommended above, and given genuine reader interest, it may well be printed word for word as it stands, even given that great accolade of the professional news story – the byline of a staff journalist.

Throughout, the expression *news story* or *news release* has been used. We do not speak of 'hand-outs'.

20.10   Feature articles

Another form of press work, often of lasting value, is the exclusive signed feature article which may be produced by a staff writer to whom facilities have been provided, or written by a public relations practitioner. If written by the PRO or public relations consultant, articles should *not* be produced speculatively. The idea should be offered to the editor of a suitable journal, and the editor should be asked:

i   Whether the idea is of interest?
ii   If so, how many words are required?
iii Are illustrations required and if so what kind and how many?
iv   When will article be published?
v   By what date is copy required?

All this can be set out in a letter. There is no need to buy the editor an expensive lunch. Once the editor has 'commissioned' the article, which will be supplied 'without fee', the writer must honour the agreement and keep to the agreed deadline or copy date. The value of the article may be perpetuated by buying reprints from the publisher.

The public relations practitioner often has access to article material which is unknown to editors and can offer a valuable press relations service of mutual benefit to the editor and to the sponsoring organization. Such articles should be published on their merits, and do not need supporting advertising *unless* and only unless, an advertisement can offer some additional information, such as a coupon offer of a catalogue, but normally one should not be blackmailed into buying needless advertisement space. Such advertisements can be refused on the grounds that they are irrelevant to the planned advertising campaign. Advertisement managers will, of course, try to sell space to firms which are mentioned in the editorial, but it is zealous salesmanship taken to the point of shortsightedness. A good feature article should be independent of advertising.

It is quite likely that the magazines and newspapers in which public relations stories, pictures and articles appear will be entirely different from those on the advertising media schedule. For example, a clock manufacturer may advertise in popular national newspapers which seldom print the company's news releases, but the news releases may well be accepted by women's magazines in which the company never advertises.

20.11 Photographs and photo captions

Editors frequently complain about the quality of photographs issued for public relations purposes. The chief complaints help to provide a check list of editorial photographic requirements.

(i) Pictures should be suitable for publication in the journal to which they are sent. The *Financial Times* does not want pin ups nor straight product shots. Trade magazines want interesting newsy pictures, not typical industrial record shots. Now that most journals are printed by web-offset-litho, more in-depth landscape pictures, and ones with grey mid-tone values, can be printed.

When ordering photographs it is therefore wise to explain to the photographer exactly what is to be photographed and how the picture will eventually be reproduced. Few photographers are equally good at photographing every kind of subject, and they need to be engaged according to their special skills. A studio photographer is rarely a good action photographer, and the specialist in photographing children is unlikely to be a first class photographer of racing pigeons. Unfortunately, very few photographers will admit this, yet editors maintain files listing scores of specialists and so do art buyers in advertising agencies.

(ii) Prints should be glossy but unglazed, and preferably on double weight paper. Editors naturally like as big a picture as they can get. However, if a picture is being distributed by post to many editors two things have to be remembered: (a) cost and (b) the risk of damage in transit. The safest practice when mailing photographs to the press is to use nothing larger than a half-plate print. If pictures can be hand-delivered, whole plate prints will be appreciated.

The reasons why editors like large prints is so that they can 'crop' them, that is cut away unnecessary parts to achieve a more artistic or dramatic composition. But if this dramatic composition is achieved on the negative, cropping becomes unnecessary and the smaller half-plate print is all the more acceptable. A good deal of cropping derives from the speed with which news pictures have to be taken with little regard for composition. Working in sympathetic collaboration with the right specialist photographer, the public relations practitioner can obtain well-composed, interesting newsworthy pictures which will enhance the editorial columns of a newspaper or magazine.

Let us take two examples to demonstrate how this can be done. Suppose the subject is a new teapot. For a catalogue it could be photographed sideways on, a straight record shot. For a product publicity shot, the teapot could be turned to a more interesting angle, photographed from a higher angle, or a woman's hand could be holding the handle and pouring tea into a cup.

For the second example, suppose we wanted an interior picture of a factory. A record shot might take in a large area, but for our purposes the camera could peep over an operative's shoulder at the job beingdone, or if more of the factory had to be in the picture the operative could occupy the foreground. With factory pictures the photographer should never tell an operative to turn from his or her work and grin into the camera.

(iii)   If the picture consists of people they should be asked to stand close together, and a more detailed and dramatic effect will be gained by taking from head to waist rather than full-length figure shots. If there is a small group, as with a presentation, subjects should be closed up so that the picture does not contain a vacant space in the middle, a fault that easily occurs when photographing two people shaking hands. Most formal groupings make very dull pictures. Few things are more uninteresting than a full-face portrait, yet this is the sort of picture most editors receive with an announcement about a new appointment or promotion.

Remember (unless a special arrangement has been made) that editors want *black and white pictures*. But *colour slides* are wanted for TV news stories. Photographers should use black and white film, not colour film from which black and white prints are made afterwards. This can be done but the black and white prints will be soft and pale, and lack the contrast of prints made from black and white film. The film pigments are different, and normally different lighting is required for black and white or colour photography.

The secret of good public relations photography is knowing what story the picture should tell, and then briefing the photographer accordingly. The photographer is not a mind reader.

Captions: why they are necessary and what they should say

Every illustration submitted to an editor *must* bear a caption which explains what the picture shows. The caption should be brief but fully informative. If people are in the picture they should be clearly and accurately named from left to right. The caption should be well attached to the print, not dangling from it so that picture and caption are easily separated. It helps to rubber-stamp the back of the print with the name and address of the sender, *not* the photographer. The best captions have printed headings stating the name, address, telephone number and negative number, the actual caption details then being duplicated on the vacant space below or above the printed identity of source.

20.12 Copyright of photographs

All pictures issued for public relations purposes must be issued *free of copyright*, and this means that the sender must *own* the copyright. The mistake is sometimes made of stating a warning by rubber stamp or caption that the picture is the copyright of the sender, but this invites the editor to reject a picture on which he presumes he will have to pay a reproduction fee. If it is not the sender's copyright there is no point in offering the picture for reproduction. Nor should the sender plead for acknowledgement or for a cutting of the reproduction.

Under the *Copyright, Designs and Patents Act 1988*, the first owner of the copyright of any work is its owner unless the author is an employee, when copyright belongs to the employer. Most public relations photography is commissioned from outside photographers who own the copyright, unless there is written assignment to whoever commissioned the photography. This can become complicated when a consultant commissions photography for a client. A transfer of assignment to the client does not normally occur until payment has been made in full to the original author and to the consultancy, and this is best established in the original contract of engagement between the client and the consultancy. This is important because in public relations pictures are distributed liberally, whereas in advertising the photography will be restricted to the client's own advertising and publicity material.

20.13 News conferences, receptions and facility visits

A news (or press) *conference* is an informal assembly, perhaps called at short notice, so that a statement may be given to reporters and questions answered. A news (or press) *reception* is a more formal and organized occasion when there is a programme of activities such as demonstrations, speeches and perhaps the showing of a videotape or slide presentation supported by hospitality which may include a bar and buffet. A *facility visit* entails taking a party of reporters on a visit to a distant location or on a demonstration ride, flight or voyage.

In organizing these events the following points should be considered very carefully:

1 Does the *news content* of the occasion warrant bringing busy journalists and others from their offices to the venue? Would not a news release suffice? It is a fallacy to believe that journalists come only for the beer.
2 Is the *date* sufficiently advanced to allow guests to print the story? As a general rule, early in the day, early in the week, early in the month, and an early enough month are excellent guide lines. It all depends on whether the story is intended for tonight's, tomorrow

morning's, this week's, next week's, or next month's newspaper or magazine. If it is intended for the women's press they are planning six months ahead and need copy at least three months in advance.

3 Is the *venue* easily accessible? London journalists often find themselves invited to two or three events occurring simultaneously. If the venues are centrally located it may be possible to cover all of them, so the convenience of the press is a point to keep well in mind. Nowadays, journalists themselves come from a variety of locations since the exodus of publishers from Fleet Street.

4 The *press material* should be slight and simple such a a brief news release and a well-captioned picture, supported by a sample if that is feasible. Elaborate press packs, loaded with irrelevant items such as a picture of the chairman, catalogues, price lists, sales leaflets, picture postcards, free gifts, house journals and company histories are definitely not wanted. The ideal press material can be stuffed in a jacket pocket or handbag.

But if more elaborate material is absolutely essential, there should be an assistant on duty who will undertake to have bulky material hand-delivered or posted to the journalist. If there is, for example, a choice of pictures they should be displayed and guests can then be invited to request prints which can be dispatched as required.

It is not very hospitable to thrust a heavy press pack into the hands of guests as they arrive – they do need hands with which to write and to handle cigarettes, drinks and food. Nor is it wise to place press material on chairs. The distribution of pictures and information should be strictly controlled and this will ensure that it stands the greatest chance of being used. On press facility journeys it is extremely foolish to distribute heavy press packs at the beginning of a journey, but better to supply a brief itinerary or background information on the outgoing journey, and to supplement this with further information, if required, during the day or on the return journey. Unwanted and irrelevant press material will be unceremoniously deposited under seats and lost!

These remarks may seem like common sense, but there seems to be a fetish that a specially designed and printed press kit must be produced, and that it must be packed with every conceivable item. All the press want and need are the essential unadorned facts which seldom need occupy more than one piece of paper. Sometimes pounds are spent on useless press packs which the majority of journalists will lose as soon as is decently polite.

Press packs become even more pointless in the press rooms of exhibitions where perhaps between one and four hundred exhibitors are supplying press information. The simple, clear, single sheets of paper will disappear into journalists' pockets; the cumbersome expensive press packs will have to be dumped by the luckless exhibition organizers when the show closes. Journalists do not come to exhibitions armed with suitcases; in fact they seldom carry brief-cases. How not to conduct press relations can be learned in one short visit to an exhibition press room.

20.14 Public relations organizations

There are five public relations organizations: the Institute of Public Relations comprises individual practitioners, and has its code of conduct; the Public Relations Consultants Association comprises corporate member firms and has its professional charter; the International Public Relations Association has senior practitioner members in some 70 countries; the International Association of Business Communicators has a British chapter; the Confederation Européene Relations Publiques links 20 European associations in 17 countries, of which the largest is the British IPR.

21
How marketing research aids advertising

There is sometimes confusing use of the terms market research and marketing research. Strictly speaking, market research is limited to research of the market but marketing research applies to all kinds of research applicable to marketing, and this includes advertising research, the subject of this chapter.

21.1 Introduction

Like public relations, marketing research is a subject on its own worthy of a separate book. Here we shall take an introductory look at the applications of marketing research techniques *before, during* and *after* advertising campaigns. Some of the jargon will also be explained.

How can research help in the finding of a copy platform, the selection of media, or in making a choice between alternative press advertisements, posters, packages or television commercials? How can research help us to find out the effectiveness of advertising during the run of a campaign?

How can we check the success or failure of a campaign after it has finished?

Can advertising be made scientific and not only creative, despite the demand by advertisers for creativity, as shown in Chapter 5.

The answer is that much of the risk and gamble can be taken out of advertising by using one or more of the many research techniques available to the advertiser.

21.2 How marketing research is conducted

Investigations can be initiated by either the advertiser or the agency, and media owners will be happy to give evidence of reader service enquiries. Very big advertisers have their own marketing research departments, so do large publishers, while most of the big agencies have subsidiary marketing research companies. There are also many independent research organizations. Some of these units use more than one research technique, others specialize in, say, shop audits, consumer panels, industrial research or opinion surveys.

It is possible to conduct the same enquiry by two different methods and get two different answers, as occurs with election-time opinion polls, or used to happen with TV audience surveys. The point is that research does not produce facts, only tendencies. Statistics can be interpreted in various ways. But the inexactitude of marketing research does not condemn it. Moreover, we are dealing with the social sciences, especially psychology, sociology and economics, and these are full of contrary schools of thought. There are 'schools' in marketing research too! Nevertheless, marketing research may be regarded by the advertiser as a form of insurance.

21.3   Social grades

Campaigns may be addressed to 'C1–C2' housewives, or a magazine may be said to have an 'A–B' readership. What do these strange symbols mean? It is a rather mercenary way of classifying or stratifying people according to occupation, interests and social background. The former expression 'socio-economic groups' has given way to 'social grades'. By grouping people in this way it is possible to organize research surveys that seek or gain information from people of either sex, different ages and different occupation brackets. Readership surveys are a good example, making it possible to discover what sort of people, as well as how many people, read various newspapers and magazines. Again, given this information, media can be selected according to the classes in the community to which the company aims to sell. Here, then, is use of scientific methods to eliminate wasteful advertising, and to make every pound spent work as hard as possible.

In Table 21.1 respondents are placed in six grades as a result of searching questions into the precise job of the head of the household. This is more realistic than the former method of grading people by their income, although this socio-economic method is still used for some surveys, especially overseas where such information may be more relevant.

It tells the advertiser of mass market goods, for instance, that the mass consumer market consists of 72 per cent of the adult population. These are the people who watch commercial television – hence the popularity of the medium for detergents, beers, confectionery, margarine, petfoods, package holidays, petrol and toiletries. Many of these

Table 21.1 *Social grades*

A	Upper middle class	The head of the household is a successful business or professional man, senior civil servant, or has considerable private means	About 2.7% of total
B	Middle class	Quite senior people, not quite at the top	About 15.2% of total
C1	Lower middle class	Tradesmen, non-manual workers, 'white-collar' workers	About 24.1% of total
C2	Skilled working class	Usually an apprenticed worker, 'blue collar'	About 27.1% of total
D	Semi-skilled and unskilled working class		About 17.8% of total
E	Those at lowest level of subsistence	Pensioners, casual workers, those dependent on social security	About 13.1% of total

products are also bought by the other grades who also watch television. Thus, TV is a more universal medium for today's staple products than any single newspaper.

21.4 Jargon of marketing research

Before going further, the rest of this chapter will be easier to follow if some of the basic jargon of marketing research is defined.

The *sample* is a number of people large enough to be representative of the whole *population* (or *universe*) relevant to the enquiry. The population is the *total number of people* (e.g. all school teachers or all motorists) who, as said above, are of value to the enquiry. The number of people in a sample may vary from as few as a dozen in a discussion group to 30,000 for the JICNARS national readership survey.

The size of sample will depend on the simplicity or complexity of the questions and the number of characteristics that exist in the population. By *characteristics* we mean different kinds of people who must be represented in sufficient numbers so that their opinions, preferences or motives are discovered. In a survey of motorists it might be necessary to go beyond sex, age and income and include owners of different kinds of vehicle, and different purposes for which the vehicles were used. Size may also depend on the degree of accuracy that is required (where this can be calculated) or the amount of money that can be spent.

As an example of cost and accuracy, it is cheaper but usually less accurate to use a *quota* rather than a *random* sample. This somewhat misleading expression 'random' should be clearly understood: it does not mean that the interviewers go out into the street and interview anyone at random. It is actually very precise and its accuracy can be calculated mathematically, whereas the quota sample is subject to human bias. A better name for random is probability, as we shall see from the following definitions.

A quota sample is made up of quotas or agreed numbers of people falling within age, sex and social grade groupings. The interviewer will be instructed to interview so many people of each type, and they are found by observation and questions. Thus, inevitably, a certain degree of error in selection can occur. But with the random sample no such human error can happen because the interviewer is given actual names and addresses and at least three attempts must be made to contact the members of this provided sample. The names and addresses are taken at random, usually by the process of selecting every nth name from the electoral roll or a membership list. (The *random walk* method may be used in developing countries, where lists do not exist, and houses are visited at intervals, say, every tenth house in a street.) The probability is that a cross-section of every kind of person in the universe will be discovered, the method working on the law of averages.

So that interviewers do not have to travel long distances between one address and another, large surveys use a stratified random sample which reduces the national random sample to names and addresses within scientifically selected polling districts.

The *questionnaire* is the document containing both questions and instructions which the interviewer has to complete for each respondent interviewed. A *diary* is a document which a respondent completes at home to show purchases made or programmes watched or listened to. Questionnaires need to be designed by experts, and this is where the psychologist enters into marketing research, devising questions, their kind and their sequence so that answers are obtained easily, simply, accurately and without causing offence.

Depth interviews are those conducted without a formal questionnaire, questions being answered freely and the interviewer writing these down verbatim, or recording them on a tape.

Opinion research seeks attitudes or shifts of opinion, and questions usually require 'Yes', 'No' or 'Don't know' answers. Most research invites *preferences* for this or that product, package or advertisement, while *motivational research* uses clinical tests – rather like intelligence tests – to identify the natures of the persons forming the sample, and then to reveal their hidden motives. With motivational research the respondents are usually unaware of the reason for the enquiry and so their answers are unlikely to be biased.

Some research is *ad hoc* – single complete enquiries – while other surveys, e.g. national readership surveys, are *continuous*. Further examples of continuous research are *consumer panels* on which house-wives are recruited and asked to submit regular reports on their purchases, or the panel used for the BARB TV audience research (using both meters to record programmes received and diaries to complete about programmes watched). Consumer panels are also used to test new products. Another form of continuous research is the *dealer, retailer, shop* or *store audit panel* of shopkeepers who are regularly visited by representatives of a research company who record stock received and stock unsold to discover sales for each brand at each shop. From the total figures it is possible to issue reports showing the share of the market held by each brand. Succeeding reports can be compared to reveal trends.

Finally, there is *desk research* which consists of the study of existing or published data ranging from internal reports to those published by the Government, trade associations, universities, banks, publishers and other organizations. It is not always necessary to undertake original research. A wealth of statistics is available from Government agencies, based on census figures, taxation, import duty, motor licensing and other sources. The Department of Trade and Industry, the Department of the Environment and HM Customs and Excise are all excellent sources of data of value to the advertiser.

Primary research consists of original research, but *secondary* research consists of surveys already conducted on which reports are available, e.g. Government statistics.

21.5   Marketing research applied to advertising (before)

Motivational and other forms of research may be used to find a copy platform, and this survey may take the form of a discussion group.

Alternative advertisements may be presented to a sample of potential customers, and evaluations made of what was remembered, liked or had a sales promoting effect. This can be done with TV commercials, members of the public being invited to a film show in a hall or private cinema. A number of commercials are shown, including the one or ones under test, and a measure is taken of the shift in brand awareness as a result of seeing the new advertising. Press advertisements can be *copy-tested* by asking members of the public to look through a folder containing a mixture of advertisements. Questions are asked to learn what respondents recall about each advertisement, and in this way the strengths or weaknesses of certain headlines, slogans, pictures or offers can be measured.

The *split-run* technique may also be used to determine the response to different advertisements. The term originated from publishing where the print run of a publication was divided between copies carrying one advertisement and other copies carrying another advertisement. Response is easily checked by replies to a coupon offer, although other methods can be adopted if there is separate geographical distribution. This can be done with a television company which has two transmitters, and different commercials can be transmitted to different audiences who can be tested next day for recall (see 21.7).

Test marketing can also be used to decide whether the right appeal or the right media are being used, assuming that a national campaign is simulated by using media such as TV or posters, but seldom press, which are typical even in a miniature campaign.

Test marketing is conducted in a test town which has retail and consumer characteristics representative of the national market, and the whole marketing strategy is tested to discover whether, over a period which allows for repeat purchases, a given percentage of the market can be obtained. If the test is successful the product is launched nationally. This should not be confused with product pre-testing which may be undertaken in the early stages of new product development.

Direct mail campaigns can be tested by sending out *trial mailings* to test response to alternative appeals or offers, and direct response marketers may also test alternative prices in this way. More people may buy at 58p than 62p, or vice versa.

Media research also aids the advertiser, and certainly helps the agency to plan campaigns and to justify schedules. Audited net sale (circulation) figures are supplied by the Audit Bureau of Circulations, while readership data are available from JICNARS.

Publishers of provincial newspapers also supply statistical details of their coverage of local markets. Information about audience figures for the previous week's programmes on commercial television are published by BARB. JICPAR and the poster industry offer data on 'opportunities to see' and 'adult site passages'. JICRAR conducts surveys of commercial radio audiences, and figures for cinema advertising are based on entertainment tax returns and there are the annual CAVIAR reports. One way and another it is possible to work out cost-per-thousand figures for reaching most media audiences.

These and other sources of media statistics are explained in greater detail in 21.9.

21.6 Marketing research applied to advertising (during)

While a campaign is running there are several research opportunities for checking its effectiveness. Using dealer audit research, it is possible to use a certain medium in one town or area and not in another control district. Sales can be checked one against the other, having first taken an earlier base period to establish a norm.

Reading and noting tests can be applied following the appearance of press or TV advertisements, each element of the advertisement being checked and given a rating. Thus so many per cent of men and so many per cent of women recalled the headline, the company name, the picture, the free offer, the copy in the box and so on right through the advertisement.

Reading and noting tests can also be used as a form of pre-testing, the advertisement appearing in a regional edition only. Testing next day can reveal strengths and weaknesses and if necessary the advertisement can be modified before it appears nationally.

Replies can be counted for each insertion of an advertisement which is 'keyed' differently for each appearance, the key being either a necessary part of the address or a coding printed on the coupon.

Advertisement expenditure by rivals can also be checked by subscribing to the reports published in MEAL Digest.

21.7   Marketing research applied to advertising (after)

The effectiveness of a campaign is often best checked by the numbers of enquiries, bookings or sales received, and these can be converted into cost-per-reply and cost-per-conversion figures which will reveal the most economical media. Cost-per-reply figures are found by dividing the cost of the space by the number of enquiries or orders received. Cost-per-conversion is found in a similar way by dividing the cost of the space by the value of sales deriving either directly or after replaying to enquiries received from readers of the advertisement. Holiday and direct response advertising relies on this method of evaluating the pulling power of media or appeals, but it cannot be applied to advertising which directs buyers to the point-of-sale. But here, continuous research of either the dealer audit or consumer panel kind should reveal whether the advertising increased sales or, which can be important too, whether it maintained them.

Dealer audit research can reveal the effect advertising has had on the movement of retail stocks and the brand share held by the advertised brand.

There are *omnibus consumer panel surveys* which combine the enquiries of different clients which may or may not be long-term, and advertising effectiveness can be checked by *piggy-backing* on one of those postal or interview surveys for a month or more.

Enquiries are sometimes carried out in the field with questionnaires to find out reactions to advertising, or the *discussion group* method may be used provided the small group is representative of the market.

The most typical form of post advertising research is *recall* (or next day recall) research, whereby members of the public are stopped in the street and asked if they read a certain newspaper or watched TV on the previous day. The respondent is then asked whether he saw a particular advertisement and what he remembered of it. This can reveal a certain amount of useful information about the impact and memorability of the advertisement. But what was the effect of the advertising? This calls for a longer and more sophisticated form of post-advertising research known as a *tracking study* of which the *Tracking, Advertising and Brand Strength* (TABS) method is one of the most refined.

A TABS subscriber receives 13 four-weekly reports covering fmcgs such as confectionery, drinks and toiletries, retailing, financial services, holidays and travel, durables, clothing and do-it-yourself goods.

These are based on a national continuous weekly tracking to show 'brand health' and advertising effectiveness across all major media. While media planners and buyers aim to obtain maximum 'share of voice' for clients, the TABS method goes beyond ordinary recall and 'might have been' effect to testing the share of 'hearing' rather than 'shouting' in respect of share of voice. It really tests the cost-effectiveness of advertising.

The technique uses a combination of computer technology and a self-completion questionnaire to monitor the strengths of reactions about the advertised brands. A sample of 500 adults, 250 of them housewives and 250 men, are interviewed each week, totalling 24,000 adults during the year in each of the 10 main TV areas. They are asked to tick scaled and other questions covering brand buying, brand usage, brand awareness, advertising awareness, brand goodwill, price image and detailed brand image. These ticks are read by an Optical Mark Reading computer and converted into scores and percentages among the target market for each of the different products or services covered.

Media consumption criteria are also analysed, covering readership of daily and Sunday newspapers, weight of newspaper reading, readership of magazines and weekend colour magazines supplements, weight of ITV viewing, Channel 4 viewing, breakfast TV viewing, listening to each of the ILR stations, and by all the different interlaced combinations of weight of ITV viewing, newspaper reading and radio listening.

TABS identifies weaknesses in both creative and media aspects of the advertising campaign by measuring real effects such as awareness, image or buying attitudes. This produces a £-per-£ assessment of the quantitative contribution by each medium.

TABS results can reveal rates of decay – the 'wear out' factor – and heritage effects where there is a halo effect from previous advertising. Linked with this are media implications concerning pattern and frequency when scheduling the appropriation, that is, whether 'drip' or sudden 'burst' tactics are advisable, and the best time to advertise cost-effectively.

21.8   Media research

Media owners research the pulling power and the audience of their media. Publishers carry out their own readership surveys to gain more detailed purchasing information than is possible with the JICNARS surveys. Individual radio and television contractors research their audiences. London Underground has published surveys of its travelling public. There are the regular CAVIAR studies of cinema audiences. There have been a number of surveys to prove the opportunities to see poster sites, and the *See You In Barking* study was an interesting one concerning public transport advertising.

The *See You In Barking* tracking study into public awareness of external bus advertising was carried out in 1987 by British Market Research Bureau for London Transport Advertising. Some 70 different bus side campaigns were measured, and about 500 adults were questioned at 40 sampling points and in home interviews. A special test campaign was run by LTA with posters of barking dogs and a message *See You In Barking* placed on 750 T-sides (T-shaped bus side posters) between mid-April and mid-May. Research interviews showed that 32 per cent recalled the poster after two weeks and 37 per cent after four weeks. Of the other campaigns tested, awareness was between 8 per cent and 63 per cent, but most scored 32 – 37 per cent.

21.9   Sources of media statistics

Media planners and buyers are aided by reliable independent sources of statistics which are described in this section. Two terms should be clearly understood because they are quite different. These are *circulation* and *readership*. Circulation means the average number of copies sold. Readership means the number and kind of people who read publications. The latter cannot be calculated simply by multiplying the circulation figure by, say, three. Some journals such as the *Financial Times* and *Reader's Digest* have very large readerships due to 'pass round' readership and long life. There is also duplicated readership because people buy or see more than one publication of the same kind.

1   Audit Bureau of Circulations

The average audited net sale is certified by the ABC on the basis of audited figures being submitted by member publishers. The net sale is the final figure after free copies and copies sold for less than full price are deducted from the print run, and the ABC figure is the average per day, week or month over a six-month period prior to June 30 and December 31. ABC figures are quoted for about 3,000 British publications. Similar bureaux exist in many other countries.

2 Verified free distribution

This is a subsidiary of the ABC and provides data on the circulation figures of free newspapers, several hundred of which are delivered door-to-door in different urban areas. They may also be given out in the street.

3 Joint Industry Committee for National Readership Surveys

JICNARS is a tripartite research organization representing the Press Research Council (newspapers and magazines), The Institute of Practitioners in Advertising (agencies), and the Incorporated Society of British Advertisers. A continuous survey, with a random sample of 30,000, produces demographic profiles on some 200 national newspapers and magazines. It uses the A, B, C1, C2, D, E social grades, which were originated for the National Readership Survey. Respondents are also questioned about ITV viewing, ILR listening and cinema-going. Figures are published every six months for January–June and July–December.

4 Joint Industry Committee for Poster Audience Research

Otherwise known as JICPAR, this organization represents the Outdoor Advertising Association of Great Britain, the Institute of Practitioners in Advertising, the Incorporated Society of British Advertisers and the Council of Outdoor Specialists. It has carried out occasional surveys of poster audiences.

5 Outdoor site classification and research

OSCAR provides a poster database, operated by the Outdoor Advertising Association through contractors (*see* 11.36).

6 Joint Industry Committee for Radio Audience Research

JICRAR produces audience reports based on diaries kept for a period by a panel of listeners. It represents the Association of Independent Radio Contractors, the Incorporated Society of British Advertisers and the Institute of Practitioners in Advertising.

7 Joint Industry Committee for Cable Audience Research

JICCAR, with similar tripartite representation, produces reports on cable-TV viewing.

8   Broadcasters' Audience Research Board

BARB measures TV audiences, both BBC and ITV plus satellite TV, using set meters and diaries completed by members of household comprising the sample. Area top tens are published weekly and are widely quoted in the press. A new contract with AGB research and RSMB Television Research commenced on 1 August, 1991 for a period of seven years. It uses a larger panel than in the past,monitoring more TV sets and more channels, isolating time-shift viewing programme by programme from playback statistics, registering age and sex of guest viewers instead of estimating them and providing daily results, if required, by electronic instead of paper methods. From the end of 1989, satellite transmissions were also monitored.

9   Media Expenditure Analysis Ltd

MEAL publishes quarterly reports on estimated media expenditure in the press and on television, and more than 150,000 advertisements are monitored each month, half of them on ITV, covering 360 product groups. It also has an on-line service. These estimates reveal what rival advertisers are spending, although the sums quoted are maximum ones since special deals will be unknown.

10   Target Group Index

TGI, run by the British Market Research Bureau, looks at TV audience research in a different and more detailed way than BARB. A panel of 24,000 adults are questioned annually to record demographic characteristics and media exposure and provides data on 400 product fields.

11   Advertising Statistics Yearbook

Published by the Advertising Association, this is a comprehensive annual survey of advertising statistics. Its contents cover advertising and the economy; cinema, direct mail, poster, radio, TV and press advertising. Advertising expenditure is given by product sector, top advertiser and agency statistics.

12   Marketing Pocket Book

This little pocket book contains a remarkable wealth of statistics of value to marketers including detailed sections on advertising expenditure. The figures are culled from numerous official sources. It is published annually for the Advertising Association by NTC Publications of Henley-on-Thames and is recommended to those studying for the CAM exams. Other *Pocket Books* are listed in Appendix 1.

13   Pan-European Television Audience Research

PETA is run by Audits of Great Britain to provide an annual survey of European TV audiences.

21.10   Lifestyle groups

Various research organizations and advertising agencies have introduced a number of analyses of consumers which classify people quite differently from the fairly simple social grading by employment which takes no account of age, mental attitude or social role. When consumers can be categorized according to the way they live or the interests they have, it is possible to identify the most appropriate media, or to extract special groups from vast data banks for direct mail and direct response marketing purposes. Some of the descriptions of these categories are picturesque, but unlike the social grades method there is no standard typology. Different research units and agencies have created their own classifications.

If we begin with what are known as *psychographic types*, of which Yuppies is the best known, there is a series of types, some expressed as acronyms. They are:

a   *Baby boomers.* People who have grown up since the baby boom of the 1960s.
b   *Baby busters.* Generation which followed the baby boom, representing smaller demand for homes and household goods in 1990s.
c   *Buppies.* Black Yuppies (see z).
d   *Crinklies.* See wrinklies (y).
e   *Crumblies.* See wrinklies (y).
f   *Dinkies.* 'Double income no kids' married couple.
g   *Empty nesters.* Married couple without children.
h   *Glams.* 'Greying leisured affluent middle-aged'.
i   *Grey panthers.* See jollies (m).
j   *Grumpies.* 'Grim ruthless upwardly mobile professionals'.
k   *Guppies.* People with special interests or hobbies.
l   *Holiday junkies.* Those who enjoy and take many holidays.
m   *Jollies.* Jet setting oldies aged 49–59 free of financial pressures.
n   *Lombard.* 'Lots of money but a real dickhead'.
o   *Managing mums.* Guilt-ridden women dedicated to their families.
p   *Markas.* 'Middle-aged re-nester, kids away'.
q   *Methuselah market.* Those within five years of retirement and well off.
r   *Minks.* 'Multiple income, no kids'.
s   *Opals.* 'Older people with active lifestyles'.
t   *Silver market.* People over 60 years of age.
u   *Ticks.* 'Two income couple with kids'.

v   *Wealthy empty nesters*. High income couples, children left home.
w   *Whannies*. 'We have a nanny'.
x   *Woopies*. 'Well-off older people' (over 55). Pre-retirement.
y   *Wrinklies*. Elderly people – in their twenties during Second World War.
z   *Yuppies*. 'Young upwardly mobile professionals'.

The ACORN, Mosaic, Super Profiles, PIN and other geodemographic systems are described in the Direct Mail section of Chapter 12, but CACI (originators of ACORN) also have their *Monica* method of ageing people, and their Lifestyles list.

The *Monica* method has been disputed but it is none the less interesting and could be 75 per cent accurate. In 1987, 43 million adults had their ages identified with 13,000 first names. It was believed that first names often belonged to periods when these names were fashionable, perhaps being associated with celebrities or royalty. Thus, it was found that Florence and Percy were retired, Pamela and Keith had young families, and Sharon and Kevin were probably young, single and without families. From this study CACI produced a database and Monica can be supplied as an overlay to the ACORN list. This takes into account that some names, such as Biblical ones, have lasted longer and are to be found in both pre-family and young family groups. Arthur and Dorothy are found in both mature family and retired groups. John was consistently popular with babies born in the 1940s and 1950s, but Robert and Gordon had the weakest age profiles.

The *ACORN Lifestyle List* uses the ACORN system as a demographic overlay to the annually updated electoral roll, a household composition analysis of a client's selected neighbourhood, an accurate age segmentation system of age bands, geographical sections to identify drive times, TV regions, shopping centre catchment areas or other geographical area criteria, ability to discriminate by surname, a wealth indicator and other facilities. There are six broad ACORN neighbourhoods, and 24 lifestyle groups which are divided into 81 Lifestyle types. Examples of the 24 groups are rural singles, affluent rural couples and families, younger traditional suburban couples and families, older singles in council areas, cosmopolitan inner city dwellers, and homesharers in affluent areas.

Super Profiles Lifestyle Groups, run by Credit and Data Marketing Services, follow a similar pattern but classified as underprivileged, council tenants, fading industrial, multi-ethnic area, aspiring blue and white collars, older suburbs, country and retiring suburbans, young married suburbs, metro singles, affluent minority and unclassified.

Behaviour Bank from Mardev is based on a twice yearly national shoppers survey and is divided into 300 psychographic/family activities. It contains details of three million households and some of its categories are business credit card users, CD player owners, fine food/wine enthusiasts, mortgage holders, non-smokers, pet owners, magazine subscribers, self-employed, stocks and shares owners, working women and so on. This is derived from the American Select and Save Survey.

Different advertising agencies and research companies have their special names for social value groups, of which the following four are quoted:

Taylor Nelson: self-explorer, experimentalist, conspicuous consumer, belonger, social register, survivor and aimless.

SRI Vals: integrated, achiever, emulator, experimental I-AM-Me, belonger, sustainer and survivor.

Y & R CCC: reformer, succeeder, aspirer, transitionals, mainstreamers, struggling poor and resigned poor.

McCann-Erickson: (men) avant-gardian, pontificator, self-admirer, self-exploiter, chameleon, token trier, sleepwalker, passive endurer; (women) avant-gardian, lady righteous, lively lady, new unromantic, hopeful seeker, lack-a-daisy and blinkered, down-trodden.

In each case they are usually different names for the same categories.

The first one breaks down like this: self-explorer (18 per cent); experimentalist (15 per cent); conspicuous consumer (20 per cent); belonger (18 per cent); social resister (10 per cent); survivor (14 per cent); aimless (5 per cent).

Such categories vary from country to country, especially those like the ACORN Lifestyle List. In the USA the Claritas Corporation's PRIZM system (Potential Rating Index Zip Markets) works on a basis of a 'birds of a feather flock together' principal and has classified 40 groups via neighbourhoods identified through the zip code system. This resembles the ACORN list based on postcodes, but indicates the variety of income, ethnic group and type of neighbourhood found in the USA. The 40 PRIZM clusters include blue blood estates, urban gold coast, God's country, gray power, blue collar nursery, towns and gowns, shotguns and pickups, single city blues, black-country folks, small town downtown, downtown dixie style, Hispanic mix, and hard scrabble – imaginative names for different grades! The full list is given in Chapter 12.

Sagacity Life Cycle Groupings are given in the *Marketing Pocket Book* (see 21.9) and these comprise Dependent (mainly under 24s), Pre-family (under 35s with households but no children), Family, and Late (adults whose children have left home or who are over 35 and childless). These are divided into White (head of household ABC1), and Blue (head of household C2DE). Sagacity groupings are compiled by Research Services Ltd.

Part Six
The Advertising Control System

22
Common law and statute law

22.1 Introduction

Advertising is subject to two types of control: legal and voluntary. There is sometimes controversy over which is the more effective, and scepticism is sometimes expressed about the strength of voluntary controls. The two are different.

The law, while warning people not be behave illegally and is preventive up to a point, can take a long time to deal with offences and court action may not occur for up to three years, simply because of the backlog of court business. Even then the law may have to be interpreted in the courts. A court decision is then subject to appeals and may finally be heard in the House of Lords. By this time it could be too late, the damage will have been done, the situation could have changed, and the penalty will be incapable of putting right a wrong. Thus, the greatest strength that lies in legal controls is their preventive effect.

Voluntary controls, which are often better called self-regulations, can also be preventive but, in the case of complaint, can be applied quickly. An offending advertisement can be modified or withdrawn (and many not even appear if there has been advance consultation), so that voluntary controls can be the more effective.

Another difference is that the two do not deal with the same offences. A false trade description can be illegal, but a misleading or exaggerated claim can offend against a code. A breach of contract is a legal tort, but knocking copy is unethical. Illegal advertising is subject to penalties, but no penalties can be exacted under voluntary controls. Law cases cost legal fees, but this is not so with voluntary controls. Yet another aspect is that, while protecting the public, voluntary controls aim to protect the good name of advertising when it is violated by unscrupulous or misguided advertisers.

On the other hand, legislation tends to be created to deter or punish offending advertisers which implies that advertising itself is a guilty practice. Thus a subtle difference exists between the defenders of the good name of advertising and the protectors of the consumer from law-breaking advertisers. Self-regulation is a form of public relations for advertising, although, as will be shown below, ethical breaches do happen, either deliberately or through carelessness or competitive zeal. However offences against the codes are seldom evil or even intended.

Nevertheless, the present extensive self-regulation system did originate to combat the extraordinary claims made for proprietary medicines in the 1930s, and it was the Advertising Association that pioneered codes of practice through the campaigning efforts of Russell Chapman before the Second World War, and Frank Bishop and Bill Needham in the 1950s.

22.2   Common and Statute law

Common law consists of civil wrongs and torts which require the plaintiff to take legal proceedings against a defendant, a judge deciding on who has suffered the greatest loss and granting appropriate remedies. Statute law requires action by the public prosecutor on behalf of the Crown, and penalties may be imposed such as probation, fine or imprisonment. The following are the most important remedies arising from the fusion of equity and common law.

(a)   *An injunction* by which the court orders the defendant to cease certain behaviour such as publication of an offensive article, book or programme.

(b)   *Specific performance* of a contract where damages would provide inadequate compensation for the plaintiff.

(c)   *Rescission of contracts* is a discretionary remedy which can be applied when it is not possible to award damages in the case of breach of contract because circumstances have changed. Thus, the contract is annulled.

(d)   *Rectification* can be effected by the court to correct the terms of an agreement which had not been accurately expressed.

(e)   *Relief against penalties* can occur when a court makes a decision on the fairness of damages such as liquidation damages decided beforehand by the parties to a contract, e.g. if a job is not completed on time.

Returning to the nature of Common law, this has grown up by precedent and case law since the Norman conquest of 1066. When pleading cases, lawyers will depend on past decisions. Unlike Statute law, it is unwritten. Typical common laws relevant to advertising are those concerning contract, slander of goods (defamation) and passing off.

Common Law

22.3 Definition

Common law consists of contracts and torts or civil wrongs, for which an aggrieved party or plaintiff can sue for redress or damages in a civil court.

22.4 Law of Contract

The law of contract applies in many transactions between advertisers and their agents or suppliers. This can include a contract of service between an advertising agent and a client, and for the purchase or hire as the case may be of advertising space, air-time, poster sites, exhibition space, exhibition stands, print, photography, videos, models, actors and so on.

It is not necessary for a contract to be in writing, although a written contract is easier to prove in court, if there is a legal dispute, but an oral contract can be valid if the verbal order is performed in good faith. Advertisements are often booked by telephone, as with the telephone selling of classifieds. Even so it pays to confirm verbal contracts in writing.

Written contracts are required if they come within the *Law of Property Act 1925* or the *Hire Purchase Act 1965*, or relate to the assignment of copyright or when a guarantee supports payment for a purchase. It is wise to be careful about assignment of contract in contracts of service between advertising agencies and clients. The agency may insist on retaining copyright until all accounts are settled. (*See* 22.16.)

A legal contract requires four elements:

i An *offer*.
ii An *acceptance* of the offer.
iii A *consideration,* both sides making a sacrifice such as payment and supply of goods or services.
iv *Consent* must be genuine, and not obtained deceitfully.

However, a new contract arises if the original offer is revised by the recipient and this is accepted by the person making the first offer. For instance, a black and white advertisement may be offered by a publisher but the advertiser may decide on a full-colour one, so that the procedure is reversed and there is a new offer, acceptance and consideration.

A contrast can be invalidated if there is a *mistake* or misrepresentation; if it is made for an *illegal* purpose; or the parties do not have *contractual capacity* because they are minors, insane or drunks.

There are four kinds of contract:

i   A *simple* contract is one not made under seal, and it can be oral, written or implied.
ii An *express* contract is one in which both sides set out the terms in words, whether orally or in writing.
iii An *implied* contract is one in which nothing is written, as when ordering a meal or accommodation which requires payment.
iv An *executed* contract exists if a task is performed and paid for, this usually being an oral agreement.

An *invitation to treat* is not an offer, and no contract is involved since there is no obligation to supply, as in the case of an advertisement or a window or store display. A shopkeeper is not bound to sell the goods on display. If a direct response marketing offer contains a coupon or order form which a customer completes that is an offer, and if this is accepted and there is an agreement to exchange goods for payment, there is a contract.

22.5   Defamation

There are two legal forms of defamation: spoken and transitory known as *slander* of a person or, commercially, *slander of goods* which is more serious than 'knocking copy', and *libel* which may be published or broadcast and can be permanent. If a person, organization or product is intentionally or unintentionally brought into disrepute the aggrieved party can seek damages from the slanderer or libeller.

To be actionable, a scandalous or libelous statement must be:

(a) defamatory;
(b) false, unless the contrary is proved;
(c) understood to refer to the plaintiff;
(d) made known to at least one person other than the plaintiff.

A simple case of libel could be a character reference which was critical and resulted in depriving a person of being a successful job applicant. Many employers will merely state the facts about employment and make no comment on performance. A bad reference could be libellous merely because it was made known to at least one other person such as a prospective employer.

Slander of goods. There are some similarities between derogatory statements as covered by the Codes and slanderous statements, as when there is severe ridicule or condemnation of rival goods or services. No doubt the EC has put paid to some of the continental press advertisements for hotels which said 'Don't stay at the XYZ hotel – it has fleas!' It is essential to ensure that comparisons are true and fair.

22.6 Passing off

When a package or 'get-up' is so designed or imitated that it may be mistaken for a well-known brand, this deception is known as 'passing off'. It occurs quite often in Third World countries where gullible customers are deceived as, for example, if a soft drink is labelled Koka-Kola.

The owner of the original brand may sue for damages representing loss of trade if:

(a) the trade name or get-up is associated with his goods in the minds of potential customers.
(b) the acts objected to have interfered with or are calculated to interfere with the conduct of business or sale of goods in the sense that there is confusion in the minds of potential customers.

A number of examples of passing off occur with products made in the Far East which closely resemble European products but usually sell at lower prices. A flagrant example was Dalu, the Taiwanese copy of Lego construction toy sets, which even went so far as to use a rectangular red, yellow and white logo which was easily confused with that of Lego. As a result of legal representations the Taiwanese manufacturers put in writing their promise to refrain from manufacturing copies of Lego products; to change the appearance of their bricks and components to avoid confusion; to use packaging which could not be confused with Lego's; and to stop using a similar logo.

Passing off can be in the form of a similar shape container where the original container was a means of distinguishing and identifying a product, and this occurs with a number of bottled products. One such case which occupied the courts for years, but was finally settled by a House of Lords ruling was that of the Jif lemon juice bottle. The juice had been marketed from 1956 in a container which resembled a lemon. The case made was that great brand loyalty was attached to this container. However, a subsidiary of the American Borden company marketed its ReaLemon in a plastic lemon similar to that of Jif. The defence was that a different brand name and label avoided confusion. Nevertheless, the House of Lords upheld an injunction in favour of Reckitt & Colman, makers of Jif.

Statute Law

22.7 Definition

Statute law consists of written laws or Acts of Parliament entered upon the Statute Book after having passed through Parliament as Bills and received the Royal Assent, together with Statutory Orders or Regula-

tions, or Statutory instruments, which Ministers may issue in addition
to Acts of Parliament.

The latter defy the democratic legislation procedure since they are
not debated or approved by Parliament, but are simply created as a
fait accompli at the Minister's discretion, even though he may be
empowered to do so by the provisions of the Act. There are probably
too many examples of this presumption of ministerial power: however,
it may be held that such laws are too urgent to await long drawn out
debate, or that they are the means of complementing existing statutes.

More than 100 laws relate to advertising, and the following are the
most important.

22.8   Advertisements (Hire Purchase) Act 1967

The object of this Act is to regulate advertisements which state hire
purchase terms. They must be set out correctly in direct response
advertisements so that the customer is told whether or not payment
by instalments will incur payment higher than the basic cash price.
Under the original *Hire Purchase Act 1965* contracts must be in writing.

22.9   Betting, Gaming and Lotteries Act 1963

The Act controls advertising of betting shops, and prohibits the sending
of betting circulars to minors. Section 10 bans any advertising which
indicates that any premises are a licensed betting office, their location
and the facilities they offer.

22.10   Business Advertisements (Disclosure) Order 1977

Here is one of those small pieces of legislation no doubt introduced
because of a recurring malpractice by deceptive advertisers. The Order
stipulates that an advertisement should always be obviously so, and
that if there is any doubt it should be headed 'Advertisement'. An
advertisement, especially a classified one, should identify that it is placed
in the course of a trade or business, and is not a private advertisement.
Similarly, 'reader' advertisements should not pretend to be editorial.

22.11   Children (Performances) Regulations 1968

Together with the *Children and Young Persons Act 1933 (Scotland
1937); Education Acts 1944–48*; those Regulations and local authority
by-laws made in pursuance of this legislation it controls the employment
of children in the making of advertisements, including TV commercials.

22.12 Civil Aviation Act 1982

Except as provided by regulations, aerial advertising is prohibited under the Act. *The Civil Aviation (Aerial Advertising) Regulations 1983*, and the *Civil Aviation (Aerial Advertising) (Captive Balloons) Regulations 1983* permit the use of banner towing, airships and for the use of both captive and free flight balloons.

22.13 Consumer Credit Act 1974

Additional regulations concerning hire purchase are contained in this Act. Consumers are given the right to cancel a contract if 'oral representations were made in the presence of a debtor or hirer', in the discussion before a contract was entered into. A typical example would be in the case of direct or doorstep selling (e.g. insurance, encyclopaedias, double glazing), and allows a 'cooling off' period of five days after the day when the customer receives a copy of the agreement. Prohibits the sending of circulars to minors offering loan facilities.

Further controls regarding credit offers in advertisements are contained in the *Consumer Credit (Advertisements) Regulations*.

In October 1989, Cheltenham and Gloucester Building Society was prosecuted under the Act for breaches committed in its mortgage advertising, and the Society was fined £3,500 for eight offences of giving more prominence to a flat rate charge of 12.75 per cent rather than the annual percentage rate (APR) of 13.7 per cent. The offences occurred on window display material, and resulted from the technical error of failing to print the APRs in bold enough type. No doubt the error was unintentional, and this example only goes to show how careful advertising personnel – advertising manager, copywriter, designer and typographer – need to be.

22.14 Consumer Protection Act 1987

A number of attempts have been made to protect the consumer against false trade descriptions and misleading prices, particularly through the *Resale Prices Act 1964*, the *Trade Description Acts* of 1968 and 1972 and the *Price Marking (Bargain Offers) Order 1979*. The need to implement such laws would seem to make a mockery of the marketing philosophy of seeking to satisfy customers, and to emphasize the *caveat emptor* (buyer beware!) nature of a free enterprise market economy. The trouble has been (and this also applies to the self-regulatory codes described in the following chapter) that offenders are rarely unscrupulous rogues but typical members of the industrial, commercial and business world. Otherwise why is an Office of Fair Trading necessary, and why have Conservative governments been obliged to legislate against their brethren?

The complex system of legislative controls of misleading prices began under Macmillan who, perhaps mistakenly, banned the system of retail price maintenance. Under this system manufacturers fixed minimum retail prices, and price-cutters were refused supplies. This led to a number of pirate retailers who made a virtue of price-cutting goods, especially cigarettes. The official idea was that by removing minimum prices, retailers could sell at their own prices, taking less profit if they chose, and the public would benefit. The unfortunate result has been 'double-pricing', fictitious 'list prices', 'price-bashing' and 'discount' pricing, in other words manufacturers published list prices which retailers could appear to sell at a discount. The 'recommended retail price' became a way of indicating a possible retail price. But the advertiser was deprived of using price as a genuine form of competition – this was left to the retailer as has been seen with the supermarket.

However, new legislation issued between 1987 and 1989 made a concerted effort to clarify the law, and to its credit the Institute of Practitioners in Advertising was especially active in lobbying for a new framework of control. The resultant *Consumer Protection Act* is consequently the most important piece of consumer legislation ever to appear on the Statute Book. Its three parts cover Product Liability, Consumer Safety and Misleading Price Indications, and they are summarized below.

Part 1. Product Liability

Under the Act, a manufacturer or retailer (who may be an advertiser) is responsible for any defects in a product. If a defect is discovered it becomes legally and not just morally necessary to recall the defective product. The following is quoted from the Act regarding the meaning of 'defect'.

(i) Subject to the following provisions of this section, there is a defect in a product for the purposes of this Part if the safety of the product is not such as persons generally are entitled to expect; and for those purposes 'safety', in relation to a product, shall include safety with respect to products comprised in that product and safety in the context of risks of damage to property, as well as in the context of risks of death or personal injury.

(ii) In determining for the purposes of sub-section (i) above what persons generally are entitled to expect in relation to a product all the circumstances shall be taken into account, including:

(a) the manner in which, and purposes for which, the product has been marketed, its get-up, the use of any mark in relation to the product and any instructions for, or warnings with respect to, doing or refraining from doing anything with or in relation to the product.

(b) What might reasonably be expected to be done with or in relation to the product: and

(c) the time when the product was supplied by its producer to another;

and nothing in this section shall require a defect to be inferred from the fact alone that the safety of a product which is supplied after that time is greater than the safety of the product in question.

Part 2. Consumer Safety: the general safety requirement

(i) A person shall be guilty of an offence if he:

(a) supplies any consumer with goods which fail to comply with the general safety requirements;

(b) offers or agrees to supply any such goods; or

(c) exposes or possesses any such goods for supply.

(ii) For the purpose of this section consumer goods fail to comply with the general safety requirement if they are not reasonably safe having regard to all the circumstances, including:

(a) the manner in which, and purposes for which, the goods are being or would be marketed, the get-up of the goods, the use of any mark in relation to the goods and any instructions of warnings which are given or would be given in respect of the keeping, use or consumption of the goods:

(b) any standards of safety published by any person either for goods of a description which applies to the goods in question or for matters relating to goods of that description, and

(c) the existence of any means by which it would have been reasonable (taking into account the cost, likelihood and extent of any improvement) for the goods to have been made safer.

Part 3. Misleading Price Indications: meaning of 'misleading'

(1) For the purposes of section 20 above an indication given to any consumers is misleading as to a price if what is conveyed by the indication, or what those consumers might reasonably be expected to infer from the indication or any omission from it, includes any of the following, that is to say:

(a) that the price is less than in fact it is;

(b) that the applicability of the price does not depend on facts or circumstances on which its applicability does in fact depend;

(c) that the price covers matters in respect of which an additional charge is in fact made;

(d) that a person who in fact has no such expectation:

(i)   expects the price to be increased or reduced (whether or not at a particular time or by a particular amount);

(ii) expects the price, or the price as increased or reduced, to be maintained (whether or not for a particular period); or

(e) that the facts or circumstances by reference to which the consumers might reasonably be expected to judge the validity of any relevant comparison made or implied by the indication are not what in fact they are.

(2)   For the purposes of section 20 above, an indication given to any consumers is misleading as to a method of determining a price if what is conveyed by indication, or what those consumers might reasonably be expected to infer from the indication or any omission from it, includes any of the following, that is to say:

(a)   that the method is not what in fact it is;

(b)   that the applicability of the method does not depend on facts or circumstances on which its applicability does in fact depend;

(c)   that the method takes into account matters in respect of which an additional charge may be made;

(d)   that a person who in fact has no such expectation:

(i)   expects the method to be altered (whether or not at a particular time or in a particular respect); or

(ii) expects the method, or that method as altered, to remain unaltered (whether or not for a particular period); or

(e) that the facts or circumstances by reference to which the consumers might reasonably be expected to judge the validity of any relevant comparisons made or implied by the indication are not what in fact they are.

(3)   For the purposes of subsections (1)(e) and (2)(e) above, a comparison is a relevant comparison in relation to a price or method of determining a price if it is made between that price or that method, or any price which has been or may be determined by that method; and

(a)   any price or value which is stated or implied to be, to have been or to be likely to be attributed or attributable to the goods, services, accommodation or facilities; or

(b)   any method, or other method, which is stated or implied to be, to have been or to be likely to be applied or applicable for the determination of the price or value of the goods, services, accommodation or facilities in question or of the price of value of any goods, services, accommodation or facilities.

From the preceding quotations it will be realized that great care has to be exercised by advertisers who make price indications.

The enforcement authority is the local authority trading standards department, which has replaced the weights and measures inspector, and is located at county council and metropolitan district level, or the district council in Northern Ireland. Damages can be claimed in the case of a faulty product; the penalty for a consumerist safety offence can be imprisonment not exceeding six months or a fine; and the penalty for a misleading price can be a fine. The penalties are not severe, but to be found guilty is to suffer loss of reputation which is poor public relations bearing in mind the resultant bad publicity in the media. Producers, importers and own-labellers are made liable for unlimited damages which cause injury or death, without proof of either negligence or contractual relationship. This implies a general duty to sell safe products, and this responsibility is additional to existing legislation, all previous legislation being repealed.

More stringent controls are placed on bogus price offers. The Government agreed with the PAI's contention that one could not categorize price comparisons as the Bargain Offers Order had attempted to do. What mattered, said the IPA, was the *impression* created by a price claim. So, section 20(1) of the Act provides:

'Subject to the following provisions of the part, a person shall be guilty of an offence if, in the course of any business of his, he gives (by any means whatever) to any consumers an indication which is misleading as to the price at which any goods, services, accommodation or facilities are available (whether generally or from particular persons).'

Services or facilities include credit, banking, insurance; foreign currency; electricity; car parks and caravan parks; accommodation extends to hotels and package holidays and to the sale of new residential property; but investment business is excluded.

In addition to the Act, a *Code of Practice for Traders on Price Indications* (see next chapter) was issued under section 25 of the Act, with the following purposes:

(a)   Giving practical guidance with respect to any of the requirements of section 20.

(b)   Promoting what appear to the Secretary of State to be desirable practices, as to the circumstances and manner in which any person gives an indication as to the price at which goods, services, accommodation or facilities are available or indicates any other matter in respect of which any such indication may be misleading.

Available from the Department of Trade and Industry, the Code is particularly relevant to 'sale prices' and the making of price comparisons in numerous situations, such as comparisons with other traders' prices and comparisons with the price of goods in different condition or quantity.

Because of the far-ranging implications of the Act considerable space has been given to it. On the question of safety, traders have to be careful about buying foreign goods (including components), since they may not comply with British (or EC) standards. In the past, there have been cases of faulty or dangerous wiring, electric-light bulbs, Christmas tree lights, and toy dolls, resulting in costly product re-calls. The problem with such re-calls is that it is not always easy to locate faulty products which have been dispersed as gifts or have been discarded.

Moreover, a firm which has assembled a product from components imported from, say, the Far East, and has done so in good faith will suffer prosecution, financial loss and blame although it did not itself make the offending component. Unfortunately the temptation is to buy in foreign components because they are cheap as a result of cheap labour.

22.15　Control of Misleading Advertisements Regulations 1988

Implementing a Council Directive of the EC, these Regulations harmonize Common Market legislation under the *European Communities Act 1972*. The Director General of Fair Trading empowers High Court actions for injunctions prohibiting misleading advertising, but only providing that the complainant has failed to obtain satisfaction from a voluntary body such as the Advertising Standards Authority. This curious creation of a last resort if the ASA has dismissed a complaint is one of the few examples of a legal alternative to a self-regulatory control. It is also an example of how Brussels may endanger our voluntary system of advertising controls.

22.16　Copyright, Designs and Patents Act 1988

Replacing the *Copyright Act 1956*, the 1988 Act restates the law of copyright; introduces new provisions regarding the rights of performers and others in performances; confers a new design right in original designs; amends the *Registered Designs Act 1949*; deals with patent agents and trade mark agents; confers patents and designs jurisdictions in certain county courts; amends law of patents; makes provisions concerning devices designed to circumvent copy protection of works in electronic form; penalizes the fraudulent reception of transmissions; and makes it an offence to fraudulently apply a trade mark.

Copyright subsists in original literary, dramatic, musical or artistic works; sound recordings, films, broadcasts or cable TV programmes; and typographical arrangements of published editions.

Copyright does not subsist in a work unless the qualification requirements are satisfied regarding the author, the country where the work was first published or, in the case of a broadcast or cable TV programme, the country from which the broadcast was transmitted.

Copyright does not subsist in literary, dramatic or musical work unless and until it is recorded, in writing or otherwise. Usually, the duration of copyright is 50 years from the calendar year of the author's death, the release of a film, a broadcast is made or the item is included in a cable TV programme.

The first owner of copyright is the author of the work, unless a literary, dramatic, musical or artistic work is produced by an employee in the course of his employment. In the latter case the employer (e.g. a studio, advertising agency or PR consultancy) is the first owner, subject to any agreement to the contrary, and creative material produced for a client remains the copyright of the agency or consultancy unless in the service agreement it is agreed to assign the copyright to the client. This assignment may be subject to the client having paid his final bill.

Copyright is therefore a very important and serious matter for those who provide professional services, and it is necessary to be clear about who owns the copyright of any creative work. There is, for instance, no copyright in an idea, but there can be in its physical interpretation. However, if the advertiser or the agency puts creative work out to a contractor, the contractor owns the copyright. If an employee produces creative work in his or her private time, copyright belongs to the author and not the employer.

Likewise, a photographer – who may be commissioned by an advertiser or agency – now owns the copyright of his or her photographs, whereas formerly only copyright of the negative belonged to the photographer. It is therefore necessary, when buying photography, to arrange for the photographer to assign the copyright, and the best method is to request such a release when ordering photography. The IPA recommends use of a detachable form bearing words such as: 'In consideration of your order I hereby assign to you as beneficial owner and for all purposes the copyright in the work to which this order relates'. Unfortunately, there is no guarantee that the photographer will respond, since he is not obliged to and is legally the copyright owner.

The 1988 Act also introduces a new element, intellectual property rights, of which there are two kinds: all written matter protected by copyright, and skill and expertise which is partly confidential. Under Moral Rights, an author or film director has the right to be identified, hence the long lists of credits which follow films or TV programmes.

These moral rights are summarized as *the right to be identified as author or director*, (section 77) and *the right to object to derogatory treatment of work* (section 80). Exceptions apply to computer programs, design of a type face, and any computer generated work, or when copyright is divested in an employer. Also, a person has the right not to have a work or film falsely attributed to him. A four-page set of Guidance Notes is available from the IPA.

A cautionary tale appeared in an article on the Act in *Public Relations* (November 1990). A PR consultancy 'undertook to produce a corporate brochure on behalf of a blue chip client... The consultancy established no written agreements with the photographers, freelance designers or design consultancy. Once several million copies of the new brochure had been printed and delivered to the client, they found themselves in the middle of disputes involving infringements of copyright and derogatory treatment.

'The consultancy had employed a design group to create a logo for the client company, which involved commissioning a freelance illustrator to draw the magpie. No copyright agreements were negotiated by the consultancy for photographic or illustrative work.

'The client asked for the magpie's tail to be shortened, and the consultancy found itself guilty of derogatory treatment of the illustrator's work'.

This account was given by solicitor Heather Leeson, the article being based on a talk given to the IPR Construction Industry Group at the Law Society. Further considerations of copyright law will be found in the references of EC directives in 22.36.

22.17   Data Protection Act, 1986

This controversial Act particularly concerns databases and mailing lists as used for direct mail advertising and direct response trading, members of the public having the right to know what data are held about them. Data holders are legally required to register their information with the Data Protection Register, and copies of the Register are available for inspection in public libraries. For a fee, members of the public may apply for print-outs of data held about themselves, *if* they can discover who holds the information and on which of their files it is held! This is likely to be impossible.

Nevertheless, registered data users are expected to observe the following seven principles: personal data shall be (i) collected and processed fairly and lawfully; (ii) held only for lawful purposes described in the register entry; (iii) used only for those purposes and only be disclosed to those people described in the register entry; (iv) adequate, relevant and not excessive in relation to the purpose for which they are held; (v) accurate and, where necessary, kept up-to-date; (vii) protected by proper security. However, if the data are kept on filing cards instead of on a computer, registration is not required!

22.18   Financial Services Act 1986

Here is more far-reaching legislation from the 1980s, concerning advertising by investment businesses and regulating the market for securities, commodities and insurance (excluding Lloyds) following the deregulation of the City, known as the 'Big Bang'. Associated with it is the authorizing body, the Securities and Investment Board, and a number of self-regulatory organizations, the Life Assurance and Unit Trust Regulating Organisation, the Financial Intermediaries, Managers and Brokers Regulating Association, the Association of Futures Brokers and Dealers, and the Securities Association. There are also recognized professional bodies such as those representing solicitors and accountants. In spite of some notable disasters and scandals, these bodies are supposed to protect the investor, and the promotion of investments are expected to conform to their rules. However, it is not easy to regulate a world in which insider trading was a normal way of life.

22.19   Fair Trading Act 1973

This Act has had a major impact on the advertising agency business, revolutionizing the old recognition and commission systems since the Act operates against monopolistic practices. The Act created a Director General of Fair Trading and staff to study how trading practices affected consumer's interests and to advise on any necessary action, becoming known as the Consumers' Charter. In November 1976 the OFT declared that the conventional agency recognition and commission system was an illegal monopoly under the *Restrictive Trade Practices Act 1976*. This did not banish the agency recognition and commission system altogether, but it did mean that the recognizing bodies (NPA, NS, PPA, ITVA and AIRC) could no longer guarantee a standard rate of commission to recognized agents. Instead, the commission rate became negotiable between agencies and individual media owners. The revised recognition agreements became concentrated on two considerations: credit worthiness – meaning adequate funds to pay media bills – and acceptance of the BCAP.

The Act adopted the new concept of *consumer trade practices*, meaning any means of undertaking the supply of goods or services. The Act covers:

(a) the terms or conditions (whether as to price or otherwise) on or subject to which goods or services are or are sought to be supplied, or

(b) the manner in which these terms or conditions are communicated to persons to whom goods are or are sought to be supplied or for whom services are or are sought to be supplied, or

(c) promotion (by advertising, labelling or marking of goods, canvassing or otherwise) of the supply of goods or of the supply of services;

(d) methods of salesmanship employed in dealing with customers, or

(e) the way in which goods are packed or otherwise got up for the purpose of being supplied, or

(f) methods of demanding or securing payment for goods or services supplied.

If he considers a trade practice to be offensive, the Director General may propose an order for the control of the practice for consideration by the Consumer Protection Advisory Committee. Upon the Committee's recommendation the Director General can ask the Secretary of State to place the proposed legislation before Parliament.

22.20 Food Act 1984, Food Labelling Regulations 1984

Food labelling laws regarding specific foods are contained in the Act and Regulations and in the *Weights and Measures Act 1985*. This legislation updates the former *Food and Drugs Act 1955*, the *Labelling of Food Regulations 1970* and the 1972 Amendment. This is an area subject to changes as new foods come on the market such as new imports and convenience foods.

22.21 Forgery and Counterfeiting Act 1981

Because English bank notes are copyright of the Bank of England, permission should be obtained before reproducing them in advertising. However, the Bank is mostly concerned about the accuracy of reproduction, being proud of its designs. It is best not to reproduce entire or flat notes, which could be cut out and used as money. Such a deception did occur when oranges were wrapped in tissue paper on which were printed English bank notes, and it was discovered that foreign seamen in the Port of London were attempting to use them as money. Unauthorized reproduction can be held to be a criminal offence under the Act.

22.22 Lotteries and Amusements Act 1976

A competition must contain an element of skill, otherwise it is a lottery, that is a distribution of prizes by lot or chance. The only legal lotteries are those run by charities which enjoy special dispensation.

Unfortunately, terms like lottery, sweepstake and free draw are very loosely used by the marketing, advertising and sales promotion worlds.

Strictly speaking, a free draw (requiring no purchase) is neither a competition nor a lottery and it is certainly not a sweepstake (of which the best example is the Irish Sweep in which subscribers may draw the name of horses which may or may not win a race). A number of free draws are strictly speaking illegal because a purchase is required such as of a newspaper or magazine containing an entry form. Some free draws sail near the wind when their aim is to at least attract store traffic.

But some operators of sales promotion schemes, such as publishers, have been literally gambling with section 14 of the Act, and official bodies such as the Institute of Sales Promotion and the Institute of

Practitioners in Advertising have condemned these illegal promotions. Up to the time of writing the Director of Public Prosecutions has taken no action, although there has been flagrant disregard for the law. For instance, the *Daily Express's* Alan Frome was reported in *Marketing Week* of September 1991 as saying that he did not care whether his promotion was legal or not. The promotion offered the chance to win the Duchess of Windsor's pearl and diamond choker valued at £70,000. Entrants had to send a £2 donation to the Great Ormond Street Scanner Appeal *and* six *Daily Express* tokens. Thus purchase was necessary, it was not a free draw and within the meaning of the Act it was a lottery.

The only get-out, if there really is one, is that on request a promoter may provide free personal lottery numbers, or the tokens may be obtained from other people's copies of the paper, or cut from discarded copies but that is a rather laughable defence. The majority of entrants will buy a copy of the journal, which is the object of the promotion. When such contempt for the law is practised it does little good for the reputation of the promoters, yet offenders have not only included the *Daily Express* but the *Daily Mirror*, *TV Guide* and the *Radio Times*.

Certain forms of contest, requiring no skill, are not lotteries. Matching halves and scratch cards are not lotteries because customers do not compete with each other. The same applies to the Bingo games in certain newspapers, which are not free draws. Spot The Ball contests are more dubious but up to the time of writing there has been no successful prosecution, although there have been court cases.

22.23   Mail Order Transactions (Information Order) 1976

This is one of the orders resulting from the advice of the Director General of Fair Trading, and it requires a statement of the trader's name and address in mail order (direct response) advertisements. For instance, it is insufficient to use a newspaper box number or an accommodation address.

22.24   Printer's Imprint Act 1961

While there are some exceptions, it is a normal requirement for all printed work to be published or dispersed to carry the name and address of the printer, but in case of a legal dispute it is in the printer's interest to identify his work.

22.25   Race Relations Act 1976

Under Section 29 of this Act it is unlawful to publish or cause to be published an advertisement which indicates or might reasonably be taken to indicate an intention to discriminate racially. The Commission for Racial Equality is empowered to institute legal proceedings where necessary to enforce the law.

22.26   Restrictive Trade Practices Act 1976

This Act applies mostly to monopolistic practices, as was seen in the ruling about advertising agency recognition and the commission system (see 22.19 *Fair Trading Act 1973*).

22.27   Sex Discrimination Act 1975

Rather like the *Race Relations Act*, this Act concerns discriminating advertisements, especially those recruiting staff in which care may be necessary to seek applicants of either sex, so that a new language has evolved with expressions like 'salesperson'. A free booklet, *Guidance on Employment Advertising Practice*, is available from the Equal Opportunities Commission in Manchester.

22.28   Supply of Goods (Implied Terms) Act 1973

This Act amended the old *Sale of Goods Act 1893* to guarantee consumers' rights under the original Act, and protects the consumer against unfair 'small print' guarantees which claim to exclude customer rights under the 1893 Act. It is a very important Act where consumers are obliged to sign agreements.

22.29   Telecommunications Apparatus (Marketing and Labelling Order 1985, Telecommunication Apparatus (Bellnoise Labelling), and Telecommunications Apparatus (Advertisements) Order 1985

When British Telecom lost its monopoly over the supply of telephones, and various kinds of apparatus became available from retailers and other suppliers, consumer protection legislation was introduced in the form of three orders, the latter applying specifically to advertising. Suppliers have to comply with this marketing, labelling and advertising legislation.

22.30   Trade Descriptions Acts 1968, 1972

Although the *Consumer Protection Act* has taken over much of these Acts (repealing the 1972 one), the requirements of a trade description remain, (now extended to services), as do false representations of Royal approval.

It is therefore important to remember that the 1968 Act contained the following requirements of a trade description which is any indication, direct or indirect, *given by any means whatever*, of any of the following matters with respect to goods or parts of goods. These requirements are still relevant: and include services as well as products.

(a) quantity, size, gauge;
(b) method of manufacture, production, processing or reconditioning;
(c) composition;
(d) fitness for purpose, strength, performance, behaviour or accuracy;
(e) any physical characteristics not included in the preceding paragraphs;
(f) testing by persons and results thereof;
(g) approval by any person or conformity with a type approved by any person;
(h) place or date of manufacture, production, processing or reconditioning;
(i) person by whom manufactured, produced, processed or reconditioned;
(j) other history, including previous ownership or use.

From this comprehensive list it will be seen that the Act's requirements can involve any statements made in advertising, sales literature, sales promotion schemes or public relations material such as news releases or scripts for videos.

There have been many prosecutions under this Act, showing that advertisers do not always check their facts, or deliberately issue misleading or untrue information. These cases range from over-optimistic claims in holiday brochures to downright lies in classified advertisements for secondhand cars.

22.31   Trade Marks Act 1938

A trade mark is defined as 'a device, brand, heading, label, ticket, name, signature, word, letter, numeral or combination thereof'. Under the Act 'it is a mark used or proposed to be used in relation to goods for the purpose of indicating or so to indicate a connection in the course of trade between the goods and some person having the right either as a proprietor or registered user to use the mark, whether with or without any identity of that person'. A trade mark may also be a logotype, but some organizations may use both. The Act requires that a trade mark must have at least one of the following characteristics:

(a) name of a company, individual or firm represented in a special or particular manner;
(b) signature of the applicant for registration or some predecessor in his business;

(c) an invented word or words;

(d) a word or words having no direct reference to the character or quality of the goods, and not being according to its ordinary signification a geographical name or surname;

(e) any other distinctive mark, but a name, signature or word other than such as fall within a–d above is not registrable, except upon evidence of its distinctiveness.

A container cannot be registered as a trade mark, as the House of Lords ruled in 1986 regarding the shape of the Coco-Cola bottle. However, as shown in the case of Jif lemon juice in 22.6 (Passing Off) there can be a remedy against imitation under common law.

22.32   Trade Marks (Amendment) Act 1984

The amendment Act makes it possible to register service marks as well as trade marks, these being marks that denote the origin of services just as trade marks denote the origin of goods.

22.33   Unfair Contract Terms Act 1977

This Act needs to be considered alongside the *Advertisement* (Hire Purchase) Act 1967 and the *Supply of Goods (Implied Terms) Act 1973*. It concerns guarantees and hire purchase agreements. A consumer who suffers loss or damage because goods are defective cannot be subject to a limited guarantee, or excluded liability, if the manufacturer or supplier was negligent. The consumer is protected from exclusion clauses.

22.34   Unsolicited Goods and Services Acts 1971 and 1975

Under these Acts the consumer is protected from the one-time racket of *inertia selling* under which he or she was sent unsolicited goods for which they felt responsible and therefore often bought under duress. The Acts render such goods the recipient's property if, during a six-month period, beginning with the day of receipt, the sender fails to regain possession, and the recipient does not unreasonably prevent possession. However, this six-month period may be shortened if the recipient requests repossession by the sender within thirty days of expiration of the six-month period. If the sender does not repossess the goods by the end of the six-month period, the goods become the property of the recipient.

The object of the Act was to deter the unscrupulous mail order practice of delivering uninvited goods on a sale-or-return basis, and the Act also prohibited the unsolicited distribution of direct mail advertisements of a sexual nature.

The classic case was the delivery of a pot of cream which, being perishable, invited consumption otherwise it would have been wasted, and this required payment although never ordered. The legal answer was that the cream should have been put in a refrigerator and kept in good condition until it could be collected.

Another provision of the Act is to protect persons from the unauthorized directory entry racket, and there is no obligation to pay for entries obtained, for instance, by a salesman tricking an office worker into signing a statement that a directory entry is correct. Incidentally, a variation on this racket is to send 'advertisers' proof of an entry with an offer of a discount for prompt payment, the 'directory' never actually appearing.

22.35   Wireless Telegraphy Act 1984

The maximum fine for broadcasting without a licence is £2,000, although it is not illegal for advertisers to buy air-time on pirate radio. However, with today's plethora of local and community radio stations, pirate radio is largely historical.

The Act aimed to ban the operation of commercial radio stations outside the authority of the broadcasting authorities, giving officers of the British Telecom Radio Interferences Services the power to seize offending equipment. For example, in one year there were 97 raids on pirates and 40 people were convicted. When some stations broadcast copyright news bulletins they tried to pay a fee to the Mechanical Copyright Protection Society, but it was refused. Pirate stations made no copyright fees for broadcasting music, nor did they pay their staff trade union rates of pay, and they exploited transmitter power and even usurped frequencies meant for authorized stations.

A more recent application of the Act refers to the use of radar speed trap detectors. While it is not illegal to import, manufacturer, or sell these devices it is illegal, under this Act, for the public to use them. The Code of Advertising Practice Committee (see next chapter) has warned that 'no advertisement should contain anything in breach of the law, nor bring the law into disrepute. Advertisers have been encouraged to take our advice before offering this kind of advertisement for publication' (ASA Monthly Report 4, September 1991).

22.36   Law and international advertising

While advertising in the UK is subject to more than 100 stringent laws, of which the most important have been quoted above, and subject also to rigorous codes of practice which are described in the next chapter, the British advertiser enjoys greater freedom than applies in many other parts of the world. Some of this liberality is due to the painstaking lobbying by the trade organizations such as the Advertising Association, Institute of Practitioners in Advertising and the Incorporated Society of British Advertisers to name but three. It may be true that some British food, tobacco and pharmaceutical companies have been able to promote products, or use promotional methods, in Third World countries which would have been inadmissible in the UK, e.g. high tar cigarettes, powdered baby milk, and medicines not approved in the UK, but the reverse is true in, say, continental Europe or North America.

A company selling in international markets has to make use of local advertising agencies and be subject to local laws. Perhaps one should sympathize with Volvo whose American advertising agents were too clever, and revelations led to prosecutions, first by the Texas attorney general and then by the Federal Trade Commission.Legal action resulted from the notorious 'Bear Foot' TV commercials which showed a large-tyre pick-up truck running over a row of cars and crushing all but a Volvo 240. Unfortunately, a witness revealed that the Volvo had been reinforced, but that supports in the other cars had been weakened! Both Volvo and their advertising agents Scali McCabe Sloves were heavily fined, and Volvo fired the agents.

The Single European Market is fraught with directives, threatened or otherwise by Brussels, contradicting national laws on what sales promotion schemes are permitted or prohibited, and national regulations on Eco-brands, Eco-labelling, packaging and other green issues. Environmentalists are more active and popular in continental Europe than they are in the UK where the activities of Greenpeace and Friends of the Earth are regarded as little more than intellectual fads compared with the political strength of the 'greens' across the North Sea. The direct mail and direct response businesses are subject to data processing rules more onerous than the British. The advertising of tobacco, pharmaceuticals and high speed cars is under so much threat that European media owners fear substantial loss of advertisement revenue. This could also affect British media circulating in EC countries.

In some cases, from an advertising point of view, there is no Single European Market, and Euro-brand advertising is limited to the legal peculiarities of each country. Harmonization is slow and is generally anti-advertising. Sales promotion (which could seriously affect packaging if it carries on-pack offers) poses some of the biggest problems.

A pan-European survey of national legislation conducted by Matthew Hooper, managing director of Interfocus, an Omnicom Group company, and published in the August 1991 issue of *Direct Response*, described the labyrinth of proposed and existing national laws which were even more restrictive than impending EC directives.

In Greece the law forbids promotions tied to product purchase, and restricts on-pack promotions.

In Spain, promotional games must be checked by the Treasury, a 10 per cent tax being imposed on the value of prizes. New legislation proposes that the market price of prizes should be added to the cost of a promoted item, the promotions agency should be named, prizes not normally retailed should not be offered, and prizes for children younger than 14 and surprise gifts should be banned. Yet another proposal is that when a promotion ends, products with promotional wrappings, must be removed. Further restrictions would be placed on game shows and prize draws. (While these proposals are being considered at the time of writing, and irrespective of whether or not they become law, they reveal the attitude of legislators to advertising and particularly to sales promotion.)

The survey looked next at France, a country of perplexing attitudes of liberality and restrictions regarding advertising. French law controls the kind of promotional offer that can be made, although three for the price of two offers are encouraged. But you are not permitted to sell two products together, unless each item can be purchased separately, which of course destroys the sales promotion idea. Goods may not be related to a lottery or any similar gaming device, nor may goods be offered at less than cost price. Promotions associated with tobacco and alcohol, including direct marketing operations, became illegal in 1991. After 1992, advertising of tobacco products was restricted to only men-related magazines, and even then the creativity is restricted. All other promotional activities for tobacco products, including sponsorship, are banned.

German advertising law bans corporate advertising, and is opposed to most free gift schemes. Generally, use of the word 'free' is regarded as deceitful in many European countries.

The German Bundesrat (Upper House) approved a new law in 1991, effective in December 1991, which obliges manufacturers to take back for recycling packaging such as boxes, cans, bottles, tubs and toothpaste tubes in which German products are sold. The British-based Industry Council for Packaging and the Environment (INCPEN), which has European members, opposed the legislation. Nevertheless, the German authorities said that unless German companies responded, a compulsory deposit of 50 pfennigs (17p) would be imposed on all packages to encourage their return. Some 400 firms, including Coca-Cola, Wilkinson Sword and Unilever, formed the Duales System Deutschland (DSD) to cooperate with local authorities and supermarkets in a massive collection campaign. Yellow bins were distributed to 11 million consumers in 1991, and bins are expected to be supplied throughout Germany by 1995.

A peculiarity of the EC desire to outlaw tobacco and alcohol advertising is that this would permit media to be truly cross-frontier because it would not then carry advertising prohibited in certain countries. This would mean economic ruin for many journals which depend on revenue from such advertising. In much of this legal minefield concerning advertising, we see the conflict between left wing and right wing principles, plus the influence of the Greens.

Green influences can be a mixture of voluntary and legal controls, and both could affect the promotion of UK exports to the continent. Germany has the enterprising Green Spot system whereby firms which subscribe to a waste collecting anti-pollution scheme are allowed to mark their packages with a green spot. An EC directive due to become effective in 1993 is aimed at controlling the volume of packaging waste, and to reduce the amount of landfill waste which can be dangerous when it contains plastic containers, biologically degradable or not.

Copyright is another area of European concern and the European Commission in 1991 and 1992 adopted a more comprehensive attitude towards the harmonization of copyright laws in the Community, requiring all states to comply with the Berne Copyright Convention, and with the Rome Convention (which covers 'neighbouring rights' – the protection of performers, producers of sound recordings and broadcasting organizations). Among the topics under consideration are harmonization of the legal protection of databases, harmonization of the length of copyright protection, moral rights, reprography; (artists) resale right and the collective administration of copyright and neighbouring rights and collecting societies. Directives may give copyright owners, including authors and performers as well as record and film producers, exclusive right to control rental of their works.

For the advertising business, ranging from direct response to TV and radio commercials, the implications of impending copyright legislation is momentous since it covers the whole cross-frontier promotional field, whether goods are advertised in only one country or in part of or the whole of the community.

Comparative advertising is a topic which has exercised the minds of the European Commission, but not without the approval of the advertising industry. This is a subject which has come within the orbit of the BCAP (Paragraph B21.1 and 2), but the Council Directive on Comparative Advertising became effective in January 1993. Its stipulations are that comparative advertisements must meet strict criteria concerning objective comparisons of fairly selected features of competing goods or services. Claims made must be objectively verifiable. Anyone making the comparison must be able to produce scientific proof of the accuracy of assertions made. A serious restriction is that advertisements must quote all relevant comparisons including those in which the advertiser's products do not make favourable comparison. This implies that companies will have to admit if their product is more expensive or less reliable.

The BCAP recommendation aims to avoid 'knocking copy' (which the Americans accept) and denigration (Paragraphs 22.1, 2 and 3), but the effects of the EC Directive on Comparative Advertisements could make it too complicated, troublesome or even undesirable to make comparisons. Typical motor-car advertising of this nature could disappear.

23
Self-regulatory controls

23.1 Introduction

Self-regulatory or voluntary controls are those without legal force which are conducted, usually in the interests of the good reputation of the industry but also to protect the public, by various trade and professional bodies. The exceptions to this are the codes of the Independent Television Commission and the Radio Authority, the *Broadcasting Act* of 1990 making it a statutory duty to enforce codes. These two codes therefore have a quasi-legal status, not being laws in themselves but having the power to require offending commercials to be withdrawn. The other codes in this chapter have no power and rely on advice and recommendation. However, as will be demonstrated, even voluntary codes do have 'teeth' and can be effective controls.

Voluntary controls have a long history in the UK, as explained in Chapter 1, the Advertising Association originating as the National Vigilance Committee in 1926, and the Advertising Standards Authority being set up as an independent and realistic control system in 1962. The problem has not been advertising but its mis-users. Advertising is like a hammer, a useful tool but a dangerous weapon in the wrong hands.

23.2 The ASA and CAP

Before discussing the two major codes of practice which control (a) all print (including poster) and cinema advertising and (b) sales promotion, it is necessary to explain the work of the Advertising Standards Authority (ASA) and the Committee of Advertising Practice (CAP) which operate jointly at the same address.

The ASA has an independent Council of 12 members, of whom only two are from advertising, under the chairmanship (at the time of writing) of the Rt. Hon. Sir Timothy Raison, MP, a director general and staff of some 60 people, plus the voluntary members of the various CAP committees. Finance comes from the Advertising Standards Board of

Finance (ASBOF) which collects a levy of 0.1 per cent of gross media rates, this being paid to ASBOF by the media or the agencies or direct by advertisers, providing an annual budget of about £2.5 million.

Substantial operational changes were introduced in 1991, the ASA handling complaints regarding all non-broadcast advertisements in the press, on posters, in cinemas, by direct mail (including mailing list and database management), and sales promotion. The ASA also monitors many categories of advertising, and issues advice. A good example has been the attention given to dubious 'green' claims.

Every month ASA case reports are published that detail complaints which have been investigated, and state the decisions taken. Examples from these reports (re-designed and issued as Monthly Reports in June 1991) will be discussed.

The CAP represents 21 advertising and media organizations, with the support of five others. Its main task is to coordinate the actions of its member organizations to secure compliance with the British Code of Advertising Practice and the British Code of Sales Promotion Practice. It has four standing committees: Health and Nutrition; Financial Advertising; Mail order and Direct Response Advertising; and Sales Promotion Practice, and is also assisted by the Copy Panel. In addition, CAP is aided by numerous experts covering specialist fields such as medicine, electronics, engineering, computers, finance and the environment.

The public have been invited to submit complaints to the ASA, and a series of advertisements has been issued over the years for which publishers have donated space. These advertisements have been characterized by a large 'tick' motif. In 1991, new advertisements were issued, one set for ASA for use in the consumer press, and another set for CAP for use in the trade and technical press. The CAP advertisements tie in with the work of the CAP pre-publication advice unit which guides advertisers, agencies and media on Code Requirements, thus preventing potential advertisements from causing offence and provoking complaints to the ASA. Here is a strength which cannot occur with legal controls, short of seeking expensive legal advice.

Examples of the two advertisements are shown in Figure 23.1 and 23.2.

The extraordinary thing is that the abuse of advertising has moved from the petty rogues who used to be investigated by the former Advertisement Investigation Committee of the Advertising Association, with constant threat of libel action by these rogues, to the modern situation where a large-staffed well-financed ASA has to contend with abuse by allegedly reputable companies. Is this the result of the more aggressive competitiveness of the free enterprise society encouraged by 11 years of Thatcherism? The monthly ASA reports, with their 'publish and be damned' policy, are remarkable collections of famous names. Moreover, whereas most of the complaints have been from a single

Figure 23.1   ASA advertisement for which publishers donate space in the consumer press

complainant some advertisements, like the Benetton new-born baby poster, produced hundreds. Is it because advertisers have become more dubious in a period of recession, or because consumers have become more money-wise and critical, or because the ASA has become better known and more efficient? Probably, it is a mixture of all three, encouraged by watchdog programmes on TV. It is said that advertising reflects society, and perhaps that is true of the end of the twentieth century.

One hundred and seventeen objections were received by the ASA about a Hennes poster which featured a photograph of a reclining model, dressed in underwear, captioned, 'Last time we ran an ad for Swedish lingerie 78 women complained – No men', according to Case Report 192 (April 1991). The factual accuracy of the statement was questioned by some complainants, but many found the poster offensive, 'mocking the previous complainants and implying that women's views were of no value'. H & M Hennes Ltd were requested to withdraw the advertisement, avoid using such an approach in future, and to seek guidance from the CAP when preparing future advertising material.

Figure 23.2 CAP advertisement for which publishers donate space in the trade and technical press

At one time there was a spate of advertisements in which famous personalities were featured. (The advertising business tends to have periods when the same idea is exploited by different advertisers) Jeffrey Archer, George Bush, Edwina Currie, Mikhail Gorbachev, Geoffrey Howe, Nigel Lawson, Francois Mitterand, Ronald Reagan, Arthur Scargill, and Margaret Thatcher have all appeared in various advertisements without permission. This could have given the impression that they were endorsing the product.

Edwina Currie protested about a Radio Rentals advertisement which used her picture and the words 'No one should turn up their nose at our free chocolate eggs'. Edwina Currie, it will be remembered, lost her ministerial job in the salmonella eggs controversy.

But the Soviet Embassy actually approved the suggestion that Gorbachev endorsed Rumbelows electrical stores!

However, the ASA emphasized the recommendations contained in clauses B17.1,2,3 of the BCAP by stating in November 1990 that some of the personality advertisements which poked fun at the rich and famous, or invaded privacy, were highly distasteful.

Particular exception was taken to a Mitchum anti-perspirant advertisement which pictured Arthur Scargill, the miner's union leader, with
the caption, 'For when you're really sweating'. At the time, the
advertisement coincided with an investigation into Scargill's handling
of union funds, from which he was later acquitted of any misbehaviour.

Although the code only advises on the seemly use of personalities
such were their exploitation by advertisers that the ASA asked agencies
not to 'launch into print without the express prior permission of the
person concerned'.

On a previous occasion, Tory MPs complained about the use of the
Prime Minister's picture in an advertisement for Harp's Premier Lager
in which George Bush, Francois Mitterand and Margaret Thatcher
were pictured above the headline 'three heated Premiers and one cool
one'. The ASA called for the withdrawal of posters advertising the
Today newspaper which showed the party leaders apparently hanging
from gallows.

Whether or not political advertisements should be truthful, and thus
come within the principles of BCAP that all advertising should be 'legal,
decent, honest and truthful', provided a dilemma for the ASA when it
received 108 complaints about the Conservative Party advertisement
'Labour's going for broke again'. But in August 1991 the ASA refused
to condemn the Saatchi and Saatchi poster, or to amend the Code, on
the grounds that it only 'expresses an opinion on a matter which is
the subject of controversy' (BCAP, clause B6.1).

Homeopathy is a contentious issue but when complaints were
received about an asthma treatment advertised by the Homeopathic
Foundation the ASA upheld the statements from the Royal National
Ear, Nose and Throat Hospital and the National Asthma Campaign
that homeopathy has never proved to have any beneficial effect on
asthma and that it would be dangerous for asthmatics to change from
conventional treatments. The advertisement had claimed that homeopathy was 'widely recognised throughout the world as a safe and
effective medicine to cure asthma'.

The ASA's monthly reports frequently refer to misleading claims in
motor-car advertisements, but the ASA also criticizes advertisements
which glamorize high-speed models, a subject of EC attention also.
When Nissan promoted the 155 mph top speed of both its 300ZX and
its Lexus, the ASA was swift to tell Nissan to stop such sales appeals
in its advertising.

Probably one of the most deceitful advertisements of recent years
was that of the Milk Marketing Board, which was condemned in the
ASA Monthly Report 1 of June 1991. Five objections were received
concerning a magazine advertisement for a preposterous competition
in which it was unlikely that prizes would be won! This was com-
pounded by the tempting appeal: '£500,000 worth of prizes to be
won – it's a piece of cake'. Entrants had to rank a list of ten reasons

why people liked frozen cream cakes with real cream in the order chosen by the competition's judges. The rules stated that 'no prizes will be awarded in the event of no entrant's statement matching that of the independent panel of judges'. The number of possible permutations was 3.6 million, making a prize winner very unlikely, and scarcely 'a piece of cake' if the expression meant 'easy'.

The ASA took the view that the greater the odds against the prize being awarded, the more prominent should be the indication of this fact, but if that advice had been followed the purpose of the competition would have been nullified. It was the purest and intentional deception, even though there was the legal loophole of the rules which said that prizes would not necessarily be won.

Sometimes, questionable advertisements are created on purpose to stir up controversy. When Datsun (original name of Nissan) brought their first car to the UK in 1969, the car (not unlike a Ford Cortina of that time) was unknown, and the import quota (and consequently the advertising budget) was small. But immense impact was achieved with a much talked about knocking-copy advertisement which asked whether a new model Ford Cortina would have the same equipment as the Datsun. Ford were furious because they were not planning a new model. The advertisement was reproduced in the tabloids, with comments on its cheeky copy, providing Datsun with truly free space to boost its meagre budget.

The Benetton new-born baby poster certainly earned its mileage of publicity, but was it all good publicity? The ASA warned against the poster appearing, but this was ignored by Benetton, its agents J. Walter Thompson, and poster site owners Mills and Allen. A record number of 1,000 complaints showered upon the ASA, and outraged members of the public also protested to the police and to trading standards officials who passed on the protests to the ASA. The baby was blood-spattered and was still attached to its umbilical cord, being held in a midwife's hands. According to Benetton, the clothes company, 'the new born baby symbolizes the beginning of life, how all human beings come into the world in the same way. It's a wonderful, profound image'. However, in Italy the company had been testing the limits of the public's indifference in many parts of the world. One of the Italian campaigns showed a priest kissing a nun. But what was the likely effect of one poster of the screaming babe which was positioned on a hoarding next to a primary school?

The ASA, annoyed that its original advice had been ignored, responded to the avalanche of complaints, however hypocritical some of them may have been, by stating the poster gave 'grave and widespread offence' and told Benetton to withdraw the poster, having 'displayed a conspicuous disregard for the sensitivities of the public'. The controversy rumbled on for more than a week with newspaper and magazine articles and readers' letters taking various stands. A further objection by members of the British public was Benetton's American spelling of the word 'colour'.

This poster provokes a number of considerations, notwithstanding the volume of good (or bad?) publicity which the controversy earned for Benetton, an odd name with which some people may have been unfamiliar. It has long been said that animals and children make the most attractive pictorial subjects, but in advertising it depends on the aptness whether they are successful or not. Lovable cats and dogs may well suit petfood advertisements, especially TV commercials. A bank (which one?) covered its press ads with numerous rabbits (why?). The shaggy sheepdog immediately arouses the response 'Dulux'! and there is no doubt that the mischievous puppy belongs to Andrex.

But children, and babies in particular, can actually obscure the identity of an advertiser or his product or service. One of the most beautiful advertisements ever printed showed a young mother playing with her baby on the bed. The picture was large and dominated the page and people talked about it admiringly. Few readers got beyond the baby and discovered that the advertiser was Sanatogen. So with the Benetton poster: what was its connection with fashion wear? Was it, as a Saatchi and Saatchi copywriter, Gideon Todes, was quoted in *The Independent* (August 30, 1991) as saying, 'a desperate attempt to cash in on a spate of successful advertisements depicting babies'?

As a result of this advertisement and other obscure Benetton advertisements people are likely to remember the name, but will this persuade them to buy Benetton fashion wear? After all, we do not forget the names of the Borgias, Al Capone, Mussolini, Noriega or Stalin. Notoriety is not the best way to fashion favour.

Other offensive advertisements followed from Benetton who were unrepentant. They even took the Henry Moore Gallery at the Royal College of Art in London for company president Lucia Benetton and creative director Oliviero Toscani to display advertisements featuring a Mafia victim in a pool of blood; a car bomb exploding; Albanian refugees hanging off the side of a hopelessly overcrowded boat; two Asians wading through a flood; and an African soldier clutching a human thigh bone. But the ad which provoked the greatest resentment was one which showed AIDS victim David Kirby dying in the arms of his grieving family.

The AIDS poster caused even greater protest than the newborn baby poster, although UK attitudes were more hostile than anywhere else in Europe. The Advertising Standards Authority banned all the Benetton ads except for the one of two Asians in a flood scene. The AIDS pressure group ACT UP launched a boycott of Benetton products.

Barbara Jacobeit-Kunert of Vienna said in a letter published in *The Economist* on February 29 1992 'The slogan on a poster depicting a young man on his death-bed is disgusting. Trying to sell fashion by "making people aware" of the tragedy of AIDS is as absurd as it is perverse. One could have supported AIDS research with the money spent on the latest advertisement. That, however would have been far less spectacular.'

The above examples give some idea of the breadth of ASA investigations which cover both complaints from the public and the result of its own independent monitoring of advertisements. An important lesson to learn from all this is that exposure, investigation and published condemnation in the ASA's freely circulated monthly reports, which are quoted by the media, is bad public relations which can be avoided by seeking the advice of the CAP before advertising is published. The problem, however, is that in a highly competitive economy advertisers will urge agencies to do the unacceptable, and agencies do not want to lose clients, any more than the media want to lose space orders.

23.3   British Code of Advertising Practice

At the time of writing the eighth edition (December 1988) is operative but new editions are published from time to time, and the latest edition may be obtained free of charge from the CAP, Brook House, 2–16 Torrington Place, London, WC1E 7HN. It contains an Introduction and three parts, Preliminary, General Rules, and Rules applying to particular categories of advertisement, followed by an appendix on cigarettes. The code is supervised by the ASA.

In the Introduction it is stated that, 'The Code establishes a standard against which any advertisement may be assessed'. Unlike some other Codes – which tend to be morally philosophical – BCAP is specific about what would be considered an offence against the Code. The Introduction also makes the important point 'everybody in advertising shares an interest in seeing that advertisements are welcomed and trusted by the people to whom they are addressed. Unless advertisements are accepted and believed, they cannot do the job for which they are designed; and if they give offence, or appear untrue, they discredit those associated with them and the advertising business itself'.

The central concern of the Code is with the *content* of advertisements, not with their attractiveness or effectiveness, or with the worthiness of what is being advertised. It is not a censor of taste, although it makes allowances for public sensitivities. Nor is it concerned with material contained in packaging, editorial material, news releases or private communications.

Part A sets out the scope, definitions, interpretation, and reference to the Code, explaining that the provisions of the Code are divided into numbered paragraphs and sub-paragraphs.

General rules form Part B, stressing that 'primary responsibility for observance of this Code falls upon the advertiser, and remains with him even when delegated, for practical purposes, to an advertising agency or other intermediary', although this does not affect the responsibility of agencies in their relations with publishers. (It will be remembered that agency recognition requires acceptance of BCAP.)

The General Rules in Part B cover the obligations of the advertiser, substantiation, confidentiality, legality, decency, honesty, and truthful presentation: general, political claims, quotation of prices, use of 'free', use of 'up to ...' and 'from', testimonials and other indications of approval, recognizability of advertisements, identity of advertisers, guarantees, and availability of advertised products.

Paragraph 14.2 refers to *switch selling* which seems to have disappeared, but was a serious problem some years ago. An apparent bargain (such as a sewing machine, vacuum cleaner or washing machine) would be advertised. However, when the salesman called he would criticize the cheap product, and seek to sell a more expensive one. The bargain model was merely a trick to sell the dearer one.

Part B also says that *all advertisements should be prepared with a sense of responsibility to the consumer and to society*. It deals with fear and distress, violence and anti-social behaviour, protection of privacy and exploitation of the individual, unsolicited home visits, and safety. The section on unsolicited home visits may not always be appreciated by those advertisers who use coupons and collect the names, addresses and telephone numbers of respondents who should not be pestered with unsolicited salesman's calls. The respondent should be given the opportunity to refuse such calls.

Under Part B comes another section which says that *all advertisements should conform to the principles of fair competition generally accepted in business,* and *covers comparisons, denigration, exploitation of goodwill* and *imitation*. Comparative advertising is now subject to the EC Directive on Comparative Advertising (see end of previous chapter). Imitation should not be confused with passing off which refers to packaging.

In Part C special categories of advertising receive attention. First, there is a substantial section C1 on *advertisements containing health claims, especially those made for medicinal and related products*. Reference is made to the *Medicines (labelling and advertising to the public) Regulations 1978*, and a list is given of the diseases and conditions in respect of which advertisements to the lay public are prohibited, and there are other ailments on which the Regulations impose restrictions on advertising. This section of the code also makes recommendations regarding *impressions of professional advice or support*. Next, *particular claims* are specified, for example an advertisement must not claim or imply a cure, nor must there be appeals to fear, or offers to refund money. Other recommendations concern *advertisements offering individual treatment*. Paragraphs C71–77 deal with *particular products* including hearing aids, pregnancy advisory services, and treatments of arthritis or rheumatism.

Section CII makes recommendations regarding hair and scalp products, CIII to advertising claims for vitamins and minerals, CIV to slimming, CV to cosmetics, CVI to mail order and direct response advertising (but see below), CVII to advertising of financial services and products, CVIII to advertisements offering employment and business, CIX to limited editions, CX to children, CXI to media requirements, and CXII to advertisements for alcoholic drinks.

From the above resumé of the BCAP it will be seen that this Code is detailed and explicit, and any advertiser, agency or media owner should be familiar with its recommendations.

N.B. Section CVI has been revised and is discussed in 23.14 at the end of this chapter.

23.4 British Code of Sales Promotion Practice

The fifth edition of this Code was published by the CAP in July 1990, is administered by the ASA, and is sponsored and supported by the same organizations as in the case of BCAP, but with the addition of the British Direct Marketing Association, British List Brokers Association, Royal Mail Letters and the Institute of Marketing. The Institute of Sales Promotion is represented on the CAP and supports both Codes. Reports on complaints investigated under the BCSPP also appear in the ASA's monthly reports.

The Code is in seven parts, Introduction, Scope of the Code, Definitions, Basic Principles, General Guidelines, Particular Cases and Legislation.

The definitions are very precise, and are necessary for a proper understanding of the code. For instance, an *intermediary* is any person or organization, other than the promoter, responsible for the implementation of any form of promotional activity. *Product* includes goods, services, property, accommodation and facilities. *Promotional products* are goods or any other benefits such as premiums, prizes and gifts offered to the consumer.

The Basic Principles (Part 4) repeat the principles of the BCAP but add fair competition, consumer interest, consumer satisfaction, fairness, the public interest, truthful presentation, substantiation, limitations, suitability of promotion to those reached by it, administration and responsibility.

The General Guidelines applying to all forms of sales promotion (Part 5) deal with *protection of privacy, children and young people* under 16 years of age, *safety, presentation* (descriptions should not overstate their quality, availability, uses or value), *quality of promotional products*, suitability of promotional products, exaggeration, participation in promotions, consumers and intermediaries, availability of promotional products, and administration, supply, refund and replacement.

Particular Cases are set out in Part 6, and these cover free offers, promotions with prizes, informing participants about results of prize contests, availability of results, protection of consumers and promoters including advertising of prize promotions, handling, free draws, games of chance, and misleading terms, charity-linked promotions, promotions and the trade, and further guidance is listed regarding other relative rules and codes.

As an example of a complaint investigated by the ASA under this code and published in the ASA Monthly Report 4 of September 1991, there was the case of *Time International*. The complainant objected to a mailing, the envelope of which had two windows. Through the first window the name and address of the recipient could be seen, and through the second window, which was surrounded in bright orange, the recipient's name followed by 'MILLION DOLLAR WINNER' could be read. The complainant considered that this presentation gave the initial impression that she had already won the competition. The complaint was upheld by the ASA on the grounds that the envelope gave the impression that the recipient had already won the prize, thus enticing the recipient to open the mailing, only to be disappointed upon reading the small print. The Authority regarded this as unacceptable and required that the presentation be changed.

23.5   Other codes

A number of additional specialized codes and voluntary controls also exist throughout the communications business, either regarding the purchase of particular media, or implicit in membership of particular bodies. These will be described, sometimes briefly, but copies of the full codes can be obtained from their sponsors.

23.6   OAA Code of Practice

Introduced by the Outdoor Advertising Association at the end of 1989, this code is supported by the 28 members of OAA whose 119,000 poster panels represent 90 per cent of all the UK's roadside poster panels. The following is a ten point summary of member's undertakings.

1 To ensure their advertising panels and surroundings are well maintained.
2 To ensure that all panels are numbered and display the name of the controlling contractor.
3 To handle all planning issues that could affect advertisers under the Town and Country Planning legislations. (N.B. The prolif-eration of outdoor advertising is controlled, and permission has to be obtained for sites).

4 To ensure advertisements are displayed for their full contract period.
5 To use their best endeavours to ensure displayed posters are legal and satisfy the ASA and CAP rules.
6 To repair any damage or remove graffiti as soon as practicable.
7 To cooperate fully in maintaining OSCAR audience data, and providing information for competitive sheetage and expenditure data.
8 To provide information required for any campaigns inspection audit selected by advertisers.
9 To comply with the OAA's General Terms and Conditions of Trade.
10 To render invoices accurately and promptly before the end of display period.

23.7 British Transport Advertising Ltd Code of Acceptance of Advertisements

While transportation advertising comes within the aegis of the BCAP, and complaints about such advertising should be made to the ASA, the advertising contractors themselves apply strict control over the advertisements they are prepared to accept. The following is the code applicable to the bus and rail advertising for which BTA is responsible, that is outside the London Transport advertising area.

'Advertisements and advertising material will not be accepted for, or retained on, display on British Transport Advertising sites if they:

1 depict murder, scenes of terror or acts of violence;
2 are calculated to demoralise, extenuate crime, break the law or incite anyone so to do;
3 depict or refer to indecency, obscenity, nudity or strip-tease;
4 are likely, through wording, design or possible defacement, to offend the general travelling public;
5 advertise firms which have been refused a permit for public exhibition;
6 might wound racial susceptibilities or those of coloured or foreign people or members of groups who may not otherwise be protected by the terms of the Code;
7 refer to religious, sacred or other politically, morally or socially sensitive subjects in a manner which might give offence, or seek to use BTA sites as a medium for controversy arising from such subjects;
8 attack a member or the policies of any government;
9 are of a political nature, whether produced by a political party or not, other than those which simply announce social activities or meetings together with the names of the speakers and the subject

to be discussed; the wording used in announcing the subject must not be politically controversial or call for support for a particular viewpoint, policy or action;

10   might foment social unrest;

11   advertise contraceptives;

12   conflict with the British Code of Advertising Practice which incorporates the British Code of Standards in relation to the advertising of medicines and treatments;

13   contain illustrations or copy which are distorted or exaggerated in such a way as to convey false impressions; are calculated to deceive the public, or contain statements of a 'knocking' or extravagant nature;

14   might adversely affect in any way the Undertaking or Undertakings on whose sites a display is required (e.g. by advertising competitive services; by the use of designs or texts which might lead to confusion or by offers of employment in competition with the requirements of the Undertaking(s) concerned).'

23.8   IPR and PRCA codes

The IPR represents individual PR practitioners and the PRCA represents PR consultancies which are corporate members. Both had similar codes, but in 1990 the PRCA introduced its Charter which expanded on the original code by stating what was acceptable as well as what was not. In 1991, the IPR amended its Code of Professional Conduct so that it was compatible with that of the PRCA Charter. The two are now similar. However, a major change was introduced in 1990 and this was the reversal of the 'payments by results' clause 9. As clause 3.9 this now reads: *A member shall not: guarantee the achievement of results which are beyond the member's direct capacity to achieve or prevent'*.

The original clause 9 banned payment contingent upon results. There was unfortunately a double meaning to this. Obviously, renewal of a consultancy contract or the future of an in-house PRO could depend on the success of their work, especially with the modern emphasis on the achievement of tangible results which justify expenditure on PR or promotion based on performance. However, the code referred to the promise of so many editorial mentions for a given sum which was impossible since it was the prerogative of editors to publish PR material if they wished. With the involvement of PR consultancies in take-over bids and government privatization share flotations plus local government performance awards, a new situation occurred in which payment by results, and the payment of bonuses, became a reality. Consequently, the clause was re-worded as stated above.

The IPR maintains a Professional Practices Committee and a Disciplinary Committee. Written complaints about abuses of the Code have to be made in writing to the executive director. The Professional Practices Committee investigates complaints and reports to Council. If the breach is serious it may be passed to the Disciplinary Committee which may take action, such as a reprimand or suspension of membership, without further recourse to Council.

23.9 Code of Practice for Traders on Price Indications

Published by the Department of Trade and Industry in November 1988, this Code supplements the important *Consumer Protection Act 1987*, described in Chapter 22. Part 1 deals with price comparisons (e.g. sale prices should refer to previous prices, and 'regular' or 'usual' prices should be stated), comparisons with trader's own previous price, introductory offers, comparisons with 'recommended retail price' sales, special events and free offers. Part 2 covers the actual price to the consumer, such as indicating two different prices and incomplete information and non-optional extras (e.g. postage and packing charges or VAT). Part 3 is concerned with price indications which become misleading after they have been given, and Part 4 covers the sale of new homes.

This Code is essential reading for anyone who indicates prices in retail displays, advertisements or in mail order catalogues. The Act and the Code does aim to stamp out some of the rackets which have occurred with so-called 'sales'.

The Institute of Trading Standards Administration has, for instance, urged car dealers to follow the price marking laws and reveal such hidden extras as delivery and number plates in advertising copy. The drive-away price can be very much higher than the list price advertised.

23.10 ITC Code of Advertising Standards and Practice

Published by the Independent Television Commission in January 1991 as a statutory duty of the Broadcasting Act 1990, but also deriving from the Broadcasting Act 1981, it is modelled closely on the IBA and Cable Authority Codes which it replaced.

Rules of sponsorship and more detailed rules on the scheduling of advertisements are published separately in the *ITC Code of Programme Sponsorship* and the publication, *ITC Rules on Advertising Breaks*.

The Code applies to all ITV services, but has separate provisions for Oracle (Teleview). Although the BCAP does not apply to broadcast advertising, the ITC has many points in common with the BCAP, and has regard to the Code of Practice issued by the Broadcasting Standards Council and to the EC Directive on Television Broadcasting. 'The methods of control open to the ITC include powers to give directions to exclude not only classes and descriptions of advertisements but individual advertisements – either in general or in particular circumstances.' Thus, whereas other Codes such as the BCAP are voluntary and self-regulatory, the ITC has the power of law behind it. This, together with the kinds of advertising it excludes from TV screens, makes it a very powerful code.

The Code sets out standards such as the separation of advertisements and programmes so that there is no confusion between the two. Advertisements must not refer to the use or appearance of any product or service in any programme. This does not mean that a product or service may not be mentioned in a programme, which is another matter entirely. The Standards go on to set out rules regarding programme performers, subliminal advertising (see later), captions and superimposed text, noise and stridency, politics, industrial and public controversy (see later), religion (see later), charities, taste and offence, discrimination, protection of privacy and the individual, appeals to fear, superstition, unacceptable products or services (see later), health and safety, motor cars and driving (see later), protection of the environment, animals, misleadingness, price claims, comparisons denigration, reproduction techniques (see later), testimonials, guarantees, inertia selling, use of the word free, gifts or prizes, competitions, homework schemes, instructional courses, mail order and direct response advertising, home shopping features, premium rate telephone services, matrimonial and introduction agencies, alcoholic drink, advertising and children (see later), financial advertising, health claims, medicines and treatments, and Pan-European or non-UK advertising (see later).

The Code then has a series of important appendices. Appendix 1 deals with Advertising and children (see later), Appendix 2 with Financial advertising, Appendix 3 with Health claims, medicines and treatments, Appendix 4 with charity advertising (see later), Appendix 5 with Religious advertising (see later), and Appendix 6 with Statutes affecting television advertising, a list of more than 50 laws which exceed those described in the previous chapter.

This is clearly a very comprehensive and painstakingly produced Code, and is necessary since TV can enter most households and be seen by almost any member of the family or the community unlike most other media which have selective readerships or audiences. The ITC Code implies a social responsibility on the part of the Commission. Anyone concerned with TV advertising in the UK should be familiar with the provisions of the Code, a copy of which is obtainable from the ITC, 70 Brompton Road, London, SW3 1EY.

Several provisions apply particularly to commercial TV, they were indicated above with the words 'see later', and are now discussed.

Subliminal advertising

Section 7 states that 'no advertisement may include any technical device which, by using images of very brief duration, or by any means, exploits the possibility of conveying a message to, or otherwise influencing the minds of, members of an audience without their being aware, or fully aware, of what has been done'. This stems from the ingenious system whereby an American amateur psychologist, James Vicary, claimed in 1957 that he had boosted popcorn sales at a local cinema by projecting hidden messages on the screen. The technique involved showing a few frames that could be seen and transmitted to the mind, although members of the audience were unaware of them.

It was used in one of the Columbo TV detective films in which a member of an audience was induced to leave a pre-view theatre and was murdered.

While subliminal advertisements are banned in the UK by the ITC, they were used humorously on American TV in 1991 by Seagram gin, Toyota, and Miller Lite beer. The Toyota commercials flashed 'sexy' and 'wild' on the screen while the presenter recited the car's technical virtues.

There have been some attempts to produce near-subliminal commercials with a kaleidoscopic sequence of different frames, but even so the message was not visually obscured.

Politics, industrial and public controversy

Section 10 says, 'No advertisement may be inserted by or on behalf of anybody whose objects are wholly or mainly of a political nature, and no advertisement may be directed towards any political end'. This is not limited to 'party political' but could include propaganda such as the press campaigns in opposition to nationalization schemes which occurred during the Wilson Labour governments. This contrasts both with the British press, and with the purchase of TV time for election campaigns in other countries. Party political broadcasts, incidentally, are allocated free of charge.

Charity advertising

Appendix 4 brings in a new form of TV advertising, and this stipulates who is permitted to advertise a charity, and announces the right to suspend any separate advertising for charities handling disaster appeals if free air-time is already being given by ITC. However, the take-up of air-time for charity appeals has been minimal, presumably because the cost is not justified.

Religious advertising

In some countries air-time is purchased by religious organizations, and Sin the USA private churches even have their own TV stations. Hitherto, religious advertisements were prohibited on ITV but, as stated in Appendix 5, after 1992, religious advertisements are acceptable to announce religious events, describe a denomination and how to contact it, or offer religious books or goods. Very strict rules are laid down concerning unacceptable advertisers, fund raising, doctrinal references, denigration, use of fear, benefit claims, faith healing and miracle working.

Unacceptable products or services

These, under Section 18, are specified as breath-testing devices and products which purport to mask the effects of alcohol; the occult; betting tips, and betting and gaming (including pools); all tobacco products (not just cigarettes); private investigation agencies; commercial advisory services (but not solicitors); guns and gun clubs; and pornography.

Motor cars and driving

Section 20 stipulates that, 'no advertisement may encourage or condone dangerous, inconsiderate or competitive driving practices or breaches of the Highway Code'. Nor may there be, 'References to top speed or acceleration'. This is also in line with EC attitudes to motor-car advertising in general.

Reproduction techniques

Obviously, TV lends itself to trick photography, but Section 27 says, 'It is accepted that on television the technical limitations of photography can lead to difficulties in securing a faithful portrayal of a subject, and that the use of special techniques or substitute materials may be necessary to overcome these difficulties. These techniques must not be abused; no advertisement in which they have been used will be acceptable unless the resultant picture presents a fair and reasonable impression of the product or its effects and is not such as to mislead'. Unacceptable devices include, for example, the use of glass or plastic sheeting to simulate the effects of floor or furniture polishes. The 'Bear Foot' commercials for Volvo in the USA, described in the previous Chapter (22.36), would have fallen foul of this provision.

Advertising and children

The TV codes have always been stricter than the BCAP regarding children, because action in TV advertisements is more easily copied.

The special Appendix 1 is very detailed and contains 18 sections. Four provisos are worth quoting.

Section 5 says, 'Advertisements must not exhort children to purchase or ask their parents or others to make enquiries or purchases'.

Section 7 says, 'No advertisement may imply that unless children themselves buy or encourage other people to buy a product or service they are failing in some duty or lacking in loyalty'. Section 7 goes further and warns that, 'No advertisement may lead children to believe that if they do not have or use the product or service advertised they will be inferior in some way to other children or liable to be held in contempt or ridicule'.

Section 9 is particularly relevant to TV and sets out rules on the restriction of times of transmission which is perhaps not easy to apply since children are apt to watch TV at all hours! Nevertheless, the Section is protective in saying, for instance, that advertisements for alcoholic drinks and liqueur chocolates, tobacco and matches must not be transmitted during children's programmes or in the advertisement breaks immediately before or after them.

Sections 11, 12 and 13 go into great detail regarding road safety, general safety and danger, and these are special areas where TV advertising could invite imitation by children if these rules are not carefully observed. For example, 'children must not be shown playing in the road', which might seem to be a natural situation in some circumstances, nor should, 'small children be seen leaning out of windows, climbing or tunnelling dangerously', while, 'small children must not be shown climbing up to high shelves ...'.

Appendix 1 is specific and needs to be read carefully by anyone who intends to use child actors in TV commercials.

Pan-European or non-UK advertising

The final Section 44 is a sign of the times! It is mindful of the requirements of the EC Directive on Television Broadcasting and the Council of Europe Convention on Transfrontier Television. The rule applies to advertisements which are addressed exclusively to audiences outside the UK, and points out that, 'An advertisement which is directed specifically and with some frequency to audiences in the territory of a single Party to the Council of Europe Convention other than the UK must comply with the television advertising rules of that particular Party'. This could apply to advertising aimed at the Irish Republic or continental Europe, remembering that with cable and satellite TV programmes can be cross-frontier.

The ITC Code is unique insofar as it is a voluntary code which operates with the power of law, using emphatic words like 'must' and is more effective than any law since it can prohibit the appearance on television of any advertisement it considers is in violation of its provisions.

23.11   ITC Code of Programme Sponsorship

Published in March 1991, this Code introduced a new element into British commercial TV which, at its inception in the 1950s, strove to avoid the system of sponsored TV so common abroad, but especially characteristic of American TV. The distinction used to be made between the British system of commercial TV with 'commercial breaks' and programmes that were independent of advertisers, and foreign services where whole programmes were sponsored.

Now, as a result of the Broadcasting Act 1990, coupled with need to find some way of meeting the high cost of producing TV programmes, especially as advertising revenue threatens to wane as a result of competition from alternatives to traditional BBC/ITV TV, we have TV contractors looking for sponsors. The take-up by sponsors during the recession of 1991 was not enthusiastic, a notable exception being Croft port's sponsorship of the *Rumpole* series. But several other programmes failed to find sponsors. For a description of other sponsored ITV programmes in 1991–2 see page 318.

However, the Act imposed a statutory duty on ITC to draw up a code which set standards and practice in the sponsoring of programmes and identified the methods of sponsorship to be prohibited or to be prohibited in particular circumstances. The Code defines programme sponsorship as, 'A programme is deemed to be sponsored if any part of its costs of production or transmission is met by an organization other than a broadcaster or television producer, with a view to promoting its own or another's name, trademark, image, activities, or other direct or indirect commercial interests'. This Code does not apply to sponsorship by religious or charitable interests, which are dealt with in the main ITC Code.

Part I of the Code deals with *Principles* among which are that no sponsor is permitted any influence on either the content or the scheduling of the programme, may not be mentioned in the programme, nor must there be any product placement (i.e. use or appearance of product in the programme) and sponsorship must be clearly defined at the beginning and/or end of the programme. *Unsponsorable categories* under Part II: specific requirements are, in respect of news programmes and news flashes comprising local, national or international news items must not be sponsored, and neither must business and financial reports when they contain interpretation or comment. Regarding current affairs, those containing explanation or analysis of current affairs must not be sponsored.

Prohibited and restricted sponsors include political organizations, and manufacturers of tobacco products, pharmaceutical products available only on prescription, and (without special approval) any other product or service banned under the ITC Code of Advertising Standards and Practice.

Part III gives Further Guidance and covers such matters as supplied programmes, coverage of events, and sponsored support material. Programme coverage of, say, sporting events may also be sponsored, even though the event itself is sponsored and advertising appears within it although, 'this must be limited to what can clearly be justified by the editorial needs of the programme itself. For example, static signs for tobacco companies at sporting events must not be located within camera sightlines for prolonged, uninterrupted periods.

Anyone concerned with sponsorship needs to be familiar with the provisions of this Code which offer new opportunities on the one hand but guard against undue exploitation on the other. It remains as controversial an area as ever, particularly where tobacco and alcoholic drink interests are concerned.

23.12 Radio Authority Code of Advertising Standards and Practice and Programme Sponsorship

Unlike the ITC regulations, the Radio Authority's Code and rules on sponsorship are contained in one volume. The address is the same as that of the ITC. As may be expected, there are similarities between this Code and both the ITC Code and the BCAP, but also some rules which are characteristic of radio.

Under Rule 2 of Section A unsuitable advertisements are listed which should not be broadcast in or around children's or religious programmes. Rule 3 lists 13 prohibited categories, and they are the same as for ITV.

Rule 4 says that presenters may voice commercials but must not (i) endorse, recommend, identify themselves with or personally testify about an advertiser's products or services; (ii) make reference to any specific advertisement when in their presenter role; or (iii) feature in an advertisement for a medicine or treatment.

A licensee (i.e. ILR station) must not unreasonably discriminate either against or in favour of any particular advertiser, according to Rule 5. They are, however, entitled to refuse advertising they do not wish to carry for legal or moral reasons. Any dispute on this point can be taken up with the Radio Authority.

Rule 6 prohibits product placement, i.e. the gratuitous mentioning of brand names in programmes.

Other rules concern misleadingness, political, industrial and public controversy, taste and offences (e.g. references to minority groups should not be unkind or hurtful), protection of privacy and exploration of the individual, superstition and appeals to fear, price claims, comparisons, denigration, testimonials, guarantees, use of the word 'free' (products or samples must not be described as 'free' unless they are supplied at no cost or no extra cost (other than postage or carriage) to the recipient, competitions, premium rate telephone services, matrimonial and introduction agencies, sexual discrimination, racial discrimination, sound effects (which must not include sounds likely to create a safety hazard to drivers), financial advertising, alcoholic drink advertising, advertising and children, medicines, treatments and health, charity advertising, environmental claims, and religious advertising.

Sound effects pose an interesting condition. For instance, simulated traffic or car noises could be distracting to a driver listening to his car radio. Charities should be recognized, registered charities, and licensees not wishing to carry religious advertising of any kind are free not to do so.

There are more detailed Appendices on financial advertising, alcoholic drink advertising, advertising and children, medicines, treatments and health, charity advertising, environmental claims in advertisements, religion, and legislation relevant to broadcast advertising.

As with the ITC Code, the regulations are detailed and explicit.

Section C deals with programme sponsorship. Whereas, sponsored programmes used not to be permitted on ITV, and there is now a special Code as described in 23.11, there had for almost a decade been certain forms of radio sponsorship, e.g. the traffic programme on LBC, using a spotter plane.

By definition, a radio programme is sponsored if it is broadcast in return for payment or other valuable consideration (which includes the programme itself) to a licensee. All programmes may be sponsored, with the exception of news bulletins. A direct link between a sponsor's commercial interest and a programme's subject matter is acceptable in all sponsored programmes.

However, sponsors may contribute to the editorial content of all sponsored programmes, except: news features, news magazines, current affairs, business/financial news or comment, programmes/documentary items of political or industrial controversy or relating to current public policy, and *endorsement* of a sponsor's product or service within editorial is not permitted.

For example, a supermarket chain which sponsors a programme on healthy eating may produce the programme, contribute to production costs and include specialist advice from its nutritionist, *but the supermarket must not make claims for, or seek to sell, its own products in editorial.*

All funding and contribution to programmes must be clearly acknowledged, and sponsor credits must be brief, precise and substantiable. The frequency of credits is specified: programme items of up to 15 minutes long must contain at least one sponsor credit, at the beginning or end, while longer programmes must contain at least one sponsor credit approximately every 15 minutes. The rules make it very clear that there must be no doubt about the *identity* of the sponsor, even to the extent of including the sponsors' advertising slogans or copylines and brand or corporate names.

Examples of suitable credits and taglines include, 'Haig Whisky, fine blended malt from the Highlands, sponsored coverage of the Edinburgh Festival firework concert', 'Weather Update with Peugeot, the lion goes from strength to strength', and 'The Fashion Report, courtesy of Lever Brothers, makers of Persil'.

Sponsors are allowed to buy advertising spots in and around programmes provided they are distinguished by, say, a jingle, from the format and style of the programme.

Finally, there is the question of prohibited sponsors who fall into two categories: (i) companies who are prohibited from advertising their products or services may only sponsor programmes with the prior approval of the Authority; (ii) children's and religious programmes must not be sponsored by companies whose commercial interests involve alcohol, tobacco, sanitary protection, family planning, contraceptives, pregnancy-testing, anti-Aids and anti-drugs.

23.13 Mail Order Protection Scheme

Known as MOPS, this scheme is operated by the national newspapers but similar schemes are advertised in magazines such as *TV Times*. The object is to safeguard that money paid to mail order traders who have advertised in the journal will be repaid if an advertiser stops trading and does not deliver an order or refund payment.

However, the MOPS scheme does not cover those advertised under classified headings, perishable foodstuffs, horoscopes, lucky charms, non-durable gardening and medical products.

Many publishers vet direct response advertisements before accepting them. There have been cases where goods have been advertised, but advertisers have not bought stocks until they knew the volume of response. By then the supply price may have risen, the advertiser could not honour his advertised price, he went bankrupt and readers lost their money. Publishers, are of course, anxious to keep faith with their readers, but they are also anxious to sell advertisement space.

23.14 Mailing Preference Scheme

Direct mail has become a major advertising medium, and careful targeting is one of its skills. Nevertheless, such is the volume of unsolicited mail that it has earned the unfortunate nickname of 'junk mail'. One of the causes of the problem is the availability of vast mailing lists and databases and the comparatively new industry of list broking. A chief contributor to this has been the government's privatization schemes and their appeal to millions of people to buy shares in gas, water, electricity, telephone services and so on. This has, in turn, contributed to financial houses becoming one of the biggest users of direct mail to sell financial services by post, simply because of the accessibility of potential clients.

The Mailing Preference Service provides the means for recipients of direct mail to ask to have their names taken off mailing lists, and the Service undertakes to notify all members of the relevant trade bodies to delete these names from their lists. This is known as the MPS Suppression File. However, this is not as simple as it seems. It may not always be possible to trace the original source of a mailing list. There can also be numerous spelling mistakes in addresses which defy the best de-duplication computer systems to detect. There are often annoying cases where multiple mailings occur for one reason or another, such as an address being on more than one list, or in more than one form.

As an example of an attempt to relieve shareholders from being annoyed by undesirable mailings notices appear in the Annual Reports of privatized companies and the following is quoted from that of National Power:

'UNSOLICITED MAIL
The company is obliged by law to make its share register available on request to members of the public and organisations. The Company therefore has no control over persons obtaining information from the register and it may result in shareholders receiving unsolicited mail. If you wish to limit the amount of unsolicited mail you receive you should write to the Mailing Preference Service, Freepost 22, London WIE 7EZ. This is a free service for members of the public'.

Another way to curb unsolicited mail is to write 'Deceased' on the envelope and return to sender.

23.15   Rules for direct marketing including list and database management

On July 5 1991 the Council of the Advertising Standards Authority ratified an extension to the scope of the British Code of Advertising Practice to regulate the use of personal data for direct marketing purposes. These rules replaced Section CV1 of the eighth edition of the Code described in 23.3.

This important extension of the Code is an example of the way in which the various specialized trade bodies can play a pivotal role in contributing to the ethics of the advertising industry as a whole. During 1990, the Advertising Association pioneered two forms of self-regulation. These were the second edition of its *Code of Practice Covering the use of Personal Data for Advertising and Direct Marketing Purposes* (first published in 1987) and *The Recommended Standards of Practice in List and Database Management for Direct Marketing Purposes*. The Code had an important link with the Mailing Preference Service, and was revised in 1990 after discussion with the Data Protection Registrar about the requirements of register entry. The point now made is that data subjects be given specific information about 'significantly different' uses which data users intend to make of their personal data, and also that they be given the opportunity to object to such use. This is incorporated in the amended Section CV1 of the BCAP.

The two documents initiated by the Advertising Association were accepted by the Association of Mail Order Publishers, the British Direct Marketing Association, the Direct Mail Producers Association, the Mail Order Traders Association, and the Post Office.

The 1991 amendment to Section CV1 takes in the essence of these regulations. It sets out the rules governing transactions of all kinds, whether for goods or services, in which the advertiser and the customer are brought into communication through an advertisement and conduct their business through the post or other means and not face-to-face at the advertiser's place of business. 'Advertisement' includes those which are mailed direct, inserted loose in a publication, appear on a videotape or cinema commercial, are delivered door-to-door, or are handed out or collected in person. 'Advertiser' includes, where appropriate, list compilers, owners, users, brokers, managers and mailing houses, and any others involved in the preparation of the advertisement or the servicing of the response.

Section CV1 (A) deals with Advertisements and Fulfilment, and covers Conformity of goods to relevant standards (e.g. a British Standard) and according to Regulations made or having effect under the *Consumer Protection Act 1987* (see 22.13), Conformity of goods to description, Goods sent on approval, Goods unacceptable for offer in mail order and direct response advertisements, the advertiser's address (which should be stated in the body of the advertisement as well as in the coupon), Mailing and Packaging, care being taken about the nature of direct response goods and their packaging since children may have access to mail, cash with order with reference to refunds and their justification, Fulfilment of the order, e.g. an advertiser should never take longer than 28 days to fulfil an order except in certain specified circumstances such as that goods are to be dispatched in a series of items, or are goods likely to require more than 28 days for delivery, media requirements such as respondent protection schemes, and Statutory Rights under the *Consumer Transactions (Restrictions Statements) Order 1976* which states circumstances in which consumers must be notified that their statutory rights are not affected.

List and Database Practice is detailed under Section CV1 (B), and emphasizes the Data Protection Principles (see 22.17) of the *Data Protection Act 1984*. Under the General Rules, list owners should be able to identify those individuals who have objected to them, suppliers of lists should satisfy themselves regarding the use to which they are put and so on in this strain.

It is pertinent to ask whether this part of the Code is not a pious hope, some mailings seeming to operate on the basis of the old computer saying, 'put rubbish in get rubbish out'. Some of the worst culprits concerning unsolicited and duplicated mailings are members of the direct marketing trade itself, who ignore pleas to stop their mailings, and anyone who has ever contributed to a charity will know that he will receive an appeal from every other charity. Getting off a mailing list is by no means easy! Many mailings are produced in-house from directories and membership lists, or accumulated databases of enquirers/customers, and so are beyond the reach of the Mailing Preference Scheme.

Section CV1(B) deals with obtaining personal data, list maintenance, mailing lists rented in and mailing lists rented out. The Code has strength where mailings are conducted for clients, or lists are supplied to clients by specialist firms, but it has little relevance to those many firms who conduct direct marketing in-house, using or compiling their own lists. As stated in 23.12, anyone can obtain a share register.

23.16   The European Advertising Standards Alliance

Formed in late 1991, the Alliance brings together all those organizations in Europe which operate self-regulatory codes of practice to govern advertising claims. With the addition of Switzerland and Austria as founder members, the Alliance reaches beyond the EC countries. The alliance works closely with the Commission, the European Parliament and national governments. It looks at the problem of complaints made in one country about advertisements that originate from another, and is consequently concerned about advertisement malpractices under the Single European Market with cross-frontier advertising. The director general of the ASA is vice-chairman of the Alliance.

Appendix 1:
Bibliography

Annuals

Advertisers Annual, Reed Information Services, East Grinstead.
Advertising Budget, The, Simon Broadbent, NTC Publications (in association with IPA), Henley-on-Thames.
Advertising Statistics Yearbook, NTC Publications, Henley-on-Thames (for the Advertising Association).
Brands and Markets, NTC Publications (for Leith & Price), Henley-on-Thames.
Drink Pocket Book, NTC Publications, Henley-on-Thames.
European Market & Media Fact Book, NTC Publications, Henley-on-Thames.
Food Pocket Book, NTC Publications, Henley-on-Thames.
Lifestyle Pocket Book, NTC Publications (for the Advertising Association), Henley-on-Thames.
Marketing Pocket Book, NTC Publications, Henley-on-Thames.
Media Pocket Book, NTC Publications, Henley-on-Thames.
Regional Marketing Pocket Book, NTC Publications (for the Advertising Association), Henley-on-Thames.
Retail Pocket Book, NTC Publications, Henley-on-Thames.
Willings Press Guide, Reed Information Services, East Grinstead.

Books

Advertising, Frank Jefkins, M & E Handbook, Pitman, London.
Advertising: What it is and how to do it, Roderick White, McGraw-Hill, Maidenhead.
Advertising Works, biennial series, NTC Publications (in association with IPA), Henley-on-Thames.
Behavioural Aspects of Marketing, Keith C. Williams, Butterworth-Heinemann, Oxford.

Business to Business Marketing and Promotion, Martyn P. Davis, Business Books, Century Hutchinson, London.
Creative Advertising, David Bernstein, Longman, London, 1984.
Dictionary of Advertising, Frank Jefkins, Pitman, London.
Effective Use of Market Research, The, Robin Birn, Kogan Page, London.
The 55 + Market, Stephen Black, McGraw-Hill Book Company (UK) Ltd, Maidenhead.
Fundamentals of Advertising, The, John Wilmshurst, Butterworth-Heinemann, Oxford.
Managing Product Recall, Howard Abbott, Pitman, London.
Modern Marketing, Frank Jefkins, M & E Handbook, Pitman, London.
Modern Marketing Communications, Frank Jefkins, Blackie, Glasgow.
Public Relations Techniques, Frank Jefkins, Butterworth-Heinemann, Oxford.
Sales Promotion, Julian Cummins, Kogan Page, London.
Secrets of Successful Direct Response Marketing, Frank Jefkins, Butterworth-Heinemann, Oxford.
The Shocking History of Advertising, E. S. Turner, Michael Joseph, London, 1952.

Trade press

Admap, Monthly, Reed Business Publishing Group, Sutton.
Advance, Monthly, Themetree Ltd, Aylesbury.
British Rate & Data (BRAD), Monthly, Maclean-Hunter, Barnet.
Campaign, Weekly, Haymarket Marketing Publications, London.
Direct Response Magazine, Monthly, Direct Response Marketing Ltd, Hertford.
Ideas, 6 yearly, Headline Promotions, Maidstone.
Journal of the Market Research Society, Quarterly, NTC Publications, Henley-on-Thames.
Marketing, Weekly, Haymarket Marketing Publications, London.
Marketing Week, Weekly, Centaur Communications, London.
PR Week, Weekly, Haymarket Marketing Publications, London.
Public Relations, 6 yearly, Institute of Public Relations, London.
Sales Promotion, Monthly, Sales Promotion Magazine, Hertford.

Appendix 2:
Useful addresses

Advertising Association, Abford House, 15 Wilton Road, London SW1V 1NJ.

Advertising Standards Authority, Brook House, 2/16 Torrington Place, London WC1E 7HN.

Association of Business to Business Agencies, Crown House, Hartley Wintney, Basingstoke, Hampshire RG27 8NW.

Association of Exhibition Organisers, 207 Market Towers, Nine Elms Lane, London SW8 5NQ.

Association of Independent Radio Contractors, Radio House, 46 Westbourne Grove, London W2 5SH.

Association of Media Independents, 34 Grand Avenue, London N10 3BP.

Audit Bureau of Circulations, Black Prince Yard, 207/209 High Street, Berkhamstead, Herts HP4 1AD.

British Association of Industrial Editors, 3 Locks Yard, High Street, Sevenoaks, Kent.

Bulk Verified Services, Black Prince Yard, 207/209 High Street, Berkhamsted, Herts HP4 1AD.

Cable Television Association, The, 5th Floor, Artillery House, Artillery Row, London SW1.

Chartered Institute of Marketing, Moor Hall, Cookham, Berkshire SL6 9QH.

Cinema Advertising Association, The, 137 Wardour Street, London W1V 4AD.

Communication, Advertising & Marketing Education Foundation (CAM), Abford House, 15 Wilton Road, London SW1V 1NJ.

Direct Mail Services Standards Board, 26 Eccelston Street, London SW1W 9PY.

Direct Marketing Association, Grosvenor Gardens House, 35 Grosvenor Gardens, London SW1W 0BS.

Directory Publishers Association, 93a Blenheim Crescent, London W11 2EQ.

Incorporated Advertising Management Association, Congress House, 55 New Cavendish Street, London W1M 7RE.

Incorporated Society of British Advertisers, 44 Hertford Street, London W1N 8AN.

Independent Television Association (ITVA), Knighton House, 56 Mortimer Street, London W1N 8AN.

Independent Television Commission (ITC), 70 Brompton Road, London SW3 1EY.

Institute of Practitioners in Advertising (IPA), 44 Belgrave Square, London SW1X 8QS.

Institute of Public Relations (IPR), The Old Trading House, 15 Northburgh Street, London EC1V 0PR.

Institute of Sales Promotion (ISP), Arena House, 66–68 Pentonville Road, Islington, London N1 9HS.

London Chamber of Commerce & Industry (LCCI), Examinations Board, Marlowe House, Station Road, Sidcup, Kent DA15 7BJ.

Mailing Preference Service, Freepost 22, London, W1E 8PN.

Newspapers Publishers Association, The, (NPA), 34 Southwark Bridge Road, London SE1 9EU.

Newspaper Society, The, (NS), Bloomsbury House, Bloomsbury Square, 74–77 Great Russell Street, London WC1B 3DA.

Outdoor Advertising Association of Great Britain, The, (OAA), 391 Strand, London WC2R 0LT.

Outdoor Advertising Council (OAC), Keeley House, 23–30 Keeley Road, Croydon CR0 1TE.

Periodical Publishers Association (PPA), Imperial House, 15–19 Kingsway, London WC2B 6UN.

Public Relations Consultants Association, The, (PRCA), Willows House, Willow Place, Victoria, London SW1P 1JH.

Radio Authority, The, 70 Brompton Road, London SW3 1EY.

Verified Free Distribution (VFD), 207 High Street, Berkhamsted, Herts HP4 1AD.

Appendix 3
CAM Certificate syllabus

Advertising

Aim

Successful completion of the module should provide candidates with understanding of two aspects of advertising. First, the role of advertising in society: its function as a method of marketing and social communication, and how advertising is controlled to avoid exploitation of the consuming public.

Secondly, the practice of advertising: the ways in which advertising is effectively planned and produced to achieve the objective outlined in the overall marketing or business plan; i.e. to economically deliver specifically defined product messages to clearly identified consumer targets.

Objectives

On completion of this module candidates will have:

a broad knowledge of the historical development of the structure of advertising; and a good understanding of the methods by which the industry is controlled to maintain a responsible service to society
a knowledge of the respective roles of advertisers/agencies/media owners
an understanding of the important contribution of advertising to 'branding' and 'image'
an understanding of the creative and

production procedures involved
a good description of media availability and characteristics
an understanding of campaign development and its measurement
relevent examples of good advertising practice

SECTION I: Organization of the Advertising Industry. General function and organization.
Origins and development of the advertising industry
Uses and users of advertising
Types of advertising, commercial and non-commercial
Professional bodies and associations

1 The advertiser
Work of an advertising department and advertising managers
Relations with the advertising agency, media owners and other suppliers

2 The advertising agency
Range of services
Recognition and remuneration. Legal status
How an agency is organized. main departments
How an agency is selected
Media independents

3 The media owner
Services rendered to advertising, including direct mail
Selling organization
The advertisement manager, role and activities

SECTION II: Planning
Advertising Campaigns

1 **Campaign development**
The mix of activities available
Relationship between above and
below the line activities
Setting campaign objectives
Steps taken in developing a campaign

2 **The advertising appropriation**
Ways of calculating a budget
Allocation
Budgetary controls

SECTION III: Creating and
Producing Advertisements

1 **The creative function**
Deciding what is to be communicated
Creative values of the different media
Establishing creative strategies
How advertisements communicate

2 **The creative process**
Steps in creative planning,
development and execution
The Creative Brief
Advertising themes and concepts
Assessing creative work, in terms of
objectives and execution

3 **The creative team**
The creative department of an agency
Function of different creative
specialists
How the team works together

4 **Basics of TV, cinema and
radio production**
TV and film production development
Scriptwriting approaches
Filming techniques
Radio production
Budgetary considerations

5 **Basics of press production**
Steps in developing a press
advertisement
Work of copywriter and art director
Basics of copy, and press design
Press production, black and white and
colour
Budgetary considerations

6 **Printing**
Types of process, letterpress, litho,
gravure, screen printing
General choice and use

SECTION IV: The Advertising
Control System

1 **Legal control**
The main areas of legal control and
the principal statutes

2 **Self-regulatory control**
The ASA and the British Code of
Advertising Practice
Controls from trade associations, e.g.
PAGB, alcohol and tobacco

3 **Media controls**
IBA, ITCA, press controls, DMSSB

Appendix 4
CAM past examination paper

Communication Advertising and Marketing Education Foundation Limited

CERTIFICATE IN COMMUNICATION STUDIES

Examination in

ADVERTISING

NOVEMBER 1991

Time allowed: THREE HOURS

All candidates are required to answer QUESTION ONE and THREE OTHER QUESTIONS (one each from section B, C and D).

All questions carry equal marks.

Rough work should be included in the answer book(s) and ruled through, but it will not be accepted as part of the candidates' answers.

Whenever possible, candidates should include examples from real life situations.

Please read carefully the instructions given on the front of the answer booklet.

SECTION A

Question One (Mandatory)

A political party is planning national advertising to establish voters' awareness and communicate its party policies.

a) Do you think the party should produce and place campaign material on an ad hoc basis or appoint an advertising agency? Give your reasons.

b) To assist their deliberations, the party's publicity committee decide to invite presentations from suitable advertising agencies.

Which important questions should the agencies ask the publicity committee before they prepare their presentations?

c) How are advertising budgets normally decided, and how do you think this political party should set its budget?

d) What are the recommendations of the British Code of Advertising Practice regarding the protection of privacy and exploitation of the individual in the political advertising context?

e) To be reactive to current events this campaign may encounter **urgent** demands for posters, press and television advertising. Explain how early planning and suitable reproduction techniques could overcome this problem.

SECTION B

Question Two

Explain why advertising is important to:

a) manufacturers

b) service organisations

c) the national economy

d) the government

e) charities

Question Three

The selection, appointment and change of advertising agency is usually an important step for the advertiser.

a) What reasons are likely to cause a change of agency?

b) How do advertisers find suitable agencies to consider for appointment?

c) Which factors influence advertisers in shortlisting candidate agencies?

d) Which key elements constitute a good agency presentation?

e) How can an advertising agency try to ensure their clients are retained?

SECTION C

Question Four

a) What essential information do you think a good creative brief should contain?

b) Do lengthy creative briefs stifle or assist creativity?

c) Assuming a successful advertisement will need to feature one major sales point, how do you think writers and designers should decide on the principal message?

Question Five

How do you think the advent of "desk top publishing", "sponsored communication" and "presence advertising" is likely to affect the advertising industry in terms of reproduction techniques, creativity and conventional origination in the next decade?

SECTION D

Question Six

The E.E.C. proposes to encourage the free flow of information to consumers with **Comparative Advertising** providing it is not misleading, or confusing and the comparison is objective and viable.

a)   How are product and price comparisons and denigration of competitors covered by the British Code of Advertising Practice?

b)   Do you think **comparative** advertisements are (i) likely to be effective, (ii) in the consumers' interest and (iii) likely to provide smaller brands with a better opportunity than larger brands to compete on a pan European scale?

Question Seven

You are asked to prepare specifications on the basis of which printers will submit production quotations.

What information will you need to provide for the printers for each of the following requirements:

a)   promotional balloons to be overprinted in red and blue?

b)   48 sheet posters?

c)   magazine loose inserts?

d)   A3 tabloid style newsheets?

e)   business letterheadings in 2 colours?

Question Eight

a)   How are television commercials produced from first concept through to final transmission?

b)   Explain how costs of TV commercial production can vary, and how it may be possible to produce low budget commercials?

c)   When and why may video be used in preference to film?

Appendix 5
LCCI syllabus

ADVERTISING, Third level (3002) – Series 2, 3 and 4
The aim of the examination is to test the candidate's knowledge and understanding of the practice of advertising within the marketing concept, and its economic and social justification.

Syllabus

1 The Nature of Advertising

(a) **Definition of advertising**

The three sides of advertising: advertiser, advertising agency and media owner, and their relationships with each other. Identifying and understanding the target audience(s).

(b) **Types of advertising**

Consumer, industrial, trade, retail, financial, corporate, recruitment, cooperative, generic and direct response.

2 The advertiser

(a) **The Advertising or Product/Brand Manager**

Managing the advertising department. Working with the advertising agency and other suppliers of services. Division of work/responsibilities between the advertising department and the advertising agency. How and why some companies operate an in-house advertising department exclusive of an advertising agency. Setting objectives and evaluation of results. Cost-per-reply, cost-per-conversion.

(b) **The Advertising Appropriation**
Different methods of deciding the appropriation (budget). Allocations for various purposes.

3   The Advertising Agency

(a)   Kinds of Agency

Full service, media independents, specialist and à la carte agencies.

Recognition or accreditation by media owners' associations. Commission and fee systems of remuneration. Effect of Restrictive Trade Practices Act 1976 and Office of Fair Trading ruling on recognition now given by NPA, NS, PPA, ITVA, AIRC. Legal status of advertising agent who 'acts as principal'. Agency-client relations, contracts of service, ownership and assignment of copyright materials.

(b)   Agency Functions and Personnel

Range of services provided by full service agencies and specialist services of other kinds of advertising agencies. Agency departments and their personnel. Plans board, review board and creative groups. Use of freelance services and buying of services.

4   The Media Owner

(a)   Types of media

Primary and secondary. Comparative costs and value. Above-the-line and below-the-line media.

(b)   Methods of selling media

Organization of the advertisement or sales department, and roles of managers and representatives. How media are sold to advertisers and advertising agencies. Use of statistics, e.g. circulation, readership and audience statistics. Cost-per-thousand sales/readers. OTS figures.

5   Creative advertising

(a)   Layout

The design of advertisements and the basic elements of design – balance, proportion and contrast. Use of display and text type, illustrations and logos. The design of coupons.

(b)   Copywriting

The writing of copy for advertisements, including headlines, slogans, sub-headings, text and the wording of coupons.

(c)   Production processes

The effect of different production processes upon creative work.

6   Other Related Activities

(a)   Sponsorship

The use of sponsorship for advertising, PR and marketing purposes.

(b)   **Sales Promotion**
Techniques to stimulate sales at the point-of-sale.

Note
Candidates should be aware of current trends in this syllabus area.

(c)   **Public Relations**
How advertising and public relations differ. Consultancies and internal departments. How public relations can contribute to success of advertising. Press relations. External house journals. Documentary films and video-tapes.

(d)   **Marketing Research**
Organizations providing circulation, readership and audience statistics.

Research particularly applicable to advertising: motivational, discussion groups, copy testing, recall, impact, reading and noting tests and tracking tests, opinion polls, image studies, consumer panels and dealer audits.

(e)   **Law and Voluntary Codes**
Statutes, regulations and common law relating to Advertising. Voluntary codes and self-regulatory procedures. The inter-relationship between legal and voluntary controls.

Examination requirements

A 3-hour examination. One question is compulsory; 4 other questions are to be answered from a choice of 9.

Appendix 6
LCCI past examination paper

LONDON CHAMBER
—— *of* ——
COMMERCE AND INDUSTRY
EXAMINATIONS BOARD

SERIES 4 EXAMINATION 1991

THURSDAY 21 NOVEMBER—1800 to 2100

THIRD LEVEL

ADVERTISING
(CODE No: 3002)

———

Instructions to Candidates

(a) *The time allowed for this examination is 3 hours.*

(b) *Answer 5 questions – the* **compulsory** *question (Question 1) and 4 others.*

(c) *Candidates* **must** *attempt the compulsory question or they will not be eligible for the award of a Pass.*

(d) *All questions carry equal marks.*

(e) *All answers must be clearly and correctly numbered but need not be in numerical order.*

(f) *Write legibly on both sides of the page. Rough work (if any) must be crossed through after use.*

(g)   If supplementary sheets are used, the candidate's number must be clearly shown and the sheets securely inserted inside the answer book. The question(s) to which they refer must be clearly numbered.

COMPULSORY QUESTION

1   There are two separate parts to this question. Part (a) requires a drawing or plan of the advertisement but should include the bold display words. Part (b) should contain every word of the advertisement and, in real life, would accompany the layout as typewritten copy.

    (a)   Draw the layout for a black-and-white press advertisement for a department store which is having a seven-day sale during which many goods will be offered at reduced prices. The layout should include rough illustrations of typical bargains.   (10 marks)

    (b)   Write **all** the wording, including prices, for the advertisement in Part (a).   (10 marks)

(Total 20 marks)

2   The full service agency often has to compete with à la carte agencies and media independents.

    (a)   Briefly describe the services provided by each of these three types of agency.   (10 marks)

    (b)   Give your reasons as a client for preferring either a full-service agency or a combination of an à la carte agency and a media independent.   (10 marks)

(Total 20 marks)

3   Briefly explain the difference between **4** of the following pairs of terms:

    (a)   a tabloid and a broadsheet newspaper
    (b)   a classified and a displayed advertisement
    (c)   a direct mail shot and a maildrop
    (d)   sheet fed and web fed
    (e)   sans serif and serif face
    (f)   a font and a family   (20 marks)

4   Write brief explanations of the following terms or initials:

    (a)   solus site
    (b)   page traffic
    (c)   piggybacking
    (d)   bleed
    (e)   camera-ready copy
    (f)   OTS

(g) TVR

(h) scc

(i) ABC

(j) BARB   (20 marks)

5 (a) Explain the difference between *a budget* and *an allocation*.
                                                       (5 marks)

   (b) Describe **3** ways of calculating an advertisement budget.
                                                       (15 marks)
                                        (Total 20 marks)

6 In direct response marketing the customer is unable to see or
   examine the goods (unless they are supplied 'on approval').
   Describe **4** devices that can be used to give customers the
   confidence to buy by post.

                                                       (20 marks)

7 (a) What are the requirements of a legal contract?
                                                       (5 marks)

   (b) In what circumstances can a contract be invalid?
                                                       (5 marks)

   (c) What constitutes slander of goods?
                                                       (5 marks)

   (d) What are the legal implications of intellectual property?
                                                       (5 marks)
                                        (Total 20 marks)

8 (a) Give **5** important questions which you would ask before
        booking stand space at an exhibition.   (10 marks)

   (b) Why would you ask these questions?   (10 marks)
                                        (Total 20 marks)

9 (a) Why is repetition considered to be one of the secrets of
        successful advertising?   (4 marks)

   (b) Decribe **4** ways in which repetition can be used to make
        advertising successful.   (16 marks)
                                        (Total 20 marks)

10 (a) Why are different advertising techniques required for
        industrial products compared with consumer products?
                                                       (10 marks)

   (b) Discuss the special merits of **4** advertising or public relations
   techniques which can be applied to the promotion of industrial
   products.   (10 marks)
                                        (Total 20 marks)

Appendix 7
The agency recognition system agreements

NPA AND NEWSPAPER SOCIETY

The recognition system applied by national and regional newspapers is as follows:

1   All matters relating to commission/discount to advertising agencies (hereinafter referred to as 'agencies') whether recognized or not (including, by way of illustration but not of limitation levels of commission/discount and the granting or withholding of commission/discount) are matters for the individual decision of each newspaper. No agreements, recommendations or advice with respect to such matters will be made by the Society.

2   It is recommended that all agencies, which are for the time being recognized agencies, should be granted credit terms. The functions of the Agency Recognition Sub-Committee shall in future be confined to all matters concerned with the credit-worthiness of applicants for recognition and the credit-worthiness of recognized agencies and all matters incidental thereto.

   The Agency Recognition Sub-Committee shall establish guidelines for the assessment of the credit-worthiness of applicants for recognition, so as to ensure consistency in its recommendations, and the guidelines established from time to time shall require the approval of the Advertising Committee. Such guidelines may be changed or expanded whenever considered necessary or desirable.

3   The Advertising Committee may, upon the recommendation of the Agency Recognition Sub-Committee make all such decisions with respect to the operation of the Recognition System as it has made in the past except that, subject only to paragraphs 4 and 5 below, all such decisions shall be based solely upon the credit-worthiness of applicants for recognition and the credit-worthiness of recognized agencies.

4   (a) In the event that the Society finds that an agency, whether recognized or not, proposes to insert in one or more newspapers of members an advertisement which is not legal, truthful, decent or honest or which otherwise fails to comply with the requirements of the British Code of Advertising Practice or any other code under the general supervision of the Advertising Standards Authority, it may recommend that its members should not accept that advertisement for insertion in their newspapers.

(b) In the event that the Society finds that an agency, whether a recognized agency or an applicant for recognition, has persistently failed to comply with the requirements of the British Code of Advertising Practice or any other code under the general supervision of the Advertising Standards Authority, or has otherwise failed to provide copy which is legal, truthful, decent and honest, it may, after giving the agency an opportunity to present its case, suspend the recognition of or de-recognize or decline to recognize that agency.

(c) In the event that the Society finds that an agency, whether recognized or not, has persistently failed to comply with the requirements of the British Code of Advertising Practice or any other code under the general supervision of the Advertising Standards Authority, or has otherwise failed to provide copy which is legal, truthful, decent and honest, it may, after inviting and receiving any representations which the agency may wish to make, recommend that its members should not accept any copy from that agency for such period as is considered appropriate in the circumstances.

5   (a) If the Society makes a recommendation to members not to accept any copy from an agency pursuant to paragraph 4 (c), that agency may, within 7 days of being notified of such recommendation, appeal to the Appeals Committee and pending the decision of the Appeals Committee that recommendation shall not take effect. No decision taken by the Appeals Committee shall affect the validity of a recommendation made under paragraph 4 (a) not to accept a particular advertisement.

(b) The Appeals Committee shall consist of two representatives from the NS and one representative each from the Institute of Practitioners in Advertising, the Incorporated Society of British Advertisers and the Committee of Advertising Practice. The Chairmanship shall alternate between the NS representatives. Each representative shall have one vote and decisions shall be taken by majority vote. All five representatives must be present to constitute a quorum.

6   An advertising agency for the purpose of these resolutions means any person, firm or company which carries on a business that includes, on a regular basis, the making of contracts for the insertion in newspapers of advertisements relating to the goods or service of other persons.

The NPA and the Newspaper Society issued *Guidelines For the Assessment of the Credit-Worthiness of Applicants for Recognition*, identical except for figures (5.4). The following reproduction of the 1979 *Guidelines* carries both sets of figures, the lower ones being the Newspaper Society and the higher ones for the Newspaper Publishers Association.

1   Adequacy of proprietor's financial interest in the business: normally evidenced in the case of a limited company by issued share capital in excess of £7,500 (NS), or £10,000 (joint NPA/NS), supported by guarantees from shareholder directors.

2   Adequacy of net working capital to enable the agency to pay its proper liabilities to trade creditors as they fall due: normally held to be 10% of *projected* annual turnover with a minimum of £7,500 (NS) or £15,000 (NPA/NS) and a maximum of £20,000 (NS), or £75,000 (NPA/NS).

3   Adequate flow of business with members of the Society to warrant the granting of credit terms in the case of an established agency, normally assessed to be £10,000 (NS) or £150,000 (NPA/NS) to have been spent with member newspapers of the NS or NPA in the previous year; and, in the case of an agency established for a period of less than one year, normally assessed by obtaining satisfactory evidence that its current level of business with such member newspapers is at the rate of £10,000 (NS), or £150,000 (joint recognition), per annum minimum and that this rate will be sustained.

4   Adequate spread of clients' business to ensure lack of total reliance on one client and the danger of loss of viability of the organization should any one client withdraw: normally assessed by a spread of turnover between not less than three clients (NS) or four clients directed between national/local press (NPA/NS), but a smaller spread will be accepted if satisfactory assurance is provided that the agency's custom is secure.

5   Evidence from past performance, if any, of ability and intent to maintain proper payment of accounts: normally assessed by ensuring no member company of the NS has had payment difficulties from the applicant agency over the six months prior to application.

6   Adequate evidence of ability to control large sums of clients' money: normally evidenced by professional financial ability of one or more director or partner (or of close contact with a professional accounting firm) and evidence of proper financial plans such as balance sheet projections, cash flow forecasts, etc.

7   Adequate evidence of ability to run the intended business: normally assessed by receipt of three satisfactory references as to the financial standing and general business ability of the applicant together with satisfactory evidence that the agency will be able to maintain a level

of business sufficient to meet all its obligations.

Certain guarantees are built into the joint NPA/Newspaper Society recognition agreement (5.5) which entitles a recognized agency to receive credit terms from member publishers, and the agency has to accept the following eight stipulations:

1   That it will pay for all advertising inserted in the newspapers promptly on the due dates prescribed by them and that if at any time it finds itself unable to do so, it will notify the Joint Committee immediately. Further, that it will at any time supply full information regarding its financial position – audited if so specified – upon request by the Joint Committee.

2   That it will notify the Joint Committee immediately of any alterations in the shareholding, proprietorship, beneficial ownership of its business, the creation of any new or additional debentures and/or charges affecting its assets and of any change of address or other alterations in the particulars furnished in the form of application for recognition originally submitted.

3   That in the event of any material change in the particulars furnished in the form of application of breach of the conditions of this agreement, the Joint Committee may suspend the recognition of the agency pending enquiry.

4   That it will not, without agreement with an advertiser charge that advertiser for any advertisement more than the price charged by the newspaper for the space occupied by such advertisement, including in addition any surcharge on that price for late payment to the newspaper, where such late payment is occasioned by the default of the advertiser. Further, that it will disclose to the advertiser, upon request, full details of any commission or discount which may have been allowed by the newspaper.

5   That all advertising placed by it shall be legal, honest and truthful and that it is aware of, will conform to and support the requirements of the British Code of Advertising Practice and any other code under the general supervision of the Advertising Standards Authority.

6   That it will conform to and support the provisions laid down by The Advertising Standards Board of Finance Limited which govern the surcharging of the gross media rate of display advertisements at the rate for the time being promulgated and which require advertisers who are clients of the agency to pay to the agency and the agency to collect and pay to The Advertising Standards Board of Finance Limited those sums required for the maintenance of The Advertising Standards Authority Limited and the Committee of Advertising Practice.

7   That in respect of any advertisement submitted by the agency for publication in any newspaper, which advertisement contains the

name or any pictorial representation (photographic or otherwise) of any living person and/or any part of any living person and/or any copy by which any living person is or can be identified, the agency will first obtain the authority of such living person to make such use of such name, representation and/or copy as is made in the said advertisement and that it will accept full responsibility for the publication of any such advertisement emanating from the agency, and hereby indemnifies the newspaper concerned against any claims or proceedings which may arise out of the publication by it of any such advertisement. Further, that in respect of any such advertisement submitted by the agency to any newspaper, there shall be implied in the contract under which such advertisement is published a warranty by the agency as set out in this clause.

8   That, except as otherwise expressly agreed in writing by the newspaper concerned, each contract for the insertion of an advertisement in any of the newspapers shall be subject to the conditions of insertion and all other conditions set out in or referred to in the Rate Card of the individual newspaper in which each such advertisement is to be inserted.

PERIODICAL PUBLISHERS ASSOCIATION

The PPA recognition requirements are similar to those of the NPA/NS as the following extracts from the Agreement indicate:

NOW IT IS HEREBY AGREED by and between the parties as follows:

1.   For avoidance of doubt it is hereby expressly confirmed that the act of conferring Recognition on an Advertising Agency shall signify only the following namely that:

1.1   The Association recommends that its members should afford credit to the Agency in each case on such terms as the individual member of the Association shall consider appropriate.

1.2   The Association and the Agency have entered into an Agreement in the terms hereof.

2.   THE Association will recognize the Agency and include its name in its list of Recognized Advertising Agents issued from time to time.

3.   THE Agency in consideration of the Recognition herein afforded:

3.1   Will provide members of the Association only with advertisements that are legal, decent, honest, truthful and uphold the standards of the relevant publication and will use its best endeavours to ensure that it is at all times credit worthy and has adequate financial resources.

3.2   Will pay for all advertisements placed by it with members of the Association promptly on the due dates prescribed and if it finds itself at any time unable to do so, or otherwise in financial difficulties, will notify the Association immediately thereof.

3.3 Will on request by the Association supply full information regarding its current financial position – such information to be certified by its auditors if so required.

3.4 Will disclose to the Advertiser, if required, full details of any commission or discount which has been granted by a member of the Association.

3.5 Will advise the Association immediately of any alteration in any of the following:

(i)   the registered ownership of its shareholding and/or beneficial ownership of its business;

(ii)   the creation of any new or additional debentures and/or charges affecting its assets;

(iii)   any new business of the Agency, its owners or officers and any alteration in the particulars furnished in the form of application for Recognition originally submitted.

3.6 Will in respect of any advertisement submitted by it for insertion in any publication, which advertisement contains the name of any pictorial representation (photographic or otherwise) of any living or deceased person, and/or any part of any living or deceased person, and/or any printed text by which any living or deceased person is or can be identified, obtain authority from any person concerned to make such use of such name, representation and/or printed text as is made in the said advertisement and accept full responsibility for the publication of any such advertisement emanating from it, and further hereby undertakes to the Association (for this purpose acting on behalf of the Publisher and printer concerned):

(i)   that it will indemnify the said Publisher and printer against any claims or proceedings which may arise out of the publication of any such advertisement. Provided always that the Agency shall be consulted prior to negotiation, settlement or defence of legal proceedings; and

(ii)   that in respect of any such advertisement submitted by the Agency to any publication there shall be implied in the contract under which such advertisement is published a clause in the terms of this Clause 3.6.

3.7 Will (but without prejudice to Clause 3.9 below), unless otherwise expressly agreed to by the relevant individual publication, conform to all material conditions of business of individual publications.

3.8 Will conform to and support the provisions of the British Code of Advertising Practice including all decisions, rules and regulations from time to time issued by the CAP Committee and/or the Advertising Standards Authority, will support fully and conform to the provisions laid down by the Advertising Standards Board of Finance (hereinafter the ASBOF) regarding the surcharging of specified media rates at the level for the times being promulgated, requiring Advertisers which are clients of the Agency to pay to the Agency and the Agency to collect and pay to the ASBOF those sums required for the maintenance of the self-regulatory system and for the purpose of ensuring that consumers are made aware of and fully protected under the provisions of the said Code; and will operate the said Mail Order Protection Scheme.

3.9 Recognizes that the Association may at any time, by the reasonable exercise of its discretion, recommend pre-payment, suspend or withdraw the Agency's Recognition if it fails to meet any of its obligations as herein specified (with the exception of obligation owing by virtue only of Clause 3.7 hereof), provided always that suitable notice of such intended action shall be given to it by the Association and that at all times it shall be entitled to apply for withdrawal of the pre-payment recommendation and/or termination of the suspension or to re-apply for recognition by the Association (as the case may be).

3.10   Acknowledges that Recognition by the Association does not entitle it to credit terms from a publisher member of the Association except only on such terms as may be offered by the said Publishers and further that nothing in this Agreement shall be deemed to interfere with the said Publisher's right to ask any Agency's client to guarantee the account for any advertising submitted.

FOR the avoidance of doubt it is recorded that the Association maintains a register available at all times for inspection by the members of the Association, which said register will contain information, required for the purposes of the Recognition System, in possession of the Association concerning the Agency.

Agency Recognition
Advertising agencies applying for PPA recognition may be asked to satisfy the following requirements:

1   *Net working capital*: £20,000 shareholders funds.
2   *Turnover*: a minimum of £200,000 of display advertising in periodicals and newspapers for the 12 months prior to application. In the case of an agency established for less than 12 calendar months evidence would be sought that the current level of billings is at the rate of £100,000 per annum and that this rate will be sustained.
3   *Clients*: a minimum of 4 clients, but a smaller spread of business will be accepted if satisfactory assurance is provided that the agency's custom is secure.
4   *Prompt payment*: evidence that the agency has, during the 6 month period immediately preceding application, paid on the relevant due dates all sums accruing to PPA members.
5   *Experience and ability of directors*: proof of professional financial ability possessed by one or more Directors or Partners, or of the

availability of adequate advice and assistance from a professional accounting firm. Evidence will normally be sought of proper financial planning, e.g. balance sheet projections, cash flow forecasts, etc, three satisfactory references as to the financial standing and general business ability of the applicant, together with satisfactory evidence that the agency will be able to maintain a level of business sufficient to meet all its obligations.

APPENDIX
Circumstances in which personal guarantees will be requested:

i   In the case of a shareholder/director of an applicant Advertising Agency who has been a member of the board of an Advertising Agency which has had a bad payment record with respect to member publishers and/or which has been unable to meet its financial obligations to them (during the period that the shareholder/director in question was a member of the board).

ii In the case of recognized Advertising Agencies which do not continue to meet the requirements of credit-worthiness and which are being considered for suspension or withdrawal of recognition, personal guarantees might be required in order to help avoid the need for suspension or withdrawal of recognition.

In both the above sets of circumstances:

a   the requirement for personal guarantees would last until the Advertising Agency gave a satisfactory payment and trading performance for a period of one year after which time the requirement would be waived.

b   personal guarantees would not be sought from shareholder directors with less than 10% of shareholding in the Advertising Agency.

c   the amount required on the guarantee in terms of personal assets would depend upon the financial circumstances of the case and the obligations of the Advertising Agency. In some cases therefore the amount would be limited and in other cases unlimited.

TELEVISION CREDIT LISTING PROCEDURES

Introduction
The ITV Association represents the 16 ITV Companies which sell air-time both on ITV and Channel 4.

For the purpose of advertising, the ITV association, on behalf of the Independent Television Companies, operates centralized systems for:

i   determining whether an organization should be listed as a Television Advertising Agency, i.e. *Agency Registration* and:

ii granting credit to advertising agencies i.e. *Credit listing.*

The Agency Registration and Credit Listing systems have been established with a view to administrative convenience for both advertising agencies and the ITV Companies, so that procedures to determine whether an organization is an advertising agency and whether it should be granted credit are not duplicated for each ITV Company. The criteria for National Credit listing have been drawn up in consultation with the Institute of Practitioners in Advertising.

The publication of the financial criteria for National Credit Listing is designed to simplify the review produres by ensuring that all advertising agencies can be fully aware of the conditions that should be met in order to be included on the ITV Association Credit List before submitting an application.

In order to achieve these objectives the ITV Association's Agency Committee ('the Agency Committee') is required to apply the financial criteria in an even-handed manner and its discretion to take account of special circumstances is therefore limited.

It is emphasized that both the Register and the Credit List are maintained by the ITV Association so that they may be referred to by the individual Independent Television Companies for guidance purposes, and that the inclusion or exclusion of an advertising agency in respect of either Registration or Credit Listing does not restrict an individual ITV Company from exercising its discretion as to whether it should pay commission or grant credit to an advertising agency.

Agency recognition

For the purpose of claiming commission from the ITV Companies an advertising agency which has placed or intends to place advertisements on ITV may apply to the Agency Committee for Registration and inclusion on the Register of Advertising Agencies maintained by the ITV Association.

In assessing whether an agency is eligible for Registration the Agency Committee seeks primarily to satisfy itself that the agency complies with all the relevant legislation relating to television advertising for the time being in force.

As a prerequisite of registration an agency agrees to abide by the Independent Television Code of Advertising Standards published by the Independent Television Commission for the time being in force and all other enactments and Codes of Practice having a bearing on the contents of commercial advertising on ITV.

An agency applying for Registration should complete the application and agreement form in duplicate and return the forms with any supporting documentation to the ITV Association. The ITV Association will then arrange for the company to be visited by a member of the Agency Committee or a representative from a television company so that a report can be given to the Agency Committee regarding the agency's suitability for Registration.

Credit Listing

Local Credit Listing

In addition to the National Credit List, the ITV Association also maintains a Local Credit List. An agency placing bookings in one ITV region only may be included on the Local Credit List. The financial criteria for inclusion on the Local Credit List are, in general terms, less stringent than for National Credit Listing. The credit review procedures are undertaken by the particular ITV company concerned and are not standardized for all ITV companies. If any agency wishes to obtain credit in more than one region it must apply for National Credit Listing.

An agency wishing to apply for Local Credit should forward registration and Credit Listing Application and agreement forms in duplicate to the ITV Association together with a copy of the latest audited accounts of the agency or group with which ITV Company they require Local Credit facilities.

National Credit Listing

The ITV Association operates a centralized system on behalf of the ITV Companies for National Credit Listing (i.e. credit facilities across the network).

The application procedures and the financial and other criteria which must be met by an agency in order to be included on the National Credit List are described below. There are separate financial criteria for 'standard agencies' and for 'large agencies'. The criteria may be reviewed periodically in the light of inflation and other changed circumstances.

A   New Application for National Credit Listing

Standard agency criteria

Agencies under this category applying for national credit listing must fulfil the requirements set out below. Group accounts and financial information, rather than accounts and information for the agency itself, are required where applicable as explained in (iii) below.

i   The agency must be included on the ITV Association Register of Television Advertising Agencies

ii   The agency must submit Credit Listing Application and Agreement forms in duplicate to the ITV Association

iii The agency must provide a statement from its auditors giving the date of the agency's incorporation or formation

iv   **Non-incorporated agencies must have partners' or proprietors' funds of at least £75,000; incorporated agencies must have total shareholders' funds of £75,000, or £50,000 if at least £35,000 is represented by issued fully paid up share capital (this is confirmed by means of the Statement of Solvency referred to at viii below).**

v   The agency must provide personal guarantees from Directors with an interest in the equity of the agency. These are referred to as Personal Directors' Guarantees. The Personal Directors' Guarantees are normally only provided for a period of one year if the criteria for continued credit listing are met.

vi   The agency must provide audited accounts which should be made up to a date *not more than three months before the date of the application*. The audited accounts should have an unqualified audit report. However, if the auditors can quantify the financial effect of the matter subject to qualification and the criteria are still met, a qualified audit report will be accepted.

vii   The audited accounts referred to in vi above should confirm that the agency has traded at a profit for at least the two years prior to the date of application. Profit in this context means profit on ordinary activities before tax.

viii The agency must provide a Statement of Solvency based on the audited accounts referred to in vi above, signed by two directors and the auditors. The Statement of Solvency must confirm that the agency's audited accounts meet the following criteria:

• share capital and shareholders' funds: Shareholders' funds are £75,000 or £50,000 if at least £35,000 is represented by issued fully paid up share capital or, in the case of non-incorporated entities, total retained reserves are at least £75,000.

• net current assets: net current assets exceed net current liabilities (current assets should not include unquoted shares, patents or trade marks).

The Statement of Solvency should also state the agency's debt to equity ratio at the balance sheet date. A ratio of debt to equity or shareholders' or partners' funds of no more than 1:1 would normally be expected. Debt is defined for this purpose as the total of loan capital, long and short-term loans (including hire purchase finance and finance leases, and loans from directors and related companies) and bank overdrafts less cash balances. Shareholders' funds are defined as issued share capital and reserves, including profit and loss account accumulations, less an amount equal to the aggregate book value of intangible assets such as goodwill and the aggregate of amounts receivable from directors and other related parties. Partners' (or proprietors') funds are defined as the capital account and reserves retained in the business.

The Statement of Solvency should also state that a cash flow forecast has been prepared for a period of at least 12 months from the date of the statement (rather than for 12 months from the balance sheet date) which confirms that the agency has adequate working capital for its foreseeable needs during the next 12 months.

Large agency criteria

It may be the case that an agency, or the group of which it forms a part, qualifies at the time of application as a 'large agency'. A large agency may submit audited accounts made up to a date six months before the date of the application (rather than the three months for standard agencies) and need not submit a Statement of Solvency and Personal Directors' Guarantees with its application for National Credit Listing. To qualify as a large agency the following criteria must be met in full:

i The audited accounts (which as referred to above should be made up to a date not more than six months before the date of application) must show shareholders' funds of at least £1 million; and

ii The audited accounts must show profits on ordinary activities before tax of at least £100,000 for each of the past two financial years.

The criteria for an unqualified audit opinion, positive net current assets, debt to equity ratio of no more than 1:1 and Parent Company Guarantees are as for Standard Agencies.

Requirement to submit group financial information

In recognition of the shareholders' ability to transfer funds between group companies, if the agency applying for National Credit Listing is a subsidiary of another UK company the audited accounts and Statement of Solvency based thereon must be for the UK group as a whole and not for the agency as an individual entity. In these circumstances as a guarantee from the parent company in respect of monies due by the agency to the ITV companies must be provided in the format set out except where the agency is wholly owned and the ultimate holding company is listed on a recognized Stock Exchange.

Where a company applying for National Credit Listing although not a member of a legally constituted group associated through common ownership or other arrangements with other companies or entities, the Agency Committee will normally require financial information for the associated companies or entities and will consider whether the agency applying and its associated companies and entities meet the financial criteria on a combined basis.

Overseas agencies

In the case of an overseas agency fully accredited in its own country, it will be required to prepay unless it is able to provide a bond or guarantee placed with a London Clearing Bank for an amount not less than the highest two consecutive months' billings.

B Agencies already Credit Listed

Criteria for continued credit listing

An agency or group of which it forms a part which meets the standard agency criteria and which is on the National Credit List will be required to provide annually:

i   a copy of its latest audited accounts 9 months from its year end, which confirm that the financial criteria set out are met; and
ii   a Statement of Solvency in the form described above.

An agency which meets the additional large agency criteria and which is on the National Credit List will be required to provide annually:

iii a copy of its audited accounts (or consolidated accounts of its ultimate holding company if applicable) seven months from its year end which is that the criteria set out for large agencies are met (i.e. a Statement of Solvency is not required).

Considerations where the criteria are not met

The Agency Committee is always prepared to discuss with agencies instances where the financial criteria for continued Credit Listing may not be met, preferably in advance of the due date for the submission of the information, so that if possible, action may be taken to enable the agency to retain its credit listing. Options for continued Credit Listing which may be considered where the financial criteria are not met include the following:

i   Management accounts
Management accounts (consolidated if applicable) which include a profit and loss account and balance sheet which show that the group has remedied the non-compliance with the criteria subsequent to the year end. If it was, in the opinion of the Agency Committee a material non-compliance with the criteria, the agency or group may be requested to submit management accounts pending final audited accounts becoming available.

ii   Personal directors' guarantees
Personal directors' guarantees may be requested by the Agency Committee and relied upon to facilitate continued Credit Listing where, in the opinion of the Agency Committee, the non-compliance with the criteria is less significant.

Where personal directors' guarantees are obtained the duration of the guarantee will be for one year but may at the discretion of the Agency Committee, be extended. The Committee, at its discretion, may not require personal directors' guarantees from non-executive directors with immaterial beneficial interests in the shares of the company or in the case of listed companies.

iii   Quarterly management accounts

If an agency has a history of profitable trading and experiences a short-term loss, provided that loss is less than 15% of shareholders' fund, it may continue to hold its Credit Listing subject to the supply of quarterly management accounts until it is back in profit.

iv   Bond or bank guarantee

A bond or guarantee placed with a London Clearing Bank or a major insurance company for an amount not less than the total of the two highest consecutive months' billings.

C   Surcharge for late payment of accounts

A surcharge for late payment of accounts will be payable as follows:

i   accounts payable by an advertising agency shall be due for payment not later than the 15th day of the month following the month of transmission.

ii   any amount not paid by the 25th day of the month next following the month in which the transmission takes place will be subject to an immediate surcharge of 1.5% of such amount; a further surcharge of 1% will be imposed in respect of the principal amount which is still outstanding on the 10th day of the subsequent month.

iii Accounts are payable on invoice and invoices will be rendered at least weekly by the ITV Companies, the invoices for the last week being dispatched by first-class post not later than five working days after the end of the month of transmission.

iv   The existence of a query on any individual item in an account will only affect the due date of payment of that individual item. In the event of any query being resolved in favour of the ITV Company, the item in query will be subject to the full rate of surcharge, subject only to the ITV Company having dealt with the query with reasonable dispatch.

Payment shall be deemed to have been made in due time if the appropriate remittance is posted by first-class post by the 24th day of the appropriate month. In months where the 25th falls on a Sunday or a bank holiday the next working day will be regarded as the due date by which the payment must be dispatched by first-class post. When the 25th falls on a Monday, that will be the due date by which payment must be dispatched. Final dates for payment in each month after which the surcharge provisions will apply will be available annually for the ITV Association. Remittances delivered by hand shall be deemed to have been made in due time if received by 12:00 noon on the due date.

In the event of an agency not paying an account by the 10th day of the month in which payment became due, the ITV Companies reserve the right without prejudice to all their other rights:

i　not to accept further bookings from the agency notwithstanding that the agency remains listed with the ITV Association for credit purposes;

ii　to recommend to the Agency Committee that credit be withdrawn.

The ITV Companies reserve the right to receive and if necessary increase the levels of the surcharges and to amend the dates on which the surcharges apply.

Index